The Diagnosis of Learning Disabilities

To Pat, Demetrius, and Wikki

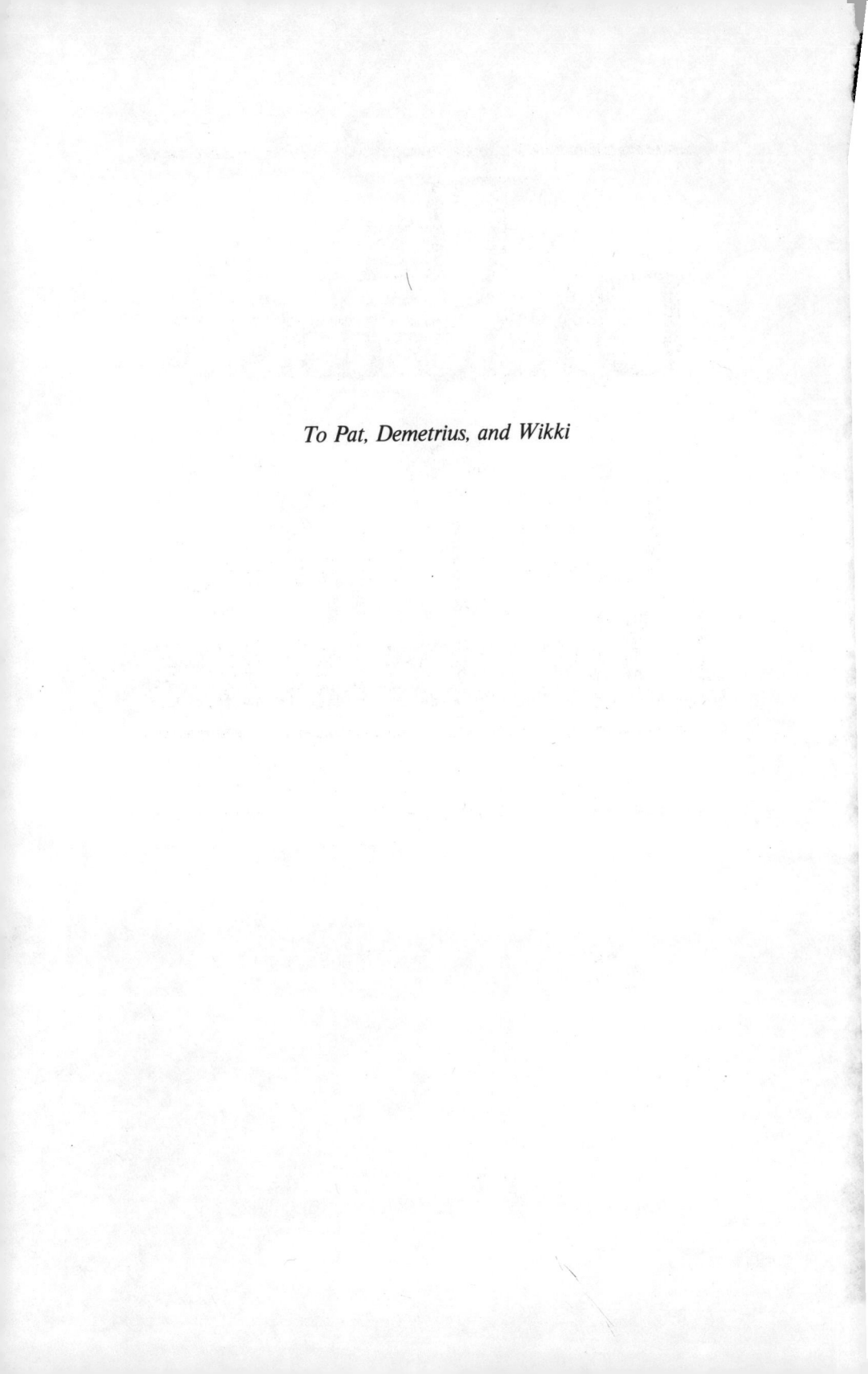

The Diagnosis of Learning Disabilities

CLARK JOHNSON

PRUETT *P* PUBLISHING COMPANY
Boulder, Colorado

© 1981 by Clark Johnson
All rights reserved, including those to reproduce this book or parts thereof, in any form, without permission in writing from the publisher.

First Edition

1 2 3 4 5 6 7 8 9

Printed in the United States of America

Library of Congress Cataloging in Publication Data

Johnson, Clark, 1944 -
   The diagnosis of learning disabilities.

   Includes index.
   1. Learning disabilities. 2. Learning ability — Testing. I. Title.
LC4704.J63   371.9   80-28462
ISBN 0-87108-236-5

Table of Contents

I	The Definition of Learning Disabilities	3
II	Etiological Factors in a Diagnosis: A Historical Perspective	25
III	Interviewing, Observing and Writing the Case Study	56
IV	Diagnosing Processing Deficits and Using Standardized Tests	89
V	The Diagnosis of Reading and Phonics Skills	118
VI	Diagnosis of Spelling, Mathematics and Written Language Skills	152
VII	The Medical and Neurological Diagnosis	184
VIII	The Motor Evaluation	228
IX	The Evaluation of Visual Perception	260
X	The Evaluation of Auditory Perception	298
XI	The Speech and Language Evaluation	319
XII	The Intellectual and Emotional Evaluation	342
XIII	The Synthetic Approach to Diagnosing Learning Disabilities	365
	Appendices	374
	Bibliography	388
	Index	415

Introduction

One of the most controversial areas in education today is the question of how one identifies a learning disability. It seems that there are three major obstacles in the way of trying to answer this question. First, the large amount of confusing and contradictory information in the learning disabilities field tempts one to conclude, as many have, that learning disabilities is nothing other than an educational myth. I, however, could not take this position because over the last century very reputable and astute researchers in a dozen professions and a multitude of countries have described the intelligent, motivated child who does not seem to be able to read adequately. The description of this child, like the ancient god Proteus, has changed its name and form again and again, but the basic description remains essentially unaltered.

The second obstacle to identifying a learning disability is the tendency to latch onto one viewpoint in the jumble of opinions so that one can describe the subject from a single theoretical orientation. This is particularly true of frameworks based on a professional discipline and therefore I have tried to use a truly interdisciplinary approach in this book. Problems, however, are best perceived when there is some kind of scaffolding to hold the information together. To do this I have used a modified factor analytic approach which I have found works well as long as one does not adhere too closely to the mathematical technique. This approach, of course, is well known in the behavioral sciences, but I believe that the broad approach used in this book is more comprehensive than is presently used in the field of learning disabilities. I have found this technique allows one to integrate medical symptoms, behavioral observations, educational-diagnostic patterns, and test results into a coherent diagnosis that can suggest a definite remedial plan.

The third obstacle to diagnosing learning disabilities is that the whole area of research revolves around comparing groups of "normal" and identified "learning disabled" students. This leads to trying to find the common characteristics of a diverse group of individuals. It is much like lumping stars, planets, astroids and comets together and then trying to find their common characteristics. Unless one distinguishes between these different bodies to begin with, one ends up with a science that cannot say much beyond they are made of matter and follow the laws of gravity. In a similar manner until we distinguish between the dozen or more different kinds of learning disabled children, we will be able to say little about them except that they are intelligent students who do poorly in school. I have therefore devoted a great deal to describing the different kinds of learning disabilities by giving their characteristics, common labels, and their course and prognosis; being fully aware that I may be wrong on a number of cases simply because there is presently no test to distinguish these types or any major research on the different types of learning disabilities. I have also avoided the temptation of making up any new labels, although I have fallen back on some old names and labels to clarify the types. Hopefully, this work will shed enough light on the labeling issue that research into this area will progress.

The whole process of accurately diagnosing a learning problem lies on the foundation of experimental evidence of how children learn. I am only too aware that in the limited space available, I have been able to give only the barest outline of the theory behind each diagnostic approach. I have included over a thousand references to help overcome this problem and hope that when researchers begin to think of the areas covered, they will begin to write review articles that are relevant to clinicians in the field. Furthermore, a day does not go by when some new finding, some new insight or review does not appear on how children learn and think. Each one of these not only outdates the book slightly, but also slightly changes the whole way one goes about diagnosing. The only way to overcome this is to include theory on why one proceedes in a diagnosis in a particular way so when new findings come out they can be fit into present knowledge easily.

Finally, I have been overwhelmed by the abundance of material in the learning disabilities field that touches on that almost mystical question of *how* children learn complex symbolic systems. Shifting through all of this, one cannot help but feel that research in the diagnosis of learning disabilities will not some day yield an important breakthrough in education and in psychology. Hopefully, this book will help in achieving these new insights.

Clark Johnson
Boulder, Colorado

Chapter I

The Definition of Learning Disabilities

A child who has at least normal intelligence, no significant emotional problems, normal eyesight and hearing, but who, even with good instruction, does not seem to be able to master basic school subjects is a child with a learning disability. The key to helping such a child is to make a diagnosis that will suggest a specific remedial treatment that will help him overcome his learning problems. The difficulty of diagnosing a learning disability involves evaluating the child's general academic, motor, emotional, intellectual, and perceptual functioning and then pinpointing which of the skills and capacities within these areas are deficient. The skills required in making a good diagnosis cut across several disciplines and require a thorough understanding of how children learn and integrate information.

Traditionally, the evaluation of the child's academic skills has been left to the classroom or reading teacher; a suspected nutritional or neurological problem to the physician; a perceptual deficit to the speech therapist or learning disabilities specialist; an evaluation of the child's intellectual capacities to the psychologist or psychiatrist; and a suspected social or environmental problem to the guidance counselor or social worker. The fragmentation of the diagnosis across different disciplines has given the child with learning problems such diverse labels as the "disabled reader," the "dyslexic," "strephosymbolic" or "word-blind" child or the child with a "brain dysfunction."

Samuel Kirk (1969), a prominent figure in the field of learning disabilities, has suggested that there be one person responsible for coordinating the diagnostic information received from the physicial, psychologist, speech therapist, and other diagnosticians, and that this person be called a Diagnostic-Remedial Specialist. It is the aim of this book to address itself to this specialist who will be called the "clinician," "diagnostician," or "learning disabilities specialist," knowing full well that this might be a teacher, reading specialist, speech therapist, or psychologist.

A good diagnosis rests on three pillars:

1. The clinician must have a sensitivity when working with people. He must be able to elicit a favorable reaction from the person being diagnosed, get him to put forth his maximum effort, and evaluate the client's behavior in an objective manner removed from his own personality.

2. The clinician must be willing to examine diverse information, particularly that which seems contradictory and does not fit with the traditional stereotypes.

3. The clinician must have a strong background of how children learn and process information, including a good knowledge of what is known about children who have learning disabilities. This last pillar is often the weakest because the information on learning and information processing is so complex and confusing and because there are few places where this information has been drawn together.

Teaching a clinician to be sensitive and unbiased cannot be done easily in the format of a book. To assist in this process, this volume is an endeavor to tie together the vast amount of information relevant to making a diagnosis, attempting to put it into historical perspective, and to outline theories of how learning takes place. This, of course, is an enormous task and liberties have been taken to reduce the confusion and simplify findings and theories. This book uses the scientific method, which assumes essentially that clinical intuition and experience are valuable but the only way progress towards consistent and universally applicable diagnostic techniques can be made is by checking all statements and assumptions with research. A great deal of this book, then, will be devoted to reviewing research studies that may appear tedious at times, but this is the only way the author knows of reducing the vast amount of inaccurate folklore and avoiding the cults of personality so prevalent in this relatively new field.

Ways of Defining Learning Disabilities

A great deal of confusion has existed about how to define learning disabilities, mostly because this disorder has been studied and described by professionals from such diverse fields as neurology, remedial reading, child psychology, ophthalmology, and psycholinguistics. Almost all definitions include three basic components: there is a significant failure in an academic area, the student has at least normal intellectual abilities, and this deficit is not due to poor vision or hearing, a medical disorder, emotional problems, or poor instruction. The issue is complex, and one can define learning disabilities from at least six different perspectives. Each may be thought of as being analogous to looking at a valley from the air, the ground, the east, the west, and various vantage points; the features are differently arranged and each view allows one to see certain details that other views do not afford, but the basic material is the same.

The first individuals to describe cases of learning disabilities were of the medical profession. They were primarily interested in LD (learning disability) children because they resembled adult patients who had brain injuries. In the latter half of the nineteenth century many cases were reported of adults with normal intellectual and academic abilities who would have a stroke and suddenly find that they either could no longer talk or "make any sense" of words. These adults were said to have "alexia" (a = not + lexia = to read) or "agraphia" (a = not + graphia = to write), and it was inferred that a particular part of their brains had been damaged by the stroke.

Morgan (1896), a British ophthalmologist, reported one of the first cases of learning disabilities, his subject a child who had normal intelligence but could not learn to read even though he tried very hard and had excellent intelligence and instruction. Morgan hypothesized that the child had a cerebral defect and was "word-blind" from birth. Other researchers, principally psychologists (Money, 1962; Critchley, 1964), have expanded this medical approach and applied the Greek term "dyslexia" for poor readers with normal intelligence, "dyscalculia" (dys = not + calculia = to calculate) for children who do poorly in arithmetic, and "dysgraphia" for those with poor handwriting. Underlying this approach is the assumption that different areas of the brain handle certain psychological processes involved in academic skills, and that children with learning disabilities have a pathological process in these areas.

The advantages of the medical approach to defining learning disabilities is that the disability is defined in terms of a specific set of processes, and this method of defining suggests clear etiological factors. This approach of defining learning disabilities has been criticized because there are apparently great differences between brain-damaged adults who had mastered academic skills and then lost them and children who have never learned them in the first place (Hermann, 1959). The medical approach also assumes that LD children have a medical dysfunction (which has never been proven scientifically), and in fact most LD children do not have just a specific reading or arithmetic problem, but exhibit many kinds of weaknesses.

A second approach closely allied to the medical approach is the symptom cluster method of defining learning disabilities. This approach assumes, as does the medical approach, that LD children are qualitatively different from achieving children and therefore exhibit special symptoms that "normal" children do not. LD children become defined, then, as those children who "reverse their letters," "perseverate," "do not know their right from their left," "have no sight vocabulary," are "easily frustrated," and the like. One of the most complete lists of the symptoms and behaviors of LD children is presented in *Figure 1*, based on Blom and Jones (1972) who reviewed the texts by Johnson and Myklebust (1964), Myklebust (1968), Vallett (1967), and Stuart (1963).

Figure 1
Behaviors Related to Learning Disabilities

A. Oral Reading Behavior
1. Confusion in letter, syllable, and word recognition
2. Reversals of letters and symbols
3. Loses place easily
4. Confusion of words with similar verbal and/or visual configuration
5. Many errors of omissions, additions, substitutions, and transpositions while reading
6. Poor use of word attack skills and lack of phonics knowledge
7. Lacks fluency in reading
8. Points to words
9. Moves ahead
10. Words and phrases lack meaning after being read correctly

B. Silent Reading Skills
1. Loses place easily and tracks words poorly
2. Points to words while reading
3. Moves head back and forth while reading
4. Erratic eye movements and unusual fixations
5. Lip movement or subvocalization (whispering) while reading

C. Perceptual Skills
1. A deficiency in visual memory
2. Poor visual sequencing ability
3. Poor visual discrimination
4. Visual-motor coordination problems
5. Figure-ground discrimination difficulties
6. Poor form constancy perception

D. Perceptual Skills
   1. Poor auditory memory
   2. Auditory sequencing difficulties
   3. Poor auditory discrimination
   4. Perseveration of beginning sounds while talking
   5. Listening ability is very poor
   6. A lack of auditory-visual integration
E. Motor Skills
   1. Lack of touch sensitivity
   2. Deficient tactile discrimination
   3. Lack of sense of muscular motion
   4. Lack of feeling of muscular position
   5. Poor handwriting
   6. Difficulties in reproducing (copying) visual forms
F. Speech and Language Skills
   1. Irregular speech development
   2. Slow speech development
   3. Speech impediments (poor articulation and stuttering)
   4. Poor verbal fluency and ability to express self
   5. Inability to blend and synthesize sounds into meaningful wholes
G. Spatial Abilities
   1. Poor position in space (spatial orientation)
   2. Poor grasp of spatial relationships of objects (up-down, over-under)
   3. Poor directional orientation (right-left of body)
H. Temporal Abilities
   1. Lack of rhythm
   2. Lack of sense of synchrony
   3. Poor orientation of time of day, days of week, seasons, etc.
I. Social and Emotional Behavior
   1. Low frustration level
   2. Poor interpersonal relationships
   3. Emotional lability (easily excited)
   4. Poor motivation
   5. Withdrawn
   6. Easily discouraged
   7. Inappropriate behavior
   8. Poor self-concept
   9. Depressed
   10. Low energy level

  11. Exhibiting the failure syndrome
  12. Tense, cannot sit still
 J. Physical and Motor Behavior
  1. Poor balance
  2. Poor posture
  3. Poor locomotion and gross coordination
  4. Poor fine motor coordination and handwriting
  5. Excessive clumsiness
  6. Ambidexterity
  7. Mirror writing
  8. Hyperactivity
  9. Confused laterality
  10. Confused body awareness
 K. Conceptual Behavior
  1. Poor memory, particularly for symbolic representations
  2. Poor association of meaning with symbols
  3. Unique patterns of conceptualization and lack of being able to abstract
 L. Attentional Behaviors
  1. Poor concentration and short attention span
  2. Poor motivation
  3. Cannot sit still, overactive

  Looking over these seventy-two behaviors and traits, it is clear that no LD child has even a majority of these symptoms, and any achieving child will exhibit a number of these symptoms from time to time and from situation to situation. In another symptom cluster approach, Wissink, Kass, and Ferrell (1975) polled forty experts in the LD field on what traits they felt most characterized LD children. They were able to obtain forty somewhat independent components and asked the experts to rate the frequency they thought these traits would appear among LD and non-LD children. By applying probability theory they also obtained a probability that the child was LD from the presence of each characteristic. Wissink, Kass, and Ferrell reported the following traits were thought by experts to be most frequently associated with LD children: poor reading comprehension, attention span, auditory-visual coordination, writing, auditory speed of perception, visualization, sound blending, rehearsal skills, and mathematical comprehension.

  The real advantage of the symptom cluster approach is that rapid identification of the problem can often be made without extensive testing. If a teacher reports, for example, that a third grader cannot seem to learn cursive, is reversing "b"s and "d"s, has difficulty remembering his directions, is a poor reader, but tries hard; one can almost immediately begin examining him for learning disabilities with a visual memory deficit, because this cluster is often associated with this kind of problem. The two main disadvantages of using a symptom cluster diagnosis are that each individual is different, so that the symptoms never cluster so neatly into patterns, and many symptoms are common to many disorders and may, therefore, cloud the issue more than clarify it.

A third way to define learning disabilities is in terms of a discrepancy between a child's potential for learning and his actual achievement. This method relies on the assumption that a child's potential — that is, maximum learning rate — can be accurately measured by an intelligence measure and that his achievement level can be measured on a standardized academic test. Then, depending on the expectancy formula used (reviewed later), if the child's achievement falls between 0.80 and 0.85, he is considered to have a learning disability. Recently the federal government wanted to adopt the formula: CA times (IQ divided by 300 plus 0.17) minus 2.5 equals LD, with CA being the child's chronological age and LD being his grade equivalent, but the formula was so heavily criticized it was finally eliminated, so now each state must develop its own definition of learning disabilities (Danielson and Bauer, 1978). The advantage of a discrepancy formula is that it allows gifted children who are achieving only at grade level and slow learners achieving much below their mental age to receive LD help. The disadvantage is that it relies on IQ testing to establish "academic potential," an old concept that has been under a great deal of criticism.

The Exclusion Approach

Another way to define learning disabilities is by essentially excluding all other kinds of handicapping conditions. *The Learning Disabilities Act of 1969* defined LD children as:

> Children with special (specific) learning disabilities exhibit a disorder to one or more of the basic psychological processes involved in understanding or in using spoken and written language. These may be manifested in disorders of listening thinking, talking, reading, writing, spelling or arithmetic. They include conditions which have been referred to as perceptual handicaps, brain injury, minimal brain dysfunction, dyslexia, developmental aphasia, etc. They *do not* include learning problems which are due primarily to visual, hearing, or motor handicaps, to mental retardation, emotional disturbance, or to environmental disadvantage.

This definition and law made learning disabilities a category for receiving federal monies in special education. For a school system to receive federal money for an exceptional child, he must be adjudicated handicapped, i.e., he must be certified as meeting the state definition of the disability by a qualified diagnostic team. The nine different categories of exceptional children are diagrammed in *Figure 2*.

This chart gives the numbers and prevalence of each handicap as estimated by the United States of Education (Gearheart, 1973, p. 3). As may be seen approximately thirteen percent of the children in the U.S. are thought to require some modification of their education.

First, there are the visually impaired who are totally blind or partially sighted with vision that cannot be corrected better than 20/200. While blind children need modifications in instruction, Jones (1961) has shown that many legally blind children, especially when given enlarged type, can learn to read with their residual vision. Children who are deaf have a handicap particularly in reading and writing, and Gentile (1969) has shown that deaf children are typically six to seven years behind their hearing peers in reading by the time they are in high school. Legal deafness is defined as a hearing loss greater than eighty decibels, and this child must learn to communicate either in sign language, finger spelling, speech (lip) reading, or a combination of these. The hearing handicapped are defined as those children with a hearing loss between twenty and eighty decibels, and the diagnosis is usually based on an examination by an audiologist.

Expressive disorders include children with speech handicaps, with about one-half of the speech impaired presently receiving services, a relatively high figure when compared with the other groups. Not all expressive disorders involve speech; there are children with orthopedic and neurological handicaps. Children with physical handicaps often face continual problems with the design of buildings and especially with getting up and down stairs, curbs, doorways, and the like. The neurologically impaired include children with cerebral palsy and epilepsy, which are diagnosed by a physician.

A large amount of schoolwork involves the processing of visual and auditory material and abstracting the relevant information. This information processing ability is what is generally referred to as intelligence. Children with a reliable IQ between 90 and 110 have normal intelligence. Taking all things into consideration, they should achieve at grade level. Children with an IQ between 80 and 90 are usually referred to as slow learners and will lag behind one or two years in all school subjects. Students with IQs between 50 and 85 are referred to as educable mentally retarded and are often taught in special education classes in the school while the "trainable" mentally

Figure 2
The Number and Prevalence of Exceptional Children

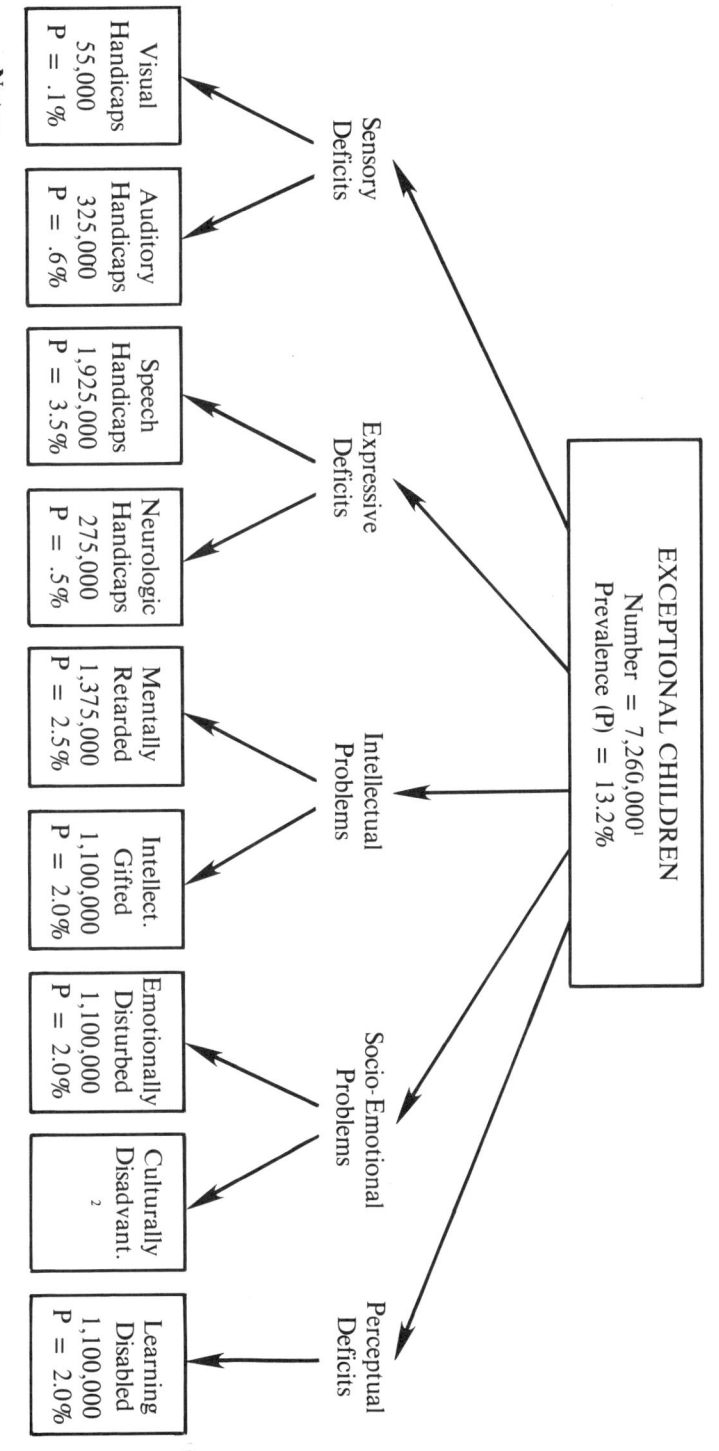

```
                          EXCEPTIONAL CHILDREN
                          Number = 7,260,000¹
                          Prevalence (P) = 13.2%
```

- Sensory Deficits
  - Visual Handicaps — 55,000 — P = .1%
  - Auditory Handicaps — 325,000 — P = .6%

- Expressive Deficits
  - Speech Handicaps — 1,925,000 — P = 3.5%
  - Neurologic Handicaps — 275,000 — P = .5%

- Intellectual Problems
  - Mentally Retarded — 1,375,000 — P = 2.5%
  - Intellect. Gifted — 1,100,000 — P = 2.0%

- Socio-Emotional Problems
  - Emotionally Disturbed — 1,100,000 — P = 2.0%
  - Culturally Disadvant. ²

- Perceptual Deficits
  - Learning Disabled — 1,100,000 — P = 2.0%

Notes:

[1] Based on a population of 55 million children in 1975

[2] No statistical information because this group was not counted as a group of exceptional children in this particular study

retarded child has an IQ between about 20 and 50 and is usually taught at a special education center. On the other end of the intellectual scale are the gifted students who are defined as having an IQ above 130. This group, because they often do well in school, is one of the most neglected groups of exceptional children.

Children with severe behavioral or conduct problems are often labeled emotionally handicapped. The diagnosis of this group usually is done by the school psychologist and is a difficult diagnosis to make because other handicapping conditions can cause emotional overlays forcing the psychologist to have to make the decision of whether the emotional problem caused the handicap or the emotional problems were the result of the stress of having the handicap. Children with social problems include the socially disadvantaged who share the experience of coming from families that do not expose them to common middle-class cultural experiences that schools assume all children possess. The programs for the disadvantaged are often referred to as "Title I" programs, because a large number of these programs are funded under Title I of the Federal Education Act of 1967. Usually, to qualify for the title programs, the child must come from a family living below a certain income level and live in a poverty-level neighborhood.

The last category of exceptional children is comprised of children with learning disabilities. This group is usually defined by exclusion—they are the children who do not fit in the previous eight categories, but still have major problems in learning to read, spell, write, solve arithmetic problems, or function in school. For the lack of any other explanation, children with learning disabilities are often considered to be children with disturbances in "perceptual functioning."

There are over 1,160,000 children in learning disabilities programs across the nation. Coles (1978) has launched a concentrated attack on defining LD children by exclusion, pointing out that this definition makes it easy to classify the unmotivated student as an LD child. He has also reviewed the research on the ten most frequently used standardized tests to define learning disabilities and has shown that they were either highly unreliable and/or did not correlate with academic achievement. His point is a good one and illustrates how a definition by exclusion in itself has many weaknesses. In fact, some of the evidence of how this definition, written mainly by Kirk, has not worked comes from Kirk himself (Kirk and Elkins, 1975) in a survey of 3,000 children in LD programs across the country. Kirk discovered, for example, that thirty-five percent of children in LD programs had IQs below 90, making them "slow learners" rather than classic LD children.

The advantages of the exclusion system is that it is fairly easy to define the child by legislative criteria without having to worry about the behaviors exhibited by the child or the cause of the disorder. Currently the federal government is reimbursing school districts about $150 per LD child. The disadvantage of this system is that it is a "waste basket" term, and a lot of children with a variety of problems end up being diagnosed as learning disabled because they do not fit the definitions of any other category.

A fifth way to define learning disabilities is in terms of a developmental lag whereby one assumes that various abilities develop at different rates, and LD children are essentially those children who are slow to develop in those areas required in academic functioning. There is a fair amount of information (reviewed later) to show that many children "outgrow" their LD problem with no intervention, which supports this position. For this reason, norms for children's ability in motor development, handwriting, written language, spelling, word attack skills, and math will be given. The disadvantage of defining learning disabilities in terms of a lag is that some children do not outgrow their problems. (Dykeman and Ackerman, 1976).

There is another way to define learning disabilities, and that is to use the procedure of factor analysis. This rather complex approach has a great many advantages over the other definitions and in many ways ties together the other definitions and will, therefore, be the one used in this book.

The Factor Analytic Approach

All the previous definitions have relied on apriori criteria based on clinical experience. Since specialists in the field do not agree on what a LD child is or what causes this condition, there are hundreds of definitions of learning disabilities. A way out of this dilemma is to perform a set of experiments that can be replicated year after year on one set of children to the next. Such experiments, however, involve examining hundreds of variables and thus require the methods of multivariate analysis. To illustrate the possibilities factor analysis can bring to the diagnosis, a hypothetical example will be illustrated.

Let us suppose that we have fifty elementary students whom the classroom and LD lab teachers agree are "true" LD children and not children placed in the lab for some other reason. This becomes our experimental group, and we could then give the children (or perhaps the children have already been given) a set of measures, which could include rating scales, physiological measures, and test scores.

The next step is to correlate these measures and develop a cor-

Figure 3
A Hypothetical Correlation Chart for Eleven Variables[1]

Variables	1	2	3	4	5	6	7	8	9	10	11
1. Aiming a ball	--	.21	--	--	--	--	--	--	.58	--	--
2. Memory for digits (ITPA test)			.32	.42	.35	.20	--	--	.45	--	.25
3. Vocabulary (WISC-R test)				--	--	.60	.60	.25	.62	--	.35
4. Attention (teacher rating)					.62	--	--	--	.40	--	.60
5. Anxiety (skin conductance experiment)						--	--	--	--	--	.38
6. Similarities (newly developed test)							.89	.65	.45	--	.40
7. Opposites (newly developed test)								.62	.41	--	.45
8. Vocabulary (PPVT test)									.61	--	.47
9. Age of the child										--	.60
10. Mother's age											--
11. Severity of the problem (years behind academically)											

[1] Nonsignificant correlations are denoted by a dash. Low correlations are in the .20-.40 range, moderate correlations by .40-.60, high correlations are above .60 in this example.

relation chart such as the one shown in *Figure 3*. A correlation simply shows how closely two measures are related to each other for a particular group of persons. This becomes the first objective information and tells us, for example, that (a) mother's age and aiming the ball do not correlate with severity of the problem and therefore probably should not be part of a diagnosis, (b) vocabulary measured by the WISC-R and PPVT are apparently measuring two different kinds of vocabulary, (c) the age of a child is very imporant in how severe his problem is, and this variable must be considered in all the tests but aiming, (d) the newly developed tests of similarities and opposites are measuring the same ability and, therefore, both tests do not need to be administered, (e) anxiety as measured by skin conductance relates highly to attention, but not to the other traits, suggesting that attention and anxiety may be a separate dimension that is related with the severity of the problem.

As may be seen, a large number of comparisons can be made with just ten measures, and some systematic way of looking at these correlations is needed. This systematic way is the mathematical procedure called factor analysis, which takes the correlation table, goes through complex mathematical calculations and comes up with factors. If each of the tests given is reliable (the next chapter will discuss reliability), and the tests are diverse enough, and the proper kind of factor analysis is performed (the author believes that oblique rather than orthogonal rotation is preferred), a set of independent factors will emerge that will correlate with each other. This factor table would look something like this for our hypothetical example:

Tests	Factor I	Factor II	Factor III
Aiming a ball	--	--	.35
Memory for digits	.25	--	--
Vocabulary (WISC-R)	.65	--	--
Attention	.45	.88	.32
Anxiety	--	.45	--
Similarities	.55	--	--
Opposites	.67	--	--
Vocabulary (PPVT)	.33	--	--
Severity	.44	.52	--

From this example (which obviously does not meet the criteria for factor analysis), one can see that three factors emerge, but the procedure does not call them anything. Factor I, however, has a marker variable (Vocabulary of the WISC-R), which in previous studies has been associated with verbal intelligence, so one might go ahead and call it a Verbal Intelligence factor.

One may now conclude that for these fifty children sampled, three distinct traits-factors-processes can be measured on this battery and that the largest factor is verbal intelligence, which is best measured by WISC-R Vocabulary, Similarities, and Opposites. The memory for digits and PPVT only correlate marginally with this factor and could perhaps be excluded in future testing, while the attention variable seems to be an all-pervasive measure and not confined to just verbal intelligence. The second factor appears to be a biological variable, but there are not enough tests to confirm this, and the third factor may well be a motor factor.

The above is only the first step helping the diagnostician decide (a) which measures can be eliminated from the battery without appreciable loss of effectiveness, (b) which tests are related and, therefore, sensitive to such variables as age, ethnic origin, race, and sex, (c) the number of different kinds of learning deficits one could expect to differentially diagnose from the battery, (d) the number of factors that are actually measured by the battery, and (e) which tests in the battery are measuring a relatively pure factor, that is a single ability, and which are measuring several abilities. Three caveats apply: first, factor structure varies from population to population so factors for normal children might be different from LD children; second, unless one uses a large population, very reliable tests, and a large number of diverse sets of variables, which include well-known marker tests, the factor analysis will be no better than armchair guessing; third, factor analysis requires a number of judgments by the experimenter and, therefore, cannot be thought of as a simple mathematical procedure that you put into the computer and it comes out all done (Cattell, 1971).

The second stage in a factor analytic study might be to give the fifty children in our example a set of criterion measures. These could be given at the beginning and end of the school year. By subtracting end from beginning scores one could then develop a variable that tells us which children made the most progress given the special instruction in the lab. We can now correlate the child's progress scores with the diagnostic battery scores and factor scores. If our criterion measures are, for example, reading comprehension, math computation, and social maturity, we can develop an equation such as:

$$\text{Progress in reading} = aA + bB + cC$$

In which A, B, and C are the three factor scores and a, b, c are three coefficients derived from the correlation of the factor scores and the criterion measures.

In fact, this formula would be the *best* possible prediction of a child's progress in the lab, for these fifty children and the formula will also predict how much variance each of the variables will account for and how much variance is due to error and measures not used in the battery (Meehl, 1965).

With this approach, one can then make a diagnostic statement such as: "John, given these diagnostic test scores and measures, will make x months of progress in reading, y months progress in arithmetic, and z amount in social development in the LD lab, while Jane with these diagnostic scores will only make half as much progress." This method of diagnosis sidesteps having to label the child and makes the most accurate possible prediction of the child's progress in the particular school districts in which the study was done. The predictions will, of course, not be one hundred percent accurate, but the factor analytic approach allows one to establish the percentage of cases which will be mispredicted. The main disadvantage of the factor analytic approach is that it does not state anything about the cause of the disorder.

What is a Diagnosis?

The English word "diagnosis" comes from the Greek word *diagnosis*, which means "to distinguish." Even today a diagnosis is a process whereby one entity is distinguished from another. Since the method of doing a diagnosis has for centuries been interwoven in the practice of medicine, most of the concepts on how to diagnose have analogies to medicine. To show how a diagnosis of a learning problem differs from a medical diagnosis, the medical diagnosis will be described.

Suppose that an individual visits his physician and tells him that he feels sick. The first thing that a physician does is to ask him for the presenting problem, which are the symptoms that prompted the individual to seek out a physician. Symptoms are any indication of disease that cannot be objectively determined, such as one's stomach hurting. The physician notes these complaints and then begins the examination, which attempts to obtain more detailed and objective information of how the person is functioning. Objective measurements of body functions such as temperature, blood count, or an observation of a rash are called signs. From the complaints and the examination, the physician then has a set of signs and symptoms that hopefully fit into a pattern called a syndrome, which indicates a particular disease.

Since the examination can reveal only symptoms present at the time, an important part of the diagnosis is the examination of the patient's case history to establish if the present symptoms are new or the result of some previous illness. The physician may also at this point order some clinical tests, which are standardized measures of the individual's bodily functioning. Finally, the physician must make a diagnosis, which has a two-fold purpose: a suggestion of what is causing the symptoms and a suggested form of treatment. If there is a treatment available, the correctness of the diagnosis is always determined by whether the symptoms subside after treatment. The last point is very important because it shows that diagnosis and treatment are very closely interwoven. If one has only one treatment plan available, then a detailed differential diagnosis is unnecessary. In the 1940s, for example, when there was only one antibiotic for treating infections, it was unnecessary to carry a diagnosis to the point of determining which type of bacteria was causing the infection.

A behavioral diagnosis is based on observations of an individual's behavior in order to remedy his learning problems. The behavioral diagnosis centers primarily on an individual's actions, although it often includes an evaluation of a client's feelings, attitudes, and problem-solving capabilities. Konfer and Saslow (1965) or Catania and Brigham (1978) should be consulted for more details. The elements of behavioral diagnosis are best illustrated by an example of an actual case. The following is a case of a six-year-old boy, Pat, who was having difficulty in the first grade and was referred to the learning disability teacher.

A teacher referred Pat to the learning disabilities teacher with the report that Pat: (a) had difficulty working independently, (b) could not follow directions, (c) was not listening in class, and (d) could not understand what was said to him. Instead of interviewing the child right away, the learning disabilities teacher went and sat in class for a few hours to observe Pat. She noticed during the observation he: (a) could not put his name on top of the paper, (b) was a "day dreamer" and tended to tune out the teacher, (c) wiggled around a lot in class, and (d) had to be reminded continually to take out his pencil.

After the observation in class the learning disabilities teacher decided that Pat had a problem serious enough to warrant putting him on her case load. She next set up a half-hour session three times a week for him. The first few sessions involved just talking, drawing pictures, and other easy activities to put Pat at ease. On the third session Pat was given an informal diagnostic survey. On a visual task and a visual memory task Pat performed at the eight- or nine-year-old level, which was well above his age of six. On a task where he had to point to and name the missing parts in pictures of common objects, he pointed to several missing parts correctly, but did not know what they were called. In two auditory memory tasks, he performed only at the four-year-old level. His poor memory was evident when Pat could not remember what he had for breakfast that morning. On a spatial orientation test he was able to put his hand "in front of," "behind," "beside," a box correctly, but when asked to draw a line "across the top" of his paper he was unable to do so. With further testing, it became apparent that he did not know the meaning of the word "across." To determine if Pat might be a slow learner or a child with an LD problem, he was given the Stanford-Binet test by a psychologist who obtained an IQ of 105 (above average).

The LD teacher now possessed the teacher's complaints, her own observations in class, informal testing results, and the score of one clinical test (the Stanford-Binet). No case history was available, so a diagnosis had to be made on the basis of the existing information. Pat seemed to have good visual abilities and most of his problems were related to memory and hearing. This lack of auditory memory would explain his inability to follow directions, why he could not remember what simple words in the incomplete pictures and "across" meant, his not listening in class, and his tendency to be inattentive to the teacher's voice. It should be noted that the symptoms of not remembering breakfast (involving visual and auditory memory) and not working well independently do not really fit the pattern of poor auditory memory. Yet the other symptoms, plus the performance on two auditory tests fit a syndrome of poor auditory memory. At the end of the year of receiving special help in auditory activities, Pat had improved greatly and was reading at grade level and was dismissed from the lab.

A behavioral diagnosis deals with analyzing the individual's behavior and trying to fit these observations and test results into a pattern, often called a syndrome. It is more difficult to make a behavioral diagnosis than a medical one, because the behavior of the individual is changing from situation to situation with the measurement of behavior not being as precise as medical measures. The first six steps in a behavioral diagnosis, however, are analogous to that used by physicians in diagnosing a disease:

1. A set of complaints are elicited from the client himself by simply asking him how he is feeling. With young children who are unaware of their own thoughts and feelings, the initial complaints are usually elicited by interviewing the child's parents and teachers.

2. An examination is performed in which the clinician tries to objectify the complaints by informally testing or observing the client.

With LD children informal testing is usually a minireplication of the classroom with the tester giving the child a school task and recording the child's performance very systematically.

3. A case history is developed by interviewing the child's parents, examining school and clinic records, and talking to the child's previous teachers.

4. Clinical tests are performed to develop standardized measures of intelligence, academic skills, perceptual and memory abilities. These are, of course, the familiar standardized tests that are so common in the school setting.

5. The symptoms, including test scores, are then fitted into a pattern (or syndrome). Unlike a medical diagnosis, the cause of learning disorders is not known and so there is great disagreement among clinicians about which symptoms comprise a particular syndrome.

6. Finally, the accuracy of a behavioral diagnosis, like the medical one, relies primarily on whether the prescribed remedial treatment leads to an abatement of the symptoms.

Since the origin of many behavioral disorders is not known, there is a strong tendency to simply put a label on a set of symptoms without making certain the suggested remediation will alleviate the symptoms. For example, a teacher may refer a child who is distractible, hyperactive, and volatile to the psychologist, who may give the child a set of tests and inform the teacher that the child has a "minimal brain dysfunction" and "learning disability," which is merely a label since it doesn't suggest any remedial treatment. If the psychologist were to report, on the other hand, that the child has an attentional deficit and is not working because of distracting auditory background activity in the classroom, or that the child can not concentrate because he is worried about whether his parents will get divorced, he is making a diagnosis.

The difference between labeling and diagnosing is that the labeling simply puts a name on a group of behaviors, while a diagnosis suggests some cause for the behaviors that can be verified by instituting the proper remedial treatment. To summarize this in Peterson's (1968) words, "The only legitimate reasons for spending time. . .in assessment is to generate propositions which are useful in forming decisions of benefit to the persons under study (p. 32)."

Three Types of Behavioral Diagnoses

A confusion over the proper way to go about diagnosing behavioral problems exists. Briefly there are three different approaches (Bateman, 1967) that have been advocated: the etiological, the process, and the behavioristic approach. Some diagnosticians use only one of these approaches and others use various combinations of the three.

An etiological diagnosis seeks to find the origin of the disorder. For example, an investigation of a child's inability to read may reveal defective vision. When the child is suffering from a diagnosable medical deficit, the etiological approach is valuable. The drawback to this approach is that the cause of many learning disabilities is simply not known. This whole issue will be reviewed in Chapter II.

The most commonly used method of diagnosing a learning disability is the process approach involving working with what are called psychological "processes," which are hypothetical constructs that can be measured by standardized tests, rating scales, or a careful examination of the child's behavior. The child would be diagnosed as being weak in a particular process such as "auditory memory," and the treatment would be to build up this process or to circumvent it without having to engage in speculating about the cause of this deficiency. The process approach will be described in Chapter IV.

The behaviorist approach reviewed in Chapter III assumes that hypothetical constructs and processes such as "intelligence," "visual memory," and the like are unnecessary to a diagnosis, and instead the clinician should simply list the observed behaviors of what the child can and cannot do. A behavioristic diagnosis might be, "Tami cannot write her letters beyond the letter 'f'," or "she knows her colors, but cannot add two-column numbers," or a similar problem. This method of diagnosis deals mainly with observed behaviors.

Sources of Information in a Diagnosis

The clinician has five basic sources of information at his disposal to make a diagnosis. He may rely on information gleaned from the child's permanent record in school; send home a family information form; develop his information from an interview with the child and his parents; make class observations and give informal diagnostic tests; and administer standardized tests. A good diagnosis should make use of all these sources, but often because of time constraints only a few of these sources are used.

The easiest source of information for making a diagnosis is often the case history, which is a record of what a person did in the past. A record of the child's performance in school is usually kept in his permanent file, which usually contains his previous grades and standardized test scores.

Permanent records have the advantage of being a quick and efficient way of obtaining information. Usually they have the disadvantage of containing little information on the individual's current functioning and may contain biased information. Records kept by schools, social work agencies, and institutions are often filled with negative information about the child because there is a strong tendency to record problems, crises, and violations of the rules without mentioning an individual's accomplishments and good qualities.

A second common source of information is the family information form, which is usually sent home before the intake interview is conducted. The family information form provides much diagnostic information and can also be a good jumping-off point for an interview with the parents. This information must, of course, be treated as biased with more defensive parents not reporting or remembering crucial information that may cast the family or the child in a bad light. The third source is the interview.

A fourth source of information can be gleaned from an informal testing situation. Informal testing involves giving the child classroom tasks that differ from standardized testing in that informal tests do not have rigid administration procedures or norms to compare the performance with that of other children. The major disadvantage of informal testing is that the tests are usually difficult to construct, and there are not established norms to determine the severity of the deficiency. Informal techniques also have the additional disadvantage of relying heavily on the clinician's opinion. If clinician A interviews a child and decides the child has primarily an auditory problem, and clinician B on the basis of his informal testing finds he or she is mentally retarded, there is no way of deciding between the two. If these two clinicians had given the child a standardized test of auditory perception (such as the Wepman Auditory Discrimination Test) and a standardized intelligence test, they could come to some objective estimate of the child's problem.

Fifth, a diagnosis may be based on standardized testing which is administered to each child in a prescribed way. A standardized test also has a specific way of scoring the performance on the test and a set of norms against which to determine how well the child did. Most standardized tests also have a body of research studies to show exactly what the test measures and how accurate it is so that a diagnosis rests on a body of scientific research.

There are also several disadvantages to standardized tests. The format of a standardized test may be more frightening to a child than an informal technique. The standardized test may also take a long time to give and yield only a single numerical score. These tests often have an aura about them that leads to quick and easy (and often incorrect) assessments. Even the name of a test is enough to cause a bias—countless children across the country have been diagnosed as having a visual closure deficit based upon poor performance on the "visual closure" subtest of the Illinois Test of Psycholinguistic abilities. Yet on closer examination, the "visual closure" subtest of this test reveals that it does not measure what is normally referred to as visual closure.

The clinician is then faced with the task of assembling this information and trying to form hypotheses about what might be wrong with the child. The case study is the usual form in which this information is presented. Depending on the situation, one person—usually the psychologist or learning disabilities specialist—may write and present a report that includes all the relevant information, or each member of a team of specialists from nursing, speech, psychology, social work, and learning disabilities may write his own report and these reports are synthesized in a case staffing. This book will assume that only one person will be writing the report, because this is the easiest way to present a unified diagnosis, although the author is well aware that in most school districts the latter method is followed.

The role of the clinician is to collect all the relevant information; to analyze the data in such a way that they make sense; to see that no area of functioning is overlooked; and to reconcile all discrepancies of the data. The clinician should then write a report that is meaningful and understandable to the persons undertaking the remedial treatment and to make recommendations that can be followed through in the child's particular situation. The author believes the clinician's other role is to be available to persons in the school and parents, to explain any questions about a child, and to follow the child as much as possible to make sure one's original diagnosis was correct and that the recommendations were followed.

Ethical Standards

It is important for every person making a diagnosis to realize that his or her decisions and statements about a child can have serious consequences for the child. A diagnostic statement may be used to support the placement of the child in a special class, to send him to a special school, or tie up valuable clinical services. It is important to express oneself in a diagnosis carefully, because what the clinician says about a child may be misconstrued by the parents or the child's teacher. It is the responsibility of the diagnostician to make sure that the words, "low IQ," "hyperactivity," "minimal brain damage," "reading disability," or similar terms are not simply copied down from the report onto the permanent folder and left there without the rest of the report to explain what the label means.

There are two main controls to ensure that the child's rights are not violated. The first is the Family Educational Rights and Privacy Act of 1974, which guarantees that all school records, test data (including IQ scores), interest inventories, health data, family background information, and teacher and counselor ratings are open to the parents' inspection. The parents also have the right to challenge any information in the child's folder and to submit minority reports. While some professionals regard this law as a threat because hostile parents might contest a valid diagnosis, the law is actually very helpful in most cases because it requires that the diagnosis be made in a careful manner with many checks and balances to ensure that the diagnosis is a valid one. The author believes that this law is a good one. In effect it says to the parents that the diagnosis is arrived at in an open and scientific manner and is always open to challenge should new evidence become available.

Chapter II

Etiological Factors in a Diagnosis: A Historical Perspective

One may conceive of the diagnostic process as analyzing the child's past in an attempt to explain his present behavior in order to modify his future. To record the child's entire past, of course, would be impossible and require hundreds of volumes of information. For this reason, a diagnosis is based on just a sampling of a very small portion of the child's behavior. The child's past is usually obtained by asking questions about how the child behaved when he was younger and his present behavior is usualy inferred from his performance on a few hours of formal and informal testing. An important question in any diagnostic procedure is which of these thousands of behaviors are important and unimportant to the diagnosis. The decision of which information is relevant must ultimately lie in what one believes is the cause of learning disabilities. If one believes, for example, that learning disabilities are the result of disturbances in visual perception, one does not devote much time to testing for auditory handicaps. Thus one's knowledge of the suspected causes (or etiology) of learning disabilities greatly influences the data one uses in a diagnosis.

The etiology of learning disabilities is not well understood, and many authorities do not agree among themselves which factors are important causes of learning deficits. As a result there is no single source or authority to refer to in order to find "the" causes of learning disabilities. A knowledge of the etiology of learning disabilities must be obtained by examining the voluminous research studies and case records on children with learning disabilities. While this is a tedious process, it pays off immensely when it comes time to make a diagnosis. For example, if the clinician knows that there is a large body of research to show that mixed laterality (e.g., being right-handed and left-eyed or vice-versa) is just as common among normal children as LD children, he will not spend his diagnostic time giving laterality tests or waste the child's time and patience by prescribing extensive remedial exercises to train for consistent laterality. Similarly, the LD specialist who knows that dozens of research studies have found a fair portion of LD children to have visual memory deficits will naturally look for this characteristic in a suspected LD child.

Establishing which factors have been implicated in causing learning disabilities is difficult, because the research on learning disabilities has appeared in such diverse sources as medical journals, journals for educational and school psychologists, books for reading teachers, and journals in the field of audiology, speech pathology, ophthalmology, and pediatrics. Since many of the causes of learning disabilities have been rediscovered again and again and given different names, this chapter will report the major etiological findings in the order of their chronological discovery. No attempt will be made to evaluate the validity of each suggested cause of learning disability, because the importance of each cause will be covered in detail in the following chapters.

To recap, a knowledge of the etiological factors in a diagnosis is vital, because it implicitly suggests what diagnostic information is valuable. The etiology of a disorder tells the diagnostician what variables to look for, how the variables relate to each other to make a syndrome, and suggests what procedures may be useful in remediating the disorder.

Early Neurological Theories

In the author's opinion the first important article relevant to the diagnosis of learning disabilities was the paper published by the prominent French surgeon, Paul Broca. In 1861 he described a disorder that he called "aphemia," but which is now called "expressive aphasia." Broca found that a number of normal adults would suddenly lose the ability to speak. These patients could carry out commands given to them, showing that they understood what was said to them, but they couldn't reply. Some patients could even express themselves in other forms, such as writing what "they wanted to say." On the basis of seven autopsies performed on patients with aphasia who later died, Broca reported that aphasia was the result of damage to the part of the brain now called Broca's area. The significance of this discovery, which has since been amply confirmed, is that it was the first time that a deficiency in a learned behavior was traced to damage to a particular part of the brain. It established that learned behavior and linguistic skills could be affected by biological changes in the body.

In the following two decades, physicians across Europe studied aphasia, finding that aphasia was not due to a paralysis of the vocal cords, because aphasic patients would under stress utter involuntary words such as "Oh damn." This situation presented a diagnostic puzzle—why would an individual lose his ability to speak and yet when emotionally upset utter some words involuntarily? This observation coupled with the heavy emphasis on introspection in the psychology of the day led to the theory that there are many stages or levels of speech. First, an individual must "think what he wants to say," then he must change these thoughts into words in the form of motor plans which move the vocal cords, and finally these speech-word plans must go to the part of the brain that innervates the vocal cords. Persons with aphasia apparently lacked the ability to perform the second stage, although in an emotional outburst the formulation stage located in Broca's area was somehow bypassed. This theorizing lead not only to the beginning of rudimentary models of how various linguistic processes function, but also to the speculation that there were dozens of areas in the brain responsible for different abilities.

In 1877, Kausmaul reported a case of a patient who not only had aphasia, but had also lost his ability to recognize the printed word. He found, however, that the patient did not have visual problems and had normal visual perception for nonwritten material such as faces, objects, and pictures. Kausmaul concluded that there was an area in the brain that was responsible for reading and suggested that this disorder be called "word-blindness." This was one of the earliest reports of an individual of normal intelligence having had a specific reading disability. The significance of this case was not well recognized at the time, and it was difficult to tell whether the "word-blindness" was part or independent of the aphasia in Kausmaul's case. The classic case of pure "word-blindness," which appears in several articles on learning disabilities, was a case described by Hinshelwood, a British ophthalmologist. In his own words:

> The patient was a teacher of French and German, and a man of intelligence and education. He was 58 years of age and had always enjoyed good health with the exception of occasional attacks of bronchitis in the winter. Of recent years, he had a large amount of mental work, and before his present visual difficulties appeared, he had considerable mental worry. He first came under my notice at the Glasgow Eye Infirmary on August 24th, 1894, and gave the following history. About one month previously he was greatly startled to find that one morning in his own house he could not read the French exercise which a pupil gave him to correct. On the previous day he had read and cor-

rected the exercises just as usual. Greatly puzzled, he went into an adjoining room, and having summoned his wife, he asked her if she could read the exercise. She read it without the slightest difficulty. He then took up a printed book to see if he could read it, and found that he could not read a single word. He remained in that condition until I saw him. It turned out that the patient remained unable to read until his death many years later. (Hinshelwood, 1917, pp. 2-3).

Hinshelwood found this patient had no change in intellectual (problem-solving) ability, had normal speech, and could write fluently and easily anything that was dictated to him. However, he could not read what he had written, leaving us with another diagnostic puzzle. The answer of how a person could not read what he had written lay apparently in the fact that there was an area in the brain like a Broca's area, which receives visual information and interprets letters into words that are then used in "thinking." In the dictation task the words were perceived auditorily so that they did not have to go through the visual interpretation area. Hinshelwood interpreted this inability to read as a loss of the "visual memory center" for letters and words and in an autopsy performed on this patient was able to find an abnormality in the area of the brain called the angular gyrus. This was, however, for an adult who had learned reading normally, and it remained for another British physician to describe the first case of a learning disability in a child.

Morgan (1896) writing in the *British Medical Journal* reported the first case of a child who had all the same symptoms of adult word-blind patients. Morgan described an intelligent fourteen-year-old boy who was normal in all school subjects except reading and spelling. After many years of regular class and special tutorial help for seven years, he could not learn all his letters and had difficulty reading simple phrases. He could also not spell even one-syllable words. Morgan is one of his interviews asked the child to write "carefully winding the string around the peg" and the boy wrote "calfuly winder the sturn rond the page." Morgan reported that this child read numbers fluently, performed mathematical operations, and could even read and understand algebra signs (Morgan, 1898). He diagnosed the boy as having "congenital word-blindness," with the belief that there were children who were born with word-blindness.

The significance of Morgan's paper cannot be underestimated, because he demonstrated that there were children of normal intelligence who were highly motivated and had received excellent instruction, who somehow couldn't learn to read, spell, or write. He showed, secondly, that this disorder closely resembled the condition of "word-blindness" found in adults with brain damage. This, of course, was to become the first etiological hypothesis: that learning disabilities were due to brain damage. Morgan also made the etiological suggestion that it was the child's memory for letters that prevented him from learning to read, spell, and write. We now had then before the turn of the century two suggested causes of learning disabilities: brain damage, and the lack of visual memory for letters and words. In many ways, even today our etiological speculation has not gone much beyond Morgan's suggestions.

It is interesting to note that the discovery of learning disabilities, as with so many other discoveries, was made independently by another person in the same year. In 1896, Kerr gave a lecture on congenital word-blindness in Britain. His talk was not widely reported, but it is of interest that Kerr's case had language difficulties as well as reading problems. This was to signal an ongoing debate of whether LD children have primarily a visual perceptional problem (as did Morgan's case) or whether they have a problem that is basically in the expression and reception of language.

Nettleship (1901), a physician who had read the reports about congenital word-blindness appearing in British medical journals, went through his patient files and found an interesting case of an individual with learning disabilities. He had seen a boy in 1882, only six years old at the time, who had normal vision but could not read words unless he spelled them aloud. Like other cases of congenital word-blindness, he had good auditory memory, but somehow could not remember visually-presented words. In spite of this, the child could read musical notes and was a good artist. Since musical notes are visual symbolic representations, it was clear that the child had a specific deficit with written material. The fact that the child could draw well suggested that the visual perceptual abilities and spatial abilities can be normal in children with learning disabilities. This finding has not been widely publicized because even today many clinicians consider a drawing made by the child an important diagnostic determinant of learning deficits. Nettleship reported that this boy, by extreme effort, learned to read and eventually became a lawyer, thus demonstrating that learning disabilities can be overcome.

A set of three more cases of children with congenital word-blindness were reported by Hinshelwood in 1902. The first was a child was two years behind in school. When Hinshelwood tested him, he was found to be behind in all forms of memory and could not obey the simplest commands. Hinshelwood realized this child was mentally retarded rather than having a learning disability and thus can be credited for making one of the first differential diagnoses in learning disabilities. His second case was a ten-year-old girl who had whooping cough and pneumonia at the age of four. It took her nine months of hard work to learn the alphabet, and after much effort she could read first grade books by spelling out most of the words to herself. She was an excellent speller and could spell many words she could not recognize by sight. Her vision was normal, and she could do fourth grade arithmetic, including multiplication. Hinshelwood suggested this child had a poor visual memory for letters and compensated for this deficiency by using her auditory memory (i.e. spelling to herself) to recognize the words. The last case reported by Hinshelwood was a seven-year-old boy who was unable to read all the letters and had gotten by in his reading assignments by memorizing the book. In spelling, the boy had to say the letters of the words to himself. For three months the boy was taken out of regular school and exposed to many short lessons each day to build up the visual memory for words. It was found that this treatment worked, and the boy learned to read first grade books fluently and began to recognize words by their visual image. In this article Hinshelwood suggests that the essential feature of congenital word-blindness is "this failure to recognize the words by their picture," and that word-blind children use their auditory memory to recognize words by spelling the word silently to themselves. He believed also that some of the children with learning disabilities overcame their problem by developing a memory for the lip movements and therefore developed a kinesthetic (body movement) memory for the words.

Thomas (1905), who worked with the Department of Education in London, did a survey of school children and found that one child in about 2,000 had congenital word-blindness. This made it a fairly rare disorder, but Thomas was able to establish that males made up seventy-five percent of the cases. This finding of the preponderance of males with learning disabilities has been substantiated many times, suggesting that learning disabilities may be an inherited sex-linked trait. Thomas therefore proposed the third cause of learning disabilities, which is some kind of inherited disorder. He reported the following cases: "One child by rapidly spelling the letters with his lips will arrive at the meaning of the word, another will trace the letters in the air or on the book with their fingers, and thus arrive at the meaning." One boy could not recognize a word visually so "if he looked at the word 'cat' it conveyed no meaning; if he had it spelled aloud to him, he could not arrive at the word; if he spelled aloud the word himself, he could not tell what it was; but immediately after he wrote it down his puzzled expression gave place to one of intelligence and he shouted the word 'cat'."

Thomas, as did Hinshelwood and Morgan, reported learning disabilities to be a disturbance of visual perception and suggested that the treatment for learning disabilities be extensive training in auditory decoding (e.g. phonics training). This suggestion, with its modern ring, was also accompanied with the suggestion that the alphabet be learned by cut-out wooden letters that would be handled.

One of the first Americans to write about learning disabilities was McCready (1910), who noted that there were now forty-one published cases of learning disabilities and that most of these were published by ophthalmologists. He named a number of cases, including the one by Kerr (1896), in which the child had not only a visual memory deficiency, but also problems with motor coordination and/or speech. He took the view that learning disabilities involved language in some way, and this might explain why some of these reports found that the children with learning disabilities also had stuttering problems. McCready's contribution was to focus attention on the auditory and motor aspect of learning disabilities. He, as did many who followed him, focused in on learning disabilities as a deficiency in language, not visual perception.

In the following year Town (1911) described in detail an entirely different type of learning disability — congenital aphasia. She described a case of an intelligent eight-year-old boy and a nine-year-old girl who learned how to function in their environment well, but had practically no speech. They could repeat almost any word said to them, showing that they did not have a hearing or vocal disorder, but they had a speaking vocabulary of only a few dozen words. These children could match and write letters, but did not know the meaning of even the most common words. Town's cases appeared to be the result of word-deafness, which is analogous to an auditory form of word-blindness. These children were unable to remember the spoken word and had extremely poor auditory memories. The papers of McCready and Town suggested, therefore, that there existed another type of learning disability caused by a deficiency in the remembering and formulating of words.

In 1917 Hinshelwood, previously mentioned, published the first book devoted exclusively to congenital word-blindness. Hinshelwood reviewed the evidence and came to the conclusion that LD children could not read because they had a congenital defect in the area of the brain involving visual memory. Among his many cases was a child with congenital word-blindness who died of pneumonia, and Hinshelwood was allowed to do a postmortem examination of the boy's brain. Hinshelwood found a lesion in the left angular gyrus, which is functionally located between the optic cortex, where visual stimuli are received, and Wernicke's area where language is processed. He therefore concluded that children with reading problems have a cerebral defect in this location. Very little has been done with Hinshelwood's finding, and in fact only one other postmorten involving a child with learning disabilities has been performed (Heller, 1963).

Clara Schmitt (1918) wrote a lengthy review of "Developmental Alexia: Congenital Word-Blindness or Inability to Learn to Read" for *The Elementary School Journal*, thus introducing learning disabilities to the classroom teacher. In her article she reported the results of an examination of children with learning disabilities. She found that all the children could recognize some words by sight with no child being completely word-blind. Each child could also match unfamiliar words even when they differed by only one letter. This reading inability did not seem therefore to be one of being unable to recognize letters. The older students could even copy into cursive writing a row of printed words they could not read. Third, she found that "the child's difficulty in every case consisted of the inability to learn phonics — to associate the sounds of letters with the letters themselves." The children given special training in phonics developed mastery in reading. Schmitt's article then was to suggest that the main cause of learning disabilities is the ability to associate the visually perceived letters with the auditory word, which the child already has in his language. This is analogous to the problem adults often have when it comes to remembering people's names; they see a familiar face, but cannot think of the auditory label that goes with the face.

The first quarter of a century of research in learning disabilities brought to the forefront four main causes of learning disabilities. First, certain neurological insults to the brain could cause behavioral disorders that closely resembled LD problems. Second, there was a type of learning disability called "congenital word-blindness" that did not affect oral abilities, mathematical performance, but did cause an extreme inability to remember the association of visual letters and the oral words they represent. Although Hinshelwood suggested fifty years ago that this was caused by a defect in the angular gyrus, this theory has been untested. If we examine *Appendix A*, we will see that this disorder affects primarily the process of intermodal symbolic memory that feeds into isolated word recognition.

Nettleship's case of a child who could read music and had artistic talent showed that it is possible to have a learning disability and have normal spatial ability, temporal sequencing, and object recognition skills. Hinshelwood's two cases are also of interest: the ten-year-old girl who could spell proficiently and do grade level math but could not read, and the seven-year-old boy could could recognize letters but could not recognize the "picture"' of the word, because the former is what one would call a "classic" or "pure" dyslexic, while the latter appears to be primarily a visual closure problem.

Third, there is another kind of learning disability called "congenital aphasia," which is closely related to language and is due to an inability to handle the auditory aspect of reading and spelling. The disorder of aphasia is placed as a defect in verbal reasoning in *Appendix A*, which is linked with syntax and auditory word perception. Fourth, scattered reports were made in which the kinesthetic channel was separated from the auditory and visual channel, suggesting some children can learn through this channel. Townsend reports a rather puzzling case in which a child apparently had a defect in auditory and visual long-term memory, although he could recognize words kinesthetically. In the author's experience, this condition does exist, but is very, very rare (with one student being remediated by teaching him Braille although he was perfectly sighted).

The Rise of Standardized Testing

In 1916 Terman published the first widely used standardized test in the United States, which opened a whole new dimension to the LD field because the processes in normal children could now be studied. This test, which became known as the Stanford-Binet, allowed psychologists for the first time to objectively measure intelligence. since the Stanford-Binet does not require any reading or writing, it can be used to distinguish objectively between slow learners and children with learning disabilities. The many studies using the Stanford-Binet that followed revealed in general that:

1. Children with below average intelligence are equally behind in reading, arithmetic, spelling, social studies, and other school subjects.

2. Children with above average intelligence are typically superior in their performance on all school tasks.

3. Intelligence as measured on the Stanford-Binet correlates moderately well (in the .50s) with word recognition, reading comprehension, and overall reading ability.

4. Mentally retarded children remained mentally behind their peers throughout their life, and there is no known educational system to bring their academic ability up to normal.

5. There is a group of children who score in the normal intellectual range on IQ tests, but who have great difficulty learning to read.

The Stanford-Binet also showed for the first time that mental ability could be measured reliably using a test. The impetus of this last discovery was to shift the interest in learning disabilities away from physicians to the realm of reading researchers and school psychologists.

After the development of standardized tests of intelligence, a great number of psychologists began developing standardized tests of other abilities. The name most closely associated with this movement was that of the American psychologist Gates, whose reading tests are still widely used. Gates' work began by designing standardized tests of word recognition (e.g. being able to recognize single, printed words) and reading comprehension. He then developed tests measuring a host of perceptual abilities, such as visual and auditory discrimination, visual and auditory memory; then he administered all these tests to various groups of children. By correlating the perceptual abilities with reading and spelling skills he was able to establish which skills were related to academic abilities and which were apparently unrelated. Gates (1926) in one study, for example, found the following correlations for normal children in the first through sixth grades:

Task	Word Recognition	Reading Comprehension	Spelling	IQ
1. Matching geometric figures	NS	NS	NS	NS
2. Matching digits	.36	.47	.37	NS
3. Matching words	.56	.72	.60	.28
4. Matching common objects	NS	.21	.27	NS
5. Associating word with design	NS	NS	.22	NS
6. Stanford-Binet IQ	.30	.50	.41	

Note: NS means correlation so small it was not significant (below .20).

This table of correlations can be used to deduce to what degree these perceptual tables are related to reading and spelling. It shows that intelligence is only slightly correlated with word recognition (e.g. reading an isolated list of words), while it is moderately correlated with reading comprehension and spelling. The task of matching words, usually referred to as visual discrimination, is very highly related to reading and spelling, particularly to reading comprehension. Interestingly, the ability to discriminate designs (i.e. nonverbal material) is not related to reading, and the discrimination of digits is only slightly related. This finding, replicated many times in other studies, shows that the matching of pictures and the like is not a good task to put on a standardized test attempting to differentiate good and deficient readers or spellers. The lack of a significant correlation between the task of associating a nonsense syllable with a pictorial design would appear to contradict Schmitt's theory that children with a reading disability have auditory-visual integration difficulty.

Since intelligence correlated with reading and with word matching, it is impossible to say how much word matching correlates directly with reading in this study. Gates (1926), therefore, did another study in which he statistically removed the influence of intelligence from the correlation between word recognition and word matching and obtained a correlation of .54. This correlation indicates that visual discrimination is a very important independent factor in reading. Gates, therefore, concluded that the ability to discriminate between words was an important factor in reading, and that lack of this skill could lead to a reading disability.

The Brain Lateralization Theory

Another development in the quest of the cause of learning disabilities was pioneered by Samuel Orton, an American neurologist who worked with the rehabilitation of brain-injured World War I soldiers. In 1928 Orton published a report in the *American Medical Association Journal* on "stephosymbolia" (steph = twisted + symbolia = symbol in Greek). His thesis was that there were children of normal intelligence who were extremely poor readers; these children had stephosymbolia, or the inability to recognize words after they had been repeatedly exposed to them. When the children were asked to reproduce what they had heard or read, they would characteristically reverse parts of the words. For example, the children would read "saw" for "was," or they would say something like they lived on "driverside ride" instead of "Riverside Drive."

Orton believed that LD children could not retain the correct order of symbols, because they had an extreme confusion between their left and right cerebral hemisphere. According to Orton the speech area (Broca's area) was normally located in the left hemisphere of the brain, and in normal children symbolic material (principally speech and reading) went to this side. Children with learning disabilities, however, had confused cerebral dominance, so that symbolic material was processed in the right hemisphere causing the child to perceive the material in reverse.

In Orton's own words: "The brain contains right and left visual areas which are exactly alike except for their opposite orientation, and we think, therefore, that the existence in the non-dominant hemisphere of engrams of different orientation from those in the dominant hemisphere cannot be lightly dismissed as the probable source of static and kinetic reversals of the spontaneous ability in mirror reading and mirror writing" (1937, p. 155).

In 1937, Orton published a full-length book giving his observations of working with children with learning disabilities. His book, *Reading, Writing, and Speech*, was comprised of only three chapters. The first chapter reviews the basic neurology of the brain and describes six disorders that had been found in adult brain-injured patients. In the second chapter Orton then suggests that there are six analogous disorders in children that are the result of a dysfunction of the brain at or near the time of birth. These six disorders are: (a) developmental alexia or congenital word-blindness, (b) developmental word-deafness, (c) developmental agraphia, which is the inability to write normally, (d) developmental motor aphasia, which results in poor expressive speech, (e) developmental apraxia or abnormal clumsiness, and (f) strephosymbolia, describing children with normal vision, intelligence, motor coordination and speech, but who cannot read.

Orton's contribution was to describe these children with learning disabilities in great detail and to point out that while they had normal ocular functioning, as soon as the information had been perceived, it became mixed up and reversed. The child would see, for example, the word "pebbles" and recognize it, but when asked to write it a few minutes later, he would write something like "pelbbse," showing that he knew the letters but not their order.

Typically, the LD child would see a word a hundred times and still become confused reading or writing it the hundred-and-first time. Orton attributed this confusion in sequential ordering to imperfect lateralization of the brain. Orton had now focused attention on three new types of learning disabilities. He found children who were normal in all respects except that their handwriting was abnormally poor. Developmental agraphia was thought by Orton to be mostly the result of left-handed children being forced to write with their right hand. Children with developmental apraxia were children who were uncoordinated, clumsy, who had difficulty hopping, skipping, jumping, and performing coordinated sequences of motor movements. Strephosymbolics were children who confused their "b"s and "d"s in reading and writing, reading such words as "saw" for "was" or "god" for "dog." They were, for the most part, atrocious spellers, because they confused the order of letters in words. Orton's emphasis on reversals suggested that the prime characteristic of LD children was the inability to orient visual material correctly in space and to sequence letters, words, and sounds. Reversals of the letters and letter sequences has now become one of the most widely accepted symptoms of learning disabilities. Orton's hypotheses that learning disabilities are caused by mixed laterality, on the other hand, has for the most part been unsupported by subsequent research, although it is still mentioned in many current texts as a cause of learning problems.

The lateralization theory did not die with Orton and is still very much with us in what is presently called right and left brain research. The observation that many LD children reverse symbolic material is so common that the idea that LD problems are caused by some defect in orientation and sequencing is obvious.

The Gestalt Movement

Behavioristic theory dominated psychology in the United States in the 1930s. Briefly, this school maintained that one should study only overt measurable behavior and not such internal constructs as attention, memory, closure, intelligence, and that all behavior should be described in terms of how the behavior was reinforced. This framework did not work well in explaining learning disabilities, because many LD children appeared to have the same external behavior and reinforcements as normal children except that they could not learn certain school subjects. An alternative to behaviorist theory was a German school of psychology named after the German word for "whole," *Gestalt*. Gestalt theory held that children learn by whole units or configurations rather than by stringing together small individual units. A behaviorist, for example, would contend that words were decoded by identifying each letter in the word and then chaining these letters together to make a word, while a Gestaltist would maintain that children recognize words as wholes in a single glance and do not have to decode each letter. This is supported by the fact that average first grade children will recognize five- and six-letter words when they are flashed on a screen for only one-hundredth of a second (Johnson, 1973).

Gestalt psychology was not well known to Americans until Ellis (1938) translated many important German works into English in *The Sourcebook of Gestalt Psychology*. Several of the articles on perception suggested that reading required seeing the words as wholes. These ideas had an impact on learning disabilities, for they led to the speculation that LD children could not perform complex perceptual activities because they could not perceive words as "wholes." This speculation also explained why some LD children, for example, could read individual letters, but not recognize words.

One article in Ellis' book was Adhemar and Goldstein's case of figural blindness. This case concerned a twenty-four-year-old laborer called Sch., who had an average education and then had a brain injury. After the injury Sch. could speak and read, but could not recognize simple drawings of objects such as may be found in coloring books. Sch's visual field was greatly reduced, and it was found that he could read only if he was given one to three seconds to recognize the word. While he read, his head moved back and forth; when his head was held stationary, he could not recognize words any longer. It became apparent with further experimenting that Sch. moved his eyes along the lines of the print and used these head movements as a source of recognizing the letters. When a few cross marks were drawn through words, he could no longer recognize the words. This was because he could not distinguish between the random lines and the print with his eyes tracing the random lines as well as the letter outlines. Sch. was also unable to make sense of perspective drawings or overlapping figures.

To the Gestalt theorist, this case illustrated that Sch. had lost the ability to perceive words as "Gestalts," because he could recognize the individual letters, but could not perceive the whole word when any distraction interfered. Two of Sch.'s symptoms — that of being unable to recognize figures as words without some kinesthetic feedback and being unable to recognize objects and words with extraneous lines drawn through them — have been reported repeatedly as being symptoms found in children with learning disabilities (Strauss and Legtinen, 1947; Kephart, 1960; Lerner, 1971, and others). This article has led to many discussions of the breakdown of Gestalt perception of words by LD children and to the development of perceptual tests using such items as overlapping figures to measure various aspects of the visual perception of Gestalt figures.

Another article in the *Sourcebook of Gestalt Psychology* was by

Wertheimer, the founder of Gestalt psychology, which described a perceptual phenomenon called "figure-ground" perception or the ability to recognize an object from its distracting background. The lack of figure-ground perception was found among very young normal chilren and adults with brain damage. This article along with Goldstein's was taken by researchers to suggest that children with learning disabilities had difficulties in reading and writing because they lacked the ability to integrate their perceptual experience into wholes.

Ellis' *Sourcebook* was to introduce into the English-speaking world a new way to look at the functioning of children with learning disabilities. Gestalt psychology provided a new set of concepts for describing learning deficiencies. First there was the concept of figure-ground, in which a child had to distinguish the important perceptual stimulus from irrelevant background stimuli. Some children with learning disabilities, for example, seemed unable to focus their attention in the classroom on the teacher's voice and instead listened to the radiator going on and off, the noise of books opening and closing, and the like. Second, Gestalt psychology introduced the concept of closure, the perceiving of individual parts as wholes. The most common example of this concept in education is sound blending, where the child "sounding out" a word must combine the initial letter sound with the middle vowel sound and the ending sound to make an identifiable word. Third, the Gestalt approach suggested that perception could be measured by giving the child tasks requiring the recognition of figures, the picking out of relevant figures from overlapping and embedded figures, and in the copying of complex designs.

During the Second World War little was done to follow up the work of Orton and the Gestaltists except for an experiment by Schilder. Schilder (1944) tried to determine if Orton and the Gestaltists were correct by presenting letters, words, numbers, pictures, and sentences to seven children who were poor readers and had normal intelligence. Schilder used a tachistoscope, which flashed visual material for a thirty-fifth of a second, in order to study the children's perception of the whole. Schilder was able to make five major observations:

1. Children with learning disabilities had normal perception of pictures, numbers, and had difficulties only with identifying letters and words. These children could repeat long number sequences and describe minor details in very complicated pictures when they were presented for just a fraction of a second. The children saw the pictures as wholes and never confused the picture with its mirror image.

2. Schilder made the surprising observation that children could recognize words just as well at one-thirtieth of a second as with an exposure of several seconds. This observation indicates that LD children were able to recognize words as wholes even at brief flashes and therefore had a disorder much different from that of word-blind adults (such as Goldstein's case of Sch., who took three seconds to recognize a word).

3. Schilder found that of these seven children with reading, spelling, and writing problems, only two of them showed any tendency towards mirror reading or writing. All of the children knew their right from their left, could follow complex commands using their right and left hands, and could correctly recognize the direction of movement of figures flashed on the tachistoscope. He took this as evidence against Orton's assumption that the basis of learning disabilities lay in right and left cerebral hemisphere confusion.

4. Only two of the seven children made right-left reading reversals (e.g. reading "god" for "dog"). All the children did, however, make visual discrimination errors by confusing, for example, L for I, T for L, g for y, M for N, m for n, indicating that the learning disability involved much more than simple confusion of letter order and direction.

5. Except for one case, the children had great difficulty in associating the right letter for the right sound in a word. For example, the child would read "as" for "at," "left" for "little," and the like.

From these observations, Schilder came up with some conclusions concerning the etiology of learning disabilities. He first concluded:

> The mirror tendency (reversals) certainly can have a new disturbing effect on the process of reading, writing, and spelling, but the mirror tendency by itself is insufficient to explain the whole picture. We come, therefore, to the formulation that the congenital reading disability is due to an incomplete function of centers. It is the inability of the patient to differentiate the spoken word into its sounds, and to put sounds together into a word. Single sounds are brought in connection with a written letter, but the written letter cannot be put together into a whole.

He goes on to suggest that this overall deficit could not be due to Orton's strephosymbolia. Schilder's experiment was able to shed some light on the problem of which factors are important in causing learning disabilities, at least for his sample of children. He found that visual perception for nonletter and nonword forms was normal, suggesting that learning disabilities are not just part of some general visual perceptual disturbance. These children also had fairly good right-left orientation, implying that Orton's cerebral dominance theory is not a very important cause of learning disabilities. The LD children could see words at a glance, indicating that they did not have a specific breakdown in perceiving visual wholes; in other words, LD children, like normal children, see words as Gestalts. Most of the LD children did, however, have problems with letter forms, and the findings suggest this is because letters have an auditory association component to them; this ability to link an arbitrary visual symbol with language being the children's principal problem.

Additive Weakness Theory

A much different approach for discovering the cause of learning disabilities was taken by Ruth Robinson. Robinson (1946) identified thirty children, aged five to fifteen, of normal intelligence who were poor readers and sent them to a team of specialists in ophthalmology, pediatrics, medicine, and other fields, and asked that each child be evaluated. She then tabulated the significant defects reported by the team members and found that many normal children had a deficit, or "anomaly" as she called it, while some of the LD children often had several anomalies. She reported the following defects for these LD children, who were primarily poor readers.

Type of Anomaly According to Specialist	Incidence In Percent	Defect Significant to Cause Reading Problem in Percent
Visual Defects	73	63
Neurological Defects	20	18
Auditory Acuity	7	Not reported
Speech and Auditory Perception	45	18
General Physical Condition	30	Not reported
Endocrine Imbalance	22	Not reported
Emotional Problems	40	32
Social Problems	70	Not reported

As may be seen, many children had more than one anomaly (and incidence does not therefore add up to one hundred percent). Robinson found in her study that: (a) pupils who were severely retarded in reading had the greatest number of anomalies, (b) visual anomalies were found in seventy-three percent of the cases, and these were significant in sixty-three percent of the cases, (c) the mere presence of an anomaly does not justify it as the cause of the learning problem, and (d) the visual, social, and emotional state of the child was very important to reading. Robinson concluded, "Reading disabilities are usually the result of several contributing factors rather than one isolated cause. Studies of the causes of reading disabilities reveal no clear-cut factors which occur only in poor readers but never in good readers."

These findings were significant because they indicated that there was not just one kind of learning disability. All children with normal intelligence who were poor readers did not seem to share the same deficit. Some had visual defects, others speech and auditory deficits, and still others social and emotional problems. Another point that her study seemed to bring out was that the normal reader may have one or two deficits, but these were not numerous enough to handicap him. The poor reader, on the other hand, may have many of these deficits or a particular combination of anomalies that would handicap his reading. An analogy to this concept might be that all bridges have girders that are imperfect and have cracks in them. The stress on the bridge is shared more or less by all its girders, so the finding of a crack in a few girders does not mean the bridge will fall down. A deficient bridge is one that contains a large number of defective girders or one where all the cracked girders are located in one critical part of the bridge. Robinson's data seems to indicate that those children who could not read had many deficiencies to cause a reading problem.

The theory of additive weaknesses helps explain why surveys of a population of children will reveal children with deficient processes such as poor visual acuity, poor memory and discrimination skills, or sequencing and coordination problems, who definitely do not have learning disabilities. These are the children with a narrow disability that is "compensated" for. *Figure 9*, which shows how a process evaluation can be done, has incorporated this theory by giving conditions where weaknesses do not result in a disability.

The Personality Maladjustment Theory

Another finding of Robinson not stressed very much by earlier researchers was that one-third of her sample had a significant enough emotional problem thought by specialists to be the prime cause of the reading problem. There had been a few psychoanalysts who had suggested that the inability to read was often a subconscious way for the child to get back at his parents (particularly the mother) with the secondary gain being that the child received a great deal of personal attention from adults. These theories were reviewed by Gann (1945) in her book *Reading Difficulty and Personality Organization*. Eleven previous investigations into reading and personality organization were reviewed; Gann felt, "that reading difficulties and disabilities are part of a larger organization, 'total personality,' and should therefore be studied in this relationship." She then developed a number of hypotheses most of which were confirmed by her study that the unsuccessful reader (the LD child):

1. feels less self-confident about himself than a normal reader,

2. shows a constriction of ego, is timid and withdrawn,

3. has more unresolved emotional conflicts,

4. feels more insecure in relation to other people,

5. has a poorly integrated ego, that is, he does not have clear goals,

6. has more neurotic traits such as greater fears, emotional resistances, and escape mechanisms,

7. has a lack of intellectual curiosity,

8. does not like reading, and

9. has exaggerated personality patterns manifested by his being either very slow and didactic, or being very fast and rushing through with the task, or being very confused and playing helpless.

Gann was then faced with the problem plaguing most personality studies; how do you measure these traits objectively? She chose the Rorschach (inkblot) tests as a personality measure, an interest-in-reading questionnaire, and had the child's classroom teachers and a psychologist rate the child. These tests were given to 102 subjects, in grades three through six, who were classified as being either superior readers, average readers, or poor readers depending on how well they read when the child's IQ was taken into consideration. She found that all three groups rated their like of teachers and school equally high, which is a surprising finding to those who believe the poor reader is "turned off to school." The superior readers were better at thinking abstractly, gave more unconventional responses on the Rorschach, and showed a basic intellectual curiosity. The average readers had the best personality adjustment, being more practical and extroverted than the other groups. They were also the least creative as measured on the Rorschach. The retarded readers were the most maladjusted of the three groups and especially exhibited the traits of being very concrete in their thinking, placing a great deal of emphasis on small details, and having difficulties relating to the adult world.

Gann's investigation encountered the same problem that most studies of personality and reading confront; namely, did the frustration of not being able to read cause the personality maladjustment or did the maladjustment cause the reading problem? Even today this controversy continues with reading specialists minimizing personality problems, while many psychiatrists claim that they can cure most reading problems by simply giving the child psychotherapy.

Although the suggestion that the etiology of learning disabilities may be due to emotional factors is an obvious one, there has been surprisingly little research on this. In fact, there have been very few comprehensive studies until Cattell and Butcher (1968) published a complex factor analytic study in which they gave academic achievement tests to children and correlated these with fifteen different personality variables. It was found that only five of these were related to achievement and summed together accounted for only a small portion of the variance. This area needs to be explored more intensely so that some light can be shed on the problem that faces most clinicians, and perhaps it can be clarified: Did the child's poor reading and spelling in school cause his current low frustration, lack of motivation, defensive and aggressive responses, or did the child have numerous personality problems that led to an academic problem?

The Minimal Brain Damage Theory

According to some experts the most important book in learning disabilities was Strauss and Lehtinen's *Psychopathology and Education of the Brain Impaired Child* published in 1947. The book was written to define the difference between retardation caused from cultural-familial and brain-injury conditions. The cultural-familial retarded children were assumed to have inherited low IQ or to have developed it from impoverished environment; therefore thought to be neurologically and perceptually normal. The brain-injured retarded were assumed to have acquired low IQ from a brain injury at or after birth; consequently having disorganized perceptual abilities.

Strauss reported that brain-injured children had the symptoms of:

1. Hyperactivity, which is the inability to organize one's bodily energy,

2. Distractibility, which results in two types of behavior — "an undue fixation of attention upon irrelevant external stimuli" and "the fluctuation in the perception of object and ground," which we now call figure-ground perception, and

3. Perseveration, which is the continuous repetition of motor patterns, such as a child who begins to color inside the lines and then cannot stop until the whole page is covered with crayon marks.

The second section of Strauss' book presented a set of tests for measuring visual perception and brain damage. He introduced the marble board test in which a child must place marbles on a Chinese checker board to make certain designs. The child with figure-ground problems would not be able to do this task, because he would become confused between the design made by the marbles and the background holes of the board. Another test involved presenting children pictures of common objects with confusing lines drawn over them. This latter task was based on reports of brain-injured, such as Goldstein's case of Sch. already discussed. Strauss also suggested that perseveration could be measured by having the child tap out various rhythms that were presented to him. The child who was perseverating would presumably tap out just one rhythm over and over again.

Strauss' contributions were the suggestion that learning problems could be caused by diffuse cerebral damage, diagnosed by the three symptoms of fluctuating attention, distractibility, and hyperactivity, now known as the "Strauss syndrome" or "Strauss triad." Although Strauss was originally interested in the mentally retarded, it soon became evident that many children with learning disabilities exhibited these symptoms. For the next two decades books for physicians, parents, and educators were published on the brain-injured child, who was often a child of average intelligence with perceptual and academic deficiencies.

In 1962 the National Institutes of Health sponsored a conference to study children of normal intelligence who learned poorly. The outcome of this conference was the establishment of a task force, chaired by Clements, which reviewed all the LD literature. Clements (1966) found that LD children had been given sixty-seven different labels. He recommended that all labels be discarded and the term "minimal brain damage" (MBD) replace them. The term MBD was recommended because the task force felt that learning disabilities were caused by diffuse brain damage that was so "minimal" that it could not be measured precisely by modern techniques. Clements (1966, p. 13) found that the ten most cited characteristics of MBD children, listed in frequency of order, were: (a) hyperactivity, (b) perceptual-motor impairments, (c) emotional lability, (d) general coordination deficits, (e) disorders of attention (short attention span, distractibility, perseveration), (f) impulsivity, (g) disorders of memory and thinking, (h) specific learning disabilities in reading, arithmetic, writing and spelling, (i) disorders of speech and hearing, and (j) minor (or equivocal) neurological signs and electroencephlograph (EEG) irregularities.

One can see from this list that MBD children primarily have attentional and perceptual problems with academic problems ranking only eighth in importance. In the following decade the term "minimal brain damage" was to appear in 600 publications, yet it never really caught on, because the term always carried with it the basic assumption that LD problems are caused by unproven brain damage. Educators, particularly, were reluctant to use the term MBD, because it implied a rather permanent organic condition and drew attention away from the fact that great strides could be made in overcoming the disorder with educational exercises.

A year later a body of parents of LD children met at a meeting for the Fund for Perceptually Handicapped Children, Incorporated, and asked Samuel Kirk to give the keynote speech. This was perhaps the most influential speech in the LD field, because Kirk described, defined, and coined the term "learning disability" to describe these children (Wiederholt, 1974). Kirk's definition and term was to become the most widespread formulation in the field and eventually the one to be written into legislation.

The Genetic Theories

During the 1950s there were a number of Swedish research studies (Hallgren, 1950; Hermann, 1959) using fairly sophisticated methods in genetics (family studies and monozygous and dizygous comparisons) that revealed a significant hereditary component to learning disabilities. The Swedish studies are especially interesting since Swedish is a completely regular (phonetic) language and therefore much easier to master, because Swedish, unlike English, can be accomplished by anyone who can learn to "sound out" words. Hermann in an examination of over two hundred LD children found that over ninety percent of these children had a parent or sibling with a learning disability. This led him to propose that learning disabilities were due to an autosomal dominant gene.

Malmquist (1958), another Swedish researcher, extended this research and found that reading problems follow a continuum rather than to be a trait that was either "present" or "absent." On this basis she strongly questioned whether this disability could be explained in terms of a single gene. To this day the question of how important genetic influences are in causing learning disabilities is largely unanswered.

The Process Theory

This theory, described in the previous chapter, became of particular interest when Guilford (1959) presented his Structure of Intellect, which suggested there were 120 different kinds of psychological processes.

Developmental Interruption Theory

The 1950s was an era of the development of many mathematical tools and experimental designs to test the ideas in learning disabilities, while the 1960s, interestingly enough, led to a resurgence of Strauss's theory that brain damage was the cause of learning disabilities. Several parental guides were published for the brain-damaged child (including Lewis, Strauss, and Lehtinen's *The Other Child* (1960) and Strauss's and Kephart's Volume II of *The Brain-Injured Child* (1955). Newell Kephart continued this work with a very influential book entitled *The Slow Learner in the Classroom* (1960), in which he presented the thesis that all intellectual and perceptual skills are an outgrowth of motor abilities. *The Slow Learner* lays out a careful sequence of motor stages that a child must go through, and whenever a child has a learning problem, it is because one of these stages of development has been disrupted. These stages begin with rolling over, creeping, crawling, static and dynamic balance, and go to such perceptual items as eye movements and directionality. In his own words:

> When development is *disrupted*, the child has either skipped a stage in development or one or more stages has been incompletely achieved. His behavior reflects the disruption: He is very good in some tasks, very poor in others. He reads difficult words and then stumbles over an easy one or one he has just read correctly in the line above. . .He takes the most devious routes to solve a problem or, on the other hand, he responds to a single stimulus as though it were all there was. His attention span is short and he wanders away from the task (Kephart, 1971, p. 44).

Kephart, then, suggested that all children go through certain developmental stages, and should any of these stages be skipped or incompletely learned, the child will have a learning disability. The treatment was obvious: "In educating the slow learner, the problem is to determine where, in the course of development, the child has broken down, and through teaching and/or therapeutic procedures, restore the course of development" (1971, p. 43). The theory that all intellectual and academic skills are grounded in the development of motor abilities was not a new theory, having been suggested by Itard (1803, 1962) and Seguin (1856, 1907) over a century earlier. Kephart's ideas did, however, become of great interest in the field of learning disabilities, because he offered a method for assessing these motor and perceptual skills (the Purdue Perceptual-Motor test) and provided extensive remedial activities for these deficits. The cause of learning disabilities, then, was the result of incomplete development in the child's perceptual and motor developmental stages before he even learned to read, spell, or write.

The Language Processing Theory

The first text to be devoted exclusively to learning disabilities was published only a year after Kirk's address. Doris Johnson and Helmer Myklebust in their *Learning Disabilities: Educational Principles and Practices* (1964) suggested that learning disabilities were due, for the most part, to defects in language processing. Myklebust divided language into various stages of processing and suggested that learning disabilities were defects in these processes. Myklebust's process approach resembled closely the breakdown one finds in texts on aphasia. For example, when one asks a person to describe a car accident he has just seen, the individual first visualizes the scene using visual imagery, then tries to find the words to describe the visualization (auditorization), then organizes these words into coherent grammatical sentences (syntax construction), and then verbalizes these thoughts (verbal expressions).

In recalling a radio broadcast, one goes through the same steps except that one must reauditorize, that is use one's auditory memory. While Myklebust's method is far more complicated than this, the diagnosis of a learning disability is essentially based upon analyzing the child's behavior in terms of the extensive literature on aphasia. This approach is still extensively used and in the process approach, previously described. Of particular interest is Myklebust's proposal that there are three types of learning disabilities, each of which is associated with a communication channel. The first is visual dyslexia in which the child has difficulty discriminating and remembering words and letters and keeping these materials in the correct orientation and sequence. Next is auditory dyslexia in which the child has difficulties in discriminating and comprehending verbal material and in reproducing and blending words into wholes. Finally there is agraphia in which the child has poor hand coordination and great difficulties in writing and drawing. Johnson and Myklebust's text is still widely used, and their three types of learning disabilities are easily understood and diagnosed using the ITPA and other commonly used tests.

The Processing Integration Theory

Gutherie (1973) tried to determine experimentally whether the subskills in reading — reading words flashed, long and short vowel production, reading consonant letter clusters, recognizing initial and final sounds, reading nonsense syllables, and auditory blending, are independent skills or outgrowths of one single reading skill. Some reading experts (e.g. Goodman) have maintained that reading is a unitary act with all the subskills being independent and contributing equally, so that one should find that an individual's reading subskills correlate highly with each other. Other LD experts (e.g. Bateman and Kirk) have maintained that these subskills are relatively independent, that LD children have a deficiency in a few of these subskills, and that treatment for a learning disability is the building up of these deficient weak areas. Gutherie gave the Kennedy Institute Phonics Tests, a test measuring these subskills, to LD children who were matched by sex, age, and IQ with normal readers. He also did reliability and validity tests and eliminated all the unreliable and invalid subtests. He found that these subskills correlated very highly for normal children with third-grade readers having mastered all eight subskills at the ninety-five percent or better level. The Kennedy test is not easy, with one subtest including reading correctly such nonsense words as "terbargib." These findings indicate that for normal readers, the various subskills are highly interrelated and the subskills result in a single integrated reading ability. To teach these children individual subskills and then build them into a basic reading skill would appear to be futile.

The disabled readers in Gutherie's study, however, behaved much differently. Of the eight subtests in which the child had to produce a response (e.g. the child reads a nonsense word) in contrast to just recognizing it (e.g. child picks one of four choices), only four correlated significantly with each other. In other words, the reading subskills of disabled readers appeared to be isolated skills, with some being well mastered and others not very well. This leads to the interpretation that one problem LD children have, is that they learn the subskills in reading in an isolated manner, and because these skills are not integrated, they do poorly in overall reading. This fits well with Kirk's notion that children with learning disabilities have great discrepancies between various processing channels.

Another area that was explored by Gutherie was the question of whether children with reading problems resemble normal readers who have just begun to read. To investigate this, deficient nine-year-olds reading on a second-grade level were compared to normal seven-year-olds reading on the same level. The scores of these two groups on the eight subskills were compared and found to be highly similar.

Both the LD children and the second graders did poorest on long vowel production, then short-vowel production, then nonsense-word production and so on. From this Gutherie concluded that disabled readers and beginning normal readers were practically indistinguishable in the skills they had and had not mastered. In other words, the LD children did not appear to have a special disability that made them "different" from other readers; they were simply behind in the same reading skills that beginning readers lack.

Finally, Gutherie tackled the problem of how many types of poor readers there are. He reasoned that if the disabled readers all have the same problem, they would all show the same pattern of deficiencies by all doing most poorly on one subtest, less poorly on the next, and so on. If there were several types of reading disabilities, one would expect different subtests to be higher for different members of the group. Gutherie discovered that fourteen of his nineteen LD children had exactly the same rank order of difficulty on four of the production tests. This suggested that they had very similar disabilities. This single experiment, if supported by other research, would go counter to the mainstream thinking in the field, which is that there are many types and varieties of learning disabilities.

Multiple Causation Theory

In the 1970s Alexander Bannatyne's 700-page book entitled *Language, Reading and Learning Disabilities* (1971) stands out as contributing the most to the understanding of the etiology of learning disabilities. Bannatyne attempted to integrate the research in brain functioning with the experimental work in language development, reading, and writing, and relate this diverse information to learning disabilities. He proposed the theory that there are four types of learning disabilities, each with a different causal agent. The first type is primary communication dyslexia, caused by the lack of a relationship being established between the mother and child during the critical period of language development (birth to four years). Children with this type of dyslexia have a limited vocabulary, slow speech development, poor physical development, and a lack of interest in auditory stimuli. They do poorly in the classroom because they do not pay attention to language and can not seem to integrate language into their experiences. They do poorly in reading because reading is language in visual form. Bannatyne suggests that these children come from homes with uninterested mothers who do not talk with their children, or depressed mothers who cannot form a relationship with their child, or angry mothers whose hostility towards their children does not allow them to form a relationship, or they are children who are institutionalized.

The second type of dyslexia is minimal neurological dysfunction resulting from some form of brain damage. There are four types of this disorder:

1. Visuo-spatial disorders that result in the inability of the child to organize things spatially. When asked to draw a man, the child confuses body parts and draws them completely out of proportion. These children have difficulties in writing their letters, in copying designs, and in various visual patterns.

2. Auditory disorders that result in children who have difficulties discriminating sounds, great difficulties with phonics and reading, and trouble in speaking and hearing. These children also become easily confused when given a set of directions or in performing tasks explained orally in class.

3. Motor-kinesthetic disorders found in children who can perceive and integrate information in normal fashion but have difficulties in expressing what they know. These children are clumsy, awkward, usually have atrocious handwriting, and when young cannot master simple skills such as hopping on one foot and skipping. Occasionally, their speech will be muffled, slurred, or jerky because of poor voice control.

4. Conceptual or integrative difficulties where the child will have difficulty, in spite of normal intelligence, in understanding abstract concepts such as more-less, larger-smaller, before-after, important-trivial, and in telling time, counting by twos or in spatial relationships.

The above four types of dyslexia are due to minimal brain dysfunction and are presumably caused by some form of brain injury. Unlike the preceding group, the characteristic of this group is a normal communicative relationship between mother and child, no other learning problems among the other sibs or parents, and usually poor spatial and integrative functions.

Genetic dyslexia is the fourth type of dyslexia, according to Bannatyne, which is definitely an inherited condition. These children have very good spatial abilities and are good at solving nonverbal problems. Since visuo-spatial abilities are apparently controlled by the right hemisphere of the brain, and linguistic processes are controlled by the left hemisphere, Bannatyne hypothesizes that children with genetic dyslexia have inherited a superior right hemisphere functioning. Since reading, writing (but not drawing), and spelling involve the left hemisphere, the child does poorly academically. These children usually come from families where several sibs have the same disorder and at least one parent had difficulties in school. Children with genetic dyslexia can usually be distinguished from children with minimal brain dysfunction by their superior spatial ability. Children with genetic dyslexia also do not have the neurological abnormalities children with MBD do.

Throughout his work, Bannatyne stresses that there are many kinds of learning disabilities caused by many different agents. He makes it clear that learning disabilities can cause dysfunctions in many domains, so that the child's motor, linguistic, visual, auditory, emotional, and cognitive functioning must be examined to determine the nature of the problem. Bannatyne also stresses that unless the remedial treatment matches the particular type of disability, the treatment will most likely be ineffective.

The Etiological Approach to Diagnosis

In a medical diagnosis the etiology of a disease is most important in specifying the treatment. In the newer field of learning disabilities there has not been enough basic research into which types of remedial activities work best with which types of handicaps. One major reason for the lack of this research is that all the various possible causes of learning disabilities are rarely presented together, as in this chapter, and accurate ways of measuring these disabilities (covered in the rest of this book) have not been developed. At present the etiological approach is based on too many hypotheses and not enough facts. The search for an etiology is important, however, because it alerts the clinician to events and responses from the client, which are valuable in making the final diagnosis.

From this chapter it is apparent that the years and years of looking for a simple specific factor that causes most learning disabilities have been fruitless. It is clear that all LD children do not have visual memory deficits, or abnormalities in language structure, or a history of clumsiness and poor motor development, or mixed dominance, or emotional problems, or poor spatial abilities, or a parent who could have passed on a LD gene. This situation leads one to the notion that there may be several causes of learning disabilities that can often lead to the same disability.

A second notion that becomes apparent is that when a child with a learning disability is closely examined, he usually shows a host of deficiencies rather than one specific symptom. It is not unusual to encounter a second or third grader, who cannot seem to pick up reading, with serious problems in discriminating letter sounds, remembering the letters that must go into words he must spell, in seeing the words as unitary wholes, in sequencing and reversing letters, and in having a fairly low frustration level and not liking school work very much. It may be that this Gates-Hinschelwood-DeHirsch-Orton-

Gann child either has one far-reaching defect in general symbolic processing, or that only the child with multiple problems will have enough handicaps to be unable to master reading. Unfortunately, the research into etiology of learning disabilities uses primarily the "two group method" in which a group of LD children is compared to a group of normal children on various traits, with those characteristics found to be significantly different in the two groups considered the variables causing the learning disability. This type of study does not reveal what percent of the children had one deficiency, which had two, or how many of the learning disabled children had no deficiencies in the variables studied.

Research into the types of learning disabilities requires giving the children in the LD group a battery of highly reliable tests measuring each of several desired traits — preferably several times to eliminate the inherent testing errors that develop in standardized testing — and then reporting the results in terms of how many of the children had each deficiency, how many deficiencies were found in each child, and answering the question of whether the deficiencies clustered into any kind of syndrome. The author has not been able to find any recent definitive investigations of this type, although Gutherie's study touches on the aspect of phonics deficiencies in LD children.

Cattell (1973) has said that history has shown that all major achievements in science have followed breakthroughs in the accuracy in measurement and suggests that until we are able to measure accurately all the various constructs in our hypotheses in the behavioral sciences, there will be little real progress. In the case of the etiology of learning disabilities, I think this is particularly true; very little definite information in regard to which factors cause learning disabilities will be clarified until accurate, noncontroversial measures of such vague terms as "visual memory," "Gestalt," and "maturational lag" are developed. Another problem hindering the research in the etiology of learning disabilities is that too many studies lump together a group of "learning disabled" children together and compare them to a group of "normal" children. This technique completely erases any individual variation within the LD group and in practice precludes any determination of whether the typical LD child has one, two, three, or more defects. When genuinely accurate measures of all these processes are developed and statistical error is reduced to a minimum, it will be possible to do an investigation which will reveal what percent of LD children had their learning problems caused by each of the 16 factors.

It is clear from this chapter that using the etiological approach to diagnose learning disabilities is almost impossible because the causes

Figure 4

Etiological Factors in a Diagnosis

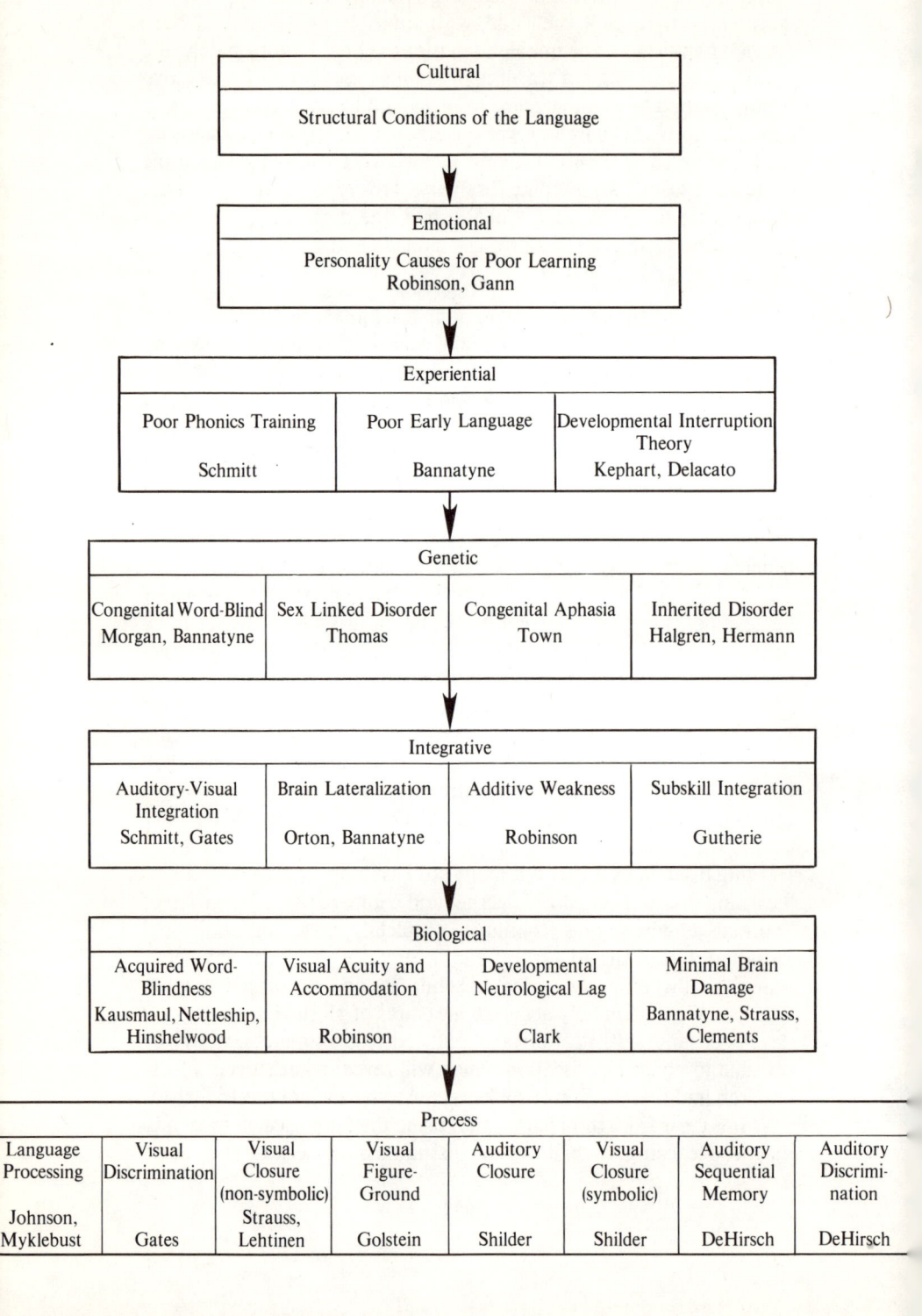

Cultural
Structural Conditions of the Language

↓

Emotional
Personality Causes for Poor Learning Robinson, Gann

↓

Experiential		
Poor Phonics Training Schmitt	Poor Early Language Bannatyne	Developmental Interruption Theory Kephart, Delacato

↓

Genetic			
Congenital Word-Blind Morgan, Bannatyne	Sex Linked Disorder Thomas	Congenital Aphasia Town	Inherited Disorder Halgren, Hermann

↓

Integrative			
Auditory-Visual Integration Schmitt, Gates	Brain Lateralization Orton, Bannatyne	Additive Weakness Robinson	Subskill Integration Gutherie

↓

Biological			
Acquired Word-Blindness Kausmaul, Nettleship, Hinshelwood	Visual Acuity and Accommodation Robinson	Developmental Neurological Lag Clark	Minimal Brain Damage Bannatyne, Strauss, Clements

↓

Process							
Language Processing Johnson, Myklebust	Visual Discrimination Gates	Visual Closure (non-symbolic) Strauss, Lehtinen	Visual Figure-Ground Golstein	Auditory Closure Shilder	Visual Closure (symbolic) Shilder	Auditory Sequential Memory DeHirsch	Auditory Discrimination DeHirsch

of learning disabilities at this period of time are a confusing mass of speculation. In order to help the reader out of this tangle *Figure 4* attempts to organize these causes along seven labels and list the names presented in the text that were associated with these causes.

Appendix A also attempts to key these etiological factors with the processes so that these factors can be organized with the rest of the book. The next chapter begins by describing the diagnosis using the behavioral observation as the basis for the diagnosis, followed by chapters on visual, auditory, intellectual, and other factors. Each of these will in turn expand the depth of this rather brief overview.

Chapter III

Interviewing, Observing, and Writing The Case Study

A valid diagnosis must rest on two activities: the collection of all the relevant information on the client and the organization of that material in such a way that it says something significant about the individual. Since the specialist rarely knows his subject from the day he was born nor has the time to observe him in a multitude of varied life situations, he must rely on interviews with the child, his teachers, and his parents to obtain this information. Interviewing is a complex art involving much more than just asking the right questions; it is a form of communication in which the interviewer projects himself in a noncritical way so that the person being interviewed feels comfortable and replies in an unbiased and accurate way. The interview must be varied from person to person, and the clinician must always keep in mind that his own personality and attitudes towards the client are influencing the interview.

The Family Information Form

Under present federal law, a school may not test or do a special case study on a child without first obtaining written permission from his parent or guardian. When the parent or parents come in to sign a permission form, a Family Information form can be given to them to fill out and return. An alternative is to use the Family Information form as an outline to the parent interview, with the interview filling out the form. This is particularly useful if the parent is defensive about being interviewed or not very well educated. Bannatyne (1971, pp. 580-583) gives a good example of a Family Information form.

Since each school district diagnoses differently and each clinician has different resources to work with, no one Family Information form will suit everyone. The diagnostician is therefore encouraged to develop his own form and to aid in this task, *Figure 5* outlines a lengthy representative form which is, if anything, overinclusive.

Figure 5
Family Information Questionnaire

I. Identifying Information:
Date_____Birthdate_____Sex_____Age_____
School_____Grade_____
Home address_____Phone_____
Is the child adopted? Yes_____ No_____ If so at what age?

II. Developmental History
   A. Pregnancy and Birth
      1. Any miscarriages or still births? Yes_____ No_____
      2. Any serious illnesses during pregnancy? _____ Were any drugs or medications taken during pregnancy? _____
      3. Describe any complications at birth (anoxia, breech birth) _____
      4. Length of pregnancy _____ Length of labor _____
         Birthweight _____ Instruments used? _____
      5. Type of anesthetic at delivery _____
      6. Did baby go home when mother left the hospital? _____
      7. Breast fed or bottle fed _____ Age weaned _____
      8. Any postnatal depression? _____
   B. Developmental Milestones. Indicate age of:
      1. Sat up_____Crawled_____Walked along_____
      2. Fed self _____Was toilet trained _____
         Bowel trained _____
      3. Said first word _____Said 2-3 word phrases _____
      4. Spoke in complete sentences _____
   C. Infant Development
      1. Describe what kind of infant the child was: _____
      2. Were there any mother-child separations during infancy? _____
      3. Describe any eating problems or lack of weight gain _____
      4. Describe any sleeping problems_____
      5. Describe any bedwetting or bowel control problems _____
      6. Describe any difficulties child had speaking _____
      7. Is another language besides English spoken in the home? Yes _____ No _____
      8. Did the child ever stop speaking at any time? _____
   D. Preschool Development. Give age at which child:
      1. Fed Self _____Put on clothes _____Button clothes _____
      2. Rode on tricycle _____Drew a man and house _____
      3. Tell time _____ Rode a bicycle _____
      4. Describe any problems at preschool age (3 to 6 years):_____
      5. Did child attend preschool or day care center?_____
         Ages of attendance _____ Describe any problems encountered: _____

      6. Did child attend Kindergarden? _____Ages of attendance _____
      Describe any problems encountered:_____

III. Educational Development
    1. Has the child been retained? Yes _____ No _____ Give grade _____
    2. Please fill in below: If the child has been in several schools in one year, please put name of each school (or location if name is not remembered)

Grade	School	How did he do?
K.		
1.		
2.		
3.		

    3. Did the child have special problems in 1st and 2nd grade? Please explain: _____ yes no
    4. Has the child received occupational or speech therapy? Please explain: _____ yes no
    5. Has the child been in any special programs?   yes no
        If yes, please specify _____
    6. Has your child been to summer school or had private tutoring? If yes, please specify _____ yes no
    7. Did the child reverse letters or numbers after 2nd grade?   yes no
    8. Has the child had motor coordination problems?   yes no
        If yes, please specify _____
    9. Does child have problems beginning and completing assignments? If so please specify _____ yes no
    10. Does child have problems in attention spans or concentration?   yes no
    11. Does child have problems expressing himself verbally?   yes no
        If yes, please explain _____
    12. Does child have problems remembering and following directions? yes no
    13. Is the child hard to organize and get on a routine?   yes no
    14. Circle below the correct description of how he is presently doing:

Math	poor average good	don't know
Reading	poor average good	don't know
Letter sounds (phonics)	poor average good	don't know
Spelling	poor average good	don't know
Writing	poor average good	don't know
Social Studies	poor average good	don't know
Musical ability	poor average good	don't know
Artistic Talent	poor average good	don't know
Athletics (gym)	poor average good	don't know

    Describe in your own words what school difficulties you see your child having: _____

IV. Present Health
    Has the child ever had: Date of illness
      1. Asthma or wheezing   yes no _____
      2. Allergies to medication or food   yes no _____
      3. Convulsions, seizures, or fainting spells   yes no _____
      4. Hearing impairment or hearing loss   yes no _____
      5. Visual problems   yes no _____
      6. Restriction on physical activity   yes no _____
      7. Overactivity or hyperactivity   yes no _____

threatening identifying information. If it is taken home, usually the mother fills out the form; a father filling it out is unusual enough to be significant and may indicate a fairly close family. The form begins by asking the child's name and birth history, which may suggest information regarding brain injury. This section is rather nonthreatening and may also reveal the overall attitudes the parents have toward the child. One important question to consider is if the parents see the child as a problem since birth or as a normal healthy child until school began.

There are a number of birth factors that are related to later intellectual and behavioral problems, including situations where the mother had several miscarriages, was older than forty at the child's birth, had babies who endured long deliveries or anoxia (lack of oxygen) at birth, or had premature babies with birthweights under three and one-half pounds. The questions about whether the child was breast fed or the mother had postpartum depression reveals information about the mother's attitudes.

The next section inquires about the famous developmental milestones that are notorious for being inaccurately recalled. Six studies comparing the pediatricians records with the mother's memory of the milestones when their children were already five or six have been reviewed by Wenar (1963). He found the following to be accurately recalled:

1. Length of gestation,
2. Overall evaluation of the delivery,
3. Age infant sat with support and sat alone,
4. Age infant crawled, stood with support, and stood alone,
5. Age infant walked with support and walked alone,
6. Whether the mother used a scheduled or demand feeding,
7. Whether child sucked his thumb,
8. Age of toilet training,
9. Recall of child's independence and aggression in first grade (mother was asked when child was eight years old),
10. Relationship of child, mother, and father.

The following were found to be inaccurately recalled:

1. Recall of health during pregnancy,
2. Duration of labor,
3. Whether instruments were used during delivery,

        8. Underactivity or lethargy   yes no _____
        9. Any hospitalizations   yes no _____
           If yes, please describe _____
      10. Any serious illness not mentioned above   yes no _____
           Please describe: _____
      11. Any serious accidents   yes no _____
      12. Does child presently take any medication?   yes no _____
           If yes, please give name and purpose _____
      13. Date of last medical examination _____results _____
      14. Date of last eye exam _____results _____
      15. Date of last hearing exam _____results _____

V. Family Background
   A. Name of father _____Age _____
      (If deceased give date and cause of death)_____
      Address (if other than child's) _____Phone _____
      Occupation and business _____Bus. phone _____
      Education _____General Health _____
      Religion _____Nationality _____Any special
      hobbies, interests, or organizations _____
      Did father have academic problems in first three grades?   yes no
      If yes, please explain _____
   B. Name of mother _____Age _____
      (If deceased give date and cause of death)_____
      Address (if other than child's) _____Phone _____
      Occupation and Business _____Bus. Phone _____
      Education _____Religion _____Nationality _____
      General Health _____Any special hobbies, interests, or
      organizations? _____
      Did mother have academic problems in first three grades?   yes no
      If yes, please explain _____
   C. Did any grandparents have significant learning problems?_____
   D. Parents are:
      Married and living together _____Divorced _____Separated _____
      Adoptive _____Fosterparents _____Relatives _____
      If parents are divorced or separated:
        a. Who has legal custody of the child _____
        b. Date of separation_____
        c. How did child react to separation _____
      Are there others living in the family?   yes no
      Please specify _____
   E. List all other children in the family
         Name   Age   School grade   Learning Difficulties
       1. _____yes no
       2. _____yes no
       3. _____yes no
   F. How does the child get along with his siblings (if any)? _____

Usually one would go through this sample form and eliminate from it all the information found in other school records and not relevant to the diagnostic system used in the school district.

    The Family Information form should begin with relatively non-

4. Injuries occurring during the delivery,
5. Forty percent of mothers forgot their babies ever crawled,
6. Whether the child was breast or bottle fed,
7. Length of breast feeding,
8. About one-third of minor illnesses and about one-half of major illnesses were forgotten.

The author knows of one case of a fourth-grade girl who did poorly in reading and on a number of language tests. The mother in an initial interview with the psychologist had said that the daughter did not really speak until the age of four. From this information it was thought that the girl had a specific language disability. However, when the social worker made a home visit and asked the mother if she had kept a baby book, the mother proudly produced the book which showed that the girl said her first word at one and one-half, talked in two word sentences at two years of age, and said ten word sentences at the age of three. A closer examination of the case revealed a very erratic mother, with many depressive tendencies, who was very busy with her career and had little time to spend with the child. In fact, whenever company visited or there was a party given, the girl was always sent to her room so as not to interfere. Slowly a picture emerged of a shy girl with little linguistic experiences who was going through a number of adjustment difficulties.

Norms for the most common milestones were assembled by Neligan and Prudham (1969); these norms were collected by nurses visiting 2,000 children while they were growing up. The first milestone, sitting unsupported, was defined as the infant being able to sit on the floor one minute not using the arms; walking unsupported as walking ten or more steps; single words as three or four words for people or objects that are correctly used; and sentences as three or more words strung together to make some sort of sense. The percentile norms for these children passing were:

Age in months of milestones passed by percentiles

	3%	25%	50%	75%	90%
Sitting unsupported	4.6	5.8	6.4	7.2	8.1
walking unsupported	9.7	10.2	12.8	14.2	15.8
Single words	8.6	9.9	12.3	14.8	17.7
Sentences	16.8	18.7	23.4	25.9	31.6

In addition to presenting the norms, Neligan and Prudham found that the relative relationship between the age of passing each of the four milestones was very low (the highest correlation was .33 and the mean correlation .20). This means that if a child is behind in one of the four milestones, it is very unlikely that he will be behind in the other three. The diagnostic significance of this is that a child being behind in one of the milestones means little, and a child behind in all of his milestones would be very unusual; also being behind in the milestones, at least in these four, does not appear to be a definable syndrome. They also compared the actual age of the milestones with the mother's memory of the milestones two or three years later and found those mothers who had children who were abnormally late in the milestones remembered the age of the milestones inaccurately and tended to place their children in the normal range. In other words, the significance of a child being late in the milestones (unless he is severely mentally retarded) is not very well understood, and extreme caution must be used when asking a parent about the age of the milestones without some reliable record.

Sometimes the Family Information form will indicate that a child who is just barely getting by in school has been extensively tutored or drilled by his parents, thus preventing his disability from becoming a severe learning problem.

A medical history on the Family Information form can be brief, because most of the normal childhood diseases do not affect learning. One is usually interested only in allergies, seizures, activity problems, illnesses serious enough to require hospitalization, and questions about medications, because they can affect classroom behavior.

The last selection of the form is the most personal and occasionally a parent will distort the truth or refuse to answer altogether. This section asks about other family members with an attempt to see if there are any genetic factors or interpersonal family dynamics that may be causing a learning problem in one of the children. Some Family Information forms also include a number of questions about the child's activities, clubs, and hobbies. This last set of questions seems to be more appropriate for the family interview than on the information form. There may also be a long list of symptoms such as cries easily, steals, eats dirt and paint, is accident prone, acts younger than actual age, or others; where the parent checks off any of the symptoms observed.

The Parent Interview

Being able to do a good diagnostic interview with parents is an art, because it involves the clinician projecting himself in such a way that the parents feel he is interested but not snooping into their private lives; that the parents feel the clinician acknowledges the child's problems but does not blame the parents for them. The diagnostician must be personal and compassionate, but not personally involved; must be able to carefully listen to everything the parents say, but not take what they say at face value; and be able to hear what is not said, as well as what is said.

Interviewing has been described in many places (Rich, 1968; Richard et al., 1965; Weins, 1976), with the concensus being that the interview should begin with an exchange of small talk to put the parents at ease and to show them that the clinician is not trying to analyze their every word or "read their minds." Throughout the interview the clinician must remember that a diagnostic interview should not give practical advice or correct mistaken beliefs the parents may hold. The danger always is that when advice is given the parents may reject it, and then the rapport of the interview is lost. A general principle is that the interview should progress from general considerations to more specific questions; from less personal areas to more personal areas; and it is best to begin with the initial complaint. The event that is perceived as causing the problem is very important, because it represents a concern, a problem the diagnostician is expected to solve. In more psychological terms it represents an anxiety, and the clinician must determine if the anxiety is based on the child's behavior or is an expression of anxiety about some other problem.

It is important to pay careful attention to the wording and tone of the first sentence of parents in the parental interview, since the most significant sentence is often the first one. The parents will be anxious at the interview, and just how they phrase their introduction tells one about what they have been feeling for many days before the interview. The parent who casually begins, "I understand you want to talk to me" or "I understand I have to sign some forms" is saying something different from a parent who begins, "We're so glad you have some time to talk to us" or "We've been worried about Helen all school year."

The interview begins with general questions because specific questions do not provide the parents with an opportunity to work in any outside concerns they may have, and specific questions tend to channel the interview in the direction of the biases of the interviewer. In this first part of the interview one must be careful of asking questions that can be answered with a "yes" or "no," because these questions can be most misleading in that the qualifying statement can be left out. When one asks, "Is your child hyperactive?", the parents may say "no." But if the question is phrased, "How active is your child?" the parents may reply that they took him to a pediatrician who rated him on a thirty point scale, and he came out with fourteen, which is not hyperactive, with the hidden implication being, of course, the parents did consider the child hyperactive enough to be evaluated by a pediatrician.

It is also difficult not to ask biasing questions during the interview; this can be helped by avoiding those questions that begin or end in "doesn't it" or "isn't it true that. . . ." Double barreled questions should also be avoided; one should not ask something such as "Does your child have reading problems or arithmetic problems or both. One's choice of words is also extremely important because some words may have such a bad connotation that it will invariably be answered in the negative. Parents who reply that their child does not have a "learning disability" may say that their child has a "learning problem," or parents who may maintain their child is not "withdrawn" may readily agree their child is "shy."

In summary, the diagnostic interview begins with the initial complaint and then general questions are asked of the parents picking up on their vague generalizations and responses and asking for clarifications and elaborations. Asking for clarifications is part of good listening. It is also valuable because parents often do not know what is relevant to a diagnosis or are too embarrassed, so they will vaguely hint at something hoping that the clinician will ask more about it.

The second stage of the interview occurs when rapport has been established, the parents have expressed in their own words who noticed the problem first, what the chief complaint is, and have given a description of the child's academic problems, activity level, mood, sibling and peer interactions, and the like. It is important to have them cite specific examples of the child's behavior and what they have done to solve the problems. The areas to be covered are listed in *Figure 6*, which is an outline the learning disabilities specialist might want to use when doing the parent interview.

This outline has been adopted from Cantwell's (1975) excellent article on interviewing for hyperactivity. The first part of the interview allows the clinician to see the problem from the parent's vantage point, and the second part focuses on the child's specific behaviors trying to fit them into some type of diagnostic pattern. The trick in a good interview is knowing when to switch from the first part to the second. The clinician should carefully observe the parent's nonverbal communication or their body language (Knapp, 1978).

When the parents begin to talk they (and often the clinician) instinctively "cover up" by such means as crossing their feet, avoiding eye contact, folding the hands and arms in front of them, and keeping the inside body surfaces (the palms) turned away. If the interview goes well and the parents feel the diagnostician does not blame them and is concerned about their child's welfare, the parents will begin uncovering themselves and give nonverbal signs that they are comfortable with the interview (Lowen, 1971).

Figure 6
The Parent Interview Form

I. Referral Source (who noticed the problem first?)
II. Chief Complaint (what prompted you to seek help?)
1. Activity level
2. Impulsivity
3. Distractibility
4. Discipline problems
5. Sibling problems
6. Mood problems
7. Poor peer relations
8. Academic problems

Recent examples of behavior:
Frequency and severity of behavior:
What has been tried to solve problem:

III. Symptom Inventory
1. School adjustment
2. Agressiveness and antisocial behavior
3. Affective state (mood)
4. Neurotic symptoms
5. Sexual behavior
6. Neurological symptoms
7. Peer relationships
8. Adult relationships
9. General health

IV. Temperament and Personality
1. Meeting strange people
2. Strange situations
3. Emotional expression
4. Affections and relationships
5. Eating, sleeping, and bowels
6. Sensitivity
7. Attitudes towards teachers and school
8. Special talents or hobbies

V. Personal History
1. Previous pregnancies and birth history
2. Infant development
3. Milestones
4. Medical History
5. Early experiences (before age of six)
6. Parent's upbringing and school history
7. Home living conditions
8. History of family illnesses
9. What parents see child doing in future

The Post-Interview Questions

1. How warm is the mother? Is she caring?
2. What is the general father-mother relationship? Who makes decisions about the child's education and welfare?
3. How motivated for change is the child? Is his family?
4. How structured is the home? How rigid are the house rules?
5. What kinds of things does the child tell parents about school?
6. Which members of the family are overprotected, segregated, ignored, disliked, scapegoated, idolized?
7. The child identified with which parent? Has he incorporated the parents' traits and values?
8. How child-oriented is the family?
9. What do parents do when they fail or make a mistake? The child?
10. How aware are the parents of the developmental stages—are they expecting too much or too little of the child?
11. How aware is each parent of the child's moods and feelings.
12. How honest and open are parents with their children?
13. What is the focus of the entire family? Is it discipline, honesty, sociability, orderliness, affluence, academics, well being, being well adjusted, or having a good time?

Reserved for the second part of the interview is an inquiry about the child's temperament and personality, trying to establish if there are any emotional problems behind the child's learning problems. At the end of the interview some diagnosticians ask the parents if they have noted various symptoms of maladjustment, such as playing with younger children, sucking the thumb, having an unusual interest in fires, or others. This should be at the end of the interview, because such questions have strong emotional overtones and often get parents worried that there is something seriously wrong with their child that they are not being told about. If the symptom approach is used, one should certainly reassure the parent that a lot of the questions are routine and do not reflect an extreme concern for the child. The symptom approach is used in many personality measure and particularly in the psychiatric interview. The disadvantage of using the symptoms of maladjustment is that the number of maladaptive behaviors is large and a fairly sophisticated knowledge of psychoanalytic theory is necessary to be able to relate these symptoms to the child functioning. The Committee on Child Psychiatry (1966) lists 583 symptoms indicating maladjustment, and to inquire about all of these symptoms is just overwhelming. A much easier approach is to inquire about the nine areas listed in the outline.

Finally, it is important for the interview to end in a positive note with some encouragement. The clinician may take notes during the interview with the parents and keep the notes for future reference, or he may take some time out after the interview and ask himself what transpired. The author finds that taking notes during the interview, while not usually resented by the parents, will tend to distract them, because in the back of their minds they always want to know what the diagnostician has and has not written down. *Figure 6* lists a set of questions one might ask oneself about the interview afterwards. These post-interview questions are often based only upon the clinician's impressions and feeling, but they can direct his attention to some area missed in the interview.

The Teacher Interview

We often forget the tremendous pressure the classroom teacher has to face. In the elementary school the teacher has twenty to thirty children crowded into a small room a little larger than a family room. In addition to trying to organize the hundreds of daily chores of teaching, the teacher must meet the constant attention that children demand. The teacher cannot therefore be expected to spend more than five or ten minutes a day with a particular child. Junior and senior high school students demand less attention, but the schools give a teacher 150 to 200 students to deal with!

The teacher interview should go from the general to the specific, but can be briefer and be conducted as one professional to another. In talking with the teacher one is usually interested in obtaining information about the following areas:

1. How does the child do in reading? This complex information processing skill is usually a weak area with the LD child. The teacher is usually able to rank the child in relation to his classmates, and one should find out if this is based on oral reading, answering questions in silent reading tasks, or the completion of worksheets. A teacher almost always bases his opinion on classroom output, and it is the LD specialist's job to decide whether the child's failure is due to poor motivation, to not understanding the assignments, or to lack of the proper automatic skills to complete the task.

2. Does the child have a problem in sounding out words? The child's ability to translate visual letters into auditory sounds is usually taught in first grade and should be thoroughly mastered by third grade. A child's phonics skills often shed light on whether the learning disability is based on weak auditory or visual perceptual skills. Some children with poor phonics have not been taught these skills adequately; others will be "late maturers" in this auditory-visual integration skill and will not develop strong phonics skills until about nine years of age, a few may have hearing problems. If the teacher is not sure about the adequacy of the pupil's phonics skills, one can ask for some of his written work and from the spelling patterns make a fair guess of the child's level on this skill.

3. How does the child perform in other academic subjects? An inability to spell with normal reading and math skills usually indicates a deficient visual memory. The child with inherited dyslexia will usually be at grade level in math computation, but will have poor reading and even worse spelling skills. Children with spatial and sequencing problems will often be low in math and fairly good in reading. A careful analysis of the performance in various subject areas can reveal the type of learning disability a child may have.

4. How good is the child's concentration ability and attention span? Attention span varies greatly from hour-to-hour, day-to-day, and from subject-to-subject. Parents will often report that their child has short attention span, but the child will spend hours in front of a TV without stirring. Boredom and frustration will also cause short attention span, so that most children with reading problems will have short attention spans while reading. When asking about concentration, one should always ask about it in relation to a particular task and whether the child is interested and capable of doing the task.

5. How good is the child's motivation? A child's day-to-day motivation for school work can be estimated only crudely in an informal interview or testing situation. The best source of motivational information is the classroom teacher, but one must be careful not to underestimate the motivation of the disruptive child.

6. Does he daydream or have unusual ideas in class discussion or on written themes? Most teachers are fairly sensitive to how well a child pays attention in class and can readily identify the child who is retreating into other thoughts. If the child has a strong emotional problem, his inner world and unusual ideas will probably be expressed in the classroom at some time or another.

7. How good are the child's relationships with peers and adults? A general idea of whether the child is a social isolate, mixes normally with his peers, or is a leader reveals a lot about whether his problem has an emotional base. How the child reacts to adults in school may also reflect his relationships at home. Sometimes a teacher may not be certain about a child's social standing and can be encouraged to use a simple sociometric technique to answer these questions. To do this the teacher can put all the children's names on the board and ask the students to list on a slip of paper three classmates they would like to sit next to, do their homework with, or work on a project with. After collecting the sheets, which may or may not require the student's name, the number of time a child is chosen gives a quick indication of where he stands socially in the class.

8. How organized is the child? Often children with good

academic abilities fare poorly in school, because they are always losing their work, forgetting to bring in their homework, constantly borrowing pencils and paper from classmates, forgetting assignments and directions.

9. How does his speech compare with his written work? LD children are usually described as being alert and answering questions put to them in class, but having very poor written work. Children with a specific language problem will also have poor written work, but their speech will often consist of "short choppy sentences" with the child being described as "nonverbal."

10. What is his handwriting like, and is he a clumsy child? The teacher is in a good position to report on the child's handwriting (fine motor coordination) and should be asked for work samples from the child. The work samples often reveal such specific symptoms as letter reversals, confusion of lower and upper case letter, letter and word transpositions, and certain spelling patterns.

11. What is the child's activity level? Hyperactivity and hypoactivity are of great interest in an LD diagnosis because of their close association with the diagnosis of minimal brain damage. Most teachers, like parents, do not know exactly what constitutes hyperactivity, but they can usually make a fairly good estimate of the child's activity level in relation to the rest of the children in the class and decide if the activity level is interfering with the child's attention span.

The teacher interview then is more of an attempt to draw out the teacher when describing the child's everyday classroom behavior. If the teacher knows the child well and all aspects of the above eleven areas are covered, the diagnostician should be able to form hypothesis regarding the child's problem.

Rating scales are very effective and can be thought of as a distillation of the person's whole experience with the rater. Rating scales are obviously more variable than test scores, but one can expect rating scales to give better overall predictions of performance than individual scores. Glazzard (1977) in one typical example tested this by giving a group of eighty-seven kindergarten children the Gates-MacGinitie Reading Readiness Test, the Gates-MacGinitie first grade reading test, and had the teacher fill out the Kirk rating scale (Kirk, 1966) on the child. The next year it was found the teacher's rating and the readiness test were equal in predicting first grade reading achievement (about seventy-two percent of the varience on the word recognition and fifty-eight percent of the comprehension) while the reading test did poorly (about thirty-five percent).

There are a number of standardized rating scales:

The ALM screening device (Cowen, et. al., 1973) is the simplest rating scale consisting of five questions measuring "aggressive-outgoing behavior" (gets in fights, restless, disrupts class, impulsive), five questions measuring "moody-internalized" personality problems (is unhappy and depressed, is moody, becomes sick when faced with a difficult problem), and one question measuring a "learning disability" (has difficulty learning). In spite of its shortness, the retest reliability is good (above .80) when children were scored on a five-point scale. The test has been shown to be a good screening measure in picking out children who developed school problems. The scale has norms for kindergarten through third grade.

McLeod (1966) has developed a set of sixteen questions that the parent marks either "yes" or "no." In one study this checklist was able to correctly identify eighty-three percent of elementary level LD children and misidentified only nine percent of children with no learning problems.

A third instrument (Rutter, Graham, and Yule, 1970) is a two-part questionnaire with twenty-six questions for teachers (with a retest reliability of .89) and a parent scale of thirty-one items (reliability of .74). The scale measures only neurotic and antisocial behavior, with eighteen questions for the parents and teachers being identical. A fourth checklist consisting of forty-three questions composed of three personality factors (conduct problems, inadequacy-immaturity, and neurotic personality problem) has been used by Quay, Morse, and Culter (1966). The drawback of this checklist also is that it has no items concerning learning.

Conners (1969) has developed a much more refined checklist that has been used in a half dozen studies mostly on the change in children's behavior after taking psychoactive drugs. This scale consists of thirty-nine items rated on a five-point scale, dividing the child's behavior into five dimensions (Kupietz, et. al, 1972) of aggressivity, inattentiveness, anxiety, hyperactivity, and sociability. Again there is no learning disability dimension to this scale, but it yields reliable scores for hyperactivity and poor concentration as well as emotional stability.

The above rating scales were developed primarily to identify emotionally disturbed students, and only one commonly available, properly researched instrument has been developed to rate LD children by the teacher. This is the Pupil Behavior Rating Scale[1] con-of attention is alertness, which is the ability to perform a fairly long and routine task and still be able to notice and react appropriately to changes in the task. Can the child, for example, do a sheet of arithmetic problems and attend to changes of directions and sign changes in the problems. The second sense of attention is whether the child can screen out irrelevant stimuli and stick to the relevant aspects of the task. This is the classic figure-ground skill, where the child will be watching a child sharpen his pencil, be thinking about where to put his book, and be talking to his neighbor about recess while the teacher is giving directions to the test.

Filtering out irrelevant stimuli can usually be diagnosed by comparing the child's performance in the classroom with his performance in a one-to-one situation. If the child shows little distractibility in the one-to-one but is highly distractible in his classes, he most likely has difficulty filtering out irrelevant activity. Usually this type of attention is broken up into "visual figure-ground" and "auditory figure-ground" problems. The child with visual figure-ground is distracted by visual stimuli, which in the classroom is usually the movement of the children. The child with auditory figure-ground problems is distracted by extraneous noises such as the noise made by the pencil sharpener in the room, the noise of notebooks being opened and closed, and other children talking during the assignment. While there are no tests for measuring visual figure-ground as described here, there is one standardized test of auditory figure-ground. The Goldman-Woodcock-Fristoe test consists of the child listening to a tape with a woman reading off various simple words in the midst of a thundering background cafeteria noise. In the author's experience this test is difficult for normal children to master, and almost all LD children have great difficulty with this task.

The third component of attention is a fairly complex variable which may be thought of as "span of attention" or the ability for an individual to hold and process a large amount of information. This is involved with how the complexity of the task affects attention. One cannot simply say a child has an attention span of a certain number of minutes, because the complexity of the task determines the attention span of the child. The difference, of course, is that some tasks require little processing and therefore become more or less automatic. The distractible child can have a span of attention of several hours for watching TV, a span of attention of thirty minutes for art, and only a few minutes for reading, which requires a great deal of processing. The excellent reader, however, for whom reading has become fairly automatic, can read for several hours without strain. We often sisting of items in the areas of auditory comprehension, spoken language, orientation, behavior (cooperation and alertness), and motor coordination. This scale was normed on several hundred children in a comparison of a group of LD children and normal children of the same age and grade. The LD students obtained, on a whole, significantly lower scores on all the items except motor coordination. The items have good reliability, and there are a number of research studies (e.g. Bryan and McGrady, 1972; Colligan, 1977) using this instrument.

Finally, the author has developed a parent and teacher rating scale (Johnson, 1980) which he has used in the schools for several years for rating the student's behavior.

Rating Attention and Motivation

Certain variables are difficult to assess in a standardized situation because they either require expensive equipment, are very dependent on the classroom situation, or require successive observations over a long period of time.

Three such variables are motivation, which can fluctuate from day to day, attention span, which can fluctuate from task to task, and self-concept, which can fluctuate from situation to situation. These three variables and their concommitment variables of auditory and visual figure-ground make up processes 1, 2, 3, 4, 10, 16 and 20 in Appendix A. Before presenting rating scales for these processes, it would be best to describe what is meant by these terms.

Self-concept is a term used to describe the way a child approaches his environment. If he has a "poor" self-concept, he will usually have a general attitude that he will fail at almost everything he does and therefore will not try very hard on any particular task. This variable is measured mostly by rating scales or self-rating scales and will be covered in the section on motivation and in the chapter on emotional functioning.

One of the problems constantly faced by the clinician is the decision of whether a child has true learning gaps or whether he cannot attend to the material long enough to learn it. In a rather philosophical paper Harris (1976) has suggested that attention can only be defined in terms of side effects of the lack of attention, such as measuring the number of times the child "looks away" or responds to conditioning. To help tease out this delicate measure, Posner and Boises (1971) have divided attention into three different components and demonstrated each has different characteristics. The first notion

[1] All standardized tests mentioned in this book will be listed in *Appendix B* with the authors of the test, the company publishing the test, and the reliability of the test.

hear teachers say a child's attention span is just one direction, or the child gets so fatigued after reading just a few paragraphs that he begins to make too many careless mistakes.

Attention and motivation are closely related; it is simply more difficult to pay attention to something that is complex or not meaningful. The child who can sit through hours of Sesame Street may only be able to watch a few minutes of a documentary on Congress. Attention span therefore must always be specified in relation to the type of task the child is performing.

Deciding the motivation of a child is most easily explained in terms of need. The culturally deprived child who sees many adults around him unemployed, whose peers tell him that school will not do him any good, and who is thinking about food or the violence he must deal with may well place little value on school and learning. The motivation of a child can often be best obtained from the teacher, because the classroom teacher has the child for an extended period of time and can usually describe his usual attitude. Observing the child carefully in a one-to-one situation where he is presented with classroom-like activities will often reveal the child's motivation by his nonverbal behavior and resentment towards being tested. The unmotivated child will usually slouch, fail to maintain eye contact, make indirect comments about the quality of the task, have flat affect throughout the testing, or ask when the task will be over; while the motivated child after the newness of the situation has worn off will usually become involved in the task (if it is set at his level), try to do more than is required, and take the task as a challenge. Another gauge that may be employed is to have the child guess if he does not know the answer. The motivated child in this situation usually gives reasonable guesses, while the unmotivated child will either give quick, ridiculous answers or continue to say he does not know.

Keogh and Margolis (1976) have recently written an excellent article reviewing about one hundred studies on attention and its relation to LD children. They suggest that attention is clearly a major component in learning in hyperactive and nonhyperactive children. Three types of attention problems are discussed and with each goes a different form of remediation. First, there is "coming to attention," which is illustrated by the child who wiggles during the teacher's directions, talking when he should be listening, and being unable to "get started" on a task until an adult prompts him. These children are frequently hyperactive and have been shown to exhibit a great deal of motor activity at the time they should be acquiring information. Whether extraneous motor activity disrupts acquisition of information or is the result of inattention is not known as far as the author is aware. Second is "decision making," which is characterized by the impulsive child who is a very fast decision maker and blurts out answers, jumps to conclusions, guesses wildly, and appears to be erratic and noisy from day to day. These children may either have a defective inhibitory mechanism, or they may have a limited number of strategies to solve problems. Third, there is "monitoring attention," which is characterized by children who cannot continue to concentrate after a task has begun. This occurs in children with figure-ground problems and also passive children who become engrossed in their own thoughts and "peter out" before a task has been completed. These three types of attention have also been related to hyperactivity by Keogh (1971).

To summarize, the distractibility of a child is related to:

1. The difficulty of the activity the child is engaged in.
2. How fatigued the child is at the time.
3. The amount of environmental distraction.
4. The child's biochemical arousal level.
5. The child's age and sex.
6. The child's motivation to do the particular task.

Because of all these variables, the test of making the child sit still for thirty seconds without moving, or trying to establish if the child is in constant movement at home as well as in school, is probably a poor test of whether a child is "hyperactive" or not.

There are few standardized tests of attention. Alwitt (1966) gave the Stroop color-word test of attention to normal and LD children matched for intelligence, age, and sex. The Stroop test (completely reviewed in Jensen and Rohwer, 1964) consists of a set of cards that have color names on them, except that these words are in different colored inks so that "blue" might be in a blue ink or a red ink. The subject's task is to read the word and the interference of the color causes a number of confusions. Alwitt could find no differences between the LD and control children.

Another test of attention is the Continuous Performance Test (Rosvold, et al., 1956), which is a revolving drum with letters presented one per second. The subject pushes a button when an "X" appears. On the second task he pushes a button only when the "X" is followed by an "A." Lapses of attention are measured by the number of times the subject misses to push a button. Dykman (et al., 1972) in an article in Myklebust's *Progress in Learning Disabilities (Vol. 2)* entitled "Specific Learning Disabilities: An attentional deficit syndrome," reviewed the evidence for attention as the main disability of LD children. A series of experiments was conducted, the first of which tested LD children on an apparatus consisting of a board with various lights that lit up, with the child having the push the appropriate button or sequence of buttons. They found that the LD children did not show sharp changes in galvanic skin reflex (GSR), heart rate, or muscle tension while doing these measures, which contrasted sharply with the controls. In fact, they could not condition the LD children, indicating that the LD children were not paying enough attention to be conditioned, or they had extremely low arousal levels.

The second study performed was a factor analysis of a battery of tests given the LD children (an aphasia test, tone discrimination, finger tapping, WISC subtest, and motor impulsivity), which found that only a test of focus of attention separated the LD children from the controls. Finally, a task very similar to the continuous performance test was administered to eighty-four LD children, and it was found that they did significantly lower on this attention test. These experiments supported the theory that LD children may have an attentional deficit, and the investigators suggest, "The child who is unable to focus his attention on the written or spoken word or on a sound cannot easily learn to read and spell."

With different measures of attention, however, the results have not been so conclusive. Doyle, Anderson, and Halcomb (1976) in a thirty-minute vigilance task found that hyperactive LD children have a definite inhibitory weakness, have erratic sustained attention, and cannot focus on the relevant stimulus; while hypoactive and normal-active LD children were much like normal children on this task of watching lights and pressing telegraph keys. Auxter (1970-1971) compared normal and LD children on a set of reaction time experiments where the child sees a light flash on and must push a button as quickly as possible. He found no differences between these groups. Kassmore (1972) listed six investigations that reported external noise affected reading performance and six investigations where this made no difference. These were normal children, and perhaps only LD children are susceptible to auditory figure-ground distraction.

Child Observation

Many clinicians find it valuable to observe the child in his classroom. The observer should sit down a few rows away and behind the child and spend time looking at other children as well. The recording of the observations can be done in several ways. An exact coding system for recording classroom behavior has been worked out by a team from the National Institutes of Health over the last eight years. The child's behavior is coded for situation, i.e. teacher asks a direct question, and there are certain responses for which the child is scored. This system codes pupils for twenty-eight categories of behavior, has reliability and validity data, and can be readily used with an inexpensively obtained manual (Jones, Reid, and Patterson, 1975).

The author has developed a simplified system for recording fifteen-minute blocks of time that can be learned in a few minutes (Johnson, 1980).

After observing in class, one may then want to observe the child in an informal testing situation. Informal testing usually involves giving the child classroom tasks attempting to keep the session as close to the classroom situation as possible. One tries to record the events as accurately as possible with a running account of what the child says and does. To record a verbatim account in longhand is too cumbersome, standard shorthand takes years to learn; instead a modified shorthand such as Notescript (Hawkins, 1964) can be used. Notescript takes only a few weeks to learn and relies on a system where vowels are left out of words and there are special notational tricks, such as putting a ring around the last letter to denote an "ing."

The Child Interview

The interview with a child differs in several ways from an interview with an adult. Child interview techniques have been described in articles on the psychiatric interview with children (Beiser, 1962; Werkman, 1965). Goodman and Sours (1967), Simmons (1969), and Rich (1968) have also written books on interviewing children. Most interviewers suggest that the interview begin by alleviating some of the anxiety of the child by asking him if he knows why he is being interviewed. If the child does not know, the clinician can explain that he has been told that the child has some problem in school and this session is to get to know the child a little better so as to help him if he does have problems. This should initiate the conversation; but with the nonverbal child, it is often best to switch to a nonverbal task, such as drawing a picture of a man, house, or his family. A more sophisticated interviewing technique is to have the child play with dolls, sand, clay, building blocks, puppets, cars, models, or table games and diagnose the problem from the symbolic messages made during the play.

Some differences between adult and child interviews are:

1. Adults are very sensitive to cues from the interviewer, so adult interviews are given in a rather bland, impersonal atmosphere with the interviewer being noncommittal and revealing little about

himself. With children, the author finds, the best interviews are those in which the interviewer is animated, a little "bouncy," and shows great interest in what the child says.

2. The child, unlike an adult, is afraid of the interviewer as an authority figure. One way to "break the ice" with young children is to be slightly (but not to an obvious degree) childish.

3. Children are usually fairly nonverbal and are likely to reply with noncommittal answers such as "I don't know," or "It's OK," or "I'm all right." With the adult this type of answer often indicates a disinterest in the interview; with the child this usually is just a lack of verbal sophistication or insight into his own feelings.

4. The child, unlike the adult, will have practically no idea who the diagnostician is or what he is supposed to do. Therefore, it is good to reassure the child that you are not going to tell his teacher or parent what happens in the session, and you just want to know a little about him.

5. Children usually do not understand the aims and goals of an interview and will not know what is relevant. Therefore, one has to ask a lot of questions and tell the child when one wants more information.

6. Children are very concrete and will likely give examples rather than describe their feelings or general behavior. An eight-year-old will, for example, not be able to answer the question "What do you do when you get angry?" because it is too abstract. He might, on the other hand, in the process of telling you about a fight he had with his mother over doing his homework answer the question "What did you do when she said,'I'll tell your dad'." The interviewer should therefore pay attention to seemingly irrelevant events and supply concrete situations to elicit general behavioral patterns.

7. The interview should be kept shorter than a standard fifty minutes used for adults. Children will begin to fidget when their span of concentration has been reached. It is best at this point to take a break and do some "fun" things such as drawing his family, writing the alphabet, or other activity, which will be used in the diagnosis.

8. The behavior elicited in an interview is usually fairly representative of the way in which the child acts with adults. The "games" or roles the child plays with the interviewer will probably be the same types of roles he plays with his parents or teachers.

9. Children, unlike adults, are highly variable from day to day. One therefore cannot generalize behavior from one interview. Too often a clinician will interview a child in one of his good days and then find it hard to believe the classroom teacher when she says he has generally bad behavior.

Finally, the interview is only as good as the skill of the interviewer. If rapport is not established or the interview cannot relate to the child's attitude, the interview will be a poor one. Because one can often get to the heart of the problem in an interview, the interview can be more efficient than a standard testing situation. The disadvantage of the diagnostic interview is that it relies mostly on verbalization, and the decision of what is "normal" or "abnormal" behavior must be judged according to the interviewer's opinion, rather than according to some standardized data. The most important element of an interview is the attention to minor details.

One can begin by asking those harmless questions that adults are endlessly asking children. What grade are you in? How old are you? What subjects do you take? What do your mother and father do for a living? More pointed questions can then be asked after firm ground has been laid. These usually require an opinion: "What subjects do you like?" What subjects don't you like?" "Do you hate it?" "Who teaches it?" "Is the teacher a bad teacher?" From the responses to these questions one should be able to decide if the interview is an open, friendly exchange, whether the child feels he is there against his will, or whether he is afraid of the interview. One can either become specific on his school problems or head the conversation to more neutral areas, such as what he did last summer (or Christmas) and what he wants to do "when he grows up." The questions should remain open, and a shy or reticent child should be encouraged to speak no matter how relevant his replies. One way to get a nontalkative child to talk is to leave painful silences in the conversation, which some children try to fill in. Children, unlike adults, usually take a long time to reply, and a mistake in interviewing children is to get impatient and fill in words for them.

It must also be remembered that a young child (usually less than six) will "yes respond" by responding "Yes" or "No" to any question, regardless of what the question is. Yes-responding can be eliminated by simply phrasing the question so the child can not answer it with a yes or no.

At this point in the interview one should have an idea of what the child likes and dislikes, what he feels good about and what makes him uneasy. From his verbal and nonverbal communication his anxieties should become apparent. What topics does he cover up on? Which questions does he refuse to answer? When does he change the subject? Make a joke? What areas cause fidgeting and breaking of eye contact? Which topics "turn him on?" From these observations one can decide which topics to leave to the end of the interview.

The next area usually elicited is the background information; from this exchange one hopes to gain an impression of the student's general intelligence, academic sophistication (cultural background), ability to stay on the topic, and fluency of speech. Ask: What are the members of your family and how old are they? What are your hobbies and interests? What athletics do you participate in? Have you ever been sick or in the hospital? Do you take any medication or pills? From this, one can get into the home life and draw him out by asking how he gets along with his sibs and parents, what do they fight about, do they make him mad sometimes? Does he get an allowance? What does his family do on weekends (or last weekend) and vacations? How much TV does he watch and what are his favorite programs?

With older children (above the age of ten or eleven), one can ask the child what his problem is and why he has a problem. This question rarely works with younger children, because they are still unaware of their problems. If one really wants to get to know the child, one can make a life space analysis, which is essentially trying to establish what the typical day is like for the child spotting his daily frustrations and rewards. One begins by asking what people live with him and ask him to tell something about each. Ask him to tell something about his house and if he has chores. Who does he talk to and what kinds of things does he talk about? Where does he sleep and does he have any roommates? Does he study and where? What are others doing while he is studying? Then getting to his average day, does he like to get up in the morning? When does he get up; does he do this on his own? How long does it take for him to get dressed? Who fixes breakfast, what are his favorite foods, and how often does he get them? To discover what happens after school, one may ask if he walks home with anybody, what does he do when he gets home? Do friends come over, and if so, how often? What are his favorite books and magazines, and are they in the home? Finally, one is interested in bedtime because this is usually a conflict situation between parents and child.

Towards the end of the interview one will want to determine if the child sees himself with a problem, whether he thinks he is crazy, lazy, or stupid, or does he know how others think about him. In the areas in which he gave inaccurate information one can test him by confronting him mildly to see if he handles the discrepancy with acceptance, hostility, denial, apathy, rationalization, or whatever response. The interview should always end on a positive note; one may usually do this by telling the child what his strong points are and explain to him that others have problems just like his. After the interview one should attempt to check the information the child has given to see how accurately he sees the situation. One must guard during an interview that a child is not just telling an adult what he thinks is socially appropriate rather than what actually happens.

The reliability of the psychiatric interview has rarely been studied. Rutter, Graham, and Yule (1970) had two psychiatrists independently interview a sample of normal children, LD children, and neurologically impaired children. The psychiatrists were only given the child's age and had to rate the child's emotional state after a half hour interview. The psychiatrists agreed with one another fairly well (correlation of .84), particularly on which children had marked emotional problems (agreeing ninety percent of the time).

The Diagnostic Report

A diagnosis relies on information gleaned from individual records, interviews with pupils, teachers, and parents, informal and formal diagnostic testing, and standardized test scores. The task then is assembling this information in a logical, coherent fashion and forming hypotheses. There are several ways for the diagnostician to do this. Each individual making a diagnosis may write a discipline report. These reports are then summarized in a face sheet to the reports or presented in a case staffing.

A second way to assembly the data is into a behaviorist report, which follows orthodox behaviorist theory where hypothetical constructs such as "intelligence," "visual memory," and "reading disability" are carefully avoided. The behaviorist analysis is described more fully in several sources; see Goldfried and Davison's (1976), or Bijou and Patterson's (1971) book. This approach in the field of learning disabilities has been called the task analysis approach after Vallet (1967).

Task-analysis is largely an outgrowth of the behaviorist school of psychology. Skinner (1954), one of the most prominent behaviorists, has suggested that the traditional diagnostic categories are nothing but vague labels that say little about the child's actual functioning. For example, a child who is mute, engages in bizarre hand motions, and does not enjoy personal contact would traditionally be diagnosed as an "autistic child." This diagnosis places the entire responsibility for the child's behavior on the child, and the label has a permanence to it implying that a child is always acting abnormal. Behaviorists would point out that perhaps the child's behavior is a reaction to an unusual environmental condition, such as being around a cold, uncaring mother and that these symptoms cannot always be observed in the child's daily life. They suggest that it would be much more meaningful and profitable to describe such a child as simply, "This is a child who does not vocalize, shows a high rate of undesirable hand movements, and does not sit in adult's laps or interact with other children." This last behavioral description is more desirable, the behaviorists argue, because it engages in overt observable behavior, implies that the child's behavior is modifiable, and it clearly points to a definite remedial plan. The remedial plan for this particular child would be to develop his speech, to reduce the undesired hand movements, to get him to sit on adults' laps, and to play with other children. The behaviorist approach at its best provides a careful description of the child's desirable and undesirable behaviors, and at its worst ends up as a long catalogue of unrelated observations.

The criticisms voiced by Skinner persist (e.g. Algozzine and Sutherland, 1977 and Vellentino, et al., 1977) who point out the problems of infering a "disability" among children who are not doing well in school and may be just underachievers. The way to sidestep the problem of infering a deficit and supporting it with often unreliable tests is to focus on direct observable behavior. The process begins by deciding which situations are relevant and then making a direct observation of the behavior in these situations. Bijou and Peterson (1971) have written an excellent review of the behavioral or "functional analysis" as they call it. They suggest:

1. Specifying the setting, which may be the classroom, child's home, or some other place.

2. Setting up a code of the stimulus and response categories, which are essentially the desired and undesired behaviors.

3. Developing an objective recording procedure, which usually means counting the behaviors in specified time constraints.

4. Estimating the reliability of the recording system, and

5. Using a method to present the data graphically.

One of the most complete methods of coding behavior is the Behavior Coding System, which codes behavior into twenty-eight behavior categories (Jones, Reid, and Patterson, 1975). Chalfant (1974) has written about using a behaviorist approach to learning disabilities in children in what he calls a "task analysis." He suggests that after the student's behaviors have been observed and recorded, that they be arranged into desirable and undesirable behaviors in an asset-deficit list. This list is simply a blank sheet of paper with a line going down the middle. On the left side the child's strengths, desirable behaviors, and capabilities are listed. On the deficit side the child's deficiences are recorded. For example, a child in the fourth grade might be observed in class and then given a set of tasks such as reading through the Dolch list of 220 most basic words, counting to 100, printing the alphabet, writing a simple passage, and doing some arithmetic problems. The asset list might then include: (a) very highly motivated, (b) can say his alphabet, (c) can count to 100, (d) good at listening in class, and (e) above average vocabulary. His deficit list might be : (a) reverses the letters "b," "d," "p," and "g," (b) unable to read forty percent of the Dolch list, (c) reverses number sequences in math, (d) eyes skip and miss words when reading.

Chalfant and King (1976) have further defined task analysis by presenting the model for task analysis. The functioning for the three kinds of sensory input (visual, auditory, and haptic) are examined in relation to six processes (attention, discrimination, memory, integration, concept formation, and problem solving) using questions that focus on the task and the child's response. He has ninety-eight questions that he asks, two examples of which are: "Does the child have unusual difficulty attending to more than one stimulus within or between the visual, auditory, or haptic channels?" and "Can the child whose motor functions are intact reproduce single rhythmic groups, but be unable to repeat the rhythmic patterns over and over as in a series?"

One of the advantages of task-analysis is that the diagnosis tends to center around actual classroom functioning, and extensive training is not then needed to begin remediating the deficits in a task-analysis. The main disadvantage of task-analysis is that it is an approach that goes only part way in understanding a disorder. To list the assets and deficits of a child's behavior without trying to cluster these behaviors into a syndrome can cause important diagnostic information to be missed. One example of this might be a child who is a real behavior problem and has the following assets: (a) tries hard when given tasks, (b) has good phonics skills, (c) knows his addition and subtraction tables; and the following deficits: (a) cannot concentrate on his work, (b) does not want to do any P.E. activities, (c) complains of headaches, (d) looks at his reading book at odd angles at times, (e) breaks into rages at times. From this one might devise a program of rewarding P.E. activities, trying to increase the child's concentration by giving him progressively longer assignments, and teaching him to hold his book correctly. Each of these could become a program for remediating the child's deficits. If one, however, went a step beyond task-analysis and tried to fit the behaviors into a pattern, one would probably come up with a completely different remedial plan and would send the child to a neurologist first because the symptoms of poor motor coordination, visual disturbances, poor concentration, and emotional lability may be due to a developing brain tumor.

Another method of writing a report is to arrange the data around the different tests administered. One might administer a Slosson IQ test, the ITPA test, and a writing sample, and then organize the report by having a section describing the test results on the Slosson, a section on the ITPA results, and a section on the writing sample with a summary section at the end of the report recommending treatment. This approach is not very impressive, because there can be so many conflicts and inaccuracies that arise out of multiple test scores that one may end up with a most confusing report. Since most LD reports are read by parents and classroom teachers, who are often only vaguely familiar with the test administered, this method of writing a report does not seem desirable.

The Case Study

The case study is the most common form for presenting diagnostic information. All the data — observations, test scores, interview material — is grouped under areas of functioning. This may be done either with each discipline on the diagnostic team reporting on their particular area of functioning or with the learning disabilities specialist drawing together all the information under various headings.

Before discussing the areas of functioning, a brief comment on how the report is written is in order, because even the most brilliant diagnosis may be ignored if it is presented in a confused manner or is poorly written. Writing a case study takes a certain amount of expertise. Since the quality of the diagnosis is often judged on the style of the report, it is important to write the report in a manner that makes it sound professional without containing an overly specialized vocabulary that cannot be understood by the teacher or parent. A few general principles should be observed.

1. Be sure to include the date of the report, child's name, age, and birthdate at the beginning of the report. Since the report will be read perhaps years from the time it was written, it is important to include the date and age at which the child was tested.

2. Reports are written in the third person and in the past tense. The word "I" or "we" should not appear in the report except in quotes. By keeping everything in the past, one avoids awkward changes of the tenses in the report.

3. Test scores, percentiles, grade levels, and so on should always be accompanied with a statement explaining the score, such as "The IQ score of 109 is in the normal intellectual range and the 3.2 grade level in reading shows that he is reading almost two years below grade level." One often includes raw scores in the report for the more qualified readers, but the untrained teacher or parent will need the

explanatory statement to understand what these scores mean.

4. Since all reports are now open information and available to the parents, it is important to insure that they are accurate. All information obtained from the case study should indicate where it came from. This allows the person reading the report to judge the accuracy of the information and prevents a mistaken piece of information being reported again and again. Also information damaging to the family or the child that is irrelevant to the diagnosis should be left out of the case study.

5. There is a tendency to "cover" oneself by couching one's statements with such words as "apparently," "possibly," "a tendency towards," and so on. If this is done too often, the report sounds as if the author does not know anything or does not want to make a judgment of what is wrong. A balance therefore must be struck between being too positive and possibly wrong and being too vague and uncertain.

6. Raw data should be left out of the report, except as illustrations to support the conclusions. The test protocols normally belong to the organization one works for, and the case report is really a summary of this data.

7. Avoid using slang or jargon in the report. Do not use phrases such as "he turned on," or he "needs TLC," or the like. The more jargon in a report, the more likelihood of its being rejected by the nonprofessional.

8. The report is most easily organized using general headings. Every report should contain a summary and recommendation section where the findings of the report are reviewed without any of the actual details of the diagnosis being discussed. Since many persons reading the report will read just this section, extra care should be taken in its execution.

9. If one does not know an item of information (such as the number of siblings or the father's name or whether the child was adopted), the best policy is to leave out mention of this fact in the report. One never obtains all the necessary information when working with children, and so one must make do with what one has. The report becomes very distracting if it contains references that this item was not known, except in cases where the information is simply not available (such as not knowing the information on the real mother because she died many years ago).

10. Every case report should be signed by the clinician so that he can be contacted later if any questions arise. If a clinician goes to the trouble of writing a case study, he should be willing to take the credit

and responsibility for the information presented in the report. By signing the report he is in effect saying he is responsible for the information and conclusions contained in it.

For more information on report writing Talent (1976) or Klopfer (1960) can be consulted. There are also a number of model case study forms that may be followed (e.g. Otto, McNemeny, and Smith, 1973). *Figure 7* is such a sample form that has been drawn from many sources.

FIGURE 7
Information Included in a Case Study

I. Identification and Referral Information
   A. Identification
      1. Name of child
      2. Date of birth
      3. Sex
      4. Race
      5. Age in years and months
      6. Grade in school
      7. Date of examination
      8. Name and address of institutions doing case study
   B. Description of Child
   C. Referral Information
      1. Father's name, address, and telephone number
      2. Mother's name, address, and telephone number
      3. Name of school and location of school
      4. Is child presently attending any special classes?
      5. Person who made referral
      6. Reason for referral

II. Family Background
   A. General Information: Age, Education, Occupation, Income, General Health of
      1. Father
      2. Mother
      3. Grandparents
      4. Siblings
   B. Home Conditions
      1. Parents' marital status
      2. Do siblings, parents, or grandparents have any learning difficulties?
      3. Are there other persons living at the home?
      4. What is the language of the house?
      5. Is the child adopted or raised by others?
      6. Does father or mother belong to any special organizations, have any special interests or hobbies?
      7. Social class of home
      8. Religion of family
   C. Observations by others of home conditions and family relationships

III. Physical Development
    A. Appearance
        1. Stature (height and weight)
        2. Body build
        3. Complexion and coloring
        4. General attractiveness
        5. Dress
        6. Posture (sitting and standing)
        7. Facial expressions
        8. Any tics, grimaces, unusual mannerisms
        9. Physical deformities (scars, bruises)
        10. Cleanliness and hygiene
    B. Development History
        1. Any difficulties with pregnancy
        2. Any complications at birth
        3. Was child premature and birth weight
        4. Age at which child first rolled over, sat up, crawled, began walking
        5. Was child breast fed?
        6. Were there any feeding or sleeping problems as an infant?
        7. Age first word, first sentence, and any unusual language development
    C. Medical History
        1. List any illnesses, hospitalizations, operations, or head injuries
        2. Has child had a diagnostic or neurological workup? If so when and where?
        3. Does child take any medications?
        4. Does child have any allergies?
        5. Is he on a special diet?
        6. Does child have any visual problems and date of last exam?
        7. Does child have any hearing problems and date of last exam?
        8. Name and address of child's physician
IV. Educational Development
    A. Age child entered school
    B. Did he attend preschool or kindergarten?
    C. School Progress

School	Teacher	Absences	General Progress
1st			
2nd			
3rd			
etc.			

    D. School Achievement Scores

Test Name	Date	Grade	Scores and Percentiles
1st			
2nd			
3rd			
etc.			

    E. Special Test (IQ, perceptual, etc.)

Test Name	Date	Grade	Scores and Percentiles
1st			
2nd			
3rd			
etc.			

    F. Has child been referred to any special program?
    G. Child's study habits at home and school
    H. Teacher's description of child's classroom functioning
    I. General school adjustment
    J. Child's future educational and vocational plans
V. Description of Present Problem
    A. Problem according to teacher
    B. Problem according to parents
    C. Problem according to remedial teachers
VI. Present Test Results
    A. List tests administered and child's scores
        1. Sensory evaluation
        2. Medical and neurological evaluation
        3. Motor evaluation
        4. Emotional evaluation
        5. Intellectual evaluation
        6. Language evaluation
        7. Perceptual evaluation
        8. Memory evaluation
VIII. The Diagnosis
    A. Suspected causes and main problem
    B. Secondary problems
    C. The prognosis
IX. Proposed Treatment Plan
    A. Weak areas to build up in a remedial program
    B. Severely deficient areas to teach compensation methods for
    C. Methods of remediating deficits
X. Summary and Conclusions
    A. Summary of case study
    B. Present findings
    C. Diagnosis
    D. Summary of remedial treatment
XI. Signature and Date of Author of Report

The clinician is encouraged to pick out a form having only those elements relevant for his purposes, since there is no point in including information which has no bearing on the diagnosis.

Summary

One of the most important aspects of making a diagnosis is the accurate collection of behavioral information about the client. For children it is recommended that information be obtained through the Family Information Form, parental interviews, and a Parent Rating Scale. Next the teacher can be interviewed and allowed to rate the child on the Teacher Rating Scale. Finally, information can be obtained directly from the child in a child interview, observing his behavior in the school setting and in doing a task analysis of his work. All these observations can be summarized in a case study, which has been outlined.

Of the major variables studied in the behavior setting, attention and motivation are the most relevant. These vary from time to time and situation to situation, so that rating scales are the best measures of these variables. In addition one should note that attention and motivation are made up of several components and must be described always in relation to a particular context or task.

Chapter IV

Diagnosing Processing Deficits and Using Standardized Tests

The LD specialist has three general plans-of-attack when making a diagnosis (Bateman, 1967). He may either do a behavioral analysis and record each individual behavior of the child, or he may look for specific perceptual and memory deficits, or he may look for the cause of the disability. The first method, the task-analysis approach, was described in the previous chapter. The second, often called the diagnostic-remedial method, will be described in this chapter along with the most common tool for measuring perceptual deficits, the standardized test. The etiological method was discussed in the second chapter.

The diagnostic-remedial method, also called the process method, makes three basic assumptions: each individual has a set of independent psychological "processes;" psychological processes can be measured by psychological tests; and children with learning disabilities have specific dysfunctions in one or more of these processes.

A psychological process is an independent structure that analyzes information received by the brain in a specific way. How the brain analyzes information is not known, and psychological processes are theoretical constructs. An example of how one might infer processes is an analysis of the task of how a child might name the pictures in a coloring book. The child must first be able to see the picture (using the visual reception process); he must then associate the picture with previously seen pictures (visual memory); then he must match the recognized visual image with the appropriate auditory word (visual-auditory integration), which involves remembering the verbal name (auditory memory); and finally he must say the word aloud (verbal expression). This task then involves six processes. If a child could not name pictures in the coloring book, the process diagnosis would attempt to find out which process was deficient, and correction for a learning disability would become a matter of giving specific practice in the deficient process to build it up to normal.

While there is some physiological evidence that basic visual and auditory processes are coded in different areas of the brain, the locations of more complex processes such as auditory and visual memory, perceptual closure, and figure-ground processes are not known. There is actually some evidence that the separate processes of auditory and visual memory are coded in the same location of the brain and are not physiologically independent.

Psychological processes, for the most part, are measured with standardized tests. A person's auditory memory might be examined by presenting him with a series of digits (e.g. he must repeat correctly the sequence 1, 8, 4, 5), or a series of unrelated words (e.g. cow, head, door, apple), or a sentence of specific length. These tasks appear on a number of readily available tests, so it is relatively easy to compare a child's performance with those of children of the same age. Should a child do poorly on an auditory memory task, provided he has normal intelligence, vision, hearing, and motivation, and the test score was a valid one, one can infer that he has a deficit in this area. In other words, standardized testing and process analysis are closely wed to each other because processes are almost always measured with a normed test. The question of how many individual psychological processes exist is still controversial. One method to get at an answer is to analyze cases of persons who perform extremely well or poorly in a particular area. Ouadfasel and Goodglass (1968) report that in their experience they have found eight independent abilities:

1. A special defect or talent for shorthand, morse code, braille, semaphore signals, and foreign languages. It is well documented that some individuals pick up many languages in a short time without trying, while others who are very intelligent and try very hard cannot seem to master a single foreign language.

2. A special talent or disability in arithmetic. There are a number of dull, mentally retarded individuals who simply cannot solve the simplest problems but who have phenomenal mental calculating skills. Similarly, there are highly gifted and verbal individuals who possess acalculia or the inability to do simple calculations without a great number of errors.

3. A special talent or disability in melodic memory, tonal discrimination, and ability to sing. There was in England a mentally retarded man, with an IQ of about 70, who was a concert pianist.

4. A specific lack of rhythm while having a sense of pitch.

Beethoven has been reported to have been unable to dance in rhythm to music.

5. A skill in drawing, independent of intelligence. Again there are a number of mentally retarded individuals who are excellent artists and can reproduce elaborate and detailed pictures of their surroundings.

6. A special deficit in the sense of direction, which may involve topographic disorientation on maps or floor plans, or manipulations in not knowing the right from the left. An example of a twenty-two-year-old girl can be found with good intelligence and good grades who majored in art, but did not know her right from her left, could not sew a dress, had difficulty turning the key in the lock in the correct direction or screwing caps on bottles, and could not read a map. In this case right-left discrimination is apparently independent of spatial ability required in art.

7. A special talent for playing certain games such as chess. A master chess player has fantastic visual memory and can remember every single move in thousands of games. Chess champions will sometimes play thirty or forty persons simultaneously (i.e. going from one board to the next) while blindfolded and being told only the opponent's last move; yet win every game.

8. A special talent or disability in motor skills and motor development. There are, of course, examples of athletes with excellent motor skills who have no particular intellectual excellence or other talents.

Standardized Testing

A standardized test is a test with a definite set of items, an exact scoring standard, and a set of norms that enables one to compare a child's performance with a reference group. Over a thousand standardized tests are presently available and information about these tests can be obtained by consulting the seven *Mental Measurements Yearbooks* edited by O.K. Buros. Buros' handbooks are the bible of standardized tests, because they give not only the name, cost, authors, publishers, and description of the test, but also have reviews of the test discussing the test's reliability and validity with a listing of all research studies using the test.

The administration of a standardized test differs from a teaching situation in that testing focuses on describing the child's present knowledge and performance skills rather than attempting to teach him anything. This unique position makes several conditions necessary for a standardized test score to be valid.

First, a standardized test must be considered a selective sample, not an exhaustive list of what the child can do. In the vocabulary section of most intelligence tests, for instance, the child must define usually only thirty to forty common words such as "straw," "regulate," "victorious," because to test a child's complete vocabulary would take several years. In spite of this, if the words are carefully selected they will correlate relatively highly (in the order of .80) with general intelligence. Because the vocabulary section is a sampling, to drill a child on these vocabulary words in remedial activities does not in any way increase the child's intelligence — instead it invalidates the child's performance on that section of the test. This is why testing companies are reluctant to allow nonprofessionals to see the tests or to have items published in books.

Second, every standardized test assumes the child is trying hard to do the task. Yet, if the administrator cannot get the full cooperation of the testee the results are automatically invalid. Since cooperation is so important on a test, every report should include a statement of how motivated the child was during the test. If the child feels the test is too easy or too difficult, he may just guess or give facetious answers. Usually, standardized tests overcome this factor by arranging the items in order of difficulty and beginning the child on items that are of medium difficulty for him.

Third, standardized tests must be administered exactly in the way prescribed in the manual. Since each child in the standardization sample was given the test in a certain fashion, to deviate from this procedure is to invalidate the norms of the test. On many standardized tests, one is often struck by individual questions that seem very outdated, irrelevant, or culturally biased — these individual items do not really "count against" the child, because the normative sample had the same ambiguous item with just the same opportunity to get it right.

One can deviate from the method of giving the test as described in the manual if and *only if* the child does not understand the item or rapport cannot be achieved. When this is done, the deviation from the standardized method should be reported with the reason it was done. In cases in which the material in the standardized test is largely irrelevant or foreign to the subject, as occurs at times with minority groups, it is better to reject the test than to administer the test not following the accepted scoring procedure.

The testing situation is, however, different from a classroom situation, because it usually has few external distractions. The child who tests out "normal" in the test situation and is still doing poorly in the classroom may have a personality clash with the teacher; may be very distractible so that he cannot function effectively in a busy classroom; or may be bored by the amount of repetition found in the classroom, but not on the standardized test.

The testing situation should yield much more than a set of scores. It should tell one how easily the child gave up, how he reacted under pressure, how he responded to praise and encouragement, whether he solved problems randomly or systematically, how the child handled his failures, and his general anxiety level. For this reason the tester should try to record as much as he can about the testing situation so that the test scores can be related to the cause of the child's problems in the classroom.

In order to test properly one should follow some basic rules. Sattler (1974) in his excellent book on intelligence testing offers over a dozen suggestions on how to test children. Some of these are:

1. When talking to the child use his first name,
2. Furnish the child with a brief explanation of why he is being tested,
3. Show confidence that he will do well on the test,
4. Watch for the child's facial cues,
5. Establish rapport with the child before beginning,
6. Praise the child for his effort,
7. Keep one's voice at low pitch,
8. Be playful and friendly when working with a child,
9. Avoid "putdowns" or situations that make a child feel badly,
10. Set clear limits of what is acceptable behavior in the testing situation,
11. Encourage the child to do his best,
12. Make sure the child does not have to go to the bathroom, and
13. With a hyperactive child simply hold his hand without making a "fuss" about it.

There are generally two different kinds of standardized tests: individual and group tests. Individual tests require that they be administered in a one-to-one situation with the administrator presenting the material and recording the child's responses. Group tests, such as the Stanford Achievement Tests or the Iowa Basic Skills Test, are administered to an entire class at one time. Under this system there are possibilities of the child not understanding the directions, not being able to read the questions, or looking onto another child's paper, and of giving up and randomly guessing. The content of these tests is also largely confined to visual items.

There are two basic types of standardized tests: normative and criterion-referenced tests. Normative tests compare a child's performance in relation to the performance of children his own age, and criterion-referenced tests determine simply whether a child has a particular skill or not. Behaviorists particularly employ criterion-referenced tests because they are interested mostly in what skills a child possesses without being interested in the child's age, intelligence, or perceptual handicaps. A great deal has been written about criterion-referenced tests (Ebel, 1971; Hambleton and Novich, 1973; Millman, 1974), because these tests are an integral part of individualized instructions whereby a child takes a criterion-referenced test to establish which module of instruction he should work at.

A good example of a criterion-referenced test is the Kennedy Phonics Test (Durrell, 1975), in which Durrell developed a set of eighteen tests measuring all the basic phonics skills, such as consonant sounds, short and long vowels, that he knew of. Durrell then gave these tests to the same children a month apart and obtained retest reliabilities on these tests. Four were found to be unreliable, so he eliminated these four tests. He then gave the fourteen tests to a group of normal readers in the first three grades and found that by third grade all normal readers could achieve at least a ninety-five percent on these tests. Without resorting to a large random sample of children across the entire U.S. or having to develop standard deviations and percentiles, Durrell was able to publish a criterion-referenced test that was reliable and valid.

It is possible to turn any normed test into a criterion-referenced test by simply establishing a particular cutoff score as passing. One might specify that if a child performs more than one year behind on a normed test, he has not met the criterion. A cutoff of one or two years behind is not very satisfactory, because a year behind in first grade means the child has not mastered the skill at all, while a year behind in tenth grade is a relatively minor deviation. For this reason an expectancy quotient is usually employed. The expectancy quotient is defined as the achievement age on the standardized test divided by the child's age times 100 (Harris, p. 212). If a child is nine years old and in fourth grade, and he is reading at second-grade or the seven-year-old level, his expectancy quotient would be 7/9 times 100, or 78. In general, a child with a learning quotient below 90 is considered not passing, although some researchers prefer to use a learning quotient of 80 and below.

Norming Population

The norming of a test refers to the characteristics of the population on whom the test was originally standardized. A perfectly normed test used in the United States could only be obtained by giving the test to everyone living in the U.S. Clearly this cannot be done, so that the norming population is randomly selected from the U.S. population. The better the sample resembles the entire population, the better the test norms.

One of the best normed intelligence tests is the Wechsler Intelligence Scale for Children-Revised (WISC-R). The WISC-R norms were established by giving the test to 100 boys and 100 girls of each age from six to sixteen making a total of 2,000 children. To make sure the test was representative of the United States population, the children came from all fifty states and were selected with the percentages based on the 1970 census for race, urban-rural backgrounds, and for social class. Another test, not so comprehensive, is the Peabody Picture Vocabulary Test, also an intelligence test which was normed on 4,000 children in 1956. But all the children in the standardization sample were white and came from Nashville, Tennessee. When giving the Peabody test, especially to a Black or rural child, one should always be aware of the limitations of the norms and consequently with whom one is comparing the testee. The normative population for most common tests is given in *Appendix B.*

Since the normative population is a representative sample of the general population, the larger the sample, the better. A general rule of thumb is that the inclusion of 100 or more children of each age is most desirable. When this large of a norming sample has been drawn from many states, the sample approaches the accuracy of an opinion poll, where the respondents resemble the entire nation within a few percentage points on almost any behavioral trait. Samples of at least fifty children in each age group yield a good sample, and normative samples of less than thirty yield fairly invalid scores.

How Scores Are Reported

Each standardized test has a "raw score," which is simply the number of items correctly answered and a "scaled score," which shows how the child did in relation to the norms. There are many types of scaled scores, the simplest of which is the age equivalent. The age equivalent is simply the average score of a particular age group of the norming population.

The child's actual age, called his chronological age (abbreviated CA), is usually expressed in years and months: one writes the year and month with a dash between so that seven years and eight months becomes a CA of 7-8. Some tests convert the months to decimal (e.g. six months equals half a year or .5 year) and this is expressed in a decimal so that five years, six months becomes either 5-6 or 5.5 years. If a child answers fifteen items correctly on the fifty items on the Auditory Reception test of the ITPA, he achieves an age equivalent of 5-5. This "age equivalent" score is often called a "mental age" or "perceptual age." A simple formula for converting age and grade equivalents is that grade equivalent equals age equivalent minus five.

The most common way of expressing scaled scores is by percentiles. A large number of tests report age or grade equivalents and then show what percentage of the children of the same age scored below and above the child on the test. In the previous example, if a child who is 5-5 received a raw score of fifteen correct on the Auditory Reception test, he would be completely average and therefore score in the fiftieth percentile, with one-half of the children above and one-half below him. Another type of scaled score frequently used is a statistical measure called the standard deviation. The standard deviation (abbreviated SD) is simply a mathematical number that is derived by taking a series of scores on the test and subtracting them from the mean, adding up these differences, dividing it by the total number of scores minus one, and then taking the square root of this. The reason the SD is so important is that it has been shown that if one graphs a large number of persons taking a standardized test, one obtains a normal curve.

Each test has a different average score: on the ITPA the mean scaled score is 36, for the IQ test it is 100, for the College Entrance Examination Boards it is 500. Now the question is, "How far does one have to deviate from the mean to still be normal?" Looking at the normal curve, one sees it is clear that there are no sharp cutoffs. It has been arbitrarily established by statisticians that any score falling within one SD of the mean is "normal."

The SD is obtained by the test maker by taking all the scores in the normative sample and calculating the standard deviation. For example, on the WISC IQ test the mean IQ score was set at 100 (that is a 100 IQ is normal), and it has a standard deviation of 15 IQ points. This means that "normal" intelligence is one SD above the mean (e.g. $100 + 15 = 115$) to one SD below the mean ($100 - 15 = 85$). On the ITPA the mean scaled score of any subtest is 36, and the SD is 6. So any score between 30 and 42 on the subtests of the ITPA is normal. It has also been arbitrarily agreed that any score two standard deviations from the mean is considered abnormal. On the WISC with an SD of 15 the "mentally retarded" child, which is what we label a child with an abnormally low intelligence score, would be 30 IQ points below the mean of 100. This is how it was decided that an IQ below

70 was the cutoff for mentally retarded. Similarly, a "genius" (or abnormally high intelligence) is defined as two SDs above the mean, or an IQ of 130.

A "normal" score is between minus one SD and plus one SD, so that sixty-eight percent of all persons score in the normal range of any standardized test. About two percent of the subjects score below two SDs and two percent score above two SDs. *Appendix C* lists the standard deviations in tenths of a standard deviation and their equivalent percentiles. This figure allows one to convert any examinee's scaled score into a percentile. The standard deviation scores are usually called "standard scores" or "z-scores" or "sigma-scores." If we want, for example, to convert an ITPA score into a percentile, we can use *Appendix C* also. A child that receives a scaled score of 26 on the Auditory Reception test, which the manual reports to have a mean of 36 and SD of 6, would then have a standard score of 36 − 26 = 10 and 10 ÷ 6 = 1.66) or standard score of −1.66. Looking at *Appendix C*, this is in the 5th percentile, or one can say that ninety-five percent of the population of his age scored above the student on the test.

Another score with which a diagnostician should be familiar is the standard error. The standard error is the amount a score on a test will deviate due to testing error for sixty-eight percent of the persons taking the test. For example, the Stanford Achievement Test has a standard error of .4 of a grade level for the reading test, which means if a girl is at the 4.2 grade level and achieves a score of 3.9, she is still within the normal range. The size of the standard error of a test tells one how accurate a test is, so if a test manual reports a standard error of 1.2 grade levels, it is not as accurate as the Standard Achievement Test, because sixty-eight percent of the scores fall in this large range.

Reliability

For a standardized test to be useful, it must have good reliability, because a test is essentially useless if it does not have adequate reliability. There are three types of reliability, with retest reliability being the most important in a diagnosis. Retest reliability is how consistently a test will yield the same score when the test is administered several times to the same person. One would hope that if one gives a test to a child and obtains a score, the child would make the same score if he were given the same test a week later.

If one gave a reading test, for example, to a fourth grader and obtained a 4.9 grade level the first time and a 3.2 grade level a week later, one is faced with the problem of which of these scores represents the child's reading level. In a diagnostic situation a 4.9

would represent better than average reading and a 3.2 a need for remedial help. The reliability of a test, then, tells the clinician how accurate the score is likely to be when he gives the test only once.

If one gives any standardized test to a number of children, one cannot expect each child to receive the exact same score on a retest. There are a whole host of factors, called "testing error," which can influence the reliability of a test. Testing error can be due to how the child was feeling that day, transitory inattention, distractions during the testing, the child making a few lucky guesses, errors made by the tester in scoring, and misinterpretations of some questions on one of the administrations. The higher the testing error, the lower the reliability. Reliability of a test is statistically derived by administering the test twice to a representative population (ideally the norming population) and then correlating the children's first test score with the second time they took the test. This method of using a correlation automatically compensates for there being an overall rise in scores with the second administration of the test.

The retest reliability is actually an index of the total testing error of a particular test. When we read in the newspaper that a child's IQ went up 45 points or that someone has taught children "how to take tests" and obtained dramatic increases in test scores, we are actually reading about retest reliability. The retest reliability does not tell one how much a particular child will vary on a test, but it does provide a good indication of what can be expected on an average from a child taking the test.

A second type of reliability is the interscorer reliability. With a standardized test it is important to determine how consistently two different persons will score the same test responses. Interscorer reliability is usually determined by having four or five trained individuals score a set of tests on which the child's response has been written down. The correlation between the scores given by each of these trained individuals then represents the interscorer reliability.

If a test has a low interscorer reliability, then the score a particular child obtains on the test is largely a function of who is scoring the test. A good number of tests used in a diagnosis of psychological processes have interscorer reliabilities between .95 and .99. A good standardized test should, as a rule of thumb, have an interscorer reliability of at least .90.

The third type of reliability is the split-half reliability, which is calculated by giving the test to a group of children and then dividing each child's test score in half, adding up the child's score on the even number of items and on the odd number of items. The score for the even and odd items for each child is then correlated, and this correlation represents roughly the split-half reliability. If the items on a test are very much alike, the correlation between the two halves of the test should be high and thus the split-half reliability provides an index of how homogeneous a set of test items is.

If a test is measuring several abilities on a single test, the split-half reliability will be low. This reliability is usually calculated by using either the Spearman-Brown or the Kuder-Richardson formula (found in most statistics books), but the formula expresses only statistical approximations of true test-retest reliability. The split-half reliabilities for the major tests in learning disabilities are given in *Appendix B*. A split-half reliability that is between .90 and .99 is very good. A general rule-of-thumb widely accepted among testers is that a test must have a reliability above .80 to be of any use in an individual diagnosis.

Although it is desirable to have high split-half reliability when measuring a unitary trait, extremely high split-half reliability in some cases is not desirable, because the only way to achieve this is to make the items on the scale almost identical to each other so that the test ends measuring too narrow a range of abilities. A lower split-half means the test is measuring a wider variety of traits and so the uniformity of a scale must always be judged in relation to what it is supposed to measured. Cattell and Butcher (1968, pp. 123-125) have disagreed with the conventional view that high retest reliability is always desirable in standardized tests, but their argument is too technical to discuss here. The more accepted view is that the validity of the test (in terms of how well the test correlates with the criterion) can only be as high as the square root of its retest reliability (Guilford, 1965). So in practice if the reliability falls below .80, the test will yield a score that is of little significance. Since one has no way of knowing on the tests with low reliabilities whether an individual score is accurate or due to testing error, it is best to avoid using tests of low reliabilities, unless the test is repeatedly given.

There are several methods for improving the reliability of a test. The first way is to increase the number of items on a test. The reason for this is that if the test has only a few items — let us say it has only thirty items for measuring reading from first to sixth grade — a child missing only one or two items out of carelessness in one of the administrations could drop as much as one-half of a grade level. If the test is much longer — say 150 items — missing a few items will change the score only a few tenths of a grade level and not significantly affect the overall performance. In general, however, a test or subtest should have thirty to fifty items to achieve a reliability of .80 (Storey, 1970, p. 5).

One would expect that a test made up of just verbal analogies, or all verbal opposites, or definitions would be more reliable than a test of equal length employing all three of these measures. The reason for this is that if the items are varied there is a greater chance for the child to misinterpret an item and to answer inconsistently because he has not developed a response set. Both retest and split-half reliability then can be increased by making the items more homogeneous. Another method for increasing test reliability is to make all the items on the test of moderate difficulty. If the test is too difficult, the examinees will tend to guess randomly at answers, and if the items are too easy, they will tend to be careless. Every standardized test, ideally, should be geared so that fifty percent of the items are missed by the persons taking the test. Test publishers can establish basals (the easiest item a particular age child would begin at) and ceilings (the item at which one stops giving the test) for any age by examining the number of items passed and failed by the various age groups in the norming population.

A rather important variable affecting reliability is the characteristics of the persons taking the test. It has been found in general that older children and adults are much more reliable than younger children — younger children do not have the concentration to be highly reliable, and they just naturally vary more from day to day. As a result split-half and retest reliability is usually reported for several age levels. One also expects reliability for groups of normal children to be higher than for groups of emotionally disturbed or LD children. Another factor affecting reliability is the range of the abilities of the individuals in the reliability study. If the sample is composed of persons varying little from each other on the test (e.g., having IQs between 90 and 110), the scores become bunched up in a limited range, and it is easier for great differences in scores to emerge relative to each other on the next administration. If the reliability sample includes mentally retarded children, normal children, and gifted children, the chance of children reversing their relative standing (and thus affecting the reliability correlation) is small. Often test manuals will report reliabilities for a narrow range of ability and statistically convert the reliability coefficient to a full range ability reliability and obtain an "attenuated" reliability. When examining reliabilities, it is therefore important to determine if the reliability is a true one or has been mathematically extended. Ideally, the reliabilities for each group of exceptional children should be reported, because LD children are usually a more diverse group than normal, although this has been rarely tested.

Finally, if the test contains many hidden implications or has trick questions, the examinee is likely to answer a question one way the first time and see the implication a second time and answer differently. This situation, of course, lowers retest reliability; therefore it suggests that all standardized tests should be as straightforward in wording of items as possible (Storey, 1970).

Ysseldyke and Salvia (1974) have suggested that the entire use of diagnostic tests be abandoned, because the reliabilities for most LD tests fall below .80. They present a chart listing the retest reliabilities of the most widely used LD tests (including the DTVP, Bender, VRT, MDT, VMI, and ITPA) and showed that the reliabilities were so low that they yielded a correct prediction of a deficiency only a few percent above chance level. The range of the LD test reliabilities was .12 to .89, with only four of twenty-three test reliabilities reaching over .80. There are a number of newly developed tests that have good reliabilities, and these tests will be reviewed later.

Validity

One often hears professionals refer to a test as a good or bad test or wish there was a better test to measure something. What they are referring to is the validity of the test. Validity is the question of whether it is applicable to the group one is testing. There are dozens of ways to determine the validity of a test, but three general types of validity seem to be the most sought after: content validity, criterion-related validity, and construct validity (Davis, 1974).

Content validity is established by examining the test items and deciding if the items appear to be measuring what the test claims to be measuring. The examining of the content is less objective, because it relies on common sense rather than a statistical procedure. For example, the validity of an auditory memory test might be questioned if the test consists of presenting pictures of familiar objects and the subject must recall what he has seen. One could say this test is not a valid measure of auditory memory, because it uses essentially visual pictures to measure auditory memory.

Criterion-related validity is established by setting some criterion for measuring an ability and then correlating how closely the individual test scores match that criterion. When a test measuring a particular ability is given to two groups, one deficient in the ability and one normal in the ability as established by the criterion, the deficient group should score significantly lower on the test than the normal group. One could, for example, test how valid a test of brain damage is by giving the test to patients who had brain surgery (and therefore were known to have brain damage) and a matched group of individuals of the same age, sex, and intelligence, without any brain damage. The number of brain-damaged patients who score normally on the test and the number of normals who score in the brain-damaged range will determine how valid the test is.

Another type of criterion-related validity is predictive validity. With predictive validity one attempts to determine how accurately a test predicts a future outcome. For example, predictive validity of reading-readiness tests, attempting to predict which kindergarten and first-grade children are ready for reading, can be established by giving the test to five-year-olds and then waiting two or three years and recording what percent of children who failed the readiness test actually became poor readers in the second and third grade.

Construct validity is a method of determining how congruent the theory of what the test measures is to what it actually measures. The most common method of determining construct validity is to give a group of representative children the test in question along with a well-accepted measure of the trait. The scores of these two tests are then correlated to determine how related they are. For example, to determine how valid a newly developed intelligence test is, one could give the new test and the Stanford-Binet Intelligence Test, which is generally accepted as one of the best measures of intelligence. If the correlation between these tests is high (say greater than .70), then one would conclude that the new test also is a good measure of intelligence.

To illustrate how reliability, validity, and norming can be used to judge the accuracy of a standardized test, the next section will apply these concepts to three process-oriented tests that are used in making a LD diagnosis.

The Illinois Test of Psycholinguistic Abilities (ITPA)

The ITPA developed by Samuel and Winifred Kirk and James McCarthy in 1961 is probably the most widely used test in diagnosing learning disabilities. This test can be given to children two and one-half to ten years of age and yields scores in twelve areas of "psycholinguistic" functioning. The experimental edition of the ITPA was published in 1961, and in 1968 the test was completely revised, renormed, and expanded. The revised edition is accompanied by one of the most complete test manuals that has ever been available with a standardized test, and the test has been administered to thousands, if not tens of thousands of children. From this manual one learns that the ITPA was normed on 962 children with about 120 children from each of eight age groups (three to ten years of age). In selecting the norm group, all the children with IQs below 84 and above 116 were eliminated as were all children with physical and emotional handicaps. The manual gives the social class, the sex, the age, and the size of the town the normative population came from. Only four percent of this population was Negro (versus 11 percent in the United States), and all the children came from middle-sized towns located in the Midwest, making it clear Kirk was choosing a sample of "average, middle-class" children (for a discussion of ethnic differences on the test see Kirk, 1972).

Besides the fact that the ITPA was normed on essentially white, middle-class children, there have been a number of criticisms concerning the validity of the test. The first form of validity — construct validity — will be discussed taking each subtest at a time.

The Auditory Reception subtest, which involves just listening and responding "Yes" or "No," is apparently measuring understanding of sentences and vocabulary (i.e. what do meteorites, bugles, or camouflage mean?). This test is very unreliable (retest reliability .40 for eight-year-olds), probably because the format allows for easy guessing. If *Appendix A* is examined, it would appear that this test is measuring verbal reasoning (process 29) and, in fact, this subtest correlates, according to the manual, more highly with IQ than any of the other ITPA subtests.

Visual perception is generally thought of as the ability to receive visual information and identify it. The Visual Reception subtest, however, involves identifying an object in three seconds and then associating it with another object of similar function. This test appears, then, to be measuring nonverbal reasoning (process 37) rather than visual identification (process 18), but since it has a reliability of only .36, it cannot be used to accurately identify this process to any degree.

The Auditory Association subtest measures the ability to extract meaning from sentences and supply a logical missing part and correlates well with intelligence, suggesting that it is another measure of verbal reasoning. In contrast to the Auditory Reception subtest, it has fair retest reliability (.70 for six-year-olds). The Visual Reception subtest involves understanding similarities of objects of similar function and has items such as pictorial analogies, which can be found on nonverbal reasoning tests. With a low retest reliability (.38), it also appears unsatisfactory for making a process diagnosis.

Verbal expression involves much, much more than the task of naming attributes of objects as is done in the Verbal Expression subtest. The use of only four items results in low retest reliabilities (in the low .40s). The Manual Expression subtest, while it fits Osgood's model of language processing, is measuring a skill that does not appear to be very relevant to school performance. It is hard to score, and a measure of more relevant problems such as motor coordination or handwriting would have been more desirable.

The Grammatical Closure subtest requires the subject to have a fair vocabulary, a knowledge of plurals and grammatical inflections, as well as being able to achieve closure. The diversity of this subtest is reflected in the fact that it has the lowest split-half reliability of the subtests. The retest reliability is fair, and this test correlates more highly with social class than any of the other subtests.

The Visual Closure subtest involves picking out objects from a very distracting background as well as visual closure. It is the only timed subtest of the ITPA, making it a "power test" and under this pressure a child's ability to scan systematically is also apparently relevant. The reliability of this subtest is only in the .60s, and it is one of those subtests that most likely is measuring a number of processes.

Auditory Sequential Memory is the ability to remember verbal items in sequence. This skill is measured verbally by presenting the child with digits, words, or sentences, and then having him repeat the items. Kirk chose to use the digit span test that appears on many intelligence tests. It is unfortunate that a more relevant task, such as having the child repeat words or sentences was not used, but in spite of this the Auditory Sequential Memory subtest is the most reliable of the subtests and is the only subtest meeting the criteria of having a retest reliability of over .80 and a split-half reliability in the .90s.

The content of the Visual Sequential Memory subtest makes it one of the most interesting subtests, because it may measure an ability very closely related to spelling. Unfortunately, the reliability of this subtest is at chance level (.36 for eight-year-olds), which means that a score could be obtained almost as accurately by rolling dice.

There are two supplementary subtests to the ITPA that are not required to obtain the total PLA score. The Auditory Closure subtest has low retest reliability and the lowest split-half reliability of the ITPA. The Sound Blending subtest is of interest, because it has a fair retest reliability and research has shown that this subtest is one of the few that actually correlates with academic ability.

Kirk and Kirk (1971, pp. 48-52) report a number of research findings concerning the use of the ITPA as a diagnostic tool:

1. Children with reading disabilities are usually lower in the automatic level, especially in grammatical closure, visual and auditory short-term memory.

2. Mentally retarded children, as mentioned earlier, are better at the representational level tests in contrast to the automatic level tests.

3. Children with Down's syndrome (mongoloids), a special kind of retarded child, show a special superiority in the motor as compared to the vocal encoding test.

4. Normal children with articulation problems also show a superiority in the representational level tests and a deficiency on the Verbal Expression subtest.

5. Spastic cerebral palsied children are inferior on representational level tests to athetoid cerebral palsied children. They are, however, superior to athetoids in the automatic level tests.

6. Lower- and middle-class Negro children show a superiority in the Auditory Sequential Memory subtest. On the test of the subtests middle-class Negroes do normally, while lower-class Negroes do more poorly. Mexican-American children do normally on the Auditory Sequential Memory subtest and are superior on the Visual Sequential Memory subtest. American Indian children are also superior in the Visual Sequential Memory subtest.

7. Partially-seeing children with vision better than 20/200 perform as well on visual as auditory subtests, indicating again that the ITPA is measuring central rather than peripheral processes.

Validity of the ITPA

Carroll (1972), a noted linguist, reviewing the ITPA in Buros' *Seventh Mental Measurements Yearbook*, has criticized it on content, criterion-related, and construct validity. Carroll begins his discussion by asking the question of whether the Illinois Test of Psycholinguistic Ability actually measures "psycholinguistic" ability. "Psycholinguistic" usually refers to the psychological processes used in language. Carroll notes that about one-half of the test items are pictorial material involving a nonverbal response. This would strongly suggest the ITPA is not measuring just psycholinguistic ability. Carrol then asks the question of what does the ITPA measure?

If one examines the content of the ITPA, one finds that there are many items similar to those found on intelligence tests. Carroll also cites a study by Washington and Teska (1970) that shows that the ITPA subtests correlate very highly (in the .80s) with Stanford-Binet intelligence scores. The examiner's manual of the revised ITPA shows the PLA correlated .49 with the Stanford-Binet IQ test and has a table for converting the PLA score to an equivalent Stanford-Binet IQ. On the basis of this evidence and more, it appears that the ITPA is not a test of psycholinguistic abilities, but a test of general intelligence.

The fact that the ITPA measures mostly intelligence does not mean that it cannot be used in a learning disabilities diagnosis. Since children with learning disabilities have normal intelligence, they should score at least 36 on the ITPA subtests. If the child is low on most of the visual subtests as compared to the auditory tests, one can diagnose a deficit in visual processing. A low score in just the closure tests or in the sequential memory tests would indicate, according to Kirk, a specific processing deficit in these areas.

Carroll in an analysis of the content of the ITPA found that the test had a number of very middle-class oriented items. For example, the Auditory Reception subtest asks such questions as "Do portals precipitate?", a statement which appears to present a vocabulary problem to the lower-class child. A low performance on the ITPA may therefore in part be due to cultural background rather than a true learning deficit.

Another question one may ask about the items of the ITPA, to decide on its content validity, is how relevant the subtests are to the problems of children with learning disabilities. Since the ITPA is used to diagnose learning disabilities, one would expect that the test would tap those functions that LD children have difficulty in. The ITPA does not have any subtest relevant to the frequently encountered problems of letter reversals, visual discrimination, remembering the sounds of letters, right-left discrimination, and auditory discrimination. Only the Visual Sequential Memory and the supplementary tests of Sound Blending and Auditory Closure measure those processes that relate to learning disabilities. This problem of nonacademic processes tapped by the ITPA and its questionable application to learning problems has been supported by Hare, Hammill, and Bartel's (1973) study in which none of the major visual and auditory ITPA subtests correlated with reading and spelling ability among third graders.

In an investigation of the criterion validity of the ITPA, Kass (1966) gave the eleven ITPA subtests and visual closure, sound blending, completion of mazes, memory for designs, and perceptual speed tests to seven- to eleven-year-old LD children with normal intelligence and reading problems. She found that the LD children were deficient in all five of the above tests, but low in only two of the ITPA subtests. These two subtests were Auditory Association and Visual Sequential Memory. This study again seems to indicate that the processes measured by the ITPA do not seem to be those processes that children with learning disabilities are weak in.

Duffy and Clair (1972) attempted to find out how well the ITPA would predict future academic progress in a predictive validity study. They correlated the WISC intelligence test subtest scores, the Bender-Gestalt figure copying test score, and the ITPA PLA administered to first graders with the Iowa Test of Basic Skills achievement scores in the third, fourth, and fifth grades. It was reported the PLA correlated only .21 and .39 with word recognition, .29 to .38 with reading comprehension, and .30 to .49 with arithmetic. These correlations were not very high and were much lower than the correlation of the Bender-Gestalt with reading. Since poor reading is usually a good sign of poor learning, one would expect a test that is supposed to pick out children with learning problems to correlate well with actual academic skills.

Another measure of the validity of the ITPA is the question of whether the subtests are really measuring distinctly separate processes or whether they are measuring one single general trait. Kirk (and the thousands of ITPA users) hold the assumption that each of the subtests of the ITPA is in fact measuring a different psychological process. There have been numerous factor analyses of the ITPA to try to establish this fact: Ryckman and Wiegerink (1968) have summarized eighteen of these studies. Although many of these studies do not agree very well with each other, because they used different types of subjects, ages, and mathematical procedures, they basically reported that there were only three, four, or possibly five factors from the ten subtests.

One recent analysis of ninety-two LD children, done by Leyton (1972), factored the subtests of the ITPA and the Wechsler Intelligence Scale for Children (WISC). He found that there were seven factors that accounted for sixty-four percent of the variance. Variance is the amount of the criterion that a test will predict, so that the seven factors accounted for approximately two-thirds of the variance of the test with everything else, including testing error accounting for the other one-third of the variance of the test scores. Each factor accounted for eight to thirteen percent of the variance, and the remaining thirty-six percent of the variance must be attributed to testing error. The first factor was a factor involving verbal comprehension and was made of three WISC subtests (Information, Comprehension, and Vocabulary). The second factor contained only one WISC subtest (Arithmetic), and this subtest was doing mental arithmetic. The third factor was a visual sequencing factor, including Picture Arrangement and Coding of the WISC and the Visual Sequential Memory of the ITPA. This indicates that this subtest of the ITPA is relatively independent and does in fact measure a type of visual sequencing, because the two WISC subtests also involve this ability. The fourth factor is an auditory memory factor and involves the WISC digits, the Picture Completion subtest of the WISC (it is hard to see why this subtest is in this factor), and the Auditory Sequential Memory subtest of the ITPA. Auditory Memory, therefore, appears to be in fact measuring a skill separate from the other subtests. The fifth factor involved two WISC subtests (Similarities and Object Assembly) and the Visual Reception subtest. The sixth factor included the Block Design of the WISC and the Manual Expression and the Visual Association subtests. The last factor is the most interesting one, because it includes one WISC subtest (Coding) and four ITPA subtests (Grammatical Closure, Auditory Association, Verbal Expression, and Auditory Reception). The factor analysis shows that the four important auditory and verbal subtests are not measuring distinctly different processes, but rather one large general process. This finding along with many other factor analyses (*see* Ryckman and Wiegerink, 1968) tends to support the position that the Auditory Reception, Auditory Association, and Grammatical Closure subtests are measuring a general oral factor. Leyton concludes his article with, "There is a false notion among many psychologists that each of the WISC and ITPA subtests assess a different dimension of ability."

Hare, Hammill, and Bartel (1973) have recently done an investigation attempting to analyze the construct validity of the ITPA. They developed ten different tasks that measured skills comparable to those found in six main subtests of the ITPA and administered these tasks and subtests to 126 third graders. They found that after these tests were factor analyzed, seven factors accounting for sixty-six percent of the variance emerged. They found first of all a written language factor that involved the tasks of reading and writing the answers to the Auditory Reception and Verbal Expression subtests (rather than hearing and answering orally), a written vocabulary test, and an analysis of a written story. This factor appears to be a written language factor much like the skill teachers refer to when they say a child's written work is poor. Interestingly, none of the ITPA subtests is related to this factor, indicating that poor written language is not measured by the ITPA subtests. The second factor was an oral language comprehension factor and included the ITPA Auditory Reception test and two other tests measuring this ability. The third factor was an oral language usage factor and included the ITPA Verbal Expression test. This analysis indicates that understanding and expressing language is distinctly different from written expression.

The fourth factor contained only the ITPA Visual Sequential Memory subtest, while the fifth factor contained the Auditory Sequential Memory showing auditory and visual memory to be separate skills. The sixth factor was the Visual Reception subtest, and the seventh was the Manual Expression subtest. The authors conclude from this study that the subtests of the ITPA are, in fact, separate and point out that the other factor analytic studies did not use other reference tests (except the WISC).

In the following year Hammill and Larsen questioned how effective psycholinguistic training is in remediating learning disabilities. This is, as already mentioned, the ultimate criterion on which to judge the basic effectiveness of a diagnostic system such as the ITPA. They found thirty-eight studies in which the ITPA was used to diagnose deficit areas and then used the ITPA as a criterion to measure the success of the remedial treatment.

Thirty-one percent of the preschool children, forty percent of the disadvantaged children, fifty percent of the mentally retarded children, and fifty-six percent of mostly LD children showed improvement after being taught by a teacher using a psycholinguistic remedial method. Between the years of 1962 and 1966, when most studies were done by close associates of Kirk, fifty-two percent of the studies showed improvement, and between only 1970 and 1973 only twenty-one percent of the studies showed improvement. It appears, then, that as the psycholinguistic method spread, the efficiency of this method became less and less until it reached the percentage rate of success found in almost any remedial method.

They concluded the effectiveness of psycholinguistic training, that is, the drilling on the process areas found to be deficient by the ITPA, has not been definitely demonstrated, and it has not been shown that one can remediate deficits as measured by the ITPA. Minskoff (1975) has tried to refute Hammill's position, citing some studies where psycholinguistic training was effective. A rejoinder to Minskoff's article is instructive, because it presents the most carefully controlled investigation of psycholinguistic training to date (Sowell, Larsen, and Parker, 1975). This study found that specific training to the child's deficits was no more beneficial than a general remedial program. Hammill and Larsen state, "We cannot help but conclude that psycholinguistic training based on the Kirk-Osgood model is unsuccessful because it does not help children improve their ability to speak or understand language, nor apparently does it aid them in academic skills such as reading, writing, or spelling....We found that the ITPA subtests generally fail to correlate significantly with reading, spelling, and arithmetic skills, and that all but the Grammatical Closure subtests are useless in discriminating good and poor readers (Hammill, Parker, and Newcomer, 1975; Newcomer and Hammill, 1975)." All this is now summarized in a book on the ITPA (Newcomer and Hammill, 1976).

Reliability of the ITPA

There are two ways to overcome the problem of low subtest reliability. The first is to give the test twice and average the scores on each subtest. This method is very impractical, because it is a rare diagnostician who has the time to give an hour test twice to a child in a space of a few days. The second method is to combine subtests into a factor score, thus essentially lengthening the number of items. For example, the forty items on the Visual Reception subtest have a reliability of only .36 (at eight-year level) and the forty-two items of the Visual Association subtest have a reliability of only .38. Common sense suggests these two subtests are very similar because both are measuring visual processing. If a child then obtained a scaled score of 42 on the Visual Reception subtest and a scaled score of 34 on the Visual Association subtest, one could find the average of these two scores (38). This average would be the child's score in visual processing. This combined factor score is much more reliable than either of the two scores, because it is now based upon two similar tasks. The danger with factor scores is that if we average two subtests that are fairly dissimilar, such as auditory memory and visual reception, the factor score is essentially a meaningless number because we have averaged, in colloquial terms, "apples and oranges." The question then becomes one of how similar must the subtests be before one can validly include two or more subtests under one factor score. The obvious method for determining the similarity of subtests is again to use factor analysis.

Based upon an examination of factor analysis studies reviewed by Ryckman and Weigerink (1968), the author proposes that the following factor scores be used in making a more reliable diagnosis:

Factor I: Auditory Reasoning Factor made up of the average of the Auditory Reception and Auditory Association subtests. These individual tests have reliabilities of only .40 and .62 and would combine to a ninety-two item subtest.

Factor II: Auditory Closure Factor made up of the Grammatic Closure test, which has a retest reliability of .72. If the supplemental ITPA tests were administered, then the average of the Grammatic Closure and the Auditory Closure subtests should be taken to make up this factor.

Factor III: Visual Reasoning made up of the average of the Visual Reception and Visual Association subtests. This factor parallels the Auditory Processing factor and can be used to determine if the child has relatively stronger auditory or visual strengths.

Factor IV: General Expression factor made of the average of the Verbal and Manual Expression subtests. Logically this does not seem to be one factor, but these two subtests correlated moderately well with each other.

Factor V: Visual Closure consisting only of this test, which has only fair test-retest reliability. The author believes calling this factor visual distractibility, or something like this, might be more appropriate.

Factor VI: Auditory Sequential Memory is a single subtest with reasonable reliability to be used idependently.

The Visual Sequential Memory test has such a poor test-retest reliability that no amount of factoring could help make it predictive; therefore it has been eliminated from this analysis. Similarly, the supplemental Sound Blending test is best left alone. This factor approach enhances the diagnosis, because it helps reduce the chance a false decision will be made because of testing error. The chance that there will be a testing error on a single subtest of low retest reliability is much higher than one would obtain by averaging two or three similar subtests.

Having discussed the inadequacies of one of the best tests employing subtests used in learning disabilities, it would be instructive to examine another not as well standardized multisubtest used in the field.

The Detroit Tests of Learning Aptitude

The Detroit was first developed in 1935 by Baker and Leland. This test is an intelligence test with norms for three- to nineteen-year-old children and is often used on children who are too old for the ITPA. The test was revised in 1967, but is essentially unchanged from earlier editions. It consists of nineteen subtests that can be divided into a number of processing areas as is done in *Figure 8*. Each of these subtests will be discussed in detail in later chapters. There are some very good points about the Detroit. First, the Detroit uses letters and sentences for their memory subtests, which is an advantage because these measures correlated higher with academic skills than nonsymbolic materials such as digits and pictures. Second, there are a number of subtests measuring apparently the same skills, so one can obtain a strong visual memory and reasoning and auditory memory and reasoning score. The Social Adjustment and Orientation subtests are also unique to the Detroit, and these two factors are certainly relevant to learning problems.

Figure 8

A Factor Approach to the Detroit Tests of Aptitude

PROCESS AREAS	MEMORY			REASONING (ASSOCIATION)		
	Test Number	Name	Number of Items	Test Number	Name	Number of Items
Visual	9.	Visual Attention Span — Pictures	(16)	1.	Pictorial Absurdities	(18)
	16.	Visual Attention Span — Letters	(28)	3.	Pictorial Opposites	(96)
	12.	Memory for Designs	(12)	17.	Disarranged Pictures	(10)
	6.	Auditory Attention Span — Words	(16)	2.	Verbal Absurdities	(20)
Auditory	13.	Auditory Attention Span — Syllables	(43)	4.	Verbal Opposites	(96)
	7.	Oral Commissions	(8)	19.	Likenesses and Differences	(32)
	18.	Oral Directions	(17)			
Social	8.	Social Adjustment A	(20)			
	15.	Social Adjustment B	(20)			
Motor	5.	Motor Speed and Precision	(371)			
Sequencing	10.	Orientation	(42)			
Verbal Fluency	11.	Free Association				
Numerical Reasoning	14.	Number Ability	(12)			

The Detroit has a unique method of computing scores. The raw scores of the subtests are arranged in order of the highest score to the lowest. The mental ages give a rough estimate of how far behind the child may be, but since no standard deviations for the subtests are reported, one cannot determine how much of a deviation from the age norms is significant. The overall score, that is IQ, is calculated not by averaging the subtests, but by finding the median (that is middle) subtest and using the formula IQ = CA divided by MA where CA is the child's age and MA is the subtest age equivalent. The use of the median is a very unconventional procedure and can be skewed by an unusually low or high test performance. It should also be noted that the median becomes more and more inaccurate the fewer subtests that are administered.

An examination of the manual that accompanies the Detroit states only that the subjects of the norming group all came from the Detroit public schools. It was apparently standardized on 150 children at each year level, but there is no description of the children's race, social class, sex, or intellectual level. The only reliability data reported was on forty-eight cases tested five months apart on the overall score. This was based, however, upon "mentally retarded, delinquent and emotionally unstable" children. The only mention of validity in the manual was a study where 4,000 children had taken a "well known individual examination" and had obtained the same IQ for the first quartile, median, and third quartile on the Detroit test. Baker (1976) reports the norming sample "was made on one hundred and fifty children at each age level including fifteen hundred pupils in the age range of six to fifteen. Each pupil was carefully selected as being in grade at age and with a group intelligence quotient ranging from 90 to 110, as stated in the Manual. This sampling from the Detroit Public Schools was considered typical of large American cities as per results of achievement tests survey reports currently available at the time. No detailed reports were computed for sex, race, etc."

In summary, there is no description of the norming sample, and the reliability and validity coefficients are essentially meaningless. Looking at the number of items in the subtests makes it clear that there are not enough items (i.e. less than 40) to lead to any usable reliability. One source has reported the retest reliabilities of the Auditory Attention Span (Words) to be .78; Visual Attention Span (Objects) .76; Visual Attention Span (Letters) .70; Auditory Attention Span (Related Words) .81; Oral Directions .77; and Verbal Opposites .82. As may be seen, only the two longest subtests have a reliability above .80. For this reason, making a diagnosis on a single subtest would be unwise. If one wanted to make a process analysis using the Detroit, it would be best to average the scores of several subtests and thus increase the number of test items along the lines shown in *Figure 8*. This averaging does not automatically insure the test is reliable, but it does improve the likelihood that it will be more accurate.

Summary of the Process Approach

Three ways of explaining how learning disabilities occur predominate. One may suppose learning disabilities are due to some brain dysfunction and try to diagnose the problem using knowledge of brain functioning; or one may assume that learning disabilities are primarily problems of behavior and therefore diagnose by describing the child's overt behavior; or one may hypothesize that there are psychological processes and LD children have deficits in certain processes. A psychological process is a hypothetical construct, but it can be measured using a standardized test. The number and kinds of processes can either be constructed using clinical experience as was done in *Appendix A*, or it may be established with very complex factorial studies. Since the factorial studies are not available, this book has chosen to use the former approach.

Just plugging in tests and subtests for each process is not a productive strategy, however, because a large number of subtests and tests are not reliable enough to use for an individual diagnosis. To repeat, if a subtest is not reliable, it has no validity, and therefore a low or high score on the test is essentially meaningless. This is why the use of the ITPA and Detroit in such a manner has led to a great deal of criticism of the whole field of learning disabilities (e.g. Salvia and Clark, 1973). To overcome this pitfall several strategies can be employed. To begin with, one should only use tests with moderate and high reliabilities. There are now a number of such tests becoming available; the most impressive is the Woodcock-Johnson Psycho-Educational Battery, which has twenty-seven subtests, seventeen of which have reliabilities above .80 at the third-grade level and the battery of tests was standardized on 4,732 children in forty-two communities.

To overcome tests with poor reliabilities, one can take shorter, more unreliable subtests and average them with other tests of a similar nature. This has been suggested for the ITPA and Detroit to yield seven broad processes: (a) auditory reasoning, (b) auditory closure, (c) visual reasoning, (d) general expression, (e) visual closure, (f) auditory memory, and (g) visual memory. Each process has a number of tasks, and each is a general ability that appears from an armchair approach to be related to academic success.

The process approach can also be made more powerful by adding in more information than simply test scores when evaluating the process. When one combines the observations discussed in Chapter III with the test scores of this chapter, often a whole picture emerges of the child's functioning. For example, a first-grade teacher may report it took her three months to teach a boy of seven or eight letter sounds, that when there is oral discussion he always contributes, that he tries hard, but he cannot seem to master his addition facts without counting on his fingers. He scores in the average range on auditory and visual reasoning tests, but the memory, particularly visual memory, test scores are low. From this, one can begin to develop a picture of a child who has memory problems, which is confirmed by his inability to learn letter sounds and math facts. Processes can then be defined by close behavioral observations of performance on certain tasks (such as reversing letters or writing in mirror writing), physiological tests (ranging from eye examinations to lab tests of arousal level), patterns on subtests of a general battery, as well as performance on standardized tests.

Some diagnosticians seem to "hit the nail on the head" in process evaluations almost every time, while others seem to miss the point a lot. Part of this is that there are many pitfalls in simply plugging a test in for each psychological process without taking into account at least a half dozen other factors. Since these factors are rarely spelled out in detail and are often relegated under the rubric of "clinical opinion," as if that were some mystical quality. A number of these factors are elaborated below:

1. One has to consider the child's previous experience, because processes that have not been used by the child will appear weak. A first-grade child who has never practiced holding a pencil cannot have a fine-motor deficit any more than a child who has learned to read by the sight word method can be diagnosed as having a deficiency in phonics.

2. Processes mature at different rates and are completed at different ages. Among six-year-olds, for example, it is perfectly normal for one-quarter of the children (mostly boys) to have weak auditory discrimination skills. To diagnose six-year-olds who have weak auditory discrimination skills as learning disabled is a mistake, because it is likely that their neurological systems will mature, and they will no longer have a problem.

3. The child's motivation and attention while taking the test affects has process score as much as any disability. One can only say a child has a true processing disability if the child can attend and concentrate on the task and still cannot do it. The reason for making this distinction is that remedial treatment for an underachiever is much different than that for the LD child.

4. Almost every process has many simpler skills required to perform the process. When a child cannot do the tasks measuring a certain processing ability, the clinician should be able to decide which

Figure 9

An Illustration of Variables in a Process Analysis

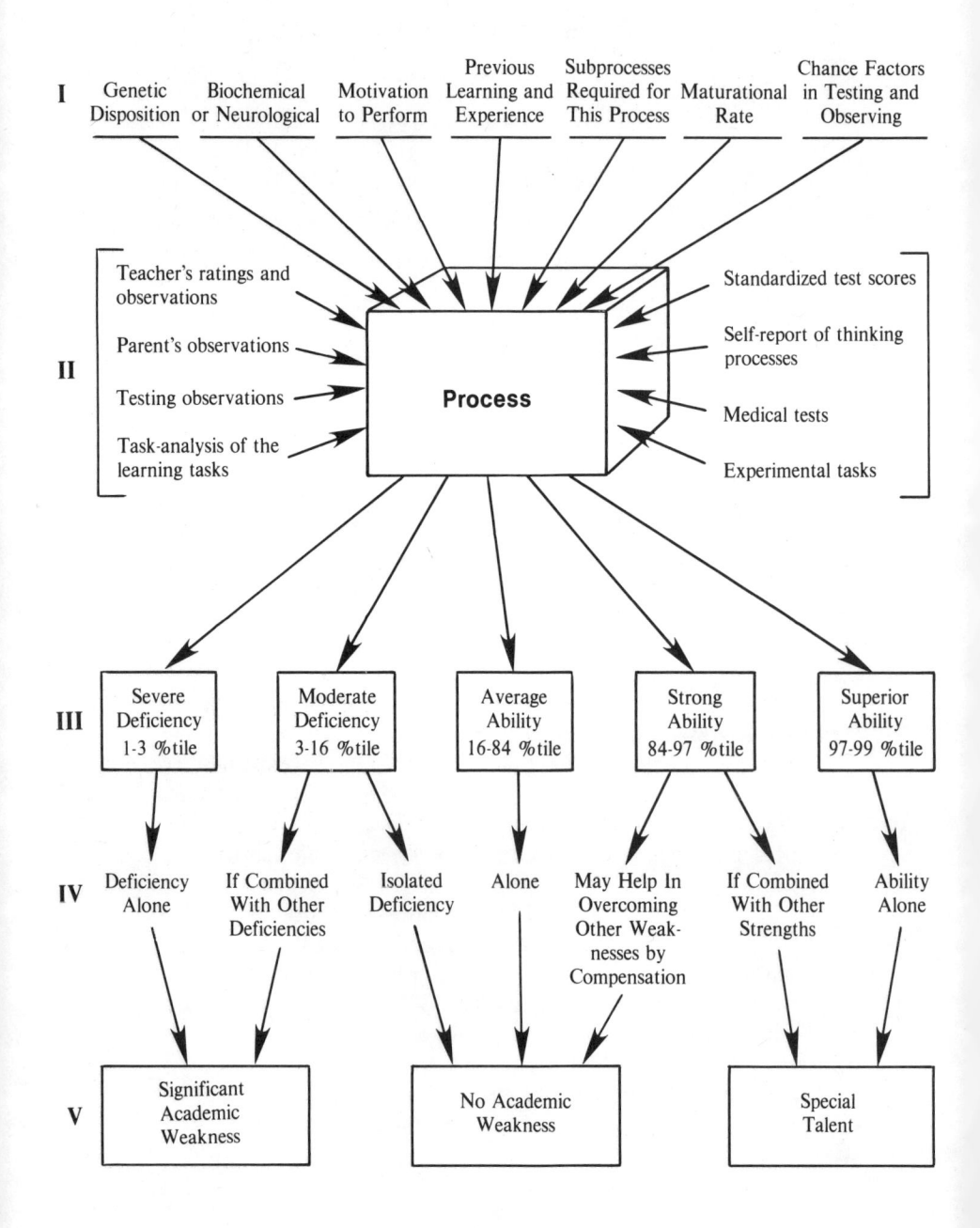

I — Genetic Disposition | Biochemical or Neurological | Motivation to Perform | Previous Learning and Experience | Subprocesses Required for This Process | Maturational Rate | Chance Factors in Testing and Observing

II — Teacher's ratings and observations; Parent's observations; Testing observations; Task-analysis of the learning tasks; Standardized test scores; Self-report of thinking processes; Medical tests; Experimental tasks → **Process**

III —
- Severe Deficiency 1-3 %tile
- Moderate Deficiency 3-16 %tile
- Average Ability 16-84 %tile
- Strong Ability 84-97 %tile
- Superior Ability 97-99 %tile

IV —
- Deficiency Alone
- If Combined With Other Deficiencies
- Isolated Deficiency
- Alone
- May Help In Overcoming Other Weaknesses by Compensation
- If Combined With Other Strengths
- Ability Alone

V —
- Significant Academic Weakness
- No Academic Weakness
- Special Talent

other processes might also be deficient. Processes are sometimes also arranged in hierarchies so that adequate acuity is required for normal figure-ground perception, adequate figure-ground is required for normal discrimination, and so forth. Since processes are not linear in nature, one cannot simply follow a simple formula or progression of processes to test, as some articles suggest. *Appendix A* makes this clear, and this is why the diagram has so many arrows in it going in many different directions.

5. In Chapter VII the various physical causes for deficient learning will be discussed. Briefly, it has been hypothesized some LD children have an inherited disorder that involves either an anatomical or biochemical weakness, which affects some of the areas of discrimination, memory, and the like. The evaluation for these then involves asking about the LD child's sibs and parents, as well as analyzing his own problems. In addition to genetic disposition, the clinician has to be alert to various neurological and physical conditions, such as faulty eye movements that may appear very similar to a processing defect.

6. Finally, a good clinician is well enough versed in testing theory that he or she knows the approximate number of times that the tests will yield spurious results because of chance factors and testing error.

A process diagnosis, which is the method that will be used for organizing the material in this book, is very complex. *Figure 9* attempts to organize this by listing: (a) the seven causes for a process strength or weakness, (b) eight different types of measurements that go into a process analysis, (c) five different kinds of degrees of the strength of the process, based on the statistical concept that a severe deficiency or superior ability lies beyond two standard deviations, moderate deficiency and strong ability lies between one and two deviations, and normal lies within one standard deviation, (d) the mitigating circumstances that could cause a deficiency to express it or be repressed, and (e) the outcome of this process.

Chapter V

The Diagnosis of Reading and Phonics Skills

In the school setting most children are referred for diagnosis because they are having academic problems. Therefore establishing where a child stands in reading, writing, spelling, and mathematics is an important part of any LD diagnosis. Besides establishing grade levels of school performance, an academic diagnosis can often give one insight into the child's intellectual and perceptual functioning, because a reading task, a spelling list, or an arithmetic problem is actually a very complex information processing problem. It requires grasping the task in proper perspective, integrating the task correctly with past experiences, sequencing the information properly, deciding on the correct answer, and then expressing the answer in a meaningful way.

The Diagnosis of Reading Problems

Reading is by far the most thoroughly studied area in educational psychology. In the twenty years from 1930 to 1950 there were approximately 1,500 experimental studies in reading that were published. The next four years, 1950 to 1954, saw almost an equal number published; this trend has accelerated until many more than this number of studies are published yearly (Smith and Dechant, 1961). Simplified vastly, experimenters have treated reading primarily as a visual act, as a linguistic process, or as a task of associating the visual symbol (the grapheme) with its appropriate auditory sound (phoneme).

Spache (1964) a prominent reading authority maintains, "Reading is first and foremost a visual act, and literally hundreds of studies show the importance of certain visual skills. The visual skills of the young child are, in our opinion, the most significant factors in his early reading success." Goodman (1967), on the other hand, believes reading is a "psycholinguistic guessing game" in which the child uses his knowledge of the structure of orally acquired language to decipher the printed word. This has been emphasized by Vernon

(1971) with his statement, "The ultimate object of learning to read is of course the understanding and memory of continuous texts.... The essential units of normal speech are phrases and sentences, which have characteristic grammatical constructions and convey meaning. The object of reading is to reconstruct these units from the printed text." Still another view by an equally prominent reading specialist, Durrell (1967), stresses the phoneme-grapheme correspondence in reading: "The essential problem with learning to read is the mastery of phonics. Any child who can speak English can learn to read it, if an appropriate program in phonics is provided him.... The elimination of poor readers, reading failures, and nonreaders usually requires only the improvement of the effectiveness of phonics instruction."

Although there is merit in all three positions, to treat reading as only a visual or auditory act is to ignore a great deal of important diagnostic information. Kohlers (1970) has summed this position up with, "If anything is true of reading, it is that it is one of our most complex forms of information processing." Since the process is so complex, it seems only practical to break it into different aspects: oral reading, silent reading, reading rate, word recognition, and reading comprehension. Vernon (1957) has reviewed this area and concluded, "The evidence of only moderate correlations between mechanical (e.g. word pronouncing) and silent reading on comprehension tests is fairly well established...." He goes on to give some representative correlations:

	Reading Comprehension	Reading Rate	Oral Reading	Word Recognition
Reading Comprehension	--	.55	.56	.51
Reading Rate		--	.52	.47
Oral Reading			--	.39
Word Recognition				--

Variables in Word Recognition

How many variables have been found to be related to reading? Holmes (1965) reviewed some five hundred experimental studies in reading and found that eighty different variables had been found in one investigation or another to be significantly related to reading. The rest of this section will review only some of the more important of these variables and try to show how they are related to reading.

1. Intelligence has been found to correlate moderately with reading achievement. Intelligence may be thought of as a global ability to process information and to make inferences from this information. Gates (1922) found that Stanford-Binet IQ scores correlated .30 with overall reading in the third grade, .35 in the fourth, .58 in the fifth, and .71 in the sixth grade. This increasing correlation was attributed by Gates to the fact that reading in higher grades requires more and more abstract thinking. In another study, Gates (1930) found that in a learning situation, first-grade slow learners (IQ 80 to 90) required forty repetitions to learn a set of words, while children with IQs between 110 and 119 required only thirty repetitions. While this is not a great difference for one word, this lag increases as the child is expected to learn more and more words.

A number of studies (Belmont and Birch, 1965; Lohnes and Gray, 1971; Lovell, Shapton, and Warren, 1964; Lovell and Woolsey, 1964) have found a significant correlation between overall reading ability and IQ. In a study typical of this kind, Reynolds (1953) compared general reading achievement of third graders with their ability to perform on a digit span, word discrimination, pitch discrimination, and oral blending task. All these variables were significantly correlated with reading, but when IQ was statistically partialled out, none of these variables was found to be significantly related to reading ability. Another example is Wilson et al. (1938), who found that the composite score on fourteen reading tests correlated .60 with the Metropolitan Reading test, while the correlation between this composite reading score and the Stanford-Binet Intelligence test was .51. In other words, there is a significant correlation between IQ and general reading achievement, IQ and word recognition, and IQ and the subskills necessary for reading. Because they correlate well with reading, intelligence tests can be used to make a rough prediction of how well a child will learn to read.

2. Some researchers have found that beginning readers are puzzled and confused about reading, because they are unaware that printed words are spoken words in visual form. Ried (1966) interviewed five-year-olds in an English kindergarten and found they were unaware, for the most part, that "reading" was different from looking at the pictures in the books, and even after several months of reading readiness many still did not know that letters stood for sounds and these letters could be blended into words. Downing (1970) has con-

firmed Ried's results using United States children and has shown that even some first graders are unaware of what reading actually is.

3. Some children are baffled when it comes to reading, because they are unaware of the word boundaries in English. Meltzer and Herse (1969) found thirty-nine first graders in a school who did not know that spaces between letters meant there was a new word. Of these, eighteen percent were actually in reading books, and the rest were doing reading readiness exercises. They tested the child's knowledge of word boundaries by presenting the child with a written sentence and having him draw a line between the words.

4. Since reading is essentially a process of translating visual letters into familiar auditory language, the child's basic vocabulary and comprehension of the semantics of the language are important. A way of measuring how much a child uses context to read was developed first by MacKinnon (1959), who found that if one simply recorded every word incorrectly read along with the correct word in an oral reading group, one could categorize the mistakes as being either contextual or graphic. Contextual errors are those in which the child misreads a word that makes sense contextually, but the letters of the word do not look like the correct word; the child might read, "Dick and Jane went home" for "Dick and Spot went home." A graphic error is one in which the child reads a word that does not make sense but resembles the correct word; the child reads, "We went out of the horse" for "We went out of the house."

Weber (1968) has reviewed the investigations on oral reading errors and has done an interesting study in this area. He sat in a first-grade class reading in the Scott Foresman readers and recorded the errors for the high and low reading group and found the following percentage of errors:

Group of Readers	Substitutes Words	Omits Words	Inserts Words	Reverses Words
Good Readers	79%	9%	9%	2%
Low Readers	82%	7%	9%	2%

Ninety-five percent of all errors were made on previously encountered words, and ninety-two percent of the errors by the good and 89 percent of the low readers were grammatically appropriate for the sentence. Weber also found ninety-three percent of these oral reading errors were consistent with the meaning of the sentence, thus showing almost all oral reading errors are of the contextual type. This hypothesis was studied more carefully by Biemiller (1970), who found the contextual errors in the first-, second-, and third-third of the first grade to be seventy-four percent, seventy-six percent, and eighty-three percent, respectively. The graphic errors for the same period were nineteen percent, thirty-nine percent, and forty-four percent (these percentages do not add up to one hundred percent, because many errors could be classified as being contextual and graphic ("The man ran away" for "The men ran away").

The research on normal readers suggests that both able and poor readers use contextual cues to decipher words; reading, therefore, is not only a visual act, but involves a linguistic "guessing game." The graphic errors so often mentioned in LD texts begin to predominate after the child has developed some reading skills. Steiner, Weiner, and Cramer (1971) found that many of a sample of the deficient fifth-grade readers did not make use of context, suggesting that there are some poor readers whose deficiency lies in not making use of their oral linguistic skills.

How a child's knowledge of grammatical structure relates to reading has been examined mostly in studies using inner-city children who speak nonstandard English (mostly the Negro dialect). Labov (1969) found these children make reading mistakes that conform to their normal language patterns, so that they have a tendency to leave out the word "did" in the sentence, "What did he do?" because "What he do?" is a standard grammatical construction in Black dialect. Harber and Bryen (1976) have reviewed seventeen studies of teaching reading using Black English to Blacks, and point out that there is presently no strong evidence that this is any more effective than teaching Black children in standard English.

5. There are a number of visual factors related to reading. The *least* important is visual acuity with a large number of investigations showing that almost all optical defects, short of blindness, do not affect reading. Even children with vision worse than 20/200 (legally blind) learn to read if they can see the print.

6. For a person to read accurately, he must be able to discriminate between the letters in the word. Visual discrimination, the ability to distinguish consistently and automatically between the letters of the alphabet, is usually measured by giving the child a letter typed on the left-hand side of the page followed by a set of random letters only one of which matches the standard; the child circles the matching letters. Barrett's (1965) review of forty years of investigations into visual discrimination of first-grade readers suggests that visual discrimination correlates only moderately with reading achievement. One of the better studies, for example, found that word

recognition on the Gates Primary Reading Test correlated between .07 to .38 with seven visual discrimination tasks. While this is not very high, it does indicate that there is some relationship between visual discrimination and reading. Meek (1925) gave four- to six-year-olds a learning task in which the child had to discriminate between various six-letter words. He reports that forty-four percent of the visual discrimination mistakes were made when the first or first two letters were alike, fourteen percent if the middle two letters were alike, and forty-two percent if the last or next-to-last letters were alike. He concluded the order as well as the type of letter affected visual discrimination.

7. Another skill closely related to visual discrimination is letter naming, in which the child is asked simply to name a particular letter. Gravel (1958) found a correlation of .54 to .58 between letter naming in the first month of school and June reading achievement in the first grade. Weiner and Feldman (1963) found even a higher correlation (.70 to .76) between letter naming in October and paragraph reading in June of the first grade. Samuels (1969) using this information decided that perhaps one way to increase a poor reader's reading ability was to systematically teach the letter names. However, in a study replicated twice, he could find no benefit in teaching letter naming or discrimination in increasing reading skills. His findings indicate that reading is much more complicated than naming letters.

8. For efficient and rapid reading one must see the printed words as whole units and not as separate letters to be individually decoded. The ability to see words as wholes is called visual closure in the LD literature. Johnson (1973) has done an investigation of developmental trends in reading words as wholes and found that when words are presented tachistoscopically, for children in the first three grades, in constrast to those in the sixth grade, the length of the word is important in recognizing the word, suggesting that inexperienced readers process words on a unit-by-unit basis. The recognition of frequently and infrequently encountered trigrams suggests that children begin to read words as wholes first in the third grade. A comparison of the recognition of pronounceable and unpronounceable trigrams revealed no developmental trends indicating that pronounceability (that is, the auditory component in reading words) did not influence recognition of nonsense words at exposure times of one-tenth to one-third of a second. The only subjects to take advantage of sequential combinations of letters (e.g. seeing "wh" or "ing" as a whole) was a high school sample. In other words, this experiment suggests that normal beginning readers start out processing words by decoding them letter-by-letter and by the time they reach

third grade, they are beginning to see most words as wholes. Under conditions where the word is briefly flashed, the auditory component to reading does not seem to be significant in the recognition of the word for elementary grade children.

9. For a child to recognize a word at a glance, he must remember the letters of the word from previous experience. Hence a good visual memory for letters (visual memory for faces and objects is apparently a different trait) is important for proficient reading. The LD child typically will see a word a dozen times and the next time not recognize it; forgetting the word in a few sentences of reading. The lack of visual memory shows itself most visibly in spelling, and in extreme cases LD children in the third and fourth grade will not remember how to print some of the letters of the alphabet.

10. Visual skills are also accompanied by analogous auditory skills. The most basic of these is auditory acuity. Deaf children with normal intelligence have great difficulty in reading, because they do not have the corresponding language structure. Children with a significant hearing loss likewise may have difficulty in reading, because they do not hear the middle syllables and endings or certain sounds of certain words.

11. A more complex auditory skill is auditory discrimination or the ability to hear the difference between two words. This skill is essential in learning how to decode reading words, and the child without this ability will be incapable of visually remembering the thousands of words in English. The child with normal visual memory and low auditory discrimination may do all right in first grade, where a lot of sight vocabulary is taught, but towards the beginning of second grade when the number of words begins to increase dramatically, he will begin to have great difficulty. Dykstra (1966) has done a careful study on auditory discrimination and its relation to reading by giving seven measures of auditory discrimination to beginning first graders and correlated this with reading at the end of first grade. Auditory discrimination, depending on the measure used, correlated between .18 to .42 with reading comprehension and between .21 and .43 with word recognition.

12. When a child is deciphering a word using his phonics skill, he will have to sound out the initial letters, the middle letters, and the final letters; then he must blend these separate sounds together to make an intelligible word. Children who lack this ability to "sound blend" have a deficit in what the LD literature calls auditory closure. In a typical study of auditory closure, Chall, Rosewell, and Blumenthal (1963) found that this skill correlated significantly with reading in the first through fourth grades. In the first grade the correlation

was .51 with silent reading; in third grade .64. When IQ was partialled out these correlations were about the same, indicating auditory closure is significantly related to reading.

13. Children with low auditory memory are often referred to the clinician, because these children do not seem to "be able to listen" and "remember directions" or "remember what they have just read." The relationship between auditory memory and word recognition is less well defined, except that many poor readers also have poor auditory memories. Rose (1958), for example, found that of all the tasks on the Stanford-Binet, the memory of digit span was the lowest in relation to the other tasks at the child's mental age.

14. Reading involves the association of the visual symbol and the auditory word. Some children seem to have adequate visual and auditory perceptual abilities, but they cannot seem to associate a particular sound with a particular letter. This visual-auditory integration skill can be measured in experiments in which the experimenter taps out a beat such as short, space, long, and the child must pick out a card with two dots, a space, and a long line. Beery (1967) found that LD children scored significantly lower on a series of auditory-visual integration tasks as compared to normal readers matched in age, sex, and IQ. Sterritt and Rudnick (1966) found auditory-visual integration tasks to correlate between .50 and .66 with reading as measured on the Iowa Basic Skills test.

The above fourteen points are just a brief sketch of the various factors involved in word recognition. Reading, however, involves much more than recognizing the individual words, or in Morency's (1968) words, "In fact...there are two distinct stages specific to the early reading process. The child first learns that the symbols which appear on a printed page represent and correspond to his spoken language. In other words, the initial stage of reading consists of decoding orthography into previously learned speech patterns. The second stage involves comprehension through arousal of associations to effect a meaningful state derived from past verbal learning."

This brief summary of the factors involved in reading is to make the clinician aware of many of the variables one must look for when diagnosing reading. Another approach is to examine *Appendix A* and variables 1 to 49.

Comprehension

The second stage, comprehension, involves the ability to abstract meaning from sentences. Comprehension varies with the subject's familiarity with the material (e.g. one can read novels more readily than physics texts) and with the complexity of the sentence (e.g. Hemingway is easier to read than Faulkner). Since the first investigation into reading comprehension by Thorndike (1917), the question of what skills are subsumed in comprehension has never been well defined.

Golinkoff (1975-76) has reviewed eighteen studies of reading comprehension and suggests that there are three major components to reading comprehension. First, there is the ability to decode and recognize individual words. She summarizes this with:

> In sum, the evidence suggests that poor comprehenders may possess inadequate decoding skills. Decoding tests using single words in isolation or textual selections find that poor comprehenders make more decoding errors than good comprehenders. And, perhaps more interestingly, the character of poor comprehenders' decoding errors may differ from the type that good comprehenders make. Poor comprehenders are more likely than good comprehenders to produce errors that do not conform to the meaning of the selection and are more likely to fair to correct their inappropriate errors. Nor is the frequency of poor comprehenders' decoding errors likely to change when they are given advance information about the passage. It is possible that there exists a group of poor comprehenders who possess adequate decoding skills although this group may be rare.

Second, there is the ability to rapidly obtain meaning from the words decoded. The research shows poor comprehenders also have poor comprehension of unfamiliar words. Furthermore, in eye-voice span experiments in which the child reads a passage in a machine and then the passage is blanked out and the child must say what the next few words are, poor comprehenders read in shorter units and do not use syntactical information. Poor comprehenders also do not vary their eye movements with the complexity of the material.

Third, one must have a good knowledge of syntax to be a good comprehender. Mosenthal (1976-77) has elaborated this area by showing that oral reading and aural processing (i.e. comprehending oral language) do not employ the same linguistic processes, while silent reading and oral language apparently do. In other words, the task of oral reading is working on decoding skills and getting the individual words correct, while silent reading, like listening, is extracting meaning in what has been called here the "intermodal" process or what Piaget has called a "schemata" (Brooks, Arnold, and Iacobbo, 1977).

Rystrom (1969) adds some caution about breaking up comprehension skills too much. He developed a test of six comprehension skills (vocabulary, syntax, recall of specific statements, recall of sequence of items, inference of an unstated fact, and evaluation of the story's reality), which correlated highly with the California Reading Test (.86), indicating that it measures what is usually considered reading. All these comprehension skills were highly intercorrelated for white and Black fourth and fifth graders and correlated .60 to .91 with a composite comprehension score. A factor analysis revealed the memory for specific details was by far the most important component of comprehension (accounting for eighty-three percent of the variance). In other words, one can break up comprehension into many different subskills, but comprehension for normal children at least seems to be a fairly unitary trait, with test items asking factual details being almost as predictive as complex comprehension tests measuring many subskills.

Gutherie (1973) performed an interesting investigation to determine if LD children were deficient in comprehension of material when they could recognize all the words in the passages presented to them. He discovered the LD children, matched with normal readers in IQ and reading level, were significantly lower in comprehension. The LD children did not, however, differ in their pattern of reading comprehension errors. Gutherie's study then seems to indicate that LD children have a general verbal comprehension problem in addition to poor word recognition skills in reading.

In light of the preceding, for the diagnostician to say that the child cannot read adequately is not very helpful. A more helpful evaluation is to determine whether the child can recognize words at sight or read silently and comprehend what he reads, or whether he can do neither of these tasks. Elementary teachers often notice that they have some children who are euphemistically called "word callers," who read aloud perfectly but do not know what they are reading. The more technical term for this is hyperlexic.

Most reading problems that LD children have are problems of word recognition. According to Winkley (1975): "It is estimated that 90 to 95 percent of the children who have trouble with reading have deficiencies in the area of word recognition, deficiencies which in turn affect reading the meaning of words, understanding what is read, or the speed of reading." Hyperlexic children whose word recognition is significantly better than their comprehension may be mentally retarded children who apparently have an exceptional skill in recognizing and remembering words; or they may be children of unusually high intelligence who read extremely rapidly (Wagenberg and Blau, 1971). Silberger and Silberger (1968-69) found in one typical second grade that five percent of the students were hyperlexic. Their cases consisted mostly of boys, although some studies have reported a predominance of girls.

The Processes in Reading

In order to diagnose a reading problem, one must be aware of the various processes involved in reading. *Figure 10* shows the various reading processes with the diagram being divided into three vertical components — visual, auditory, and the intersensory aspects of reading. The lowest level of visual reading involves the basic letter skills, which comprise such elements as visual acuity, letter orientation, letter discrimination, and visual closure. On the auditory side, the child must be able to hear the various letter sounds so that he knows that "bad" has a /b/, and /a/, and /d/ sound. Letter sound recognition involves such skills as auditory acuity, sound sequencing and discrimination, and auditory closure.

Figure 10 **Processes Involved In Reading**

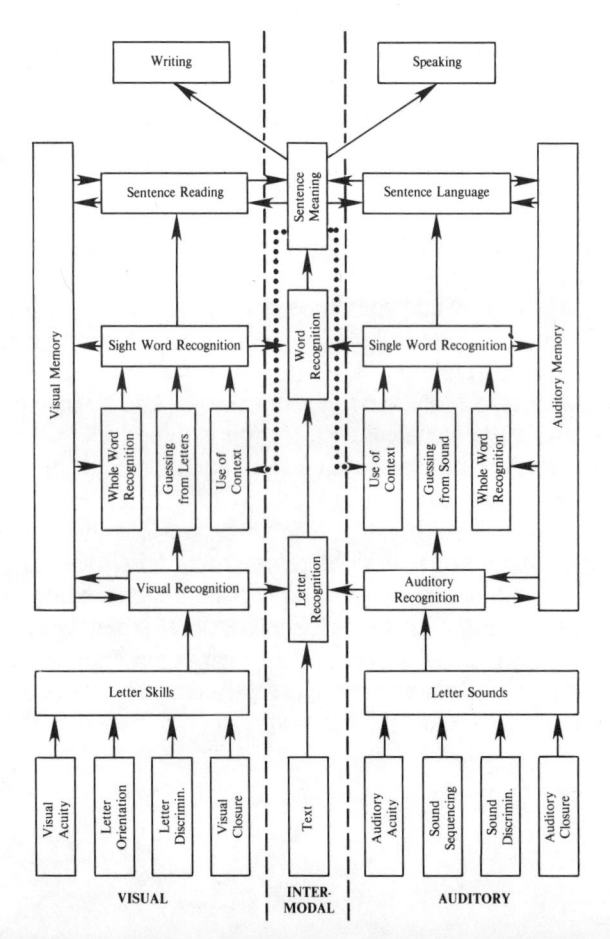

Basic visual skills combine to form the recognition of letters, which in turn interacts with visual memory for the letters. Beginning readers may have to consciously employ all the letter skills to recognize letters, but after a little experience with them they perceive the letters instantly and automatically. In other words, more experienced readers go from the visual text directly to recognizing the letters and this is shown by the center of the diagram representing automatic intersensory processes. Since this immediate visual recognition is related to previous experience with the letters, it requires visual memory. A parallel situation occurs with the auditory side of the chart, with auditory memory being involved in word recognition. One can see now that LD children who are in the third or fourth grade and still reverse letters have a deficiency with their visual recognition abilities, while those children who cannot hear, for example, the difference between "bet" and "get" have a defect in the auditory recognition skills.

Visual recognition of letters along with recognizing words as wholes (via visual memory), guessing a word from a few prominent letters, and the use of a context word from previously read words are the processes necessary for sight recognition of words. Since the use of context is a significant factor in word recognition there is a feedback loop with sentence meaning, which helps to decipher individual words as illustrated by the dotted lines in the diagram.

On the auditory side, when the printed word is associated with language and it is decoded and processed into a form that is neither auditory nor visual, word recognition is placed in the intersensory column. Finally there is reading by phrases and sentences where the reader actually skips over many of the nonfunctional words and extracts the meaning from the sentences he has read. At this stage, the individual will often miss typographical errors and will be unable to recall exactly what was said, but can explain what the text was about.

The above diagram of reading processes shows that one could have reading difficulties with either visual or auditory processing at the level of basic perception of the letters and sounds, or in the integration of these units into words, or in the more complex process of extracting meaning from phrases and paragraphs. Several authors have noted this and have made the point that there are at least two main types of poor readers: those with visual dyslexia and those with auditory dyslexia. Johnson and Myklebust (1964) and Jordan (1972) have described these types clearly and have made lists of characteristics of each so that a child can be readily categorized into one type or another. The characteristics of visual dyslexia are: (a) letter discrimination problems, (b) a tendency to reverse and invert letters, (c) transposition of letters, especially in spelling, (d) poor visual abilities in drawing, copying, puzzles, and similar activities, and (e) poor sequencing of days, weeks, etc. The characteristics of auditory dyslexia are: (a) auditory discrimination problems and being unable to rhyme, (b) inability to hear part of a word and guess the rest of it, (c) cannot synthesize sounds into wholes, (d) silent reading is better than oral reading, (e) especially poor word attack skills, and (f) mispronouncing and leaving out sounds in words.

If one wants to use an informal test of reading and word attack skills or to do criterion referenced testing, one may refer to *Figure 11*, which lists these skills by grade level. This particular outline was used in a middle-class district and was taken from objectives used in the Wisconsin Reading Design and other curriculum materials used in the district.

Figure 11
Decoding and Word Attack Skills for Reading Arranged by Grade

		Grade
1.	Auditorally discriminates between the regular consonant sounds in initial position.	K
2.	Produces the regular consonant sounds.	1
3.	Auditorally discriminates between the regular consonant sounds in final position.	1
4.	Auditorally discriminates between the regular short vowel sounds: o as in ostrich, e as in Ed, u as in umbrella, i as in Indian, a as in apple.	1
5.	Produces the regular short vowel sounds.	1
6.	Produces the long vowel sounds.	1
7.	Recognizes the long vowel sign: a, e, i, o, u.	1
8.	Auditorally discriminates between the regular short vowel sounds and long vowel sounds.	1
9.	Decodes two- and three-letter words that have short vowel sounds.	1
10.	Substitutes initial consonant to form new words.	1
11.	Substitutes final consonant to form new words.	1
12.	Substitutes medial vowel to form new words.	1
13.	Decodes words with same phonogram/phonemic pattern: e.g., at, cat, bat.	1
14.	Reads the preprimer level Dolch sight words.	1
15.	Reads the primer level Dolch sight words.	1
16.	Reads the grade one level Dolch sight words.	1-2

17.	Produces the consonant blends in isolation: bl, br, cl, cr, dr, dw, fr, fl, gl, gr, mp, nd, pl, pr, qu, sc, sl, st, str, sw, scr, sm, sn, spl, sp, squ, sk, spr, tr, tw, -st, -nt, -nk, thr.	2
18.	Decodes words with consonant blends.	2
19.	Substitutes initial consonant blends to form other words.	2
20.	Identifies forms and sounds of consonant digraphs in initial position: sh, ch, ph, th, wh.	2
21.	Identifies forms and sounds of consonant digraphs in final position: sh, ch, gh, ng, ph, th, wh.	2
22.	Decodes four- and five-letter words that have regular short vowel sounds.	2
23.	Decodes words where the vowels are long.	2
24.	Decodes words with final consonant blends.	2
25.	Decodes words ending in v-c plus silent "e": e.g., make, smoke, bone.	2
26.	Decodes consonant variants: e.g., s — has, see; g — garden, large; c — music, ice.	2
27.	Decodes long e and i sound of "y."	2
28.	Decodes vowel dipthongs: oi, oy, ou, ow, ew.	2
29.	Decodes words in which vowel is controlled by "r": e.g., far, fur, bar, more.	2
30.	Forms compound word with two known words: baseball.	2
31.	Identifies root/base words in inflected forms of known words: e.g., helpful-help, darkness-dark, unhappy-happy, recall-call.	2
32.	Decodes words in which final silent "e" is dropped before adding ending: e.g., smoke-smoking.	2
33.	Identifies sounds and forms of consonant digraphs in medial position: e.g., wishing.	2
34.	Decodes vowel digraphs/vowel teams: oa, ai, ay, ee, ea, ie, ei.	2
35.	Identifies sounds of "a" followed by l, w, or u.	2
36.	Decodes suffixes: e.g., less, ful, ness, er, est, ly	2
37.	Decodes prefixes: e.g., un, re, dis, pre, pro, ex, en.	2
38.	Identifies multiple sounds of long "a": e.g., ei-weigh, ai-straight; ay-day; ey-they.	2
39.	Decodes words with vowel digraph/vowel team irregularities: e.g., bread, heart.	2
40.	Reads the grade two level Dolch sight words.	2
41.	Decodes silent "k" in kn: e.g., know.	3
42.	Decodes silent "gh": e.g., though	3

43.	Decodes words ending in "ed": e.g., ed-crooked; t-looked.	3
44.	Decodes "dg": e.g., edge.	3

Permission granted by Jefferson County Schools, Lakewood, Colorado.

Informal Reading Inventories

Informal reading inventories, referred to as IRIs, are reading tests that have no established norms. These tests usually have a list of individual words to be read followed by a set of paragraphs typical of each grade level. The oldest and still most frequently used word list is the dolch list consisting of 220 basic words, which were chosen to make up sixty-five percent of the words found in average printed texts.

Johnson (1971) in a reexamination of the Dolch list points out that the list is over forty years old, and the words were selected in a rather arbitrary manner. He then compared the Dolch list with a modern frequency count of words and concluded that the Dolch list was outdated. Soon afterwards, Otto and Chester (1972) published a list of the 500 most frequently used words based on the American Heritage word count, which employed careful sampling of school texts and library materials used in the third through ninth grade. These 500 words accounted for three-fourths of all the 840,875 words sampled in grade three.

Harris and Jacobson (1973), using a slightly different procedure counting every single word in the first through sixth grades of the six basal readers used most frequently in the United States, developed a graded word list of 332 of the commonest words making up fifty percent of the words encountered in the basals. This graded word list appears in their *Basic Elementary Reading Vocabularies* (1972) and is, in the opinion of the author, the word list that should be used in constructing up-to-date IRIs. With a disabled reader in the upper grades, one may be less interested in "basic" words and more concerned with "functional" words, which are the words encountered in everyday life, words necessary to know to operate effectively in society. For example, the words "income tax," "alcohol," "typewriter," are important functional words not found in the usual primary reading books. An excellent list, broken down by grade levels, of 500 basic words and 1,500 functional words can be found in Otto, McNenemy, and Smith (1968, p. 189).

Informal inventories take many forms, but recently they have become more consistent in their content. The construction of these inventories was first fully discussed by Betts (1957, Chapter 11). These inventories should meet the following requirements (Otto and Smith, 1970; pp. 129-131):

1. Be constructed of materials actually being used in the classroom; usually a graded basal reader is used.

2. Be made of passages selected from the middle of the materials rather than introductory or ending passages.

3. First grade level should have approximately 100-word passages, followed by five comprehension questions; second and third grade levels with 150-word passages followed by six comprehension questions; levels fourth and above with 150-word passages followed by eight questions.

4. The comprehension questions should deal with literal meanings, meaning that can be inferred from the passages, and vocabulary questions from passages.

IRIs are graded into three levels of performance (Killgallan, 1942; Morton, 1968). The first is the Independent Reading Level, which is the grade level of the passage the student can read orally with ninety-nine percent accuracy and ninety percent comprehension. The student should read independent level passages with no outside help. The second is the Instructional Reading Level at which the child reads orally with ninety-five percent accuracy and with at least seventy percent comprehension. At this level the student needs some teacher supervision when reading. The third is the Frustration Level at which the child reads at less than ninety percent oral accuracy and fifty percent comprehension.

The difficulty of the passages in IRIs may be determined by either using a passage in a basal reader of a certain grade level or using a readability formula. Readability formulas (such as the Dale-Chall formula) are usually complex equations involving the length of words in a passage, the number of nouns and verbs in a sentence, and the number of words in a sentence resulting in a grade level (Dale and Chall, 1948; Spache, 1953). The utility of these formulas has been reviewed by Chall (1958), Bormuth (1967), and Klare (1963); and in general these formulas are poor measures of reading level and probably should not be used. Far better, in the author's opinion, is to have the grade level of the passages determined by a consensus of several experienced, competent teachers.

IRIs usually involve giving the child a series of eight passages, one from each grade level and having the child read the passage aloud. While the child is reading, the teacher marks any mistakes on a record book containing a copy of the passage, double-spaced, followed by the comprehension questions. The teacher usually marks any omissions, words in the test not read by the student, by circling the word in the booklet. Substitutions are marked by writing the word read over the actual word; words making sense in the context of the sentence are much less significant than words clearly the result of a wild guess. From analyzing a number of substitutions, one can determine if the child is making "reversals" (reading "saw" for "was"), visual errors (reading "bog" for "dog"), or auditory errors (reading "eated" for "eating"). Insertions are words that do not appear in the text, and these are written where they appear with a caret. Again these by themselves mean little until one can see if they form a pattern. Mispronunciations are marked by crossing out part of the word and writing the pronunciation over the word as phonetically as possible. Repetitions occur when a child reads a word or phrase twice; this is scored by placing an R over the word. A few repetitions are not considered significant, but many repetitions indicate spatial confusion or a habit of repeating words to gain time to decode the next one. A child having difficulty with phonics and decoding will often hesitate in reading a word. Hesitations are usually scored with a check mark over the word. The pattern of hesitations often shows which sounds and letters the child has difficulty with.

In addition to having the child read aloud and answer comprehension questions orally, many informal inventories also include a set of graded paragraphs to measure the "hearing" or "listening capacity level." These passages are read by the teacher to the student, and then the student is asked the comprehension questions. The hearing level is the highest passage of which the child can comprehend at least seventy percent of the material. This level is usually considered the child's maximum comprehension level: a high score in the listening level and a low one in oral reading would indicate the child has visual dyslexia; a low listening and oral reading level would indicate auditory dyslexia or low intelligence.

A complete description of informal reading inventories can be found in Johnson and Kress' *Informal Reading Inventories* (1965). Since these tests are numerous and their test characteristics are unknown, they are not reviewed in *Appendix B*.

Recently, several IRIs have been published in book form. While not meeting the requirement of using the specific material the child is using in the classroom, the IRIs meet many other requirements for informal testing. Siviroli's (1965) *Classroom Reading Inventory* is an excellent IRI consisting of ninety-five pages of interesting passages, comprehension questions, graded word lists, and spelling surveys with informal norms for the independent, instructional, and frustration level. Another whole system is *The Teacher's Handbook of Diagnostic Inventories* developed by Mann and Suiter (1974). This notebook consists of diagnostic inventories to evaluate spelling, reading, handwriting, and arithmetic which are on duplicator masters.

One may ask the important question of whether IRIs are any more accurate than a standardized test. Daniel took a sample of about thirty-five second and third graders and had teachers rank their grade placement. These placements were then correlated with well-constructed IRIs and the Gates reading test. Both the IRI and the Gates agreed about the same degree (.60 to .65) with the teacher's placement, indicating that IRIs are not particularly more accurate than standardized tests.

Reading Readiness Tests

Reading readiness tests are designed to be given to kindergarten and first-grade children to establish if they have sufficient perceptual skills to begin reading. These tests are of special interest in a reading diagnosis, because they contain standardized measures of skills a LD child is likely to lack. The latest edition of Buros describes thirty-two reading readiness tests, only ten of which have sufficient normative information to assess how useful the test is. These tests are carefully described and evaluated in Farr and Anastasiow's *Tests of Reading Readiness and Achievement: A Review and Evaluation* (1969).

In order to do an effective evaluation of prereading skills, one must be familiar with the tests, know their limitations, and choose one with good test characteristics. The major readiness tests will therefore be briefly reviewed:

1. The Anton Brenner Developmental Gestalt Test of School Readiness consists of five subtests with norms based upon 750 kindergarten children aged four and one-half to six and one-half years with a retest reliability of .55 to .75, making it a little too unreliable for an individual diagnosis.

2. The Gates-MacGinitie Reading Readiness Tests consist of nine subtests and are the most thorough readiness tests, requiring two hours (in two or three sessions) to administer. The test was normed on 4,500 children in thirty-five communities, and the kindergarten score correlates moderately well (about .60) with first grade reading achievement.

The Gates tests rely on the child recognizing the pictures in the test. Paston and Patrick (1944) attempted to test the knowledge of the picture recognition in first and second graders by having the children name the pictures orally. It was found that under these conditions the children only identified forty-five percent of the pictures correctly. Seventy-one percent of the children, however, could pick out the correct picture after having the four word choices in the test read to them. This investigation illustrates how simple factors such as choice of pictures can turn a reading test into a different task.

3. The Lee-Clark Reading Readiness Test is a short twenty-minute test consisting only of three subtests normed on 328 children, and it has fair reliability (split half .87) except for the concepts test (.52). One study (Hopkins and Sitkei, 1969) found that the Lee-Clark predicted first grade reading achievement better than a standardized IQ test. The Lee-Clark has good validity and has been found to correlate about .50 with reading achievement in first grade.

4. The McHugh-McParland Reading Readiness Test takes about an hour to administer and is composed of four subtests. Each one of these tests, except the visual discrimination subtest, can be used by itself because test-retest reliabilities are above .80. The test was normed on 2,600 children and is one of the more useful of the readiness tests.

5. The Metropolitan Reading Readiness Tests are the most widely known readiness tests and were standardized on 12,000 children in the first grade. It is made up of six subtests that are relatively short and have low split half reliabilities (.50 to .86), making an individual diagnosis from the subtests inadvisable. This test takes sixty minutes to complete, and the total score is relatively reliable (.91) and a fair indicator of future reading skill. Singer (1970) notes that bilingual children may encounter some handicaps on this test, and Metropolitan scores may be much lower for this group.

6. The Murphy-Durrell Reading Readiness Analysis takes an hour and is made up of three subtests. This test was normed on 12,000 in twelve different states, and the subtests, except learning rate, have good reliabilities. The correlation of this test with later reading was .65, which is very good and comparable to other reading readiness tests.

In summary, there are numerous reading readiness tests tapping a large number of "prereading" skills, but only about a half dozen of these are standardized well enough to be of much benefit to the diagnostician. The reading readiness test can be used by the clinician with older children if converted to criterion-referenced tests with an eighty to ninety percent passing criterion, because they give an accurate measure of prereading skills that should be mastered to read regardless of age. For more information on criterion-referenced measurements, Ebel (1971), Hambleton and Novich (1973), and Millman (1974) can be consulted.

Silent Reading Tests

The evaluation of reading beyond kindergarten is usually measured with a silent reading test. These tests are designed to be administered to a whole group of children at once and are given every year in most school systems. Dozens and dozens of these tests are listed in Buros and Farr's excellent book, *Reading — What Can Be Measured?* (1969). *Appendix B* lists the reading tests that cover the entire elementary grade range, not just a few grades, and are adequately normed.

Silent reading tests, like readiness tests, usually have various subtests, but caution must be used to select these. The titles of the various subtests are often misleading, because the tests themselves vary greatly in what they are measuring. Farr has found, for example, that simple reading vocabulary is measured in twenty-six different ways on reading tests.

Below is a review of six major silent reading tests, all of which can be administered individually or to a group. One may want to use a group test for an individual diagnosis because the standardization, reliability, and validity of many group tests are superior to individual reading tests.

Before covering the silent reading tests, it might be instructive to examine the limitations of standardized reading tests. Newkirk (1975) suggests that "Any standardized test is only a measure of performance at one time," and that one cannot treat the score as a definitive measure. Second, "A standardized reading test purports to measure the student's reading ability by having him read passages which may be of no interest to him," and he cites an experiment where fourth graders made higher scores on high-interest passages than on low-interest passages. Third, "The type of reading comprehension measured on reading tests is not the type of comprehension needed for most kinds of reading," with Newkirk arguing that rarely does one in real life read just 100 words and then answer a half dozen comprehension questions on it. Nor do the investigations show the skill in interpretation of literary selection to be related to comprehension measured on standardized tests. Fourth, "The rigid time restrictions create an unrealistic environment for the testing of reading." Fifth, "Tests of reading comprehension tend to overemphasize factual recall of relatively insignificant facts." This observation is borne out by Howard Langstone's investigation of the Metropolitan Reading test, which found one-third of the comprehension items were not crucial to understanding the paragraph. Sixth, "Because of standardizing procedures, many standardized tests may be inappropriate for low socio-economic and minority groups." Seventh, "Reading tests may actually test pre-existing knowledge as much as they test reading comprehension." This statement is supported by Allington's et al. (1977) investigation, which showed third graders could answer between five percent to sixty-five percent of the comprehension questions on the Diagnostic Reading Scales, the Durrell, Gilmore, and

Gray, without ever having read the passages. Silberberg and Silberberg (1977) have also cautioned that group tests, which will be reviewed here, cannot be readily interchanged with individual tests. As with all standardized tests, a high level of reliability is desirable; Tinker and McCullough (1962) recommend that a reliability coefficient of .90 or above is desirable; in the high .80s is satisfactory, but in the low .80s is unsatisfactory, except when making group comparisons.

One may ask the question of how well standardized tests compare with teacher ratings in predicting reading achievement. Morgan (1960) compared first grade reading achievement with teacher's ratings and two IQ tests (the Peabody Picture Vocabulary Test and the Pinter-Cunningham) and found that the tests predicted the child's future reading achievement better than evaluation based on teacher's staff conferences. Kermonian (1962), on the other hand, obtained the opposite result: teachers' ratings in the first grade were as accurate as the Metropolitan Reading Readiness Tests, with the two measures correlating very well with each other (.73). Kermonian also found that teachers with more than ten years experience did much better in predicting future reading achievement than those teachers with less than ten years experience.

Below are the six major reading tests:

1. The Burnett Reading Series has been standardized on 44,000 students in the first through twelfth grades. It yields a score in word recognition, reading comprehension, and vocabulary. At the elementary grades, word identification skills are also measured, although there is some question of whether these tests actually measure word identification (Farr, 1972). The test takes fifty minutes to administer, and the retest reliabilities are not reported.

2. The California Reading Test, which is part of the California Achievement Battery, is a series of tests that measure a number of reading skills from first to twelfth grade. The elementary level is composed of about five subtests, some of which are simple word recognition while others are school related tasks, such as alphabetizing and reading graphs. The test was normed on 38,000 children from all the fifty states. The individual subtests are too short to yield reliable scores with, for example, the second grade reading comprehension subtest having a retest reliability of only .59. The reliability of the total test is fairly high (e.g. .88 for first grade), but the Gates-MacGinitie and Stanford Reading Tests have better test characteristics.

3. The Gates-MacGinitie Reading Tests are a revision of the popular Gates Primary Reading Tests. The Gates-MacGinity measures word recognition and reading vocabulary in first through twelfth grade. Reading rate above the second grade is also measured. The test at the primary grades consists of fifty pictures of common objects with four accompanying words; the child must circle the word that best describes the picture. The comprehension section involves thirty-four paragraphs with four pictures, and the child reads the paragraph and circles the appropriate picture describing the scene or action in the paragraph. The reliability of these two subtests is fairly high, and the test is very "pure" in that it does not involve knowledge of opposites, alphabetizing, punctuation, or other skills often found in reading tests.

4. The Metropolitan Reading Test is part of the Metropolitan Achievement Test and was standardized on 27,000 children in forty-nine states. It yields a word recognition, reading comprehension, and general language skill score for first through ninth grades. This test has good reliability for each subtest (.79 to .96) and has good validity (Robinson, 1965).

5. The SRA Reading Test was normed on 70,000 children and yields a total reading, a word recognition, and a reading comprehension score for first through ninth grades. The reliabilities of these subtests are very good. The vocabulary subtests require recognizing words in context, and these are identical to the previous words and contexts in the reading comprehension paragraphs, so this subtest must be considered contaminated. The reading comprehension section is a set of interesting paragraphs and good comprehension questions.

6. The Stanford Reading Test is part of the Stanford Achievement Battery and is considered by some (Traxler, 1972) one of the best silent reading tests. The test comes in five levels and three different forms, and the individual subtest reliabilities are good. The test yields a score for word recognition and reading comprehension at all levels, with the first through third grade test also including a study skills section. The test was normed in fifty states using 850,000 pupils, and grade levels and percentile scores are available.

The first step in making a reading diagnosis is to establish the grade level at which the child is reading. The simplest way to do this is to use a group reading test. Unlike the individual reading tests, these tests can be administered to several suspected LD children at once and by a nonspecialist. In certain circumstances the two or three suspected LD children in each class can be treated with a reliable group test early in the school year, in the school library or cafeteria,

Diagnostic Reading Tests

Diagnostic tests are administered in a one-to-one situation, and thus reducing the screening time considerably.

The question often arises about what grade level of the test one should use. Should one test the child at the grade level he is in or at the grade level he is reading at? If one wants to establish which children fall into the lowest five or three percent of the school, then one should test him using grade level material. However, to obtain an accurate measurement of the child's reading level, Fisher (1961) has found in a study of 1,041 children that out-of-grade tests are better. the child's errors are recorded in detail to determine exactly where the child is having difficulty. These tests usually have an oral reading test that consists of eight graded passages to be read aloud, eight paragraphs to be read silently with comprehension questions, and a section measuring word attack skills. Often a listening comprehension scale is included where the administrator reads a paragraph to the child and then asks him to answer comprehension questions regarding the paragraph. Hayward (1968) has suggested that each diagnostic reading test should meet the following criteria: (a) the subscores should represent meaningful areas for providing remedial instruction, (b) the subscore reliabilities must be sufficiently high (above .90) for an individual diagnosis, (c) the intercorrelations among subtests must be sufficiently low (below .65) to warrant a differential diagnosis, and (d) the test should report norms in terms of grade level, geographic distribution, community type, and numbers of children.

Monroe (1932) in her pioneering work developed ten categories of reading mistakes:

1. Faulty vowels, which is simply reading a vowel in the word incorrectly such as reading "dig" for "dug" or "not" as "note."

2. Faulty consonants, which is mispronouncing or altering one or more consonant sounds.

3. Reversals, which is defined as interchanging b, d, p, q, u, and by reading such words as "dig" for "big," "squirt" for "spirit," the complete reversals such as reading "was" for "saw," "left" for "felt," and text reversals where the child reads "once there was" for "there was once."

4. Addition of sounds in which the child inserted one or more sounds as reading "track" for "tack," "pussie" for "puss."

5. Omission of sounds as reading "farm" for "farming."

6. Substitution of words, where a child substituted a word having no consonant or vowel sounds similar to the test word or not related to the test word by reversed letters.

7. Repetition of words, where a repetition was tabulated each time the child repeated one of the test words.

8. Addition of words, such as reading "saw his four little feet" for "saw his four feet." Each addition was counted.

9. Omission of words, which is simply the leaving out of a word in the text.

10. Refusal and words aided are simply the number of words where the child said he did not know or where he hesitated more than fifteen seconds and the word was read for him.

The retest reliability of the sum of all these ten categories of errors was .97, showing that when a passage of 500 words is given, one can obtain a highly reliable score for oral reading errors. Monroe also included in her book a set of norms for the reading errors for various grades. The average for each of the reading categories is included in the table below, because, as far as the author can establish, nowhere else are the percentages of errors presented for a large sample of normal children. Listed are the percentages of each type of error based on the errors made by over five hundred children with normal reading ability using 500-word passages and retest reliability for fifty children done six months apart on a 500-word passage.

Percentage of Oral Reading Errors of Normal Readers

Grade	1.5	2.0	3.0	4.0	5.0	Reliability
Vowels	10.2	8.6	6.0	3.4	2.0	.94
Reversals	6.6	5.6	3.6	1.8	1.2	.93
Addition sounds	6.2	5.2	3.2	1.4	0.8	.91
Omission sounds	3.2	3.0	2.6	2.2	1.8	.77
Substitutions	1.4	1.0	0.6	0.4	0.2	.82
Repetitions	4.2	3.2	2.2	1.6	1.0	.76
Additions words	0.8	0.8	0.6	0.2	0.4	.55
Omissions words	0.4	0.2	0.6	0.8	0.8	.60
Refusals	5.0	2.4	0.0	0.0	0.0	.95
Total errors	46.2	37.6	23.6	14.2	8.8	.97

Monroe also compared the number of errors of LD children with normal children and found that the LD children made significantly more errors in the following areas: faulty vowels, reversals, omission of sounds, repetition of words, consonant sounds, addition of sounds, and in total reading errors. She was able to categorize her poor readers into four groups using the types of reading errors; those children who made excessive errors in the sounds of words (altering vowel and consonant, adding and omitting sounds in words), who would nowadays be called children with auditory dyslexia; those making excessive errors in the orientation and sequencing of letters and words, who also had a tendency to repeat words read and are now called children with visual dyslexia; those who had a combination of the two above and were sometimes the most severely handicapped readers; and those who made excessive errors under the pressure of speed, characterized by excessive omissions of sounds and words. This last group usually learned under a system emphasizing context cues, and Monroe considered their difficulty to be an emotional reaction.

There have been extensive analyses of standardized reading tests, one of the most relevant being Winkley's article on "What do diagnostic reading tests really measure?" Winkley (1971) did a content analysis of nine diagnostic reading tests (including the Durrell, Gates-McKillop, Spache, and Stanford) that revealed that these tests used essentially ten different tasks to measure prereading skills. These prereading skills included naming letters (in three tests) and selecting printed words containing phonemes heard in the word (covered in four tests). All the diagnostic tests contained three or more subtests of word recognition skills; only seven of the nine had subtests of syllabication skills. In the area of reading comprehension, however, only the Stanford Diagnostic Reading test provided a breakdown of the child's comprehension skills. Using the extensive charts in this article, the diagnostician can, at a glance, pick out the skills thought to be important to reading and determine which tests measure these skills. Winkley notes, however, that "most of the instruments cannot be used to determine a child's chief area of skill deficiency," and "It is not possible to pinpoint specific problems in the areas of vocabulary, comprehension, or the rate with the instruments." Moreover, "No single test, group or individual, assesses all subskills of word recognition from knowledge of consonant sounds to ability to select the accented syllables in an unknown word."

Below is a brief description of the nine most commonly used diagnostic reading tests:

1. The Diagnostic Reading Scales by Spache (not to be confused with the Diagnostic Reading *Tests*) measure a number of skills from first to eighth grade. There is an A and B paragraph for each grade level, with the A being equivalent to the first semester of the year and the B to the second semester. One can obtain a very reliable (above

.90) word recognition, oral reading, silent reading, and listening comprehension score from this test. The scores on the word recognition, oral, and silent reading were found to correlate highly (.79 to .87) with the California Reading Test in a sample of second graders and highly with (.90 to .92) the Durrell and Gates oral reading tests. This test also comes with a phonics test, but its reliability is not reported. The passages of the Spache are interesting, and the test allows for the missing of many "little words" without severely penalizing the child.

2. The Durrell Listening-Reading Series is an improvement of the older 1933 Durrell Analysis of Reading Ability. The Durrell Analysis of Reading Difficulty has a set of graded paragraphs for first through ninth grade to obtain an oral, silent, and listening comprehension score. It also measures word recognition under untimed and flash (one-half second) presentation as well as having subtests for letter naming, letter sounds, word attack skills, and reading speed. The Durrell Listening-Reading has only the reading and listening of words, phrases, and paragraphs, but is normed on 20,000 children. Bormuth (1972) criticized this assumption about listening comprehension and calls it the "folklore of reading instruction." In spite of this, the Durrell has good test characteristics being normed on a large sample of children with the individual subtests having good reliability.

3. The Gates-McKillop Reading Diagnostic Tests are very compact and comprise seven subscales measuring oral reading using eight graded paragraphs (with no scale for reading speed), flash (half-second) presentation of single words and short phrases, word attack skills using nonsense words such as "spack," auditory blending, oral spelling, and auditory discrimination. The drawback of this test is that there is no reading comprehension subtest; the entire test was normed on only forty children per grade; and no reliabilities are available for the test.

4. The Gilmore Oral Reading Test measures oral reading ability, comprehension of material, and rate of reading for the first through eighth grades. Norms on the Gilmore test are based upon 1,620 pupils from five states, and the retest reliabilities for oral reading accuracy, reading comprehension, and reading rate are all very good (.84 to .89). The Gilmore is considered by some to be the best of the standardized tests in its accuracy of oral reading of meaningful material (Harris, 1972). There is some doubt concerning the validity of the test, because it measures comprehension ability with an oral test. One wonders about the appropriateness of testing reading entirely with a test of oral skill.

5. The Silent Reading Diagnostic Tests cover only the reading range of second through sixth grade. The test consists of eight different subtests: word recognition of individual words, reading words in context, oral reading errors, syllabication, word blending or word synthesis, beginning word sounds, ending sounds, vowel and consonant sounds, and results in a total reading score. It takes about eighty minutes to administer and was normed on 2,500 children. The split half reliabilities for the subtests are between .80 to .95, which is very good. This makes it a valuable test, except for the fact that it cannot be used with first graders.

6. The Stanford Diagnostic Reading Test is another diagnostic test that goes from 2.5 to 8.5 grade levels. This test consists of seven subtests: reading comprehension, word recognition, auditory discrimination, syllabication, beginning and ending sounds, blending and sound matching. It is designed to be given to groups of children and therefore does not resemble the other oral reading tests. The measures of the subtests consequently are rather complex. The test was normed on about 150 children per grade and has good subtest reliabilities, but unfortunately cannot be used in first grade.

7. The Peabody Individual Reading Test (PIAT) is one of the most frequently used individual achievement tests and has a word recognition and reading comprehension subtest. In the word recognition subtest, the examiner says a word and the child points to one of four words. Reading comprehension is measured in the conventional way of answering comprehension questions. The PIAT was normed on 200 children per grade from a diverse background, and the reliability of the word recognition section is excellent (.94 in third grade) and fair for reading comprehension (.73 in third grade). No other reading skills are measured on the PIAT. One weakness of this test is that it always involves choosing one of four choices, so that guessing can be done fairly easily.

8. The Wide Range Achievement Test (WRAT) is probably the most widely given academic screening test and has a reading section that shows the child a list of about 100 words and has him read the words aloud. This test measures only word recognition and does not require the child to know what the word he is reading means. The WRAT was standardized on about 100 to 600 children at each grade level in seven states. The test reports such a phenomenally high reliability (.98 and above) that Merwin (1972) suspects foul play. It should be kept in mind when giving this test that it is only measuring a very narrow reading skill — the ability to pronounce very difficult words. Bray and Estes (1975) have compared PIAT, WRAT, and

California Test scores with teacher ratings for forty-five LD children and found these tests to be comparable.

9. The Woodcock Reading Mastery Tests are a fairly recent battery of five subtests in the format similar to the PIAT, but consisting of very reliable subtests measuring basic reading skills. The scales are letter identification, word recognition, word attack, and reading comprehension in which the child reads three words, e.g. "boy, girl; man. . .," and must fill in the appropriate fourth word (in this case "woman"), which requires a fair amount of conceptualization as well as reading, yet it shows good reliability in the elementary grades (.85 to .95). A passage comprehension test is included, employing an infrequently used cloze method of measuring comprehension. The child reads a sentence such as "Dusty went out in the rain. See how wet. . .is." to himself and then fills in the missing word, which in this case would have to be "he." The test also has a procedure by which one can obtain a criterion-referenced score using ninety-six percent, ninety percent, or seventy-five percent cut-off score.

The reason for giving the different parts of reading tests is that these skills have been shown to be relatively independent of each other as demonstrated by Vernon's correlations at the beginning of this chapter. More recently Leibert (1968) compared the scores of sixty-five third graders on an IRI and a silent reading test (the Gates Advanced Primary test) and found that a lower word recognition score was found on the IRI than on the silent reading test, and that some children would misread an important word orally and still get the comprehension questions correct. A fairly large difference was discovered between the IRI score and the silent reading score, suggesting that generalization from one kind of test to the other cannot be readily made. In a study of 178 children ranging from first to sixth grade, Kirby (1970) found the scores of the Gray and Gilmore oral reading tests to correlate poorly with silent reading scores or those derived from the cloze method of scoring comprehension. Spache (1950) compared the Diagnostic Reading Scales, the Durrell, and the Gray and found that these oral reading tests were very much alike and measured the same skill. The Diagnostic Reading Scales, the Durrell, and the Gates-McKillop were also compared by Eller and Attea (1966), who also obtained a high correlation between the word analysis of the different tests and the oral reading sections of these tests. The Durrell (old edition) was one-half grade lower than the Reading Scales and one-third grade lower than the Gates-McKillop.

The research indicates that one oral reading paragraph test is much like another, but there can be large discrepancies between scores on these tests and silent reading tests. This is not surprising, since oral reading requires several skills not required in silent reading. Good oral reading calls for reading each word exactly, while silent reading requires reading long passages and abstracting meaning from the words read. With only a limited time to diagnose a reading problem, one wants to spend the time with the child getting to know him, and therefore individual reading tests are the tests of choice. Of these the Spache and Durrell appear to be the best suited and least likely to yield a faulty score because of testing error.

Phonics Concepts

An important aspect of reading is the ability to decode letters and letter combinations into words. The child who has not mastered this skill must rely on his visual memory to memorize the letters in every single word. This allows the child to master perhaps one or two hundred words, but beyond this he must learn phonics. Children who have severe auditory problems that result in the child being unable to hear the difference in the sounds in words will have problems in learning to read, mainly because they cannot learn to apply phonics to decoding words. Phonics is not easy to master, especially with English being a conglomeration of four or five distinctly different languages. The child must begin with simply hearing the differences between the forty-four sounds in English — a skill some children of normal intelligence do not master until nine years of age. Next, the child must remember which letters must go with which sounds, and this auditory-visual integration is apparently lacking in many LD children until the age of eight. Adults often forget that the task of remembering, for example, that a "p" has a /p/ sound is a difficult memory feat for the beginner. Phonics also involves breaking up words into meaningful letter components, so that phonics rules can be applied. If the child were to analyze the "ch" in "chide" into the separate /c/ and /h/ sounds, he will be lost just as he will be if he does not look for the silent "e" at the end of the word. Finally, phonics involves putting the individual sounds of letters together again to decode the whole word.

The research into phonics (Chall, 1967) shows that the average child learns to read fluently whether he learns by phonics or by the sight-word method although the phonics method appears to be slightly better. But, as Bannatyne (1971) puts it, "Children taught to look-and-say will eventually develop a somewhat crude phonemic analysis and blending attack to use on new or different words." Just memorizing the phonics rules, of course, does not make the child a good reader, and because a large number of words are exceptions to the phonics rules "each word has to be learned by rote memory in association with the only distinctive feature of the word, namely, its memory in context" (Bannatyne, 1968). The classic example is, does one spell /bow/ with the answer being "bow" in a dog's bark, "bough" of a tree, and "beau" for a girl's lover and, of course, one should not confuse it with a bow of an archer.

The twenty-six letters form about sixty-five letters or letter combinations that make the forty-four sounds in English (Leton, 1968). These sixty-five letters are essentially the phonics rules a child must master. The question always arises how regular is English and how many phonics rules are there? Hanna and Moore (1953) examined the phonics rules and claimed that English was, contrary to popular opinion, very regular. They found that English was eighty-seven percent regular with single consonants being predictable over ninety percent of the time. Hanna (et al., 1967), in a test of this fact, programmed a computer with 111 vowels and 92 consonants rules. This computer, which is completely logical, could spell only one-half of 17,000 words given it and essentially refuted Hanna's earlier finding. One problem with this investigation was that he used far more words than any school child would encounter in beginning reading. Leton (1969) redid Hanna's study using 190 preprimer words and 770 primer words and found a ninety-six percent and eighty-five percent accuracy in the phonics rules. This indicates that while only half of the total words in English are regular, almost all those easy words encountered by beginning readers are regular. Most of the phonics programs capitalize on the fact that 340 of the 500 most common words are monosyllables, which are far more regular than the rest of the words in English (Hodges, 1968).

Learning phonics by rules is not easy because a sound like /a/ in "hat" appears 592 times in a set of about 7,000 words and is pronounced /e/ in eighty-one percent of the words, /a/ in seventeen percent, and /u/ in two percent of the words. The child, of course, has no way of knowing which way it will be pronounced in any new word he encounters, and when he uses a large number of phonics rules (such as Hanna's) he finds that many of the phonics rules are incorrect more times than they are correct. Clymer (1963) went through phonics books and found forty-five common rules and then applied these rules to 2,600 words found in basal readers, discovering that only eighteen rules applied seventy-five percent or more of the time. Only thirty rules predicted the pronunciation of the word correctly in over fifty percent of the words that they applied to. For example, the rule that the "c" followed by an "h" is pronounced /ch/ held for 103 words and was correct one hundred percent of the time, while the rule "when two vowels go walking, the last one does the talking" (e.g. the first vowel is silent) applies to 309 words and is incorrect more times than it is correct. Clymer's list can also be used to discover if a rule is worthwhile to teach or diagnostically to test for, because some rules such as "kn" is pronounced as "n" are correct one hundred percent of the time, but this rule accounts only for eleven words in English. Bailey (1967) has expanded Clymer's work to include the entire vocabulary in eight basal readers (5,773 words) and is to date the most complete set of phonics utility rules. When specifically testing for word decoding skills, one should test for examples of rules that have good utility (they hold seventy-five percent of the time) and occur enough to warrant the use of the rule (more than about ten words). This would leave us with about twenty phonics rules.

To measure phonics skills one may rely upon informal methods, the phonics sections of diagnostic reading tests, or standardized reading tests. There is a problem with using the standardized phonics tests, because they usually begin at the third or fourth grade making them useless for children with severe reading problems.

Most of the oral reading tests have some sort of informal phonics measures. The Diagnostic Reading Scales have eight supplementary phonics tests. These include the naming of the sound which goes with each of the consonants; the blending of digraphs such as *sh* and *dr*; the reading of common two- and three-letter combinations found in words such as *ell*, *ow*, and *ing*; the blending of nonsense words; the naming of letter sounds, the substitution of an initial letter in a word so that the child is presented with the word, such as *find* and asked to pronounce the word as if the *f* were an *m*; and a thirty-word auditory discrimination test.

The Durrell Analysis of Reading Difficulty has a subtest in which the examiner says a word like "hall," and the child must pick out one of four words which begins with the same sound as the word; then the child must do the same for the first two letters; then words that end the same as a particular word; and finally words that begin and end with the same sound as the orally presented word. The Durrell also has a subtest in which the child gives the sounds for letters and a test in which the child must write a very uncommon word that sounds as it is spelled, such as "tonometer" and "isotherm."

The Gates-McKillop Diagnostic Reading Tests contain a subtest that presents the child with letters, and he must give their sounds, and a test of where the child must read nonsense words such as "spack." The use of oral reading tests over an informal battery is that the reading test has norms. The most commonly used phonics tests are:

1. The Kennedy Institute Phonics Test (Guthrie, 1973) can be obtained by writing to Guthrie. The test has norms for first through third grades and measures eight phonics abilities. These tests have very good reliabilities but, unfortunately, poor norms.

2. There are six phonics subtests for the Diagnostic Reading Scales, but unfortunately no information on their standardization is available. The six areas are: consonant sounds, vowel sounds, consonant blends, common syllables, blends, and letter sounds.

3. The McCullough Word-Analysis Tests measure seven phonics skills and are normed for fourth through sixth grade. The reliability of the subtests is good, and they were normed on twenty-three classes, each taken from a different school. The McCullough measures initial blends and digraphs, phonetic discrimination, matching letters to vowel sounds, sounding whole words, dividing words into syllables, and root words.

4. The Phonics Knowledge Survey Test measures fifteen phonics skills for first through sixth grades, but has no norms or reliability.

5. The Stanford Diagnostic Reading Tests, which are well normed and have very reliable subtests, include subtests in auditory discrimination, syllabication, beginning and ending sounds, blending, and sound discrimination. The tests have norms for 2.5 to 8.5 grade levels. Since they also yield a reading recognition and comprehension score, these tests are convenient to use as a phonics and reading test.

It is clear from examining the phonics tests that they are not close to the quality of the reading, spelling, or arithmetic tests. One reason for this might be that most diagnosticians and reading teachers use an error analysis on the reading test to infer if the child knows phonics rather than falling back upon another standardized test to measure this ability. For example if the child spells "cut" kut, "bread" bred, "edge" eg, "look" luk, it becomes clear that he knows the phonics rules, but for the life of him he cannot remember "what the word looks like".

There is also a question of whether one wants to break up phonics skills into so many different skills; most likely phonics is something a child either has grasped and can apply to almost any situation (e.g. he has mastered the major phoneme-grapheme correspondences in English), or it is a system that is fairly alien to him and does not help his reading or spelling.

Of the few investigations into phonics, the most often quoted is Dolch and Bloomster (1937), who found that, in the sample of children they used, the children with a mental age below seven years were unable to learn phonics. They also found a correlation of .41 to .52 between phonics skill and intelligence. Many authors have pointed out that this finding is nonsense, because there are tens of thousands of kindergarten and first-grade children who learn phonics relationships before this age. Tiffin and McKinnis (1940) gave a phonics test to children in the fifth to eighth grade and found that this skill correlated .70 with the Stanford reading tests and .66 with reading comprehension on the Iowa reading test. Even at these advanced grades, phonics skills appear to be closely related to reading proficiency.

Diagnosing a Reading Problem

If a child has a learning disability, it is most likely to show up as a reading problem, because reading is such a complex skill requiring the integration of dozens of processes. The diagnosis of a reading problem lies in establishing the child's reading level and, in the case of the LD student, determining which processes are deficient. One may do this either by giving a battery of visual and auditory tests measuring discrimination, figure-ground, memory, closure, and other factors, or by giving the child passages and carefully recording his mistakes in reading and deducing from these mistakes what processes are deficient. The former method is essentially the method recommended by the ITPA; the latter approach is recommended by the oral reading tests and IRIs.

Besides the fact that many of the process tests have low reliabilities, there are several reasons for beginning a diagnosis with an analysis of reading instead of administering process tests. First of all, the process tests are very narrow in the skill that they tap. Auditory memory is an important skill in reading, and this process involves memory of phonics rules, memory of words, of the meaning and facts presented in the passage, and many other complicated skills, yet the "Auditory Sequential Memory" subtest of the ITPA involves the recall of a series of random numbers. Clearly, these tests are measuring a very limited aspect of auditory memory, and the assumption that recalling a few numbers and isolated words measures the identical skills necessary to read is to make a rather shaky assumption. Second, a careful analysis of process tests measuring visual skills reveals that these tests almost always involve the manipulation of pictorial (nonverbal symbolic) material. The performance tests of the Wechsler Intelligence Scale for Children (WISC), the visual subtest of the ITPA, all the visual subtests of the Detroit save one, the Beery Visual-Motor Integration test, and the Bender-Gestalt test use pictures, not letters, words, or numbers. This is unfortunate, because there is a fair amount of evidence that pictorial material is processed in a completely different area of the brain (see Chapter VII) and, as has already been mentioned, the investigations of Gates have shown the correlation between pictorial reasoning and reading is very small. In other words, many of the LD process tests measure essentially skills unrelated to reading. This author has sat through many case staffings where the child to be placed in the LD program would be found to have no process deficits as measured by the difference of auditory and visual subtests on the ITPA or Detroit, yet it was clear that this child was well motivated, intelligent, and several years behind in reading.

The approach of analyzing reading processes through a diagnostic reading test involves comparing the child's performance on the word recognition, graded oral paragraphs, silent reading paragraphs with comprehension, and word attack skills on nonsense words. The child's rate, errors, and method of word attack are carefully recorded and discrepancies between these tasks then become the basis of diagnosis. Boder (1969) has suggested that children then be grouped into three categories:

Group I comprises the largest number of children with learning disabilities who have deficits in auditory processing and in integrating the letter with the correct sound. In reading, these children read words as wholes and have a tendence to make nonphonetic errors such as reading "funny" for "laugh;" "human" for "person." In other words, they rely heavily on context and not on deciphering letter sounds.

Group II are children with a visual channel deficit who read words phonetically with a tendency to have to sound out every word, even when they have seen it many times before. These children have particular difficulty in spelling and make errors in omitted letters in common words spelling words like said, "sed"; right, "right".

Group II has an impairment in the auditory and visual channels. These children have such a severe problem that they still may be nonreaders by high school. When reading they may still reverse letters, unable to spell regularly spelled words, and use random guessing when encountering words.

After a silent reading test has established that the child has problems in reading, then an oral reading and phonics test can be used to find out whether the child has visual, auditory, or word attack problems. From these the examiner can determine if the child knows his phonics rules, is reading consistently from left to right, has to sound out simple and complex words, or can understand the passage read to him.

Chapter VI

Diagnosis of Spelling, Mathematics and Written Language Skills

Spelling

Spelling is a skill closely related to reading, and it is usually more difficult for the child to master because it requires producing a response with no clues or context to allow guesses. Spelling is of special interest to the diagnostician, because there are many LD children who outgrow their reversals, poor visual perception, and reading problems and are left with only a severe spelling problem. Since there are now dictionaries, secretaries, dictaphones, and the like, a specific spelling problem is not considered by society as severe a problem as reading.

Spelling is a complex skill, but essentially the spelling of regular words requires a careful application of phonics, while the spelling of about one-half the words in English requires memory of which letters go into the word. One must remember "through" is an "ough" word, that "pebbles" has two *b*s, that "cope" is not spelled "coap," and the like. In LD texts the ability to remember the letters in words is referred to as "visual memory" and as a rule of thumb a child's spelling ability is the best measure of his visual memory. Although spelling is considered "visual" memory in contrast to "auditory" memory, this is questionable, because there is some evidence that words presented either visually or auditorally are probably coded in the auditory mode and meaning is coded in an intersensory mode.

It is instructive to talk with good spellers, because they report that they can look at a word and tell you if it is correct or not. This involves a high degree of visual recognition memory, and good spellers can tell if they have *ever* seen a word before. The good spellers often visualize the word broken into syllables and under close questioning will report "seeing" the word not in the typeface they originally saw the word, but in standard type. Interestingly enough, excellent spellers do not have particularly good visual memory for nonsymbolic material and report that they do not remember clothes people wear, places they have been and the like any better than everyone else. This supports the notion that symbolic and nonsymbolic material is coded differently. Children who are poor spellers typically report that they cannot tell by looking at a word if it is spelled right, so that to ask them to go back and correct their work for spelling is often futile. This also explains why spelling tests where the child is presented with four words and must merely pick out the misspelled one is a difficult task for an LD child. Recognition memory, or simply determining if a word is correct or not is much easier than recall memory for the LD child. Some spelling tests (e.g. the PIAT) employ the recognition technique, while others employ recall (e.g. the WRAT).

Recognition tests must use harder words to make them comparable to recall tests. Recognition tests lend themselves more to guessing, and one cannot observe such characteristics as letter reversals, grasp of phonics generalizations, handwriting speed and quality, and number of erasures. Learning disabilities specialists also prefer the recall over the recognition method because it yields important clues as to how the child is processing words, because misspelled words can be analyzed in the same manner as oral reading errors.

Spache (1941) reviewed the factors that could cause a spelling disability and reported the following variables to be related to spelling: auditory and visual acuity, auditory discrimination, vocabulary knowledge, phonics skills, motor coordination and handwriting, intelligence, emotional and perhaps genetic variables. He reports that in several dozen studies spelling correlated with both reading, intelligence, and vocabulary knowledge on an average of .60.

Research in Spelling

The research in spelling dovetails with the research in reading. The first standardized test in spelling was developed by Buckham (1913), and Gates (1926) did the first major study in spelling. He reported that spelling and reading both correlated about .60 with the ability to discriminate small differences in word pairs, only about .20 with copying designs, and nonsignificantly with a spatial task, and that spelling correlated only .22 with a task associating a nonsense word with a nonsense visual figure. When IQ was statistically eliminated, the correlation between word discrimination, which is so important to reading, and spelling was still .54. Curiously the auditory-visual association task, a task resembling phonics, correlated practically not at all with spelling.

Monroe (1932) found that reading and spelling ability correlated .81 for normal children and .85 for LD children. She concluded, in reference to spelling, "The correlation coefficients are so high that it seems that we must be measuring an achievement which is greatly dependent either upon reading or upon the same factors which underlie the ability to read." What Monroe's findings suggest is that poor readers are poor spellers and vice versa, and the psychological processes underlying reading, which have already been extensively discussed, also underlie spelling.

It remained for Russell (1937) to do the classic experiment of matching on age, grade, and intelligence for sixty-nine poor spellers with sixty-nine good spellers in the third, fourth, and fifth grades. Spelling correlated .39 and .27 with intelligence for the good and poor spellers, respectively. Visual acuity and hearing acuity were not related to spelling except in two isolated cases. Reading speed and accuracy were on an average a year lower in the poor spellers. Russell found the following percentage of written spelling errors:

Type of Error	Hearing Disabled	Poor Spellers	Good Spellers
Additions	5%	6%	4%
Insertions	11	9	9.5
Omissions	39	39	42
Substitutions	37	36	33
Transpositions	4	4	5
Phonetic errors	4	4.5	6

These fascinating results parallel the reading errors and show that even children who are hard of hearing make the same errors as the LD and normal child. The only significant differences were in a test of oral spelling, where the poor spellers used a letter-by-letter approach, while the better spellers spelled more syllable-by-syllable. These data argue against the theory that the LD child has a special defect or a missing process that causes his spelling disability. Russell went on further to train these children on new words using the kinesthetic method. Of the poor spellers eighty-two percent learned well by tracing the words, and twenty-eight percent did poorly. Of the normal spellers thirty-two percent did very well using this method, and sixty-eight percent did poorly. This bears out the feeling of teachers that the laborious tracing method works best for the poor student. In this portion of the study Russell also noted that while both groups tried equally hard to learn the new words, seventy-six percent of the good spellers and eight percent of the poor spellers used a systematic method of learning the words.

Russell (1943) followed this study up with an investigation of the relationship between reading readiness scores in first grade and spelling in the second grade. He found spelling correlated: .41 with mental age, .16 with chronological age, .80 with word recognition and reading comprehension, .81 and .85 with naming of the upper and lower case letters, .50 with auditory discrimination of word pairs, .87 with naming letter sounds, .26 with rhyming of ending sounds of words, and .85 with spelling nonsense words. Again the closeness of spelling and reading processes are so high they are remarkable.

In still a third study, Russell (1955) compared the spellers of the fifth and sixth grades who were in the lowest twenty-seventh percentile and the highest twenty-seventh percent without any consideration of intelligence and found that the lowest spellers were significantly lower on the perceptual speed, reasoning, and total IQ on the Primary Mental Abilities (PMA) test, but were equal to good spellers on the spatial reasoning section of this test. This finding should lay to rest the idea that poor spellers somehow might have lower spatial abilities and reemphasize that poor spellers lack the general verbal processing skills that many poor readers also lack.

Horn (1957) has reported that one-third of the words in the dictionary have more than one pronunciation. He also found that one sample of first and second graders who had received a healthy dose of phonics spelled the word "those" 44 ways and the word "circus" 148 different ways! Clearly, the forming of an image of what the word should look like is necessary to spell a great number of words.

Holmes (1959) took a completely different approach to spelling and reasoned that spelling diffrences among college students at Berkeley would be due almost all to personality differences, since these students are screened carefully for academic and intellectual traits. This is based upon the contention of psychiatrists who say only certain rigid personality types have the patience to be excellent spellers. Holmes found in an elaborate investigation that only nine percent of the variance in men and three percent in women was due to any kind of personality variable. Allen and Ager (1965) essentially found the same results in a factor analysis of abilities of twelfth grade students.

Cahen, Crown, and Johnson (1971) have reviewed the spelling research and found that familiar and easy to auditorally discriminate words are easier to spell. Visual configuration or the serial order of the letters are not related to spelling. The most important factor, however, is whether the word "looks like it sounds." Unfortunately computer tests show only forty-nine percent do (Simon and Simon, 1973).

One of the few studies aimed at the spelling capabilities of LD children and other psychological processes is the investigation of fifty normal third-grade children by Bannatyne and Wickearajate (1969). It was found that spelling correlated .29 with recognizing a figure from memory (the BVSMT), .33 with copying a design from memory (MFD test), .33 with standing on one leg, .42 with a test in which the child writes the numbers 1 to 12 down a page with both hands simultaneously, which Bannatyne calls unlearned ambidexterity, .40 with sound blending of the ITPA, and nonsignificantly with the ITPA Auditory Closure, Auditory Sequential Memory, and Visual Sequential Memory, an auditory discrimination task, and a test of letter span similar to a digit span test. When the top twenty-five spellers were compared with the bottom, there were significant differences in all the above tests that obtained significant correlations with spelling. Bannatyne's results are interesting because the traditional auditory variables, except auditory closure, were not significant, while visual and motor factors were. Since sound blending, the only auditory skill that correlated with spelling, also correlated .37 with the memory for designs, this suggests that sound blending requires visual-spatial sequencing. Balancing on one foot correlated with spelling, according to Bannatyne, because balancing neurologically involves the integration of visual perceptual and kinesthetic information. Bannatyne citing a number of diverse findings in neurology and models proposed:

1. "Spelling is facilitated by an overall intact function of the motor and kinesthetic aspects of the C.N.S. (central nervous system). . . ."

2. "Because sound-blending is a sequential vocal-motor multi-articulating process" it must depend on motor patterns used to form words.

3. "Spelling does not involve the visual sequencing of designs," but involves the sequencing of sounds in the motor speech areas of the brain.

4. "The visual memory element of spelling is not concerned with any form of sequencing."

Another set of investigations by Boder (1969, 1973), reviewed at the end of Chapter V, uses spelling patterns to diagnose learning disabilities. She suggests normal readers spell seventy to one hundred percent of the reading sight words and can sound out their reading words while "dysphonetics" can read fifty percent of the sight vocabulary and have few phonics skills. Another group, "dysledetics," read phonetically and sound out each word and can spell phonetic words only, while "alexics" have low reading, letter confusions, and mirror writing and cannot spell nonphonetic words. Camp and Dalcourt (1977) developed a spelling test of phonetic and nonphonetic words for fourth through sixth grades and report this test correlates .95 with the WRAT. Based on this they could categorize children into phonetic and nonphonetic spellers, although about one-half their sample was a mixture of these types.

Finally, Beery, Westerman, and Wilkinsen (1971) use a sensory modality preference to categorize spelling disabilities. Westerman's technique, while more lengthy because the child has to be pretested to determine which words he can already spell, yields more information, namely, the most efficient way to bring up the child's spelling and his most efficient sensory channel. This system is diagrammed in *Figure 12.* While Westerman's diagram is very complete and lists all possible approaches, it is an armchair approach with no research yet to back it up. A simpler and less complete method is to try to categorize the spelling into the following areas:

1. He may come from a poor linguistic or cultured background, so that he really does not use or know the meaning of words he is to spell. In some inner-city areas children do not pronounce or use the words typically found in spelling books. This leads to low motivation, poor spelling, and often poor reading abilities.

2. The spelling lesson may be extremely boring. The traditional way of memorizing twenty words a week can be very dull and lead to a low spelling score. Motivation is an important factor in spelling.

3. The child may have poor auditory decoding or phonics ability and therefore cannot use the additional cue in sounding out the word. This lack of phonics will show up in an analysis of the child's errors. An examination of the misspelled words will tell one if the child has mastered phonics or not and often whether he heard the word correctly.

4. The child may have a poor memory for the irregular letters in the words. This child will make errors such as spelling "round" and "rond" or "should" and "shud." These children are often referred to as having "visual errors" and will reverse letters and confuse capital and lower case letters. The most prominent aspect of their spelling is the misspelling of the most frequent, commonly used words.

If one wants to use an informal test or to do criterion-referenced testing, one may refer to *Figure 13,* which lists the spelling skills keyed by grade level. Of course, if the school district one is working in has a similar behavioral objective list, that list should be used. This particular list is used in a middle-class district and was taken from objectives used in the Wisconsin Reading Design and curriculum materials.

Figure 12

A Process Analysis of the skills required in spelling

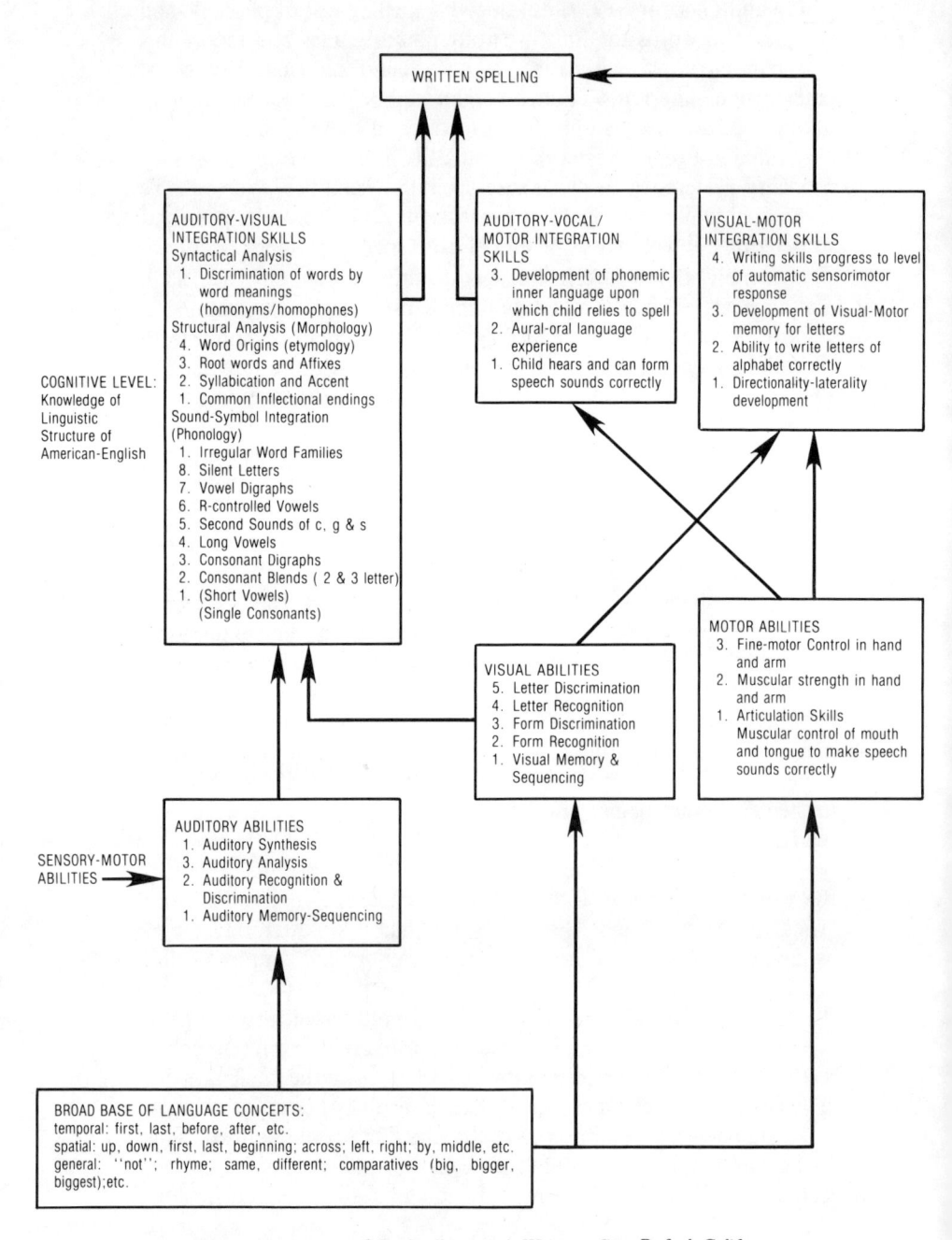

WRITTEN SPELLING

AUDITORY-VISUAL INTEGRATION SKILLS
Syntactical Analysis
1. Discrimination of words by word meanings (homonyms/homophones)

Structural Analysis (Morphology)
4. Word Origins (etymology)
3. Root words and Affixes
2. Syllabication and Accent
1. Common Inflectional endings

Sound-Symbol Integration (Phonology)
1. Irregular Word Families
8. Silent Letters
7. Vowel Digraphs
6. R-controlled Vowels
5. Second Sounds of c, g & s
4. Long Vowels
3. Consonant Digraphs
2. Consonant Blends (2 & 3 letter)
1. (Short Vowels)
   (Single Consonants)

AUDITORY-VOCAL/MOTOR INTEGRATION SKILLS
3. Development of phonemic inner language upon which child relies to spell
2. Aural-oral language experience
1. Child hears and can form speech sounds correctly

VISUAL-MOTOR INTEGRATION SKILLS
4. Writing skills progress to level of automatic sensorimotor response
3. Development of Visual-Motor memory for letters
2. Ability to write letters of alphabet correctly
1. Directionality-laterality development

COGNITIVE LEVEL:
Knowledge of Linguistic Structure of American-English

VISUAL ABILITIES
5. Letter Discrimination
4. Letter Recognition
3. Form Discrimination
2. Form Recognition
1. Visual Memory & Sequencing

MOTOR ABILITIES
3. Fine-motor Control in hand and arm
2. Muscular strength in hand and arm
1. Articulation Skills
   Muscular control of mouth and tongue to make speech sounds correctly

AUDITORY ABILITIES
1. Auditory Synthesis
3. Auditory Analysis
2. Auditory Recognition & Discrimination
1. Auditory Memory-Sequencing

SENSORY-MOTOR ABILITIES →

BROAD BASE OF LANGUAGE CONCEPTS:
temporal: first, last, before, after, etc.
spatial: up, down, first, last, beginning; across; left, right; by, middle, etc.
general: "not"; rhyme; same, different; comparatives (big, bigger, biggest);etc.

From Westerman, G.S. *Spelling and Writing*, San Rafael, Calif: Dimensions Publishing Co., 1971, pp. 24-25. Used with permission of the author and publisher.

Spelling tests are another way to assess the child's spelling skills. The usefulness and validity of spelling tests have been recently reviewed by Spores and Yee (1973), who found that there were only seven tests on the market that had enough technical information to be used with confidence. These tests are:

1. The spelling section of the Metropolitan Achievement Tests was normed on 27,000 children in forty-nine states. The first and second grade tests do not contain spelling items, the third and fourth grade spelling tests consist of writing thirty words dictated by the teacher, and it has good reliability. The spelling test at the fifth and sixth grade level consists of spelling forty words dictated by the teacher. This test is not so practical, because there are no items for first and second grade children.

2. The California Achievement Tests were normed on 15,000 children in all fifty states. The spelling test for the first and second grade consists of spelling twenty words read by the teacher. At grades four, five, and six, the child reads twenty-nine sets of four words and marks the word that is misspelled, or if all are spelled correctly marks "none of the above." These tests are rather short, and the split half reliability is only .57, which is very low.

3. The SRA spelling test was normed on 71,199 children from all regions of the United States. The split half reliability for spelling ranged from .89 to .92 at all age levels. There is no spelling test for grades one and two, but in grades two to four the child spells twenty-five words dictated by his teacher. At the fourth through ninth grade level the child is presented with forty-six sets of four words and must mark which one is spelled incorrectly with a fifth option of "none of them."

4. The spelling section of the Stanford Achievement Test is considered one of the best achievement tests. The Stanford was normed on 49,000 children. The spelling consists of the teacher reading off thirty words, and the child writes the words for the second and third grades. This test has excellent reliability (split half .94) and is a test of choice for this grade level.

5. The spelling section of the Gray-Vataw-Rogers General Achievement Tests was normed on 60,000 students in first through ninth grades with fair reliability. The spelling test takes fifteen minutes, which is a dictation test for first through third grade, picking which (if any) of the four words are misspelled.

6. The Spelling Errors Test is a scale devoted exclusively to spelling but is deficient because it was normed only on fifty children. It will therefore not be considered further.

7. The Wide Range Achievement Test (WRAT) is probably the most often given individual screening test in the United States. The spelling scale can be administered in less than ten minutes and measures spelling from kindergarten (such as writing the letters in one's name) to college level. There are forty-five words to be written from dictation ranging from first to fifth grade and another forty-six words to measure spelling in children eleven years and older. This test has a good split half reliability, although its retest reliability is not reported.

Johnson and Olds (1981) have also developed an academic screening test that overcomes some of the problems of the WRAT. The spelling section is arranged so that the odd numbers are regular words, the even irregular words, so an extensive cue analysis can be made to establish the type of learning disability the student may have. The arithmetic section contains eight problems of each basic process, carefully cued for grade level and process, so a math cue analysis can be made. The reading section consists of a continuous story with each paragraph being a grade level more difficult. The whole test takes about twenty minutes to administer. It has the unique feature of being obtainable on a cassette tape for most common microcomputers that will do the entire cue analysis and suggest teaching modules to overcome the learning difficulty (Olds and Johnson, 1981).

8. The Peabody Individual Achievement Test (PIAT) is an individual measure. It determines spelling by showing the child a page with four spellings of a word, and the adminstrator says the word and records which one the child points to. There are eighty-four words to cover first to twelfth grade. The test was normed on children from several reagions in the United Stated and has a retest reliability of .78, which is just shy of the acceptable .80 for individual tests. Part of the problem with reliability is that the PIAT is set up so a child can guess a set of words easily and inflate his score.

Spelling is of particular interest to the diagnostician because older LD children have a specific deficiency in spelling. The inability to spell adequately is also a symptom of learning disabilities that is the most difficult to remediate, so that those children who learn to read and can solve mathematical problems may still be very poor spellers. The research in spelling shows quite clearly that speiling and reading are highly correlated, and to find a child who can spell well and cannot read well is extremely rare.

One can perform the very same error analysis on spelling words as on reading words, so no new tools are necessary to analyze spelling mistakes. Russell's important investigation into spelling errors on good and poor spellers shows that poor spellers do not make any qualitatively different kinds of mistakes than good spellers, except that poor spellers tend to spell letter-by-letter while good spellers spell by syllables.

Of the spelling tests, the WRAT is one of the most convenient and yields a fairly reliable score. It takes only about ten minutes and covers spelling from kindergarten to the college level. If a more reliable spelling score is desired, the appropriate level of a test such as the Stanford Achievement Tests may be used.

Figure 13
Spelling Skills Arranged by Grade

	The student spells with 90% accuracy:	Grade Level
1.	Consonants.	1
2.	Short vowels.	1
3.	Phonetically regular consonant-vowel (c-v) nonsense words when dictated to him: e.g., ba, ub, up.	1
4.	Regular c-v-c words: e.g., bug.	1
5.	Words ending with double consonants: e.g., will.	1
6.	Preprimer level Dolch sight words.	1
7.	Primer level Dolch sight words.	1-2
8.	Isolated consonant blends: bl, br, cl, cr, dr, dw, fl, fr, gl, gr, -mp, -nd, pl, pr, qu, sl, st, str, sw, sc, scr, sm, sn, sp, spl, spr, squ, sk, tr, tw, -st, -nt, -nk, thr.	1-2
9.	Words beginning and/or ending with consonant blends: e.g., mask, drum, splash.	2
10.	Isolated consonant digraphs: sh, ph, ch, th, wh, ng, -ck.	2
11.	Words containing consonant digraphs and short vowels: e.g., ship, which.	2
12.	Words ending in v-c plus silent "e": e.g., cake.	2
13.	Words containing long vowel digraphs: ee, ea, ai, ay, oa, oe, ow, ie, ue, ei.	2
14.	Words with variant consonant sounds for c, g, s, -dg: e.g., ice, large, has, edge.	2
15.	Plurals ending in -s or -es.	2
16.	Words containing long e and i sounds of y: e.g., why, happy, monkey.	2
17.	Words containing vowel diphthongs: oi, oy, ou, ow, ew.	2
18.	Words with r-controlled vowels: er, ir, ur, or, ar.	2

19.	Verbs with inflectional endings: e.g., jump, jumps, jumped, jumping.	2
20.	Words containing al, au, aw.	2
21.	Words with two sounds of oo: e.g., foot, moon.	2
22.	Words ending in c-v-c pattern whose final consonant must be doubled before adding ng, er, ed, y: e.g., bat, batted.	2
23.	Common words with silent letters: e.g. knife, talk, light, catch, write.	2
24.	Common compound words.	2-3
25.	Common contractions.	2-3
26.	Words which drop the final silent "e" before adding suffixes: ie, er, ing, ed, est: e.g., take, taking.	2-3
27.	Words in which f is changed to v in plural form: e.g., knife-knives, calf-calves.	3
28.	Words containing prefixes and suffixes: dis, en, in, un, re, pre, -or, -er, -sion, -ful, -ness, -tion, -ly.	3
29.	Words in which y is changed to i before adding es: e.g., hurry, hurries; baby, babies.	3-6
30.	Alphabetizes and uses guide words in the dictionary.	2-6

Permission granted by Jefferson County Public Schools, Lakewood, Colorado.

The Definition of Arithmetic

Arithmetic, used here to denote mathematics commonly taught in elementary school, is the ability to understand and solve problems involving number, quantities, spatial relationships, temporal relationships, and size relationships. The child who cannot perform adequately in arithmetic may not know his numbers, computation facts, decimals and fractions, be unable to arrange the numbers spatially, or be unable to solve "word problems." To treat failure in arithmetic as the result of a single disorder is obviously to oversimplify.

Some LD children will read several years behind their grade level, but perform at grade level in mathematics. These children have what may be called dyslexia with normal spatial abilities, visual and auditory memory, and have a specific disability in associating words with the written symbol. Such children with specific reading problems perform well on nonverbal tasks (e.g. the WISC Performance IQ tasks, the ITPA and Detroit visual subtests, the design copying and drawing tasks) but do much more poorly on the verbal tasks of the WISC, ITPA and Detroit, and on auditory discrimination tasks. Children with dyslexia will often reverse their letters and not their numbers, because there are fifty-two letters (lower and upper case) for the child to remember and only ten digits, putting a much smaller load on the visual memory. There are, however, children who reverse numbers as well as letters, and transpositions (913 for 931) are much more common than reversals (a backwards 2).

Dyslexia contrasts greatly with individuals with acalculia, who read normally but have arithmetic skills far below age level. Reading involves a rather passive process, and if the child can move his eyes left to right along the lines and can recognize the words, he can read. Arithmetic, however, requires a more active process of organizing numbers in columns, remembering numbers to carry, and understanding spatial relationships. Persons with acalculia either cannot remember their math facts or have serious spatial organization problems. A number of authors (Strauss and Werner, 1938) have suggested that acalculia is associated with two other neurological symptoms — right-left confusion, finger agnosia (no sensation in the fingers) — and is the result of a spatial disturbance. The finger agnosia is an interesting symptom, because it suggests that when children begin learning arithmetic they do use their fingers, and lacking a feeling in the fingers, they do not learn these basic concepts. These three symptoms, known technically as Gerstmann's syndrome, will be discussed at greater length in the next chapter. Children with spatial confusion usually get the columns of numbers confused and have great difficulties understanding fractions, length, distance, and time relationships, because these require visualization of space.

A third type of arithmetic problems are those children who have dyslexia and acalculia, but normal intelligence. Children with both these disorders have apparently a disorder in general symbolic processes. These children will do well in problems involving pictures, objects, spatial relationships, but do poorly with letters, words, numbers, musical notes, and the like.

Research in Arithmetic

The research in math disorders is very sparse. A large amount of the research is involved with explaining the development of mathematical ideas in terms of Piagetian theory, which is very interesting but of little practical value to the LD diagnostician. For example, Copeland's (1970) 300-page *How Children Learn Mathematics* gives details on how to test for all the Piagetian stages. Bartel (1975), in a more relevant approach, suggests there are five general causes of a math disability: (a) ineffective teaching, (b) perceptual disturbances of size, shape, and time, (c) problems of directionality including getting numbers in the proper columns, (d) difficulties in abstract thinking, and (e) reading problems. Twelve specific factors are inability to: (a) match numerals to objects, (b) associate numbers with numerals, (c) recognize part-whole relationships, (d) understand mathematical principles, (e) know the addition, subtraction, multiplication, and division facts and do the processes, (f) understand place value and decimals, (g) decide which process to use in a problem, (h) learn cardinal and ordinal sequences, (i) understand the meaning of process signs, (j) recognize the numerals visually, (k) tell time, and (l) learn the value of coins and making change.

Werdelin (1958) has done an outstanding factorial study of mathematical ability of normal secondary students that used thirty-six tests of ability. He found five clearly distinguishable factors. In order of their importance:

1. A numerical factor involving knowing the basic addition, subtraction, multiplication, and division facts,

2. A verbal factor that corresponds closely to verbal intelligence,

3. A visual factor composed of spatial tests such as visualizing objects rotated in space,

4. A deductive reasoning factor composed of problem-solving tests such as solving syllogisms (this differed from factor 2 in that syllogisms, for example, can be solved nonverbally as well), and

5. A general math reasoning factor that involved spatial and visual logic that was specific to math.

Finally, Aiken has done one of the few reviews of the research in math. In a review of nonintellectual variables (1970) he reported the studies on attitude and interest in math showed it was related to math skill only at the high school level, and in single studies of general anxiety and math, these variables were not related until about the sixth grade and older. In general the studies of emotional variables failed to find these related to math ability. Also, in studies in twelve countries, males were superiors to females in math ability at the secondary level.

Aiken (1971) in a review of intellectual variables reports only two isolated studies with inconclusive results done at the elementary level. In a review of language factors and math (1972) he reports a fair amount of evidence that math problem solving and reading ability correlate about .40 with intelligence partialled out. On the California Achievement Test in grades one to four, arithmetic reasoning correlated .64 and .70 with reading vocabulary and comprehension, .68 with English mechanics, and .59 with spelling. Arithmetic computation correlated between .42 and .53 with these four measures. It has also been demonstrated that vocabulary skills correlate with math problem solving and that training in vocabulary specific to math helps increase math skills. Part of this can be explained by the fact that math and verbal abilities both correlate with general intelligence, which is apparently an intermodal process. However, when intelligence is accounted for there is still a correlation between math and verbal abilities. One could propose that even though math involves a lot of spatial ability, many math problems can be solved verbally. Murray, cited in this article, found that some students used verbal processes to solve geometry problems. This can be done by saying to one's self, for example, "this is an equilateral triangle; that means it has three sides; in the book it says if it is equilateral then the angles must be equal, etc." which is admittedly slow, but will come out with the same answer as a more intuitive, spatial approach.

Diagnosing Arithmetic Problems

When diagnosing an arithmetic problem one usually begins by establishing if the child can count. Counting involves two skills: the auditory task of saying the numbers in order and the visual task of associating these numbers with actual objects. One can simply ask the child to count from one to twenty-three or some odd number and record if he has learned his numbers. Any child with normal intelligence and a good educational background should do this task after the first half of the first grade, unless he has an auditory memory problem. A child who cannot count in sequence may have a specific sequencing problem. Such a child will usually not know the days of the week, or the months of the year in the correct order, and will most likely also reverse his visual letters in reading and writing.

After the child has counted aloud, he can be presented with various numbers of objects (blocks, poker chips, paper clips) and asked "How many are there?" When the child is counting five objects, three objects, twenty-two objects, etc., one can watch carefully to see how the child goes about the task. Some children must line all the objects in a straight row, others with spatial confusion will leave the objects in a heap and count objects twice or miss some. General manual dexterity can also be measured as well as color naming skills if multicolored blocks are used. If the child has difficulty counting he may have a lack of one-to-one correspondence. This is the realization that objects remain the same number no matter how they are spatially arranged. Preschool or retarded children with mental ages below five will have to count a set of objects repeatedly when they are simply pushed around because they believe the quantity will change with its spatial configuration.

One-to-one correspondence (Piaget, 1954) can be formally tested by laying out two rows of eight objects about two inches apart and telling the child, "This row of objects are yours and these are mine. Now I'm going to take these away here (remove two objects from examiner's side) and now who has the most?" If the child answered correctly, then remove four objects from his side and ask "Who has more? Who has less?" Then remove two from your side so both sides are equal with four objects and ask "who has more now?" If the child answers they are the same, he knows the concept of more-less-same, and one can proceed. Replace all blocks and then push examiner's blocks together so they are about an inch apart and ask, "Now do I have more, the same, or less?" One should never ask this latter question putting "the same" last in the sentence, because some children will "yes respond" by simply repeating the last thing they heard. Also if less than eight objects are used initially, problems may arise. If the child believes the amount changed with the spatial arrangement, he does not have one-to-one correspondence and should do fairly poorly in arithmetic reasoning.

The next step is to see if the child can write the numbers. Here the child is given a blank sheet of paper and asked to write his name (this is so if paper gets mixed up later, it can still be identified) and then the numbers to about twenty-seven. If the child reverses a number or gets them out of order, he most likely has visual dyslexia also. If he does this task correctly, it does not mean too much, because compared to other school activities it is fairly easy, although the writing of the numbers could also reveal poor fine-motor development and spatial deficiencies.

The next step is how well a child can copy numbers. When the numbers are placed on a sheet and he copies them below, the task is much easier than writing the numbers. However, when the task is copying two- and three-digit numbers from the board, the child with poor visual memory may look at a number and by the time he has looked down on his page he may have forgotten it, reversed the orientation, or scrambled up the order of the numbers. This again is due to poor visual memory and explains why some children can do worksheets, but cannot copy assignments correctly.

Next one is interested in the auditory-visual integration of the child. This is measured by presenting the child with a number, and the child writes the number from dictation. Children with auditory dyslexia may be especially poor at this task and will also have great difficulty with their arithmetic facts. The reason for this is that remembering $(2 + 2)$ or (7×6) or $(7 - 3)$ requires auditory memory. These children should also have difficulty with remembering assignments, chores around the house, in learning foreign languages, remembering tunes or jingles, etc.

A child's ability to add can be measured by simply giving him a random sampling of problems or a standardized test of arithmetic. The problem with most standardized tests is that they often combine word problems, fractions, and addition, subtraction, multiplication, and so no easy diagnosis can be made. A test that does yield pure computation socres is the arithmetic section of the California Achievement Tests. In the Upper Primary booklet there are fifty addition, fifty subtraction, fifty multiplication, and fifty division problems with separate norms. The advantage of having fifty problems ranging from first to fifth grade is that this number of problems puts a stress on the child's system and will therefore be likely to reveal any weaknesses. A large number of problems crowded on a single sheet of paper such as the California Test also resembles classroom work. If a child fails on some of the arithmetic problems, he should be encouraged to employ his fingers or making of marks to get the right answer. By watching, one can determine if he understands the concept of addition and if he can remember what he has learned. A child who cannot count on his fingers may have finger agnosia, and some children with really poor memories may have to look up at a number line or any row of objects in the room to perform the simplest computations. Being able to understand place value is of great importance in math, and Smith (1973) in an investigation of 300 second graders found twelve skills that were prerequisites to correcting using place value.

Multiplication is fairly easy if the child can remember the multiplication tables. The multiplication process involves merely remembering these tables and being able to add. Children who cannot consistently and reliably add or have problems in organizing their work will have difficulty in multiplication. The best way of determining just what the problem is, is to give a series of multiplication problems and watch the child do them, noting what kinds of mistakes are made.

Division is much more difficult because the child is forced to be able to: estimate a divisor, to place the estimate in the correct column based on a knowledge of decimals and "places," to reliably multiply, to subtract if the number is smaller, then go back and correct himself several times if the number is larger to get the correct answer, and to begin this process again without losing his train of thought. Any child who cannot do these steps correctly or systematically will not be able to do the division of two or more numbers. Again a task analysis of how the child proceeded and the mistakes he made will be the most reliable diagnosis of his difficulty. One finds children who have "the right idea," but who make many "careless" mistakes and therefore usually get the wrong answer. These children have to be taught to see if their answer makes sense so that they know that when one divides 100 by 13, one doesn't get an answer of several hundred.

There are numerous math skills that are taught in elementary school ranging from the math facts to abstract operations, such as fractions, telling time and measurements. *Figure 14* lists a fair number of these and gives the grade level at which they should be mastered. The sequencing and time skills are usually not mastered by a number of LD children, because they often have temporal sequential deficits. This often shows up in process testing, because questions such as naming the days of the week or months of the year are on IQ tests, language tests, and process-oriented tests such as the Detroit.

Figure 14
Math Skills Arranged By Grade Level

	Skill	Grade

A. General

1.	Can demonstrate one to one matching of objects.	K
2.	Can group related objects based on similar attributes.	K
3.	Can identify objects that do not belong in a group when given criterion.	K
4.	Can correctly use the terms "more than," "less than," "most," "least," "fewest," "largest," "smallest," "same as" when given two or three groups of objects.	K
5.	Can orally count by rote from 0 to 10.	K
6.	Can orally identify written numerals from 0 to 10.	K
7.	Can match written numerals to groups of objects from 0 to 10.	K
8.	Can order written numerals from 0 to 10.	K
9.	Can write numerals from 0 to 10.	K
10.	Given an incomplete sequence of one-digit numerals, can identify missing numerals.	K
11.	Can demonstrate the definition of addition by combining groups of objects.	K
12.	Can demonstrate the definition of subtraction by removing objects from a group.	K
13.	Can identify coins by value in cents.	K-1
14.	Can use term "equals" interchangeably with "same as" and can use the symbol " = ."	1
15.	Can demonstrate place values of ones and tens by manipulating objects.	1
16.	Can orally use ordinal numbers, first through tenth.	1

17.	Can count, recognize, order and write written numerals from 9 to 99.	1
18.	Given an incomplete sequence, from any numerals group between 1 and 99, can identify missing numerals.	1
19.	Can read, write, and use the "+" and "=" symbols correctly in an equation.	1
20.	Can read, write, and use the "−" and "=" symbols correctly in an equation.	1
21.	Can read and write the basic addition facts, in vertical and horizontal form, from 0 to 20 at an automatic rate with 100% accuracy.	1
22.	Can read and write the basic subtraction facts, in vertical and horizontal form, from 0 to 20, at an automatic rate with 100% accuracy.	1
23.	Can read, write, and use the inches (") and foot (') symbols correctly.	2
24.	Can state the number of: a. inches in a foot b. inches in a yard c. feet in a yard	2
25.	Can measure a given object to the closest whole or fractional part using inches, feet, yards, centimeters, and meters.	2-5
26.	Can count orally by rote by 2's, 5's, and 10's from 0 to 100.	2
27.	Can assign place values to three-digit whole numerals.	2
28.	Can compute addition problems with sums from 20 to 10,000.	2
29.	Can state the freezing point of water and identify it on the thermometer.	4
30.	Can read, write, and use the ounce (oz.) and pound (lb.) abbreviations correctly.	4

B. Fractions

1.	Can demonstrate ½, ¼ and ⅓ as parts of a whole using manipulative objects.	1
2.	Can read and write ½, ¼, and ⅓.	2
3.	Can demonstrate an understanding of the meaning of fractions, denominators, numerators, and fraction bars.	3
4.	Can read and write fractions for all visual models.	3
5.	Can compute equivalent fractions by multiplying or dividing numerator and denominator by any given whole number.	4
6.	Can convert improper fractions to mixed numbers and vice versa.	5
7.	Can reduce fractions to their simplest form.	5

8. Can express any whole number as a fraction. 5
9. Can add proper fractions and improper fractions. 5
10. Can subtract proper and improper fractions. 5
11. Can multiply all fractions. 6
12. Can divide all fractions. 6
13. Can construct and solve equations using fractions based on teacher dictated story problems. 3-6

C. Time and Calendar

1. Can read and write the time from a clock and in written form (e.g. 7:15):
   a. to the nearest hour — K-1
   b. to the nearest half hour — 2
   c. to the nearest quarter hour — 2
   d. to five minute intervals — 3
   e. to the nearest minute — 3
   f. to the nearest second — 4

2. Can state:
   a. the number of hours in a day — 1
   b. the number of minutes in an hour — 3
   c. the number of seconds in a minute — 4

3. Can read and write dates in:
   a. numerical form — 3
   b. written form — 6

4. Can read the days, weeks, months, years, and seasons from the calendar. 3

5. Can state:
   a. the days in a week in sequence — 1
   b. the number of weeks in a year — 3
   c. the months in a year in sequence — 3
   d. the number of days in a year — 3
   e. the seasons in a year — 3

D. Multiplication

1. Can demonstrate the definition of multiplication as repeated addition. 2-3
2. Can read, write, and use the "$\times$" and "$=$" symbols correctly in an equation. 3
3. Can read and write the basic multiplication facts, in vertical and horizontal form, from 0 to 10, at an automatic rate with 100% accuracy. 3
4. Can multiply numerals by 100. 4
5. Can multiply two-and three-digit numerals by one-digit numerals demonstrating the application of place value:
   a. without regrouping — 3-4
   b. with regrouping — 4
6. Can multiply two-, three-, and four-digit numerals by two-digit numerals demonstrating the application of place value (with and without regrouping). 4

7.	Can multiply three- and four-digit numerals by three-digit numerals demonstrating the application of place value (with and without regrouping).	5

E. Division

1.	Can demonstrate the definition of division: a. by separating a large number into equal subsets (partitioning) b. by demonstrating ratio, whereby the larger number (dividend) is a number of times larger than a given number (divisor)	2-3 3
2.	Can read, write, and use the "÷" and "—" symbols correctly in an equation.	3
3.	Can read and write the basic division facts with no remainders in "÷" and "—" form, up to 81÷9, at an automatic rate with 100% accuracy.	4
4.	Can divide all numerals up to 100 by one-digit numerals: a. without remainders b. with remainders	 3 4
5.	Can divide three-digit numerals by one-digit numerals, demonstrating the application of place value.	4
6.	Can divide four-digit numerals by two-digit numerals demonstrating the application of place value and estimation (with and without remainders).	4
7.	Can divide up to five-digit numerals by two-digit numerals (with and without remainders).	5

F. Decimals and Percents

1.	Can demonstrate the definition of a decimal as a fractional number in which the denominator is always ten or a multiple of ten.	5
2.	Can identify from a set of numerals those which are common fractions and those which are decimal fractions.	5
3.	Can read and write decimals through thousandths.	5
4.	Can order a set of decimal fractions from smallest to largest.	5
5.	Can rewrite fractions whose denominators are 10, 100, and 1,000 in decimal form.	6
6.	Can convert ½, ¼, 1/5, 1/3, 2/3, and 1/10 to decimal form.	6
7.	Can round off decimals to the tenths, hundredths, and thousandths.	6
8.	Can convert common fractions and mixed numerals to terminating decimals.	
9.	Can convert terminating decimals to common fractions and mixed numbers.	6
10.	Can define percent as a common fraction in which the denominator is always one hundred.	6

171

11. Can read, write, and use the "%" sign correctly in any numerical situation.   6

12. Can convert common percents to decimals and vice versa.   6

13. Can convert percents to common fractions and vice versa.   6

14. Can construct and solve percentage and decipal equations based on teacher dictated story problems.   6

Permission granted by Jefferson County Public Schools, Lakewood, Colorado.

Tests of Arithmetic

There are a number of group tests that measure arithmetic processes in the elementary school range. Seven of the better standardized group tests are:

1. The Bobbs-Merrill Arithmetic test is a test that measures the child's ability to understand concepts and solve problems and his computational skills. This test was normed entirely in Baltimore using 4,000 children per grade in the first through ninth grades.

2. The Emphoria Arithmetic Test is a test that is hard to administer and has many deficiencies in its standardization. The normative group is not described and does not yield grade levels (just percentiles).

3. The SRA arithmetic test is a fairly well-conceived test, which places a fair amount of emphasis on computational items. It measures math concepts, reasoning, and computation.

4. The arithmetic section of the Stanford Achievement Tests is well normed, using 850,000 children from all fifty states. The test yields a math concepts score that emphasizes basic mathematical reasoning, a math application score, which is essentially solving "word problems" in math and a computational section. All three sections have high reliability and good validity. The test is, however, long and takes about an hour and one-half to take (in two sessions).

5. The arithmetic section of the California Achievement Test is very well normed and covers math skills from first grade to the second year in college. The elementary grades have very good computational sections along with the ability to solve word problems and other math concepts such as money, time, weights and measures, fractions, and percents. This test has good reliability, especially for the computational sections and has been found to correlate moderately with intelligence (.42 with the California Mental Maturity test).

6. The Comprehensive Tests of Basic Skills measures math skills from the second to twelfth grade and requires eighty minutes to take.

It has good subtest reliabilities and was normed on 170,000 children. It measures computational skills, concepts and application of math skills, and is comparable to the other major group math tests.

7. The Stanford Diagnostic Math Test is an extensive test requiring two hours and fifty minutes to administer. It is designed, however, to be given in a group setting and has norms for the 2.5 to 8.5 grade level. This test was normed on 15,000 children and has split half reliabilities between .89 and .98.

8. The arithmetic section of the Metropolitan Achievement Tests goes only from the mid-third grade level to mid-ninth grade level and hasn't been revised recently.

Some individual arithmetic tests are:

1. The Wide Range Achievement Test (WRAT) has an arithmetic section comprising a set of about fifty problems ranging from simple counting to logarithms. Because the test covers such a wide range there are only a few addition and subtraction problems and a fairly strong concentration of problems using the reduction fractions, decimals, and the like. It does have one advantage and that is the problems are mixed, so the child must observe the correct sign to solve the problem. LD children often have the tendency not to look at the sign and this only shows up on tests where the problems are mixed.

2. The Key Math Diagnostic Arithmetic Test is a detailed individual arithmetic test that has fourteen subscales each with ten to twenty problems. The test has norms for kindergarten to ninth grade and is broken into three areas. It measures content (counting, fractions, and geometrical concepts), operations (the four operations plus a scale for mental arithmetic and numerical reasoning), and applications (word problems, money, measurement, and time).

Analysis of Written Language

The analysis of a child's written language is of special importance in the LD diagnosis because written expression is the most complex symbolic system that the child must master. Auditory receptive language is the easiest, and children can understand sentences spoken to them before they learn to speak, next is spoken language mastered almost completely by age five; then learning to read, which is a visual symbolic system based on spoken language. Reading is much easier than writing, because the child utilizes only his recognition memory and can employ phonics rules to decipher difficult words and does not have to formulate ideas and organize these ideas on his own. Written language requires, in addition to handwriting skills discussed in the motor skills chapter, memory of letter forms, an understanding of the highly abstract and confusing punctuation system, and spelling, one of the most difficult and enduring deficiencies of LD children. Knowing how to write well is actually knowing a language (symbolic system) based on another language system (reading) based on still another language system. It is a common experience to find the typical LD child to have slightly deficient language in preschool, be a nonreader in the first few grades, and from the fourth grade on up be able to survive in all the academic skills except written expression, which is almost always atrocious.

Compared to reading and oral speech, there is practically nothing on the evaluation of written work. As far as tests go there are only one formal and one informal test of written expression. This is unfortunate, because written language is very sensitive to the problems of the LD child and written work is much more convenient to analyze than either a tape recording of a speech sample or the procedure of carefully recording every reading error. I suspect that the reason for this area being so ignored is that it is so complex that no one has felt qualified to venture into it.

The evaluation of written work can begin by having the child copy a few sentences. This allows one to evaluate the quality of the handwriting, check for letter reversals, see how fast a child can write under optimum conditions, determine how many times he must look at the original in copying (a crude measure of visual memory), and get an idea if there might be visual acuity or perceptual problems. Next have the child write all the lower case letters of the alphabet, then all the capital letters. Usually one specifically asks the child to print rather than to use cursive, because these letters are more easily reversed and are easier to analyze. Printing the alphabet allows one to determine if the child remembers all the basic elements in writing, and children with very poor visual memories will often avoid words beginning with certain letters they know they reverse, or they will do such things as put capital letters in the middle of words.

While the child is writing the alphabet, one should note if he must say the letters aloud before he can write them (that is reauditorize them) and if he must go back to the beginning every time he hesitates. Following this, one can give the child some dictation to see how well he can spell and whether he knows his punctuation by using a few sentences with at least one question and a quote. This should reveal if the child knows how to capitalize the beginning of a sentence, put a period at the end, perform the more complex punctuation, remember the sentence long enough to write it without asking for it to be repeated, hear the word boundaries, form his letters accurately and rapidly, and spell the basic primary words. Lastly, the child can be asked to write something on his own. He may be asked just to write a story, or he may be shown a picture and asked to write about his picture.

Figure 15 gives the various writing skill competencies by grade level so that the diagnostician can evaluate the writing sample in terms of the written skills mastered.

Figure 15
Written Language Skills

A. Sentence Writing and Punctuation:

1. Can use and determine proper ending punctuation in sentences:
   a. period at end of declarative sentence — 2-3
   b. question mark at end of interrogative sentence — 3
   c. exclamation point at end of exclamatory sentence — 5

2. Can use commas correctly in a sentence:
   a. in a series — 3-6
   b. after phrases and clauses — 5-6

3. Can write sentences containing quotations with correct use of quotation marks and commas. — 5-6

4. Can identify, describe, and write compound sentences by combining related simple sentences with a conjunction and comma. — 6

5. Can use periods correctly:
   a. end of sentences — 3
   b. in initials — 3
   c. in abbreviations — 4

6. Can use an apostrophe correctly:
   a. in a contraction — 4

7. Can use a colon correctly:
   a. writing the time — 4
   b. to introduce a list — 6
   c. after the name of a speaker in a play — 6

8. Can use a hyphen correctly:
   a. to separate syllables — 6
   b. when two words function as modifiers — 6
   c. for numbers between 20 and 100 — 6
   d. to connect parts of words — 6

9. Can underline correctly: titles of books or articles and other words that should be in italics. — 6

B. Paragraph Writing:
   1. Can write three or more sentences about one topic. — 3-6
   2. Can describe and use the correct paragraph format with indentation and topic sentence. — 3-6
   3. Can organize given sentences in sequences according to chronological, logical, or historical order. — 3-6

C. Parts of Speech:
   1. Can identify, describe, and write nouns. — 3-4
   2. Can identify, describe, and write verb forms in all tenses. — 3-4
   3. Can identify, describe, and write adjectives and adverbs. — 5
   4. Can identify and write all pronoun forms. — 5
   5. Can write sentences with subject-verb agreement. — 6

D. Proofread and Correct:
   1. Can identify and correct any punctuation or capitalization, given sample sentences. — 4-6
   2. Can identify and correct any structural, punctuation, or capitalization errors given a sample paragraph. — 4-6
   3. Can identify and correct any structural, punctuation, or capitalization errors given a sample five-part letter. — 5
   4. Can identify and correct errors in original writing. — 4-6

E. Letter Writing and Composition Writing:
   1. Five-part friendly letter:
      a. can write a friendly, five-part letter using the correct format and punctuation, including heading, greeting, body, closing and signature. — 4
      b. Can address an envelope by writing the address and return address correctly. — 4
   2. Can write three or more paragraphs about a given or chosen subject in composition form including the title, introduction, and conclusion. — 5-6
   3. Can develop a plot for a story to include a beginning (who, what, where), a problem, a high point of climax, a solution, and a satisfying ending. — 4-6
   4. Can read about and research a given topic and write a research paper. — 6
   5. Can correctly outline and gather ideas and information to be given in a written paper or oral speech. — 6

Permission granted by Jefferson County Schools, Lakewood, Colorado.

The evaluation of written language has been hampered by the fact that there are few standardized measures. There are the Slingerland

and Jordan tests, which have short dictation tasks to measure some aspects of written language; the DiComp system, which is a system for analyzing any written composition; and Myklebust's Picture Story Language Test. The DiComp system (Marzano and Di Stefona, 1977) is primarily designed for the secondary student and requires such a complex system of scoring that a workshop in this system is recommended. Its norms are complicated and the description of the norming group is very vague. Myklebust's test consists of a very old picture (1920s) of a boy about eight years old dressed in a suit playing with some dolls. It took some forty years to collect the norms, and the written compositions are scored for total words, number of sentences, words per sentence, syntax, and abstractness of the theme of the story. The norms are for every other age from seven to fifteen.

Myklebust (1965) found that total words did not correlate with auditory receptive language or auditory expressive language (in the measures used by Myklebust) except for seven-year-olds and correlates well with age (.59) in normal children. Dyslexic children were significantly lower in Total Words in their stories than normal children in all ages for which the norms are available (seven to fifteen years of age). Total Sentences did not correlate with either receptive or expressive auditory language or with chronological age in normal children. Dyslexic children were significantly below normals in the seven to eleven age range on this skill. Words per sentence correlated significantly with auditory receptive and expressive language for seven year olds only. It also correlated highly with age (.71) for older children writing longer sentences, but the dyslexics had the same number of words per sentence as the normals, suggesting that while LD children are briefer in their writing, they do not have noticeably impoverished sentences. Syntax did correlate significantly (in .30s) with oral expressive and receptive language and with age, but surprisingly the dyslexic children were lower in syntax only at the nine to eleven age level. Myklebust found this to be unrelated to oral receptive language (except for seven year olds), but related to oral expressiveness.

Johnson and Hubly (1979) have developed a Written Expression Test that consists of a color picture, an extensive scoring manual, and norms for first through sixth grade. Each compostion takes about six minutes to score and yields a score for number of words, clause length, punctuation, grammar, spelling, handwriting, and paragraph development. The characteristics of this test and the relationship between these written language skills and word recognition and reading comprehension is available (Hubly and Johnson, 1980).

Diagnosing An Academic Problem

The art of diagnosing a learning disability has come to a definite point in the last half century and has stopped. Almost every school system recognizes that there are children not having emotional or motivational problems with normal intelligence who have specific academic problems. The practice of observing the child in class, giving the child an individual intelligence test and achievement battery, administering some process tests such as the Beery, ITPA, and Detroit is now widespread in LD programs. This enables one to fairly and accurately categorize the child into the right funding category and takes the first step of labeling the child, but it is not a proper diagnosis, because it does not suggest the proper treatment for remediating the child, and it does not provide a prognosis or course of the disorder.

The process of diagnosing learning problems will never raise itself to the level of a science with any authority or prestige currently shared by doctors, psychologists, physicists, and the like until it is able to (a) develop reliable measures of learning processes, (b) be able to classify learning disabilities into distinct types, and (c) make an accurate prognosis for each of these types of learning disabilities. The whole field of learning disabilities will be revolutionized when diagnosticians will be able to say in a staffing something like, "John has a visuo-motor dysfunction type of learning disability and research has shown that eighty-five percent of the children of his age overcome this problem in eighteen months if given extra help in hand-eye coordination." To help the clinician find his way among all the material covered in this chapter, it is suggested that there are at least the following types of LD children with the following patterns of performance on the academic evaluation:

1. There are LD children who because of bad school experiences, poor home conditions, different cultural values, and emotional problems are poorly motivated in the classroom. These children usually make failing grades in school and do poorly in achievement testing. They are usually found in the fifth through tenth grades and often do particularly poorly in math computation, because they have not bothered to learn the boring math facts. They can be identified by interviewing the teacher and by observing their nonverbal behavior during the testing. These children say they do not know the answer when items become difficult, whip through and make careless mistakes, and sometimes do much better when challenged with a statement like, "You cannot do this." Poor motivation also shows up when the child does well on the basic process tests and does not make

classic reversals, substitutions, and the like while reading or solving math problems.

2. There are LD children who do poorly in school because they cannot concentrate long and consistently enough to pick up the academic skills. These children are easily distracted by irrelevant noise and movement, perform significantly better in one-to-one testing than in group situations, and have the concomitant problem of being very disorganized. The author has found these children to be hyperactive sometimes and sometimes not, and many respond to stimulant medication whether they are hyperactive or not. On testing they score much lower than they are "capable of" by everyone's judgement, and if attention is increased by medication, their classroom performance and individual testing scores usually rise markedly. These children can be recognized also because they "fall apart" on any long task (such as reading comprehension of paragraphs) while doing well on brief tasks. Kindergarten and first-grade children with this problem typically have low auditory memory and discrimination skills. Other visual perceptual skills, particularly in the hand-eye coordination area, are also low, indicating that at this age these factors are all linked to a general immaturity.

3. There are LD children with visual perceptual problems who have a great difficulty integrating, processing, and understanding visual information whether it is symbolic material or not. These children score low on the visual tasks of the WISC, ITPA, Detroit, Beery, and others, and they have difficulty copying and keeping words and letters in the correct orientation. Reading is difficult because of its visual aspects; math is not much better because counting, graphs, fractions, spatially organizing division problems, etc., require much nonverbal reasoning and written expression is extremely poor. Their oral reading is marked by omissions, substitutions, losing place on the line, reading reversals, and the like. In extremely rare cases one finds that these children can spell better orally than when they write the words.

4. A more common disorder than the one above are children who are normal visually on nonsymbolic material and in auditory tasks, but have a specific difficulty in processing letters and words. These LD children usually score in the normal range on the WISC, ITPA, Beery (except for the Detroit subtests using letters and words), but are still years behind in reading and usually not very far behind in

math. They read hesitantly making reversals, transpositions, omissions, and substitutioins, and their spelling is marked by misspelling the most commonly encountered words such as "there" as "ther," "does" as "dos," "which" as "wich," and so on. Often these children will have a parent or sib with the same problem, and teaching them to spell visually, auditorally, kinesthetically, does not help because they have apparently a defective visual memory center, which often affects the child's visual discrimination, closure, and short-term memory for letters and words.

5. There are some LD children who have severe language processing problems and normal visual abilities. These children can print the alphabet from memory, read many common sight words fairly automatically, but have difficulties in learning phonics, comprehending what they have read, and expressing themselves in writing. Since reading is a symbolic system based on oral language, the child will often read as he speaks, that is use wrong tenses without realizing his mistake, leave off endings, read questions that have reverse subject and verb as declarative sentences, and the like. These children also typically have low Verbal IQs on the WISC, score low on the ITPA and Detroit verbal items, but do fairly well on the visual tasks.

6. Since all the perceptual processes of discrimination, closure, and short-term memory rely on recognition of material encountered in the past, there are children who appear to have perceptual handicaps that are based mainly on gaps in their instruction. Such children show unusual deficits in areas that do not make a pattern, have fairly good memories, and learn their deficient skills at a rapid rate. On the other side of the coin, children with true perceptual problems may not appear to have unusual deficits, because someone has overtrained in these areas. Reversals, a good indication of visual perceptual problems after first grade, may be absent from the child with a visual perceptual problem because he has been carefully overtrained in this area. This is why it is crucial to obtain an educational history before making an LD diagnosis.

7. Some LD children, in fact a majority of those that are not high auditory or visual learners, have a deficit in associating the visual symbols in reading with their auditory language. These children, with extensive work in phonics and other techniques, will be able to learn on the basic first- and second-grade reading level. Yet when faced with a moderately long paragraph at this elementary level, their reading will suddenly go completely off so that they will read, "and they were going" for "that was a gate" before catching

themselves. New words, except those drilled, will often be hopelessly mispronounced. These children often have good coordination, do not exhibit the usual symptoms of distractibility and hyperactivity, except that they are usually "burned out" by the whole process of reading. The typical auditory and visual tests are usually low (in the slow learner range), the children do not fit nice patterns such as reversals, substitutions, etc., and often after a year of intense instruction the child progresses in math and in general information, but reading is so poor the student often needs a self-contained classroom.

8. There are some LD children who may be a little weak in reading and math, but have specific disability in spelling. These children can encode words as required in reading but cannot remember the letters that go into words. This inability to spell is actually a defect in visual symbolic memory, and this trait is not particularly related to intelligence or even visual memory for non-symbolic material. These children are of two types in the author's experience — younger children in the primary grades who have difficulties in written expression and older junior high age LD children who have "outgrown" their reading disability. Pure cases of a visual memory deficit are fairly rare and usually there are other symptoms involved.

9. Some children have specific problems in remembering things that the LD texts commonly call long-term auditory memory. In many ways these children are the hardest to teach, because there is essentially no teaching method to increase memory except drill and repetition. These children seem poor in most areas, have special problems in learning their math facts, forget their reading skills almost completely over the summer, and may seem dull and nonverbal because they cannot ever remember even what they did over the weekend. They usually do not have any particular channel that is stronger and therefore do fairly well on the exercises at hand, but cannot seem to integrate this into previous learning. Often the teacher after a year will be very discouraged and demand another IQ test because the student resembles a slow learner so much.

10. Some LD children are proficient in the isolated skills of reading, know their phonics rules, but cannot integrate these into whole units. Some of these children have simply received poor reading instruction, but there are a few who have no closure. These children typically can sound out all the parts of words, but they cannot put them into a whole word. This ability to see things as wholes,

to derive a pattern from its pieces, also extends often into the understanding of abstract concepts, such as telling time or getting the main point out of a story. In the auditory mode, the child cannot seem to sound blend except with laborious practice and overtraining.

11. It is common to find that children with genetic dyslexia also have a lack of right-left discrimination and visual and auditory sequencing. These children do not know what month Christmas is in or the order of the seasons. When they read they have a lot of reversals, may have difficulty reading left to right, and do not know how to go systematically from one alternative to the next in a multiple test situation. Orton has said that this is the primary characteristic of LD children, although the author has found that almost always these symptoms are found in conjunction with poor visual memory. Several authors have suggested that the right-left orientation goes away after the age of ten and is no longer part of the learning disabilities problem. Whether there are children with just sequencing problems has not been resolved, but the author suspects that there are.

12. Many LD children have specific problems in short-term memory, which is involved in the immediate retention of arbitrary symbols. Since much of reading and spelling is involved in remembering arbitrary letters and making words out of them, short-term memory is important in skill development even if the long-term memory is normal. These children can do the tasks assigned to them if they are given sufficient visual cues, but typically they have difficulty in such tasks as copying off the board, are almost incapable of doing mental arithmetic, and take much longer to do things. Short-term memory also codes into long-term memory, and so their general information may also be poor.

13. There are LD children who can perform academic tasks as long as they involve sensory input and a minimal amount of organized output. These children, for example, may have a good vocabulary according to a picture vocabulary test (such as the PPVT), but when the child is asked to define even the simplest words, he cannot. Similarly, these children test normal or even high on individual achievement batteries where one and two word answers are required, but they cannot write a paragraph or "put their thoughts down on paper." They have a specific defect in oral and written expression, which may be due to either the visual motor aspects of writing and speaking, or more commonly, in the syntactical aspects of speaking that interferes with their expression.

One could go on with dozens of other hypothesized disorders that could be recognized from patterns of how the child performs doing academic tasks. The above are only some of the major ones observed in a rather informal way. Hopefully when LD specialists finally begin to agree on a common vocabulary and a set of subcategories of learning disabilities, the type, course, and prognosis of each of these will be developed, and the specialist will be able to predict the correct therapy and outcome of a learning disability as accurately as a physician does a disease.

Chapter VII

The Medical and Neurological Diagnosis

A comprehensive diagnosis might begin with the biological aspects of the child, an examination of his genetic makeup, height and weight, sexual development, physique, pre- and post-natal history, diseases and injuries, medications and diet, and neurological status. These topics will be discussed in this chapter along with their relationship to learning disabilities. The medical evaluation should obviously be left to the physician; but the learning disabilities specialist should be fully aware of what a medical examination entails and the significance of various medical findings. It is important for the clinician to be aware of any biological condition that could affect the diagnosis for the reason that while doctors are well trained in medicine, they are not always well trained in learning disabilities. In fact, one standard pediatrics textbook with over 1,500 pages on diseases of children has only two pages devoted to learning problems; another, *The Textbook of Pediatrics* (Nelson, 1964) devotes nothing to learning disabilities.

At present there have been few environmental influences attributed to learning disabilities. Ott (1976) in a study done in a windowless school found that the type of fluorescent lights affected the students' learning. High voltage lines near residential housing has also been suggested, but not substantiated.

Genetic Variables

Since the discovery of new techniques in the last decade to evaluate the genetic aspects of behavior without contaminating the results with environmental factors, there has been a renewed interest in the inheritance of psychological traits (Vandenberg, 1969). These techniques employ essentially a correlation between identical and fraternal twins. Parents are often mistaken about whether they have identical or fraternal twins, and these two types of twins are raised usually more or less in the same way. The only difference between these twins then is that identical twins are genetically identical, and fraternal twins are no more genetically similar then two siblings. If one takes some trait which is determined hardly at all by environment, such as the length of the fingers on the hand, one obtains a correlation of about .50 for siblings, .50 for fraternal twins, and almost 1.00 for identical twins. These correlations show that finger length is almost one hundred percent inherited where the correlations for some totally environmentally determined trait, such as the child's social security number, would be .00 for identical and fraternal twins. With psychological traits, for example, Shields (1962) reports that the intelligence scores of identical twins raised in separate families correlated .77, identical twins raised in the same family correlated .76, and fraternal twins raised together correlated .51. As may be seen, intelligence neither follows the correlations of 1.00 for identical and .50 for fraternal, nor does it follow the correlations of .00 and .00; rather it suggests that heredity accounts for more than one-half of the determination of intelligence. It is also well known that IQ is not the only psychological trait that is genetically influenced. Vandenberg (1967) in a review of the inheritance of psychological traits found a genetic influence for (a) perceptual factors such as copying designs with blocks, picking out hidden figures, identifying a figure with missing parts; (b) motor skills such as hand strength, tapping as rapidly as possible, and operating a telegraph key; (c) verbal abilities; (d) spatial abilities such as recognizing rotated figures in space; and (e) some personality factors.

Genetic abnormalities may also influence a child's learning ability. It is well known that Down's syndrome, which is the result of an additional forty-sixth chromosome, causes mental retardation. Kleinfelter's syndrome, which occurs in one in five hundred males, is the result of an XXY sex chromosome combination (instead of XY). These children are not usually identified until adolescence, and then only because they have atrophied testes. No intellectual or learning problems have been associated with this syndrome (Burnand, Hunter, and Haggart, 1967). The female counterpart is Turner's syndrome, who are females who inherit only one X sex chromosome (instead of XX) and have a larger number of physical abnormalities — the most prominent being an absence of ovaries. Turner's syndrome has been shown to have the same intelligence distribution as normal children, but they have a specific defect in directional sense, spatial abilities, and mathematics (which requires spatial ability). Girls with Turner's syndrome also score on an average twenty IQ points higher on their Verbal than Performance IQ on the WISC. Turner's is to date the only chromosomal abnormality linked to learning disabilities (Green and Perlan, 1971).

With it fairly well established that some psychological traits appear to be significantly influenced by genetic variables, one would expect that some of the deficits found in LD children might also be genetically determined. Fisher as early as 1905 reported a case of a learning disabled six-year-old girl with a maternal uncle who was also word-blind. Stevenson (1907) a few years later found a family where there were six cases of learning disabilities in three generations and concluded that this trait must have been inherited. Little was done in this area of genetics until Eustis (1947) did an investigation of a family with thirty-three members. He tested each member for the five symptoms that he believed to be closely associated with learning disabilities: left-handedness; unusual body clumsiness; late speech development; speech defects; and a specific reading disability. he found that forty-eight percent of these family members exhibited one or more of these symptoms with a few members exhibiting all five. This pointed quite strongly to the inheritance of several LD characteristics. Walker and Cole (1965) examined all the families with three or more children in a middle-class suburban school (grades two through twelve) and were able to isolate seventy-five children of normal intelligence with significant spelling difficulties. Eighty-three percent were males, and a careful analysis provided strong evidence that spelling disabilities ran in families. In another approach Owen (1968) compared the academic performance of parents of LD and control students on the WRAT and high school English grades. The fathers and mothers had significantly more poor grades and the fathers scored lower on the WRAT reading but not math.

The first extensive investigation into whether learning disabilties were inherited was done in Sweden by Bertil Hallgren. Hallgren (1950) compared the case histories of 79 nonreaders with normal intelligence with 212 carefully matched normal children. He found that sixty-four percent of the nonreaders had problems before they entered school and that eighty-five percent of these LD children had another member of the family who also was a nonreader. The pattern of this disorder revealed that specific reading disabilities were *not* sex linked as one would suppose from the higher incidence of learning disabilities in males. Hallgren also found that this disability was due to a "monohybrid autosomal dominant" trait, meaning that if a person with that condition married a mate with the same trait, seventy-five percent of the children on an average would be affected. If a person with this learning disability married a person without any learning problems, fifty percent of the children on an average, would have the learning disability. Another interesting conclusion of Hallgren's was that this learning disability, unlike height, IQ, hair color, and personality traits, is due to a single gene rather than a combination of several genes. Before generalizing these conclusions to American children, it should be noted that Swedish is a completely regular language, there are no exceptions to the phonics rules so a LD child in Sweden is more like a "pure" word-blind child than his English-speaking counterpart. It should also be noted that there are several other genetic interpretations of Hallgren's data (Sladen, 1971). Modern genetics tell us that if it is due to a single gene, it is extremely likely that this defect is caused by a biochemical disorder with one enzyme being defective. By way of speculation, it also suggests that the part of the brain that is involved in visual memory (perhaps the angular gyrus) has a specific enzyme reaction that the rest of the brain is lacking.

Hermann and Norrie (1958) followed up this study with an examination of forty-five sets of twins at least one of whom had a learning disability. They discovered that both children of all the twelve pairs of identical twins had the learning disability. Of the thirty-three fraternal twins, both twins in thirteen pairs had learning disabilities, and twenty-two pairs had just one twin with a learning disability. This trend was greater for twins of the same sex, and these facts again are evidence that learning disabilities in the Swedish word-blind sense is a dominant genetic trait. Bakwin (1973) has also reported eighty-four percent concordance for identical and twenty-nine percent concordance for fraternal twins.

Malmquist (1958), another Scandanavian, has marshalled a great deal of evidence to show that reading skill is not something that is present or absent, but ranges in gradual gradations from superior reading to deficit reading. At what point in this continuum does this single autosomal gene manifest itself? Part of the problem of whether a learning disability might be due to one or several genes is a matter of what kind of learning disability one is talking about. Malmquist was concerned with children who were six months, one year, or two years behind in reading, while Hallgren and Hermann were concerned with persons who had reading and writing problems their entire life and who often had other motor and perceptual disturbances. On the other hand, the deviation of a child from the norm on a reading test could be accounted for by environmental influence interacting with a genetic defect. Until more research is done in this area one must conclude that some kinds of learning disabilities are inherited and others appear to be the result of a normal distribution of a trait.

McGlanman (1968) after studying the research on genetics has suggested that there are two types of dyslexia, one which is inherited and one which is caused by a neurological dysfunction. He suggests that these two types have the following characteristics, which can be used diagnostically to differentiate the two types:

Characteristic	Hereditary	Neurological
A family history of dyslexia	yes	no
Abstract reasoning	good	poor
Arithmetic skills	good	poor
Attention span	good	poor
Visual motor coordination	good	poor
WISC Similarities subtest	high	below average
WISC Block Design	average	below average
WISC Verbal vs. Performance IQ	Perf. higher	Verb. higher

McGlanman's article (which expands Critchley's view) reflects current thinking that the child with inherited learning disabilities will be an alert child with good attention span, normal mathematical skills, and a fairly specific problem in reading; while the child with a learning disability due to brain damage will have far wider problems in concentration, abstract reasoning, organization, and motor coordination. Little research, however, has been done in the area of differentiating these two types of learning disabilities. Silver and Hagin (1966) gave a battery of ten tests to a group of familial (inherited) LD children and a group of organic (neurological) LD children. They used a multiple criterion to differentiate these groups and found the familial children had more speech and directionality problems than the organic children; in fact, when these children were tested as adults thirty percent of the familial and zero percent of the organic individuals still had speech defects. The organic children were significantly lower than the familial on a figure-ground test.

Sex Differences

Most surveys of learning problems indicate a considerably higher incidence of learning problems among boys than girls. Twenty-three studies of sex ratios among LD children have been reviewed by Blom (1972) and Critchley (1964, pg. 65), with the lowest ratio being two boys to one girl and the majority showing four or five boys to one girl. Mumpower (1970) has given sex ratios for 7,000 children referred to a diagnostic center, broken down by type of problem, and boys outnumber girls regardless if their diagnosis was low mental ability, speech, neurological problems, vision or hearing losses, physical or emotional conditions. In Blom's review of sex differences, strong support is presented that among normal groups of school children, girls do better in reading, spelling, reading comprehension; while boys score higher in mechanical reasoning. Maccoby and Jacklin (1974) have recently devoted a whole book to reviewing the 2,000 books and articles on sex differences. They suggest there are eight myths, four definite differences, and eight unanswered questions about sex differences. The *myths* are (based on their briefer article in *Psychology Today*): (a) girls are more "social" than boys, (b) girls are more suggestible than boys, (c) girls have lower self-esteem than boys, (d) girls lack motivation to achieve, (e) girls are better at rote learning and repetitive tasks, (f) boys are more "analytic" than girls, (g) girls are more affected by heredity, boys more by environment, (h) girls are "auditory," boys more "visual." The four *differences* are: (a) males are more aggressive than females, (b) girls have greater verbal ability than boys after adolescence, (c) boys excel in visual-spatial ability, which develops after adolescence, and (d) boys excel in mechanical ability beginning again in adolescence. Bentzen (1963) has reviewed a diverse literature that shows sex differences are very pervasive. For example, 125 to 135 males are conceived for each 100 females, but with the higher death mortality rates in males, this figure declines to 105 males to 100 females at birth. Three to four times as many males as females have articulation defects and stuttering. Bentzen also reviewed the medical information on biological maturation as measured by skeletal age and age of eruption of permanent teeth and concluded that boys are biologically a year behind girls at the age of six and probably also that far behind neurologically. From this he concluded that to insist that boys perform as well as girls in academic tasks in the first grade is unreasonable and suggests that there be a different entrance age for boys than girls. This lag in neurological maturation is one possible reason for girls being better readers than boys. Dystra (1966) found girls did significantly better than boys on three auditory discrimination and two reading tests in the elementary grades. Boys also have a higher incidence of visual and hearing defects, infantile autism and schizophrenia, delinquency and behavior disorders.

Bannatyne (1971, Chapter II and VI) has extensively reviewed the sex differences on many tests and concludes that there is a genetic predisposition toward the development of the right cerebral hemisphere, which processes spatial information in boys, while girls have a stronger predetermination toward developing the left hemisphere, which processes language. Since Bannatyne believes LD children have normal spatial abilities and poor linguistic abilities, it would make sense that boys would be more likely to have an LD problem. He bases part of his argument on the fact that boys have twice the incidence of left-handedness (which is related to right cerebral hemisphere) than girls. There have also been some experiments by Kimura (1963) which suggest that the left hemisphere becomes differentiated about a year earlier in girls than boys. In spite of this evidence, Bannatyne and others admit that there is not enough evidence to definitely say that the difference in sex ratios of LD children is due to some genetic or developmental mechanism. Dwyer (1975) has argued persuasively against this position by citing data by Preston that shows that in Germany, where most elementary teachers are males, boys do better than girls on reading achievement tests and the rate of reading disabilities is higher for girls than boys.

Another theory places the blame for these sex differences on the school system. These advocates point out that elementary schools are manned almost totally by fairly verbal women and this provides a model for the girls in class. Furthermore, the values of the school system — an emphasis on nonagression, punctuality, neatness, and expressing oneself — are all traditional feminine values causing boys to have a much harder time relating to the school experience.

Still another theory for this sex difference is that our culture reinforces girls to engage in verbal activities and boys into mechanical activities. Dwyer has marshalled a fair amount of evidence to support this contention, including such facts that children rate reading as a feminine activity.

The diagnostician should be aware of the sexual differences in the children referred. Boys, because they do have higher rates of metabolism and are encourage culturally to engage in more aggressive and nonverbal activities, may be more likely to be referred because they stand out in class. The clinician must then carefully screen out those boys who are simply rowdy and not very interested in school from the true LD child. When evaluating children in kingergarten, first, and second grade, it should be kept in mind that the norms on standardized tests that average the responses of boys and girls will be biased against males, who will be on an average about six months below the norms. There is also more of a chance that boys will have very good spatial and mechanical ability (which is measured in only a few tests used by LD specialists) and may have low verbal abilities, which will interfere with their learning of academics. These are, however, only trends, and there are many girls who are active with excellent mechanical abilities who have learning disabilities, just as there are highly verbal, compliant boys.

Diagnostic Significance of Age.

The child's age is one of the most important factors in determining how a learning disability expresses itself; unfortunately this complex issue is overlooked by many clinicians. One event closely connected with age is the problem of spontaneous remission — those cases that "cure themselves" with no intervening treatment. Clark (1971) in a careful examination of one-fourth of all Scottish children entering school in one year (1,538 children) found that eleven percent of the seven-year-olds with normal intelligence were deficient in reading. In the third grade with no special help being given to the children only four percent of the normal IQ children were reading significantly below grade level. In the fourth grade this number had fallen to one percent and remained at this level for successive grades. In other words, ninety percent of the children initially diagnosed as LD children had a spontaneous remission. Clearly, these figures argue strongly against the push for early identification of learning disabilities. Taking these findings another logical step, one could reduce the number of reading failures in the United States by over three-fourths by simply waiting until the third grade to begin teaching reading to those children who do not seem to be ready to read. Children who wait to learn to read apparently pick this skill up much more rapidly than younger children. A most dramatic illustration of this occurred in World War II when the army took 400,000 illiterate soldiers and taught eighty percent of them to read at fourth grade level in a mere sixty days. Supporting these findings was a study by Langman and Rabinovitch (1968) who followed twenty-six good and twenty-six poor first-graders receiving no special help. After a few years all the good readers remained good readers, while sixty-one percent of the poor readers were reading at grade level. An even more suprising study was done by Rawson (1966), who followed up a group of white middle-class children diagnosed between 1930 and 1947 as being dyslexic. All these students graduated from high school and many went on to college and received graduate degrees. These studies raise the question of whether LD might just be a maturational lag — a theory proposed by several researchers such as Bender (1958). Dykman and Ackerman (1976), however, have reviewed the evidence for this theory and find many LD students to be just as far behind in their mid-teens as they were in the primary grades. This would argue against a lag and more for a permanent lag, which is another name for a processing deficit.

The various investigations that follow LD children through several grades indicate that many children with normal intelligence who do poorly in the first few grades develop the readiness skills for reading, spelling, and arithmetic (such as directionality, ability to concentrate, visual discrimination and memory for symbolic material, auditory discrimination and memory for symbolic material, the ability to integrate the visual and auditory symbol) by the age of six, while others, including a majority of deficient first- and second-graders develop these skills at about the age of eight. It is the author's impression that oral language skills are mastered by normal IQ children between the age of four to six; visual discrimination for letter and words between six and eight; auditory discrimination of sounds in words between six and nine; the consistent discrimination of right and left between six and eight; and the ability to match a visual symbol with an auditory sound between seven and ten.

It becomes clear that making a diagnosis on a six or seven year old is fraught with inaccuracies and the burning question becomes: Can one distinguish between those children in the primary grades who will have a long-standing learning disability from those who will outgrow the problem without treatment?

Koppitz (1971) studied 137 children who had deficient Bender Gestalt Tests, of whom ninety-one percent were described as restless and hyperactive, fifty-four percent as having low frustration levels, and forty-three percent as being explosive as rated by their teachers. Koppitz found that after five years of treatment, twenty-four percent were able to return to the regular classroom and forty percent remained in a LD lab. Others received intensive psychiatric care or were placed in other programs. Of the eight characteristics recorded in the initial diagnosis, not one (including the Bender) could predict which children would improve enough to return to the regular classroom. DeHirsch, Jansky, and Langford (1966) gave thirty-seven different tests to a sample of kindergarten students and then waited to see how these tests correlated with first- and second-grade reading. This investigation, which is one of the most thorough, found twenty of thirty-seven tests they gave predicted reading, writing, and spelling achievement well. Hyperactivity, distractibility, and impulsiveness of kindergarten was a poor predictor. While performance on a pegboard task and the Bender Gestalt was a good predictor. Of fourteen language tests, the ability to imitate tapped patterns and auditory discrimination and the ability to retell the story of the three bears were especially good predictors. Of special note was that IQ (all children had IQs between 85 and 115) was a poor predictor (eleven out of twenty). The good readers showed defects on one or two areas, while the deficient readers were low on many of the tests. Twenty of the thirty-seven tests were maturationally sensitive; when the failing readers were compared to the children with just maturational lags, no single test differentiated these groups other than the failing readers were low in all different types of tests. When the correlations of each of these tests of reading in the second grade were examined, they were almost uniformly in the .30s, indicating that no particular ability was better at predicting later academic performance. The low correlations also indicate that a great many children outgrow a deficiency in a certain area at least to the extent that it doesn't affect their academic ability. These correlation studies do not, however, show which child does and doesn't outgrow his disability. In a search through the literature, this author has found little about which tasks can predict the child will outgrow his disability beyond the suggestion that the more severe the disability, the less likely he will outgrow it (Frankenberg, 1976).

To recap, the child is continuously developing and acquiring new skills as he matures. With change in age the manifestation of learning disability changes, so that some symptoms at one age are unimportant at a different age. To overgeneralize, the "typical" LD child goes through various stages: at age three, the mother may notice that he or she is slow in talking; in kindergarten, the teacher may be concerned about his drawings, which will be very distorted and immature with the child often being more active than the other children; in first and second grade, he or she will be reversing his letters and be unable to learn the basic sight words, but the speech at this age will be normal, although the child will have great difficulty discriminating sounds. At this age the drawings will be fair, but the child will not know his right from his left, and if he or she has a tendency to be hyperactive, the hyperactivity will be very noticeable with the teacher complaining that the student "cannot keep his hands off the others," has trouble staying seated, is so easily distracted that schoolwork cannot be completed. By the third and fourth grades, the LD child has mastered the basic sight words and can read somewhat by sight (especially if given special help) and does fairly well in other subjects not requiring reading. At these grades much of the subject material is taught orally, with the amount of reading kept at a minimum, but the child stands out because he or she cannot master phonics. By now the child, however, is coordinated and knows his right from his left and rarely reverses his letters and words anymore. The teachers will often report that he or she seems bright, because the child always has has hand up to answer questions, but "can not put it down on paper."

In the fifth and sixth grades, the child who has a severe reading problem confined to spelling and written work. In adolescence, he or she may sometimes become an avid reader, with the majority of his problems confined to spelling and written work. In adolescense, a majority of the hyperactive children "outgrow" their hyperactivity. The LD child at this age usually can read and write, but reading is very fatiguing to him and when he writes he must constantly consult the dictionary. The constant exposure to words, especially if done in a controlled situation as a lab, has paid off, and the child has built up images for these words so that he can sight read — if he has not been completely turned off to school. It has taken him much longer, and the tremendous work and strain involved usually reflects itself in the fact that he hates to read for enjoyment. The inability to spell, however, remains the most persistent symptom and perhaps a spelling test the only test that can be given in adulthood to establish if a person has ever had a learning disability. The author has also noticed that there is another stage in the mid- to late-twenties when some individuals report that they outgrow their spelling disability. Connected with this maturational issue is an interesting account by Yakavlev and Lecours (1967) that shows the age at which each area of the brain matures. The reticular formation, for example, responsible for arousal, does not mature completely until ten years of age. And, while age is important, birth order apparently is not (Vockell and Bennett, 1972).

Physical Description

Sometimes a clinician will become so wrapped up in specialized testing that he will forget that valuable diagnostic information can be obtained from the careful observations of the client's appearance and manner. *Figure 16* lists items to look for when working with the child with a possible learning problem. A systematic way to evaluate these is to observe the general stature of the child and begin at the head and work down.

Figure 16
Physical Factors To Consider In A Diagnosis

I. Stature
1. Complexion and attractiveness — light, dark, same as parents?
2. Height — abnormally short or tall (endocrine dysfunction)?
3. Weight — nourishment, hypothyroidism, body image?
4. Build — exomorphic, mesomorphic, endomorphic?
5. Posture — rigid, at ease, sloppy, alert, writing posture?

II. Physical Description
1. Hair — thin (electric hair), dirty, unusual style, two or more whorles?
2. Head — symmetry, circumference?
3. Eyes — focus, gaze, dialated (drugs?) bulging (exothalmia), eye contact, hyperteliorism, epicamphal fold?
4. Ears — malformed, asymetrical, soft and pliable, no ear lobes, low-seated ears?
5. Lips and tongue — hairlip scar, tongue raw (vitamin deficiency) high-steeped palate, furrowed tongue?
6. Throat — thyroid, tracheotomy scar, Adam's apple in boys?
7. Secondary sex characteristics — developed, underdeveloped?
8. Hands — signs of suicide, needle marks, evidence of physical labor, tremors, nails, single palmar crease, abnormal finger prints, curved fifth finger, syndactalic fingers or gap between second and third?
9. Legs — coordination, gait, nervous movement, third toe longer than second, gap between first and second toe?

III. Medical Signs
1. Activity level — hyperactive, lethargic, depressed, tense and anxious, calm?
2. Alertness — lapses of consciousness (seizures), sleepy?
3. Mannerisms — tics, nervous habits, avoidances?
4. Attention span — alert, easily tired, distracted by visual or auditory ground, bored with task?

5. Spatial and temporal orientation — awareness of space and time, easily confused, sequencing problems?
   6. Voice and speech — too loud, soft, lacking rhythm, word finding problems, voice tense, hoarse, stuttering?
IV. Social Signs
   1. Body language — inappropriate, exaggerated, lacking, defensive, open, uses gestures in place of words, body language contradicts verbal?
   2. Dress — overdressed, inappropriate, clean, dirty, style, sloppy, conservative?
   3. Body odor — preculiar smell (metabolic disorder), bad breath?

A child's height and weight can give clues about the child's self image and his nutritional status. Hallahan and Cruickshank (1973) and Shneour (1974) have reviewed the evidence linking malnutrition with learning problems in children. To summarize this complex field: the animal studies show that protein deprivation can lead to learning deficits; this fact has been confirmed on children in a number of South American investigations, particularly when the deprivation occurs in the first year of life. The problem with generalizing these findings to children of the United States is that peasants in South America eat, say, one piece of meat every few months, and it is hard to imagine a U.S. family not having enough money to be able to afford a pound of hamburger a week. Birch and Gassow (1970) in their excellent book *Disadvantaged Children: Health, Nutrition, and School Failure* extensively review the nutritional status of poor Americans and find their eating habits to be very inadequate. For example, in Washington, D.C., sixty-five percent of 460 Negro preschoolers were found to have anemia, a strong indication of poor nutrition. It must also be considered by the clinician that being underweight might be due to a thyroid malfunction or to anorexia nervosa, which is the refusal to eat because of emotional problems. In teenagers, a mild weight loss may also be due to a fad diet. Being overweight may be due to a metabolic problem, or more likely to compulsive eating.

Kagan (1966) found that eight- to ten-year-old children are sensitive to height and weigh variations; when they were asked to pick out their own silhouetted outline from nine examples on the wall, the children accurately picked out their profile with the sole exception of very tall and short children, who chose outlines closer to the average height for their age. Kagan has also shown that boys, but not girls, between the ages of eight and ten were aware of their height, and the short boys felt inferior. The shorter and more muscular boys tended to be more impulsive. Simon (1959) reports, however, that a child's body type at four or five years of age did not correlate with his school readiness.

Scattered reviews of physiological factors exist: de Queros (1976) suggests a number of LD children have vestibular disorders; Read (1975) found children with anemia had decreased attention and persistence, and a decrease of activity; Lott, Wheelden, and Levy (1970) found that children with histodemia—the inability to metabolize an amino acid in protein—developed normal intelligence, but abnormal speech; and Kasl (1974) has reviewed the effects of a number of biochemical abnormalities and learning problems.

Physical attractiveness should not be discounted as an unimportant variable. Wilson and Nais' (1976) book on sexual attraction has reviewed a great deal of the literature in this area. When 400 teachers were shown a report card that was accompanied by either a photograph of an attractive or a plain child, the teachers rated the child as having a higher IQ, having parents more interested in education, and as getting along with his peers better when it was accompanied by an attractive photograph. Another study (Dion, 1972) gave female students in education a description of a seven-year-old's misconduct. When the description was accompanied by a photograph of an attractive child, the misdeed was mostly excused, but when accompanied by the plain child's photograph, it was assumed that the misconduct was his usual behavior. It should be pointed out there is a flaw with these experiments, and that is classrooms teachers have much, much more information at their disposal, so one would expect that the physical attractiveness of the child would have a much smaller influence on the teacher's judgement. This factor should, however, be kept in mind when making a diagnosis.

One very interesting set of studies recently done has involved examining children with learning problems for physical characteristics common in children with Down's syndrome. These characteristics (Gellis and Feingold, 1968; Gardner, 1969) include fine electric hair, two or more hair whorles in the back of the head, the head circumference larger than normal, an epicanthus fold in the eyes, hyperteliorism (eyes spaced abnormally apart), malformed ears, asymetrical ears, soft pliable ears, low-seated ears, no ear lobe, high-steepled palate, furrowed tongue, a single transverse palmer crease (Simian line), fifth finger curved inward, the third toe longer than the second, partial syndactalia (two adjacent toes or fingers fused), and a large gap between first and second toes. Waldrop and Goering (1971) found that average school children have one or two of these physical anomalies, but hyperactive boys had more anomalies. In fact, the more hyperactive the boys, the larger the number of physical abnormalities, suggesting that it may be possible to judge the amount of prenatal insult by the number of minor abnormalities (Waldrop and Halverson, 1971). In a surprising study Waldrop, Bell, and Jacob (1976) discovered that forty elementary school girls rated by their teachers to be inhibited, inattentive, and fearful had a significant number of abnormalities. The number of anomalies correlated .38 with IQ and .27 with motor coordination, but did not correlate with verbal or mathematical achievement, education of the mother, or height and weight of the child. These investigations have a great deal of promise and may eventually make a careful physical examination an important part of a LD diagnosis.

Prenatal and Natal Factors

The diagnosis of minimal brain damage figures heavily in the diagnosis of learning disabilities. It is thought by some that prenatal traumas and birth complications are a major cause of minimal brain damage, making a careful birth history an important part of a diagnosis.

Anderson and Kelley (1931) were one of the first to investigate the relationship between birth complications and learning problems. They compared the rate of birth complications of one hundred deficient readers of normal IQ with one hundred normal readers and found the following rates:

Condition	LD	Normal
Birth injuries	5	0
Neurological complications (epilepsy, etc.)	15	14
Surgical operations	57	46
Number of infections	248	259
Blows to the head	7	7

As may be seen, there are few differences between these groups, indicating that physical complications do not seem to play a large role in learning disabilities.

Kawi and Pasamanick (1959) are usually credited with doing one of the most complete studies in the field of prenatal influences and learning disabilities. They found 205 LD children referred for learning problems who had birth certificates and hospital records in Baltimore. They then matched each of these children with the child who received the next birth certificate. The two groups were compared on a whole host of prenatal and natal variables to find out which factors were related to learning disabilities and which problems occurred equally in both groups and, therefore, were not a specific cause of learning problems. Below is a list of just a few of these variables, the percentages of their occurrence in each group, and their significance (with n.s. being not a significant difference).

Variable	LD	Normal	Significance
Mother older than 39	3.5	2.0	n.s.
Father older than 39	7.3	6.3	n.s.
No previous pregnancies	33.7	49.7	n.s.
Labor less than 5 hours	18.6	17.6	n.s.
Labor more than 30 hours	5.2	2.4	n.s.
Premature (under 2,500 grams)	11.5	4.6	sig.
Maternal complications	45.4	18.1	sig.
Forceps delivery	29.3	31.3	n.s.
Caesarian delivery	1.5	.5	n.s.
Breech birth	.9	.5	n.s.
Previous spontaneous abortions	22.1	20.6	n.s.
Child abnormal at birth (physician's obs.)	7.8	3.9	n.s.

These figures show that only the prematurity (child under five pounds and the health of the mother during pregnancy appear to affect later learning. In other words, one must be very cautious in deciding whether a child has had subtle brain damage because the pregnancy was difficult.

Birch and Gassow (1970) reviewed the evidence from many quarters and found that low birth weight leads to an increased rate of cerebral palsy, mental deficiency, epilepsy, behavior disorders, reading disabilities, stabismus, and autism. The IQs of children with low birth weight (defined as 1,500 grams or less or about 3.5 pounds) was on an average of five points lower. Nine of ten studies have found premature children to have a higher incidence of personality disorders.

Lyle (1970) compared the birth history of normal and LD children and concluded that twenty-two percent of the difference (actually of the variance in a factor analysis) between these groups could be accounted for by birth complications. The difference is not so clear in studies not using retrospective data, however. Denhoff, Hawsworth, and Hawsworth (1971) rated 178 children for the amount of birth stress at the time of birth. One year later they rated these children on their general development, and when they reached second grade gave these same children the WISC intelligence test, the WRAT achievement test, and the Meeting Street Screening Test (MSST), which measures perceptual and motor coordination. The correlation between these tests and birth stress was insignificant (.02 to .10), the neurologist's judgment at birth, however, correlated .18, .21, and .30 with the WISC, WRAT, and MSST, respectively. The neurologist's judgment at the end of the first year correlated .28, .20, and .38 with the WISC, WRAT, and MSST, respectively, showing that birth complications do not greatly influence later learning to any large degree. These low correlations show that a judgment of later ability based on birth complications alone, leads to one being wrong most of the time. A similar study (Hardy, 1970) found that children with poor birth histories (low Apgar scores, elevated Bilirubin blood levels, and birth weights under 1,500 grams) were more likely to be minimally brain damaged, have lower IQs, and have failures in reading. Balow, Rubin, and Rosen (1975-76) have reviewed twenty-eight studies on perinatal events and how they affect reading and report a fair number of studies that show some relationship between these events and reading.

Medical Variables

There are a number of medical conditions linked with learning disabilities that the clinician should be aware of. The first area of interest has been the suggestion that LD children do not metabolize vitamins correctly. Cott (1972) has written a nontechnical article on treating 500 children with behavior disorders and learning disabilities with large doses of vitamins (more specifically one to two grams of Niacin, one to two grams of ascorbic acid, 200 to 400 milligrams of Pyredorene, and 400 to 600 milligrams of calcium pentothenate). He found few side-effects to what is usually thought to be massive doses, and reported it took on an average of two to six months for the vitamins to affect the child's behavior. He reports "extremely encouraging" results with LD children, particularly those who are hyperactive. If this theory is borne out, then the inability of the body to metabolize vitamins may be added to the list of causes of learning disabilities.

Feingold (1975, 1976) claims that some children are allergic to food colorings in food, and these children become hyperactive (HA) and develop learning problems when eating food with dyes in them. A number of research studies report that the Feingold diet does not work, except perhaps on less than five percent of HA children who may be allergic (Spring and Sandoval, 1976). In this vein, Pihl and Parkes (1977) have sent hair samples of LD and normal children to be analyzed by atomic analysis for trace elements. The LD children were significantly higher in cadmium, lead, and manganese and lower in cobalt, suggesting an improper metabolism of trace elements. Dunn (1976) also reports that twenty percent of one sample of LD students had abnormally high lead levels in a hair analysis.

Still another theory is that many children with behavior and learning problems have undiagnosed cases of hyper- or hypoglycemia. One occasionally encounters LD students who will change their behavior drastically after lunch, depending upon what they eat, although the author in about fifty cases could find only two such cases where this appeared to have occurred.

The author feels that these biochemical causes of learning disabilities are promising, but even if they are correct, will only apply to a small portion of the LD population. The question, of course, becomes which of the two or three children in a hundred can be cured by restricting their diet, and this question will not be readily answered until some easily administered method of assessing the child's metabolism is developed.

Another important area where the clinician may be involved is with students with suspected seizures and activity level abnormalities. The difficulty in determining whether the child has an activity or seizure problem is compounded by the fact that emotional problems may make the child restless, tense, nervous, hyperactive, or slow and lethargic and cause him to have unusual tics, shaking of the body, and periods where he will gaze into space. With the teacher many times too busy to carefully observe the child, and physicians usually treating emotional problems as outside their realm of knowledge, the diagnostician is often placed in the awkward position of gathering the information on the child's behavior to decide if the behavior is medically or emotionally based.

Activity level refers to the amount of movement the child engages in. In the school one is concerned with three kinds of activity: basal metabolism rate, inappropriate activity closely related to hyperactivity and distractibility, and motor activity due to immaturity in young children (first and second graders).

Basal metabolism is the rate at which the cells of the body burn energy, and this is mainly regulated by the thyroid gland. When the thyroid gland produces too much thyroxin, the individual begins to show signs of hyperthyroidism — restlessness, nervousness, irritability, quick movements and speech, and a large appetite in spite of the fact that the individual is thin. These children are extremely active and often irritable and may even have a slight swelling in the neck (where the thyroid gland is located). The opposite, hypothyroid, results in the child's general weakness, lethargy, being excessively fatigued, having dryness of skin, and nervousness. Contrary to popular belief, obesity is not a common symptom of hypothyroidism (Chatton, Margen, and Branerd, 1968). There is one inborn condition, congenital hypothyroidism, which apparently does not affect intelligence, but results in a specific disability in communication, especially depressed speech. While these descriptions are of extreme cases, there are many in-between states that can be diagnosed in a series of laboratory tests (usually a Basal Metabolism Rate, a Protein-Bound Iodine and Radioiodine test). Green and Perlan (1971) note that there is now an inexpensive laboratory test of thyroid functioning, which some day may be used as a routine screening test in the schools. Cavenaugh (1948) has reported one investigation that screened 660 children in the Santa Barbara schools and found that eighteen percent had thyroid deficiencies sufficient to be two years behind in physical maturation. The typical hypothyroid child lacked initiative and drive, seemed lazy and unwilling to complete assignments, tired easily, and did not perform up to his intellectual potential. Dunn (1976) reports an investigation in which twenty percent of the 144 LD students had abnormal glucose tolerances.

Children who are "hyperactive" are different from children with high activity rates. Hyperactive children appear to be constantly in motion, squirming while working, out of their seat a lot, touching and pushing and talking to their classmates and the like. Yet studies of the overall activity level of these hyperactive children show that they do not move any more than normal children. What makes them appear to be constantly in motion is that their motion is inappropriate. The "hyperactive" child moves and squirms almost always because he is distracted by his environment during a task that requires concentration. In other words, hyperactivity is closely related to distractibility: the more demanding the task, the more distracting the situation, and the more likely the child will lose his concentration and move his body.

A seizure is actually an abnormal electrical discharge across a portion of the brain. This abnormal discharge may be due to a prenatal trauma or it may spontaneously develop any time during childhood. Most seizure disorders result from no known reason, although occasionally it is the result of a severe head injury or a developing brain tumor. A long-standing seizure disorder is called epilepsy, and Crickshank (1967) has done extensive work to show that epileptics have numerous kinds of perceptual and memory disturbances as well as learning disabilities. There are three general types of seizures, each recognizable from a different set of symptoms. First, there are petite seizures, which are difficult to recognize because they often cause lapses of consciousness lasting less than fifteen seconds. The child will just blink or "stare into space" or develop a "blank expression" for a few seconds and afterwards will have forgotten what was said just preceding and during the seizure. These can, if they are long enough, be distinguished from daydreaming by calling the child's name while he is staring. If he responds, it probably was not a seizure, because the child cannot respond in the middle of a seizure. Petite seizures usually begin at the age of four to twelve and most children outgrow these seizures by the ages of sixteen to eighteen.

Psychomotor seizures result in involuntary trembling or contraction of a portion of the body. In petite seizures the abnormal electrical activity just affects the part of the brain controlling consciousness, while in Jacksonian seizures the motor area of the brain is involved. The part of the body that moves first can reveal where the seizure originates and which side of the brain is damaged. The involuntary movements may be as mild as some facial grimaces and drooling, or as severe as the whole half of the body contracting. Grand mal seizures can be easily recognized because the child looses consciousness and usually falls to the ground. Falling to the ground is the result of the muscles relaxing in the initial part of the seizure, which is soon followed by the epileptic "fit" where the muscles begin to violently contract. Repeated seizures without regaining consciousness in-between are called "status epileptus" and require immediate medical attention. Afterwards the child is very tired, sometimes very cold, and usually wants to sleep about half an hour. Grand mal seizures, like the others, may begin at any age. The clinician should always be aware that many other medical conditions such as a high fever can cause a seizure, and there are other diseases, notably hypoglycemia, that will cause shaking and loss of consciousness. The diagnosis of a seizure disorder is usually made on the physician's observation and an electroencephalogram (EEG), because each type of seizure has a characteristic EEG pattern (Folsom, 1968).

Hyperactivity

The diagnosis of hyperactivity has a long history beginning with the great epidemic of encephalitis that occurred during World War I. Encephalitis is a virus that attacks the nervous system and may cause temporary and sometimes permanent paralysis. After the individual recovers, he usually shows no abnormalities on the neurological examination. However, some patients who recovered appeared to be hyperactive, restless, and had uncontrolled outbursts of aggression (Bond and Partridge, 1926). These symptoms were soon explained in terms of the behavioral aftereffects of brain damage that occurred after encephalitis. The association between distractibility, impulsivity, and hyperactivity continued until many neurologists began to assume that children exhibiting these symptoms must be brain damaged in some subtle way. In 1937 Bradley made a rather startling discovery — benzadrine, the only stimulant known at the time, seemed to calm down hyperactive children. From this observation was born the theory of the paradoxical effect, which essentially stated that stimulants normally increase the activity of children, but in brain-damaged children, stimulants have the opposite effect of calming them down. Then came Strauss' and Lehtinen's book on the education of the brain-damaged child, which asserted that hyperactivity, distractibility, and perseveration were the cardinal symptoms of brain damage. Through this route hyperactivity was treated by most LD specialists as an expression of a brain dysfunction, even though Strauss' original study contained no control group and his brain-damaged children had an average IQ of about 70. This set of symptoms is essentially indistinguishable from what is now called minimal brain dysfunction.

Weery, Weiss, and Douglas (1964), using twenty-eight seven- to twelve-year-old hyperactive children of normal intelligence selected solely on the symptom of hyperactivity, found the hyperactive children did not differ from the control children in maternal age, birth weight, ordinal position in the family, number of spontaneous abortions by mother, total pregnancies, or birth complications. The only difference was that the HA children were more irritable (e.g., excessive crying, sleeping, and eating disturbances) as infants. Of particular interest was that there was no difference between the HA and normal children in either the EEG patterns or in the number of major neurological abnormalities. In other words, the hyperactive children were not just children with the symptoms of minimal brain damage whose hyperactivity could be attributed to birth trauma. Weery (1968) summarizes his position with, "The majority of nondefective children (i.e., where the reason for referral is behavioral and educational) either have normal electro-encephalographs and neurological examinations or minor abnormalities which are of uncertain cause and significance." He goes on to suggest that a medical examination appears to have little importance in a routine clinical assessment of the nondefective, physically healthy, hyperactive child. There are also a number of studies (e.g. Schulman, Kaspar, and Thorne, 1965) to show that the total amount of activity of HA children is no more than for normal children. Overall activity is usually measured by having the child wear a self winding watch that runs on body movement and then seeing how long these watches run after they are taken off the children.

Finally, no review of hyperactivity would be complete without mentioning three recent books on the subject. Cantwell (1973, 1975) has edited a collection of excellent articles in *The Hyperactive Child* (Vols. I and II) that review the evidence and suggest, briefly, that most brain-injured individuals are not hyperactive; that the cardinal symptoms of hyperactivity are distractibility, impulsivity, and excitability, which may also manifest itself in such symptoms as aggressiveness, learning problems, low self-esteem, etc.; that most HA children also have poor gross and fine motor coordination; that HA children have slower reaction times; that only half of HA children have soft neurological signs; that families of HA children have a much higher incidence of mental illness (fifty percent have other family members with a psychiatric diagnosis, including sixteen percent of the fathers and four percent of the mothers also diagnosed as hyperactive); that three-fourths of HA children have a marked decrease in the symptoms with age; and one-third of HA children have a long history of antisocial behavior. Safer and Allen (1976) believe hyperactivity should be defined as "a persistent pattern of excessive activity" with the major symptoms being inattentiveness, learning impairment in thirty-three percent of HA children (behavior problems in eighty percent, immaturity in seventy percent), with the minor symptoms being impulsivity, peer difficulties, and low self-esteem. They also report nine studies using LD children with a median of thirty-nine percent of these children being hyperactive. They also report the percentage of symptoms of fourteen HA children and fourteen controls matched for IQ, sex, and age (with a mean age of eight years and a mean IQ of 110). Millichap (1968) reports that eighty-four percent of HA children show improvement with Ritalin and sixty-nine percent with amphetamines. Interestingly, Gittelman-Klein (1976) gave Ritalin to non-HA, non-behavior LD students and reports this stimulant did not improve performance on Verbal IQ or academic tests, but did improve performance on visual perceptual tests including Performance IQ that involves time limits.

To summarize, it is best to treat hyperactivity as an independent syndrome not related to brain damage. This disorder, characterized by distractibility, impulsiveness, and inappropriate movement when the child is engaged in a task, affects a few percent of the children, and in eighty percent of the cases can be controlled by stimulants. When diagnosing this disorder one must always keep in mind that emotional problems, inappropriate curriculum, hormonal imbalances, immaturity, and other factors can cause hyperactivity.

Friedland and Shilkret (1973) have suggested the term "defensive hyperactivity" to refer to children who are hyperactive around certain people (e.g. the teacher) and certain situations (e.g. reading) and is clearly due to an emotional problem. Marwit and Stenner (1972) make a similar distinction. The diagnosis of hyperactivity is best done by making direct observations of the child under a varied set of conditions. The activity level and distractibility of a child is hard to evaluate by a standardized test, but can be rated in relation to other children in similar situations. The measurement of HA in children has been reviewed by Sandoval (1977).

When diagnosing hyperactivity one must be aware that total activity of HA children is no greater than that of non-HA children (Cantwell, 1975). The HA children just have more inappropriate movement. One must also realize that activity that is observed in the physician's office or the diagnostic session does not correlated with other measures of HA or whether the child will respond to medication (Stealor and Neumann, 1974 ; Zrull et al., 1966). Almost all HA children can control their hyperactivity for a half hour interview or testing session, and therefore HA should be evaluated by those in contact with the child over a period of time using a rating scale that compares the child with children his own age and sex. The Hyperactivity Kit (Johnson, 1980) contains a parent booklet explaining HA and different ways to treat it, a clinician's manual that reviews the research in the area including the studies evaluating modes of treatment, and three rating scales. The first scale is for parents, the second for the teacher, and the third is a coded fifteen-minute observation form that can be used for outside observers.

The Neurological Examination

One cause of learning disabilities already described in this chapter is the inability to read due to an inherited genetic trait; another probable cause of learning disabilities is some insult to the nervous system either before, during, or after birth. One way to determine if the child has an organic type of disability is to give the child a neurological examination. While only a neurologist is qualified to do this, the diagnostician should know how the nervous system is examined and what kinds of information the neurological examination can and cannot reveal. Hopefully, the trained learning disabilities specialist should also be able to understand and interpret the results of a neurological report.

To greatly simplify, the neurologist cannot examine the brain directly and therefore must rely on the study of reflexes and other peripheral (everything but the brain) nervous symptoms to infer brain functioning. While the neurological is excellent in determining whether the patient has developed a tumor, blood clot, or other pathology, it is not as effective in finding long-term defects or what is known as diffuse damage (damage that is spread out over the whole brain). There is also considerable evidence that children who have suffered brain injury at an early age behave much differently from persons receiving the same injury later in life. For example, adults who have damage in Broca's area will become mute, while children with the same injury will have little or not speech problems apparently because younger children have a more pliable nervous system that allows one area of the brain to take over for another part.

The standard neurological exam takes about half an hour to an hour to administer, with the neurologist usually beginning by establishing rapport. The neurological usually involves testing the twelve cranial nerves, the motor system, the body sensations of hot, cold, vibration, touch, and pain; and the reflexes (Paine and Oppe, 1966). The neurologist begins by examining the head for any asymmetries. During the examination the neurologist carefully notes any asymmetry of the muscles of the face and any drooping muscles such as one eyelid being lower than the other. A lack of symmetry indicates damage to one side of the brain. Then the cranial nerves (those nerves going to the brain outside the spinal cord) are examined in order.

The first cranial nerve transmits the sense of smell from the tongue and back of the throat to the olfactory lobe of the brain. Its functioning is usually measured by having the patient identify and match various smells from bottles that have the odor of camphor, peppermint, etc.

The second cranial nerve is the optic nerve, which transmits the information from the eye to the occipital region of the brain. The optic nerve is examined by an ophthalmoscope to see the fovea. A deformation of this disk indicates a tumor in the area behind the eye. The pigmentation and condition of the blood vessels in the eye can also reveal information about the patient's general health.

The third, fourth, and sixth cranial nerves are responsible for eye movements, and these are examined by having the patient follow a penlight or the tip of a pencil as it moves in various directions. The physician also examines the optokinetic reflex by moving an object right to left to observe if the eyes make quick jerks in the opposite direction. If they do so in a rhythmic fashion, the patient has a normal optokinetic reflex. The pupilary reflex, involving the second, third, and fourth cranial nerves, is also tested by shining a bright light into the eye and noting if both pupils of the eye contract.

The fifth cranial nerve carries the tactile sensations from the face to the brain and also carries the motor messages from the brain to mouth muscles that are involved in chewing. This nerve is examined by having the child to indicate with his finger where he is being touched when touched on the face by a feather with his eyes closed. He is also asked to move his mouth in the motion of chewing an imaginary object.

The seventh cranial nerve innervates all the muscles in the face except those involved in chewing. The patient is usually asked to close his mouth and blow his cheeks in and out. The blowing of the cheeks should be performed only on children nine years and older, because younger children have not developed the coordination to do this (Rabe, 1969). Masklike faces indicate the child may have had encephalitis or the mobius syndrome (Schain, 1972). The child is then asked to stick his tongue straight out, move it right to left touching each corner of his lip, and then to try to touch his nose and chin. If the tongue deviates to a side then he's trying to put it straight out, it indicates brain damage on one side of the brain. Clumsy tongue movements might explain an articulation disorder, but have no great neurological significance beyond this.

The eighth cranial nerve is the auditory nerve, and the child's hearing is tested. The ninth and twelfth cranial nerves innervate the tongue and are responsible for making speech sounds. Besides testing deviation to one side, the neurologist usually listens to the child's speech to see if the child has adequate articulation. The four- or five-year-old child should be able to make words containing labials, linguals, and gutterals.

The tenth cranial nerve innervates numerous internal organs (stomach, liver, lungs), and the eleventh cranial nerve innervates the muscles in the neck.

After the cranial nerves are examined, the neurologist usually asks the child to close his eyes and then touches him in two places simultaneously such as hand and hand, right hand left face, left hand right face and has the child point to where he has been touched. A child of six should not make more than one error in twelve tries.

The neurologist may then check for finger agnosia by having the patient close his eyes and stretch out his fingers. The neurologist touches two fingers simultaneously on one hand and asks how many fingers are between the two touched fingers. Since this test is rather difficult for young children, the test of Kinsbourne and Warrington (1962) may be used.

The neurologist also examines the sensory nerves from the body to the brain by having the patient close his eyes and report when he feels a pin prick. The patient is pricked by an ordinary straight pin on various parts of his body to locate any parts of his body that are insensitive to pain. This may also be done with a feather or a cotton ball to check if the neurons involved in touch are intact. A lack of feeling (tactile agnosia) is caused by degenerating nerve pathways or a deficiency in the sensory cortex of the brain.

The measurement of the motor skills is an important part of a neurological because a dysfunction of certain parts of the brain will fail to give the muscles nerve impulses and cause the muscles to eventually lose their tone, strength, and coordination. The strength of the muscles in the four extremities is usually measured by having the child push and pull against the examiner's grasp. Any rigidity, spasticity, or lack of smoothness is noted for further evaluation. Hand coordination, which involves the coordination of twenty-five muscles, is measured by having the child touch alternately his thumb and index finger, thumb and third finger, thumb and ring finger, etc. A child of six should be able to do this fairly rapidly in a smooth rhythm. Another common neurological test is to have the child touch his nose with his forefinger, then the examiner's index finger held about a foot away, then back to his nose while the examiner slowly moves his finger and observes these movements for jerkiness or incoordination. The child over three years of age should be able to place a raisin in a medicine bottle or marbles in a small-mouthed container with ease and be able to tap his finger on the table rapidly and smoothly. More complex movements for older children are examined by having the child lace his shoe or button his clothes. At this point the neurologist may ask about the milestones or in Paine's words, "The motor milestones. . .have admittedly only a limited correlation with intelligence, but inquiry should always be made concerning these dates, since abnormal delay in maturation of motor function implies a neurological disability unless it can be explained on the basis of factors outside the nervous system." If the child does very poorly on any of these more general screening measures, the neurologist can give an extensive set of tasks to locate the exact muscles that are not functioning.

Gross motor coordination is usually measured by having the child stand on one foot, walk heel-to-toe with his eyes open and closed. Any abnormal clumsiness or inability to balance would indicate a disturbance in the vestibular system or the cerebellum of the brain. The coordination between the different sides of the body is measured by having the child hop alternately on one foot and the other and then skip across the room. Any normal first grader should be able to do this. Another common test is to wad up a piece of paper and have the child catch, throw, and kick the paper. Especially of interest is whether there are any significant differences in coordination of body sides.

No neurological exam is complete without an examination of the famous knee jerk, patellar, and Babinski reflex. The Babinski is elicited by running one's thumb along the sole of the foot and observing if the patient fans his toes. The curling of the toes is normal for all but infants, and the patellar reflex involves striking the elbow in the same fashion as the knee. Consistently elicited abnormal reflexes indicate neurological damage located in the spinal cord.

Finally, the neurologist investigates the "higher" or "central" processes of the brain involving discriminating right from left, body image, and the processing of symbols (speaking, reading, writing, and calculating). The child of seven should be able to discriminate his body sides by following commands such as "put your right hand on your left ear." The child then writes his name, the alphabet, and a few sentences, copies some designs, and sometimes solves simple arithmetic problems. These tasks indicate if the child has aphasia, apraxia, spatial disorientation, or right-left discrimination problems, although sometimes the child will be diagnosed as having dyslexia, dysgraphia, or perceptual problems based on these tasks. Further information about the neurological examination can be found in Touwen and Prectl's *The Neurological Examination of the Child with Minor Nervous Dysfunction* (1970), Paine and Oppe's *Neurological Examination of Children* (1966), Schain's *The Neurology of Childhood Learning Disorders* (1972), and Bray's *Neurology in Pediatrics* (1969).

One of the few investigations into the reliability of the neurological examination was performed by Rutter, Graham, and Yule (1970), who had two neurologists independently examine a group of children without either knowing the history of the child or whether he was a dyslexic, a child with known neurological disease, or a control child. The neurologists used an exam that took only half an hour. They found that no one sign was a sure indication of abnormality, but ninety-nine percent of the normal children and the children of normal IQ with a reading problem (dyslexics) had less than eight abnormalities, while seventy-eight percent of the neurologically impaired group had more than eight abnormalities. They also ran a reliability check on each measure and found an interrater reliability between the neurologists to be about .80 for almost all the signs, except the reflexes, which had very low reliabilities. The reliability of the overall neurological status was .88 for the normal children and .80 for the physically handicapped, showing that the neurological exam can be standardized like any other test.

The investigation also revealed that LD children did not differ from normals on handedness or mixed laterality, eye or tongue movements, the gross motor tasks of hopping, throwing, kicking, threading beads, finger-thumb opposition, muscle tone, and the eliciting of most reflexes. The LD children were significantly inferior in fine motor tasks, right-left differentiation, constructing designs with matchsticks, and complexity of their speech. Myklebust (1973) sent LD and normal controls to a pediatric neurologist and reports the examination could not distinguish these two groups. None of the 137 signs examined were related to learning disabilities, although the LD group had a few more total signs. Adams, Kacsis, and Estes (1974) in a similar study found only a few neurological signs that distinguished LD from normal children, but these were too unreliable to distinguish the groups.

Walker (1965) tried to determine if there weren't special neurological symptom patterns associated with various perceptual and spatial abilities as measured by standardized educational tests. She gave a series of twelve tests measuring such areas as visual and auditory discrimination, memory, and figure-ground relationships and correlated these results with standard neurological tests. She found essentially there was no relationship between the commonly used LD measures and the neurological examination for these six- to nine-year-old children and concluded, "No consistent association of perceptual, visuo-spatial or coding deficits with finger gnosia, associated movements, Oseretsky or Prechtl findings, nor with reading disability." Walker also concluded, "The greater the 'neurological' loading...the greater was the likelihood of extensive perceptual, viso-spatial and coding weakness." In still another study, Boshes and Mykelbust (1954) had eighty-five seven- to eighteen-year-old LD children examined by a neurologist and then compared those children passing the neurological examination (probably those with a "genetic" disability) with those that showed significant neurological problems (probably the "brain-damaged" group). They found that there were no differences between these two groups in their social adjustment, silent or oral reading ability, spelling achievement, or sound blending ability. They concluded that the neurological status of a child was not related to the behavioral or academic achievement when IQ was carefully controlled for. Critchley (1964) in his volume on *Developmental Dyslexia* reiterated this by stating that the symptoms of poor right-left discrimination, finger agnosia, and the like are found in younger children and may be part of a general developmental lag, but they are "peripheral" and "not essential" to the diagnosis of a learning disability.

Forrest (1968) gave neurologicals to seventy-five LD children, seventy-five siblings of LD children, and seventy-five normal children matched on age, sex, and IQ. Of all these children only four had definite neurological signs (three were from the LD group and one was from the normal group) showing how rare neurological problems are among LD children. The neurologist in Forrest's experiment did not know from which group the child came from and was unable to find any difference in dominance, motor overflow movements, choreiform movements in the extended arms, and walking on the balance beam. He did, however, obtain differences in tappings patterns presented auditorily, right-left discrimination, the alternating tapping of fingers, and the face-hand test where the child must say when he is being touched on the face and hand when his eyes are closed. The mothers of the LD children in contrast to the control group also reported that their children were more irritable in infancy, were colicky babies, talked poorly, had poor listening skills, were hard to communicate with and had more temper tantrums.

In general, the presence of a particular neurological sign or even a set of neurological signs does not indicate a learning disability. Expanding this, the neurological examination does not seem to be extremely important in making a LD diagnosis, unless there are such gross neurological abnormalities that specific neurological damage may be certain or if there is a sudden deterioration of behavior that may signal a disease such as a developing tumor. Some authors, however, suggest a special pediatric examination (Keele, et. al., 1975).

Minimal Brain Damage

Minimal Brain Damage (MBD) or minimal cerebral dysfunction refers to a set of symptoms or behaviors that suggest brain injury, but the symptoms are so mild that no real brain damage can be established. MBD is usually diagnosed on the basis of a set of overt behaviors especially hyperactivity, distractibility, and impulsivity; electroencephlographic (EEG) recording the brain wave activity; certain test score patterns such as great scatter between subtests; or on the presence of numerous soft neurological signs and the absence of hard neurological signs.

A series of reports were done on this syndrome, but it was not applied to children with learning disabilities until Strauss and Lehtinen's book (1947) on the education of the brain-injured suggested that these children could be identified by their "hyperactivity" (p. 24), "lack of orderliness" (p. 25), their exhibiting the "phenomonon of distractibility" (p. 25), "perservation" (p. 27), and their perceptual disturbances in visual and auditory figure-ground, tactile-motor sensations, and perception of rhythm. They also suggested brain-injured children had thinking disorders such as not being able to conceptualize and think abstractly. While Strauss presented these symptoms as those of a brain-injured child, he did not present any evidence to support his contentions. Three of these symptoms — hyperactivity, distractibility, and perservation — were to become known as the Strauss syndrome.

Strauss' concept of brain injury has been criticized by Stevens and Birch (1947) who pointed out that: (a) there is not evidence that these symptoms necessarily mean that there has been brain injury, (b) known cases of brain injury do not necessarily exhibit the Strauss symptoms, (c) the term "brain-injured" implies children with these symptoms have a permanent, untreatable condition (and some outgrow it), and (d) the diagnosis of these symptoms is an oversimplification of the whole issue of brain injury. These few articles were the extent of the interest in MBD until 1962, when a conference on learning disabilities in Oxford reviewed all the dozens of labels that had been given children with normal intelligence who had learning problems and agreed to label these children as having a "minimal cerebral dysfunction." This same year Clements and Peters published their influential paper in the United States entitled "Minimal Brain Dysfunction in the School-Age Child" and the term MBD caught on and over 600 papers with this name in their title appeared in the next ten years.

Clements and Peters began their historic paper by suggesting that many of the children who were seen in child guidance centers and subsequently diagnosed as having personality problems actually had minimal brain damage or a simple maturational lag. They found that teachers tended to describe MBD children as bright but lacking self-control, having frequent temper outbursts, being high-strung and nervous, and who were working below their intellectual capacity. They listed nine symptoms of MBD with the caution that any one child will only have a few of these symptoms. The symptoms most suggestive of MBD were:

1. Specific learning deficits such as poor spelling or a specific reading problem,
2. Perceptual motor deficits particularly in writing and copying and distinguishing figure-ground relationships,
3. General coordination deficits with the child being clumsy and awkward,
4. Hyperkinesis or hyperactivity,
5. Impulsivity in which the child must touch everything he sees, say things without thinking, and commit antisocial acts without being able to control himself,
6. Emotional liability with the child being high-strung, irritable, agressive at times, and sometimes bursting out crying for little reason,
7. Short attention span where the child is distractible except when facing something of great interest,
8. Equivocal (soft) neurological signs including poor muscle coordination, confused laterality, and slow speech development, and
9. A borderline or abnormal EEG.

The answer to whether MBD is an independent entity lies in the research. In an investigation to statistically establish which symptoms were actually associated with MBD, Paine, Werry, and Quay (1968) examined eighty-three school-age children from above average socioeconomic backgrounds who were classified minimally brain damaged on the basis of either an abnormal EEG, abnormal neurological signs, or psychological findings accompanied by excessive clumsiness. Forty-six percent of this MBD group had no prenatal or birth complications, and only eleven percent had a definite history of birth complications or prenatal trauma. Furthermore, fifty-nine percent had normal EEGs, forty-three percent of the sample had no neurological abnormalities other than clumsiness, and seventy-five percent had no right-left orientation problems. The Verbal-Performance discrepency on the WISC was only slightly higher than one would expect from a normal population. The data from the history, the neurological examination, the behavior ratings by parents and teachers, the EEG, and the psychologists' observations during testing did not correlate with each other, indicating that the search for various types of syndromes within the MBD group is probably futile. However, the following observations and measurements appeared to be associated with each other:

1. Perceptual deficits, difficulties in body image, and dyspraxia,
2. Clumsiness in small and large movements, poor penmanship, and minor shaking of the limbs (choreoathetosis),
3. Prenatal and natal conditions and history of the brain injury,
4. Abnormal EEG findings and postnatal insults.

These data suggest rather strongly that MBD is not a clear-cut disorder, and its diagnosis relies a great deal on whether one decides to accept EEG evidence, or test data, or the neurological examination as evidence of brain damage.

In 1971 Wender published a book devoted solely to MBD in children, which summarized much of the literature on MBD. Wender reported that the literature showed that about fifty percent of the MBD children had soft neurological signs; birth complications such as prematurity and breech birth were associated with MBD, but it was rare to find clear-cut brain damage; MBD occurs in five to ten percent of the school population; boys outnumber girls in a ratio from nine to four boys for each girl with MBD; and many children with MBD apparently outgrow their problem. Another interesting area explored by Wender was the changes in the symptoms with age. As an infant the MBD child was usually hyperalert, excitable, and a "colicky" baby; as an infant he was destructive, nonaffectionate, and unable to listen to simple commands. As a toddler (age two to four) he had a short attention span, social problems, and a low frustration level as noticed in preschool. In the first grade the major complaint was hyperactivity; by the third grade academic problems were prevalent; and in adolescense he often had difficulty with peer relationships, antisocial behavior, and was often behind in reading. Some children outgrew their problem in postadolescence and others continued to have difficulty throughout their lives in the area of impulse control. Finally, Wender lists his own eleven symptoms of MBD: motor hyperactivity, dyspraxia, verbal hyperactivity with flight of ideas and an inability "to stop thinking" at night, short attention span and concentration, poor impulse control that results in a low frustration tolerance and antisocial behavior as well as recklessness and accident proneness, defective sphincter control (enurisis and encoptesis), extraversion and unresponsiveness to social demands often accompanied by poor peer relations, increased emotional lability with a "low boiling point," anhedonia or the inability to experience pleasure, low self-esteem, excessive anxiety with one-half to two-thirds of MBD children having significant learning problems in spite of good intelligence.

No review of MBD would be complete without discussing two other neurological signs often thought to be the more important indicators of MBD than those discussed above.

Choreiform Movements

Choreiform movements are minor trembling in the hands that can only be elicited under certain conditions and are thought to be the result of poor cerebral control. The famous child neurologists, Prechtl and Stemmer (1962), briefly reviewed many studies touching on this subject and developed a neurological test for these "distinct chorea like twitchings of the extremeties and the head." They did a systematic study of fifty children aged nine to twelve who had normal intelligence, no clear neurological signs or psychiatric symptoms, but who showed clear muscle twitches as picked up on the EEG. They found the twitching in one hundred percent of the tongue, face, neck, and trunk, but only eighteen percent in the arm and leg muscles. Also in ninety-two percent of the cases the eye muscles were affected in spite of the fact that almost all of the children had normal reflexes (eighty-two percent), normal muscle tone (seventy-six percent), and normal EEGs (eighty-six percent). Ninety percent of children with choreiform movements were also reported to have a severe reading problem. This led to much speculation about the relationship between neurological factors and learning disabilities until Rutter, Graham, and Birch (1968) did a careful comparison of choreiform movements in a normal group of seven- to nine-year-olds, a group of retarded children, and a group of carefully selected LD children. They used the traditional measure for choreiform movements—of having the child stand barefoot with his legs together, arms outstretched, and eyes closed for forty seconds with the instruction not to move at all. It was discovered that previous activity greatly affected the presence of these movements, and it was experimentally controlled for this condition. The person examining the hands for choreiform movements did not know which child had a learning problem, so biases could be reduced. It was found that twice as many boys exhibited choreiform movements as girls, that there was a consistent relationship between this measure and other neurological signs, and that when IQ was taken into consideration there were just as many LD children with choreiform movements as the normal group. There was also no relationship between these movements and classroom behavior as rated by teachers.

In summary, choreiform movements had been thought to be a reliable indicator of minimal brain damage and related to learning disabilites, but a more carefully done investigation using a control group has shown this, like so many other signs of brain damage, to be unrelated to learning disabilities.

Finger Agnosia

Agnosia is a term first used by Sigmund Freud (1891) to describe a condition in which the patient with normal sensory abilities would be unable to recognize a common object. In 1930, the German neurologist Gerstmann proposed the well-known "Gerstmann's syndrome" composed of four symptoms: finger agnosia, right-left discrimination, acalculia, and agraphia, which he thought were the major signs of brain injury to the right parietal lobe.

Strauss and Werner (1938) introduced finger agnosia to the field of learning disabilities in an investigation comparing seventeen mentally retarded children who were good at calculation with twenty-three retarded children of comparable IQ who had an arithmetic disability. They found a large difference in these groups with the children having the calculating disability also having finger agnosia. Benton, Hutcheon, and Seymour (1951) have carefully repeated this experiment and obtained no relationship between finger localization and arithmetic ability for either normal or retarded children. Hermann (1959) in his study of dyslexia in Denmark found that forty-three percent of normal readers aged nine to eleven and thirty-seven percent of normal readers twelve to fifteen years of age had some right-left confusion; while word-blind children had seventy-five percent and sixty-three percent confusions for the same ages. He also found one-third of the LD children had finger agnosia and concluded, "The many points of similarity between the symptoms of Gerstmann's syndrome and of constitutional dyslexia make it highly probable that congental word-blindness is dependent on the same disturbances of directional function which is responsible for the symptoms of Gerstmann's syndrome" (p. 134).

Finger agnosia is tested either by having the child simply close his eyes with his hands outstretched and touch a particular finger lightly and have him report which finger was touched, or by using a set of standardized tests developed by Kinsbourne and Warrington (1962) in which two of the child's fingers are touched and he must report how many fingers are between the touched fingers. Benton (1968) has found that, "Between the ages of three and four, the child can localize his thumb, but treats his fingers as indistinguishable units; by the age of six he is able to localize tactile stimulation on his fingers with his eyes open; and by the age of ten, ninety-nine percent of the children can localize fingers with eyes closed." He also found that finger localization correlated .22 with speed of putting paper clips into a box and .18 with the ability to tap one's fingers rapidly.

Benton has also launched a formidable attack on the whole notion that Gerstmann's syndrome is just a set of four symptoms. He examined one hundred patients with parietal disease and tested each patient for right-left discrimination, finger localization, writing ability, calculating skill, constructional apraxis, visual memory, and reading. He then correlated these seven symptoms in all possible combinations and found these symptoms correlated with each other between .43 and .56 in all combinations. From this he concluded that each of these symptoms affected reading, writing, and calculation to the same degree, and that these parietal symptoms were therefore not specific to arithmetic abilities as suggested by Gerstmann. This finding was supported by Naidoo's (1972) careful comparison of children who were retarded readers, children who were retarded spellers, and normal children on Kinsbourne and Warrington's test. He found no difference between these groups on finger agnosia, but there were significant differences between retarded readers (but not retarded spellers) in right-left discrimination and visual memory. In another comparison of several hundred normal and LD children aged six to ten, Reed (1967) found no relation between finger agnosia and reading in the six-year-olds and in the ten-year-olds, and there were few differences except that the LD children tended to have more finger agnosia errors in the right hand only.

One other rare condition that the clinician should be aware of is syneshesia, which is a rare condition in which the individual can "see" sounds. From birth he has an unusual neurological condition in which auditory input and emotions cause the person to visualize colors (Marks, 1975).

Testing the MBD Child

Putting all the evidence together, it appears that the clinician will encounter a few children with gross neurological abnormalities. These children should be immediately referred to a neurologist, because these abnormalities are frequently associated with brain tumors or epileptic conditions. There will be another group of children — perhaps one-third — who will have minor neurological variations that can be found on occasion in completely healthy children. The most prominent of these MBD signs is abnormal gross and fine motor clumsiness, confused right-left discrimination, distractibility and poor organization. Hyperactivity may or may not accompany these symptoms and is probably best treated as a separate syndrome. The clinician may either diagnose children with these symptoms as "minimally brain damaged," or he may opt for the diagnosis of attentional deficit. The MBD label is not a very helpful one because: (a) it does not suggest any form of remediation, (b) studies of the incidence of birth complications of normal and LD children suggest that MBD is not closely related to any cerebral damage, (c) it is not a snyndrome, because there is little agreement on what the symptoms of this syndrome are and few children have most of the symptoms of this syndrome, (d) the classic measures of MBD including the EEG (to be reviewed later), choreiform movements, and finger agnosia, clumsiness and hyperactivity do not discriminate between MBD children and normal children with any degree of accuracy, (d) there is some evidence that one of the cardinal signs of MBD hyperactivity is biochemical rather than due to brain damage, and (e) a lot of the symptoms of MBD, expecially clumsiness and right-left discrimination, are so similar to the characteristics of late maturing children that MBD in young children may be simply another name for "late bloomers." This leaves us with the excellent suggestions of Gomez to abandon this syndrome entirely and to simply describe LD children as being also a "clumsy child," a "hyperactive child," a "perceptually handicapped child," or a "distractible child."

Measures of Brain Damage

The question of whether a dichotomy between organic and familial LD children really exists rests heavily on the issue of whether brain damage can be measured with any degree of accuracy. One of the major stumbling blocks for the clinician using brain damage tests is that almost all of the measures of brain damage were developed on adults, particularly soldiers with war injuries and stroke victims. Brain-damage tests for adults are easy to design, because the subjects possessed the skills tapped by the test before their injury and no control for mental age has to be made. Children are so variable and are growing so rapidly that the task at one age (e.g. write your name with the left and right hand) is totally inappropriate at another age (e.g. kindergarten). As a result tests of brain damage for children require careful standardization with great attention to mental age.

Below is a brief review of some of the most frequently used tests of brain damage:

1. One of the most frequently used measures of brain damage is the electroencephalogram (EEG). The EEG is a machine that records the electrical activity of the brain, usually by using six quarter-inch metal cups that are placed on the skull to pick up the small electrical current (in the order of one hundred millivolts or one hundred times less than a flashlight battery) that is generated by the brain, amplifies it, and records this electrical activity on strips of paper. While the EEG is normally used to evaluate a brain dysfunction, it is not a very exact measure of mild brain damage. About eighty to ninety percent of individuals with known brain damage and fifteen to thirty percent of normal individuals have abnormal EEGs. Because as many as one-quarter of normal individuals have abnormal EEGs, an EEG by itself does not definitely determine the presence of a brain dysfunction. Part of the reason why the EEG is such a gross measure is that the electrode is averaging the activity of thousands of cells and measuring this through one-half inch of bone, blood vessels, and other skull tissue.

In an early study Hanvik (et al., 1961) tried to determine how closely an evaluation of brain damage based solely on an abnormal EEG correlated with an estimation of brain damage based on psychological testing (using the WISC, Bender, Seguine Form Board, Porteus Mazes, Ravens, and WRAT) and a neurological examination. They found that the ratings of the EEG records done by two independent physicians correlated only .64 with each other, and that they agreed on seventy-one percent of the records as being abnormal versus the fifty percent one would expect for chance level. The EEG then correlated only .04 with the medical examination and .40 with the psychological testing. This study was on seven- to fourteen-year-olds referred to a child guidance clinic primarily for emotional problems, but it does show the EEG does not have good reliability or correlate closely with other brain-injury measures.

Aryes and Torres (1967) compared three groups of eight- to twelve-year-old children: a group of poor readers who also exhibited the symptoms of hyperactivity and short attention span, a group of children waiting for remedial reading instruction (LD children without Strauss symptoms), and a randomly selected control group. Forty-seven percent of the hyperactive group, fifty-five percent of the remedial group, and twenty-nine percent of the control group had EEG abnormalities. Both the hyperactive and dyslexic groups had statistically significant, more abnormal EEGs, but it is of interest that the added set of Strauss symptoms did not apparently have more brain damage using the EEG as a measure of brain damage. Hartlaze (1971) also reports no EEG differences for children with reading, spelling, or arithmetic problems.

Hughs (1971) did an extensive investigation of the EEG patterns of 606 children between the ages of eight and eleven who had WISC IQs above 90. Children failing a vision test, with hearing difficulties, or with high anxiety were excluded from the study. Of these randomly selected children, thirty-seven percent had abnormal EEGs as determined by an expert who did not know if the child was normal or had a learning disability. Hughs reports a correlation of .84 to .95 between two independent experts and a reliability of .85 for records taken four to six weeks apart. Below is the incidence of abnormal EEG recordings for normal and LD children who were matched for age, sex, and the classroom they attended.

Types of Abnormal EEG Pattern	LD Children	Controls
Slow waves	22%	13%
Sharp waves (epileptiform)	5%	6%
Positive spikes	20%	15%
Extreme spindles	2%	1%
TOTAL	49%	35%

As may be seen, the LD children showed slightly more abnormal waves, but there were no statistically signficant differences between the types of abnormalities encountered. This study based on such a large population shows fairly clearly that the EEG is of little diagnostic significance in making an individual diagnosis of brain damage. In summary, the overlap between brain-injured children or children with LD problems and normal children is so great that this instrument must be used in conjunction with other instruments (Freeman, 1967). It might be added that newer techniques of hooking

EEGs to computers might greatly revolutionize this area so the EEG will become a useful diagnostic tool (Goleman, 1976).

2. The second most common method to diagnose brain damage, particularly minimal brain damage, is to use behavioral symptomology by examining the individual for the Strauss symptoms. This had already been discussed in this chapter, and the relationship between these symptoms and brain-injury is a tenuous one. Ernhart et. al. (1963), for example, report that hyperkinesis is not associated with brain damage.

3. The third most common indicator of brain damage is the presence of "soft" or "borderline" neurological signs. These signs are basically minor neurological abnormalities that can be found occasionally in healthy individuals. They include clumsiness in fine and gross motor tasks, choreiform movements, overflow movements, slight reflex abnormalities (especially if reflexes on one side are brisker than the other side), eye movement abnormalities, finger agnosia, mixed laterality, inability to discriminate right from left, inability to wink alternatively, and awkward gait in walking (Schain, 1972). Routh and Roberts (1972) had eighty-nine MBD children examined by an interdisciplinary team and were able to find a relationship between soft signs and academic ability. However, when intelligence was controlled for (with lower IQ children having more soft signs), there was no relationship. Black (1976) reports the same results.

4. The marble board test was first proposed by Strauss as a measure of figure-ground perception. This test consists of a square board with indentations much like a Chinese checker board and a set of marbles. Herbert (1964) has reviewed the marble board studies and found that most investigators did not control for IQ. When IQ was taken into account, the brain-injured did as well as the controls.

5. The Bender Gestalt test was first developed by Bender in 1938 and consists of nine designs on four-by-five cards, which are copied one by one on a blank sheet of typing paper. The original test was unstandardized, but Koppitz (1960) developed a scoring system based on 1,055 students in kindergarten through fourth grade. Koppitz's system has a reliability of .89 (Billinglea, 1963) and is very easy to learn. In general, the validity of the Bender as a personality instrument has not been supported (Billinglea, 1963). Bender believed that brain-injured individuals produce loosely organized designs with many distortions and rotations. The test is sensitive to intelligence (correlations of about .50 to .70), so this must always be controlled for.

There have been many studies of the validity of the Bender in diagnosing brain injury. Hanna (1958) attacked the belief that rotated figures meant brain damage by reviewing fifty studies that had very mixed results, and in an experiment showed that by simply changing the width of the cards one could reduce the number of rotations in one-third. Charost, Spivack, and Lewin (1959) found no correlation between the Bender and EEG abnormalities in children. Goldberg in a rather devastating experiment gave the Benders of fifteen patients with clear-cut brain damage and fifteen psychotic patients to trained psychologists and their secretaries. The secretaries did better in differentiating these groups than the psychologists, with only one-half of the judges doing better than chance. Stoer, Corretto, and Curnutt (1965) had psychologists sort the Benders of a control group, brain-injured patients, and schizophrenics matched in age, sex, and intelligence, with the clinicians not being able to reach any accuracy above chance level.

6. The Minnesota Percepto-Diagnostic Test is based on a study of the Bender, which showed that only two of the nine figures discriminated brain-injured subjects from normals when age, sex, and IQ were controlled for (Fuller and Laird, 1963). This test consists of various forms of these two Bender figures with an extensive set of norms taking into account such factors as age, sex, and Full-Scale IQ on the WISC. In spite of this refinement, the Minnesota has not been much more accurate in diagnosing brain damage, probably because it involves copying only two designs.

7. Benton's Visual Retention Test consists of copying ten geometrical figures on blank half sheets of paper after the subject has seen the design for ten seconds. In one study Benton (1955) found that four percent of the normal and twenty percent of the brain-damaged children scored in the defective range, while eleven percent of the normal and fifty-five percent of the brain-damaged children scored in the borderline category of this test. In other words, if defective and borderline scores are considered, sixty-six percent of the brain-damaged children will be identified, but twenty-four percent of the normal children will be misclassified. The retest reliability of this test is good (.85), and interscorer reliability is high (.95).

8. The Graham and Kendall Memory-for-Designs Test consists of fifteen designs that are viewed for five seconds and then must be reproduced from memory. The test was standardized on 535 children and has norms for the ages eight and one-half to twenty years of age. The retest reliability is good (.81), and a study by the authors using 243 adult brain-injured patients and a control group found this test to

correctly identify one-half of the brain-injured and misclassified only four percent of the normal individuals. This test does discriminate the desired population, but it is wrong fifty percent of the time. Anglin (1965) compared normal and brain-injured adults on the Bender and Graham-Kendall and found these tests correlated .61 with each other, but neither could separate brain-injured and normals effectively.

9. The Goldstein-Sheerer tests of abstract and concrete behavior is an unstandardized set of tasks involving the construction of figures using matchsticks, the building of cubes in three-dimensional patterns, classifying designs (red and green circles or all squares, etc.), and classifying objects such as a spoon, penny, pair of scissors into categories. Halpin and Patterson (1954) matched fifteen brain-injured children with control children for age, sex, and intelligence and found that only the stick test discriminated between these groups, and there was so much overlap between the groups that the test was not a very valid measure of brain damage.

10. The Porteus Maze test consists of a series of paper mazes that are standardized on an unknown population, and Porteus (1959) has cited a number of studies to show that the maze test and no other standardized IQ test shows a deficit after a lobotomy (where the fibers in the frontal lobe are cut to calm the patient). He has similarly made the claim that his test is very sensitive to brain damage. Since there is no description of the norming population, and the reliability of the test is not known, little has been done with this test.

The mazes of the WISC, which are well standardized, could be used, but the retest reliability of the WISC mazes is only .69, which makes them not very accurate for an individual diagnosis. It is therefore advisable that until more research is done in this promising area and a better standardized version of the mazes is published, that mazes should not be used to assess brain damage.

11. The Trail Making test consists of a sheet of paper with fifteen quarter-inch circles randomly scattered over it with each circle containing a number. The examinee's task is to connect the circles in numerical order as fast as possible. Davids, Goldberg, and Laufer (1957) gave this test to normal, cerebral palsied (who were considered brain damaged), and emotionally disturbed children matched in age, sex, and IQ. They found the Trail Making test correlated well (.60) with IQ. They also obtained a significant difference between all three groups with the normals doing best, then the emotionally disturbed, and finally the brain damaged. Camp (1965) gave the Trail Making test to a large group of nine- to fifteen-year-old children seen at a children's diagnostic center and published norms for this test by IQ

level. They were not, however, able to establish if this test does in fact distinguish brain-injured children from normals.

12. There are a few aphasia tests that can be used with children. One may use a test such as Goodglass and Kaplan's (1972) *Boston Diagnostic Aphasia Examination*. These aphasia tests consist of a set of tasks such as repeating words, observing pictures with absurdities, listening to and reading simple paragraphs, and writing some sentences. Although aphasia is considered a form of brain damage, Goldstein, Landeau, and Kleffner (1960) reported that thirty-two percent of a group of aphasics had no abnormal neurological signs, and sixty percent had no abnormal EEGs.

13. Another measure of brain damage is "psychometric scatter," which is frequently used by psychologists and ITPA specialists. Scatter refers to the discrepancy between subtests on a multisubtest scale such as the WISC, ITPA, or Detroit and is based on the notion that the more brain damaged a child, the more discrepancies in test scores. Berko (1955) has reviewed this concept and found retarded brain-injured children had much greater variability between the items than normals on the Stanford-Binet. Rutter, Graham, and Yule (1970) have more recently reviewed this literature and pointed out that one-quarter of the normal population have a discrepancy of fifteen IQ points, and studies on adults such as Denneril's cannot be used to generalize to children. They cite one careful study showing that only one-fourth of a large population of neurologically impaired children referred to a clinic had a large Verbal-Performance IQ discrepancy. In another study, sixteen to twenty children with a twenty-five point discrepancy had definite brain damage compared to ten to twenty children referred who did not have this discrepancy. In Rutter, Graham, and Yule's own study, fourteen percent of the children with brain disorders had a significant Verbal-Performance discrepancy as compared to the seven and one-half percent of the control group with no brain damage. To sum up, the classic psychometric scatter as measured on the WISC is not much more accurate than any of the other measures of brain damage.

14. The Aryes battery has been suggested as a tool to diagnose brain damage, but the reliabilities of the Aryes subtests are so close to chance level that no accurate diagnosis can be made.

A review of the above individual tests shows clearly that at present there is no single test that is accurate enough to reliably select the brain-damaged child from the healthy child. The unsuccessful attempts to find such a test have lead to the theory that brain functioning is so complex that only a battery of tests will ever diagnose brain damage. Einhart (et al., 1963), specifically, gave a whole battery of tests to preschool children and found that no single test was very accurate, but when he combined the scores of these tests he was able to identify seventy-five percent of the brain-injured children and misidentified only ten percent of the normal children. The use of a battery of tests makes a great deal of sense for several reasons (Haynes and Sells, 1963). A battery overcomes the problem of the reliability of a single short test and the problem that there are so many different types of brain damage affecting several different functions, which must be measured by a variety of tasks. The battery also reduces the chance that a normal subject will be classified as brain damaged because he performed poorly on one test due to some idiosyncracy of the tests.

One of the best examples of a test battery approach is the brain injury test first developed by Halstead (1947) and later refined by Reitan. The Halstead-Reitan battery consists of over twenty tests and takes many hours to administer. The success of this battery with adult patients is fairly impressive; in one study (Reitan, 1974a), this battery was given to 112 patients and it correctly predicted eighty-nine percent of the focal lesions, ninety-six percent of the diffuse lesions, and of the focal lesions sixty-six percent were correctly diagnosed in the proper quarter of the brain. This prediction was made by Reitan examining the test results, which proved superior to a statistical prediction based on test scores. In a study of brain-damaged children (Reitan, 1974b) using the WISC and over a dozen other tests, the WISC Full-Scale IQ was the test score that most accurately discriminated between brain-injured and normal children. Following this in order of accuracy was the WISC Verbal IQ, a speech making test, the trail-making test, the Seashore, finger tapping, and time sense, with the tactile test being so poor that about one-third of the children were misclassified. These findings are not so impressive, because the normal children had an IQ presumably around 100, and Reitan's brain-injured groups had a mean IQ of 78. This explains why the WISC Full-Scale was the most sensitive test and raises the question of whether any of Reitan's battery would be sensitive to the problems of LD children, who have by definition normal intelligence. In another investigation Reitan and Boll (1973) compared a control group (IQ = 110) with a MBD group of children with behavior problems (IQ = 107) and a LD group (IQ = 100). They report that there was no difference between the LD and MBD group on the twenty-one tests of the Reitan battery, except for Verbal and Full-Scale IQ; that there were no differences between the MBD and control group on all twenty-one variables except Verbal IQ. This would indicate again that the Reitan battery is not very effective for diagnosing MBD or LD in children.

In a summary of the complex field of tests for brain damage, Yates (1964) concluded that all the tests except the WISC were poorly standardized, that they all had inadequate norms, and the reliabilities of these tests were too low for an individual diagnosis. A decade later, one must arrive at the same conclusion. There are now a few more well-standardized tests of visual perception such as the Bender, Beery, Graham-Kendall, and some auditory discrimination tests such as the Wepman, Woodcock-Goldman-Fristoe, but these tests are used routinely in a learning disabilities diagnosis and can hardly be considered specific indicators of brain damage. It therefore does not seem feasible, as many have suggested, to graft the aphasia model onto a learning disability diagnosis when there is still no solid research that damage to a specific area of the brain will cause a specific processing deficit or that this deficit can be picked up consistently in a battery of psychometric tests. Pond (1961) has summarized, "In spite of the vast array of tests and observations available, many investigators are still forced to the same painful conclusion: There are. . .no absolutely unequivocal clinical signs, psychological tests or physiological tests that can prove a relationship between brain damage and any particular aspect of disturbed behavior."

Chapter VIII

The Motor Evaluation

A diagnosis should include a description of the child's motor coordination. Depending upon the clinician's orientation, the motor performance of the child may be treated as a significant clue to the cause of the child's learning disability. Students of Kephart, Barsh, Getman, Doman, and Delacato, and to a lesser extent Frostig, are likely to examine fine and gross coordination, because they believe that the root of all perceptual and academic problems lies in a motor dysfunction. Most others will tend to treat motor disabilities as relatively separate abilities with little relationship to learning problems.

Types of Motor Skills

There are many ways to divide body movement skills. The most precise way is to treat the problem on a muscle-by-muscle basis. This, however, becomes impractical because there are approximately 610 muscles in the body, and a simple motor sequence such as swinging a bat involves as many as twenty to thirty muscles. Muscles also work in groups with complex relationships to bones, ligaments, and tendons. For instance, when the child has to write his name, twenty-five muscles begin to move to adjust for the movements involved in making each letter.

The most commonly used method for classifying motor movements is to divide them into gross and fine motor movements. Fine motor coordination consists of those movements involving the hands, fingers, and wrist, while gross motor coordination involves all other movements as those in walking, running, skipping, and throwing a ball. Developmentally gross motor coordination precedes fine motor coordination: at age one, when the child is walking and can direct his hands to a desired location, he is still unable to grasp objects between his fingers and thumb or perform fine motor acts such as twisting tops off jars. A more complex system was developed by Guilford (1959), who was able to establish the various types of motor abilities by giving a large number of tasks to adults (mostly Air Force personnel) using factor analysis to isolate seven independent motor skills. The five gross motor types are:

1. General strength and overall muscle tone. For muscles to work efficiently they must be exercised. Any lack of muscle tone or general weakness in motor movements indicates that the individual has not used the muscles much or, more rarely, that the individual is suffering from some type of muscular disease. Neurologists are especially interested in muscle tone and strength, because if the brain does not constantly send signals to the muscles due to some form of brain damage, the muscles will lose their tone; muscle strength therefore can indicate brain damage. Muscle strength is usually measured with a dynamometer, which is a small spring device that is squeezed with the hand and reads the pressure of the grip in pounds.

2. General reaction time or the speed at which an individual will react to a stimulus with his whole body. Overall reaction time can be measured by having the child lie flat on the ground face down and having him stand up as fast as he can on a signal. The average seven-year-old should be able to get up to a standing position in less than two seconds. Reaction time can also be measured by observing how fast a child can do jumping jacks, run a short distance, or clap his hands. Finger tapping, where the child places his hand on the table and taps the table as rapidly as possible with his index finger, is the usual measure of fine motor reaction time. A normal child can do this rapidly with both hands with his nondominant hand being about ten percent slower.

3. Static balance, which is the ability to maintain one's balance while standing. The commonest measure of static balance is to have the child stand on one foot for as long as he can. The average boy can balance for ten seconds on the preferred foot by the time he is four-and-one-half to five years old. Girls can do this task on an average at five-and-one half to six years of age. The simpler task is with the child having his eyes open, and is easier because he has the added visual clue to help him maintain his balance. The average boy with his eyes closed can stand on his preferred foot for five seconds at the age of five-and-one-half to six, and girls can do this first at the age of six-and-one-half to seven. When giving this test, the child may move his hands to help him maintain balance, and children who cannot do this either have a problem with the vestibular system (the three semicircular canals in the inner ear) or have poor gross motor development.

4. Dynamic balance, which involves maintaining balance while one is moving. The traditional way to measure this is to have the child walk the balance beam — a two-by-four board with the child

walking on the four-inch side. It is ten feet long and a few inches above the ground. If a balance beam is not available, dynamic balance can be measured by having the child walk tandem by placing the heel of his foot in front of his other foot while walking on a strip of masking tape placed on the floor. The average four-and-one-half year old should be able to walk in this fashion across the room without any support, and at five-and-one-half he or she should be able to walk tandem backwards.

Cooke (1968) has given balancing tests to fourth, fifth, and sixth graders and found these balancing scores correlated .15 to .32 with the California Mental Maturity Test (an IQ test) and the Iowa Basic Skills test. Balance and basic language on the Iowa correlated .32 in the fourth grade. Walking the balance beam has been carefully standardized by Seashore (1947), who showed this test has a reliability in the .80s if three trials are given. This skill increases gradually from five-and-one-half to eleven-and-one-half when the performance levels off. Seashore's study offers norms for the ages of five to eighteen. Another study (Espenshade and Eckert, 1967, p. 163) found a correlation of .34 between the score obtained walking the balance beam (dynamic balance) and the length of time standing on the one-inch beam (static balance).

Hopping is another task that involves dynamic balance and the four-and-one-half year old should be able to hop on one foot across the room. Dynamic balance for fine coordination is measured by having the child put one dot in a series of circles that are only one-eighth inch in diameter.

5. Gross body coordination, often called general agility, which is how the child moves when he is walking, sitting, and generally moving about. Gross motor coordination can be informally observed by watching the child play or in the standard physical education exercises of timed jumping jacks, running, and throwing and catching a ball. Fine motor coordination is simply hand and finger dexterity and can be assessed by having the child copy designs, draw a line between two parallel lines placed one-fourth inch apart without touching either line. Fine motor coordination is usually a major concern to teachers, because it is involved in handwriting.

The above classification system is only a rough way of dividing motor skills so that they can be readily described by the clinician. In actual fact, one finds that many motor activities involve a combination of the above skills, specifically, when the child throws a ball he uses static balance to stand, dynamic balance to shift his weight to the appropriate foot, gross motor coordination to move his arms back, fine motor coordination to hold the ball correctly, and hand-eye coordination to hit the target. The normal child is able to coordinate all these separate abilities into a single smooth act so that one cannot tell where one type of skill begins and another ends. Children with motor dysfunctions, however, will do poorly in some or all of the above areas, and their throwing will appear to be jerky and clumsy. Besides the six types of motor acts there are also various basic components to a motor act.

Components of Motor Acts

A child's perceptual skills are very highly developed when compared to motoric skills; a child only a few months old can see as well as an adult, possesses most of the visual perceptual skills of size and form constancy, visual discrimination, depth perception, and the like (Reese and Lipsitt, 1970), but can barely grasp objects at seven months, does not walk until a year, and cannot throw a ball until two years of age. For convenience a motor skill in a diagnosis is usually broken into four components. The motor performance of older children is more difficult to analyze, because the movement is smoothly coordinated and one part blends into another. With younger children or children with motor dysfunctions the components can often readily be seen. Below is an example of a motor sequence of a nine-month-old child who scored in the average range on an infant intelligence scale.

At the age of nine months Demetrius had the opportunity to observe his parents plugging and unplugging the vacuum cleaner. One day when he was playing with the cleaner, he came across the loose plug. He grabbed it and began crawling across the floor to the nearest outlet. On his way across the room he encountered a set of pillows, and without hesitating scrambled over the pillows until he came to the wall with the plug. He then began pushing the plug into the bare wall missing the socket by as much as a foot. This continued for a while until he caught sight of the outlet again. He then placed his left hand on the outlet (covering up the holes) and tried to push the socket into the outlet with his right hand. He made six or seven unsuccessful attempts and then began crying in frustration.

First, there is a motor goal or what the person decides to do. In the example, the baby saw the plug and the wall socket, and his motor plan was to put the plug in the socket. He then began scrambling across the pillows without any thought of which muscles to move. To carry out the motor goal one must know how to do the act and the knowledge of how to move the muscles to perform the appropriate act, which is called the motor plan. In the above example, the infant was unable to put the plug in the two holes because he did not have a motor plan, which was illustrated by his attempts to plug in the plug with the left hand covering the outlet. In patients with cerebral disease, such as that caused by a stroke, one can observe a striking example of an individual with a motor goal who loses his motor plan when the patient will suddenly be unable to light a cigarette or brush his teeth anymore. Third, there is motor coordination or the actual movement once the individual has the correct motor plan. In the example, the infant after he realized he must put the plug in the holes, began pushing the plug into the wall, missing the holes by a few inches each time. He knew what to do, but his muscles were not responding in the desired way. Finally, there is motor strength to perform the act. Some children cannot do handstands or throw a large medicine ball, because they are not strong enough.

The Measurement of Gross Motor Skills

Compared to the measurement of reading or intelligence, there is very little published on the measurement of motor skills. One reason for this is that motor skills are relatively independent skills, so that the nineteen different motor skills of the Purdue Motor Test correlated all below .30 (Aryres, 1965), which is very close to chance level. This means that there is not any apparent overall gross motor ability, and a measure of motor proficiency using one skill, such as ball throwing, will yield an entirely different result if another skill, such as skipping, is used as the task of measuring gross motor proficiency. This independence of motor abilities also means that a child trained in one skill will probably not realize any improvement in another motor skill.

The four commonly used methods for evaluating motor skills are: estimating performance by observing the child play, comparing his motor skills on tasks with a normative chart, using informal tests of motor skills, or using a standardized test of motor performance. When observing the child informally, one should look for the symptoms mentioned in the neurological examination. Kephart (1960) has suggested examining the following seven attributes of motor skills:

1. Whether the midline is crossed, with the midline being an imaginary line splitting the right and left sides of the body. This plane extends out in front of the individual and "crossing the midline" is the ability to move one's hands and arms across this line without any significant deviation in movement. Normal children under eight months of age will not cross the midline when playing with an object; when moving an object from one side to the other, they will change

hands at the midline. Kephart measures crossing the midline in school age children by placing two "X"s on the blackboard on either side of the standing child. He is then given a piece of chalk and asked to connect the "X"s. If the line the child has drawn has any jumps or significant deviations in the line in the middle, it is taken as evidence of difficulty in crossing the midline. Midline difficulties may also be examined by having the child follow an object with his eyes that crosses the midline. The eyes of children with midline difficulties will deviate while passing this point.

2. The smoothness of movement is also important. The muscular system is organized so that each muscle is opposed by another muscle, with one muscle contracting when its opposite relaxes. A normal child will have good control of these opposing pairs, and his movements will thus be smooth and flowing. Almost all children have had extensive experience with running, jumping, hopping, and balancing by the time they enter school and should be able to perform these activities in a coordinated manner. They should also be able to perform them with a grace and rhythm. Any real jerkiness would indicate a motor dysfunction and, if severe, a neurological examination should be considered.

3. A normal child will have approximately the same gross motor dexterity in his right side as his left. Any significant deviation of coordination of body sides would indicate that there might be brain damage in the opposite hemisphere of the brain.

Consistency of handedness exists between and within motor acts. Children who switch hands while doing something so that they appear right-handed one minute and left the next have no firmly established handedness. This in children over four or five is often (unless the person is truly ambidextrous) a sign of immature motor development. The switching of hands in the middle of a task is rather unusual and indicates a significant confusion of handedness. Usually it is remediated only if it interferes with the child's work. The child is given a complete laterality evaluation, which decides which hand he or she should use.

5. Continuity exists between a visual-motor task and a simple motor task not requiring vision. It has been observed that children under the age of six rely on their vision not only to guide motor behavior, but also to control it. For example, a four-year-old often cannot stand on one foot when his eyes are closed, but can do so with open eyes. Similarly in handwriting, most children can begin a motor pattern such as writing a string of cursive "b"s and after a few can continue the motor pattern without having to look at their writing.

Older children can continue the pattern with their eyes closed with little difficulty. Children of school age should be able to write letters and words on the board with their eyes closed, because they have the motor plan. Children behind in motor development with inadequate motor plans will have to use their eyes to do these activities.

6. Impulsivity of motor control suggests that the overall control of the energy in motor movement is not well established. Children who are hyperactive are classic examples of impulsivity, because their energy spills out in such actions as fidgeting, wandering around, and in the making of large explosive-like movements rather than fine well-coordinated movements.

7. One should always make the distinction between splinter skills, which are autonomous motor patterns developed as a result of a great deal of practice, and motor skills that are an integral part of the individual's overall functioning.

Another motor phenomenon described by Cratty and Martin (1969) to be looked for is motor overflow. When a child below the age of six is asked to do a task with one hand, he can frequently be observed moving his other hand while the task is being performed. This is a motor immaturity and apparently the brain has not yet completely differentiated both sides of the body. Children over six or seven should show little no overflow. The informal observation of a child's motor functioning then involves recording what motor activities he can and cannot perform, some statement about motor strength, and a careful observation for the above seven phenomena.

The second way to evaluate motor abilities is to use a normative chart. These charts must, however, be accepted cautiously, because they are usually based on small samples (Gesell's norms had less than forty children) that often come from the unrepresentative population of college professor's and graduate student's children. Furthermore, "average age" at which the child is able to perform the task varies from a criterion for passing from fifty percent to ninety percent of the children. A fairly representative normative chart appears in *Figure 17,* which was derived from the norms presented in Cratty and Martin's excellent book, *Perceptual-Motor Efficiency in Children* (1969). These norms were derived from the research of ten experimental studies with the norms for less than one year of age omitted, because children of this age should be examined by a pediatrician.

Figure 17
Norms For Gross Motor Skills By Skill Areas

Agility and Coordination	Motor Speed	Rhythm	Static Balance	Dynamic Balance	Motor Strength
Kicks ball (2 yr.)	Gets up from lying on back in 1.5 sec. (7 yr.)	Consistent walking rhythm (2 yr.)	Stands alone (1.1 yr.)	Walks alone (1.1 yr.)	Pushes body up (2.5 yr.)
Throws ball overhand (2 yr.)	50 yd. dash in 8.5 sec. (10 yr.)	Jumps in place (2.5 yr.)	Raises one foot (1.1 yr.)	Walks backwards (1.5 yr.)	Catches 16'' ball (4 yr.)
Double jump takeoff (2 yr.)		Hops 3L then 3R pattern (7.5 yr.)	Stands on one foot one sec. (2.5 yr.)	Walks up steps (1.9 yr.)	Throws 16'' ball (4 yr.)
Stops a rolling ball (2.5 yr.)		Hops R-L-R-L pattern (8 yr.)	Stands on one foot five sec. (3.8 yr.)	Kicks ball forward (1.9 yr.)	Does 20 situps (10 yr.)
Jumps in place (2.5 yr.)		Jumps and hops on one foot (8 yr.)	Stands on one foot ten sec. (5 yr.)	Walks sideways, backwards (2 yr.)	Throws softball 50 ft. (F=10 yr.)
Broad jumps (3 yr.)		Opens and closes hand alternately (10.5 yr.)	Balances on one foot with arms folded (4.5 to 6 yr.)	Walks on tiptoes (2 yr.)	Throws softball 80 feet (M=10 yr.)
Jumps three steps (4 yr.)		Taps both feet and fingers on table simultaneously (11.5 yr.)	Balances on one foot with eyes closed (7 yr.)	Walks on balance beam (3 yr.)	Does 20 modified pull-ups (M=10.5 yr.)
Runs, stops, starts and turns (4 yr.)		Taps feet while making circles with fingers (12.5 yr.)	Crouches on tiptoe (6.5 to 7 yr.)	Hops on one foot (4 yr.)	Does 1 modified pull-up (F=10.5 yr.)
Jumps 10'' (4.5 yr.)			Stands on one foot tiptoe (14 yr.)		Does 3 modified pull-ups (F=14.5 yr.)
Catches bounced ball (5 yr.)				Walks heel-to-toe (4.5 yr.)	
Arm action proper in running (5 yr.)				Walks heel-to-toe backwards (5.5) yr.)	
Jumps using arm movements (5 yr.)					

Agility and Coordination

Throws ball with proper movement (7 yr.)

Jumps over 16" high (9 yr.)

Catches tennis ball with one hand (9.5 yr.)

Throws tennis ball 8 feet and hits 10" target (M = 10 yr.) (F = 14 yr.)

Key:
yr. = years old
M = for males
F = for females
R = right
L = left

The third way to evaluate a child's motor performance is to rely upon an informal survey test of motor development. There are a number of tests of this nature, the Purdue Perceptual-Motor Abilities Test being the most popular in this field. The Purdue has been closely associated with Kephart's theory of development and was standardized by Roach. The test consists of eleven subtests scored on a four-point rating scale. For example, when the child walks the balance beam he receives four points if he "walks easily," three points if "occasional difficulty but reagains balance," two points if the child steps off the beam once, and one point if he is "off balance" over one-fourth of the time. The norms for this test are based on fifty students each in grades one to four. There are some apparent mistakes in the reporting of the norms, because the reported mean for walking the balance beam is 8.90 in first, 9.74 in second, 9.04 in third, and 10.42 in fourth grade, so that one must conclude that third graders have poorer balance than second graders. In spite of this, Meier (1971) gave the Purdue to LD and normal students and concluded there was no difference between these groups on the Purdue. Given the inadequacy of the norms and scoring, one must consider this test simply an informal survey.

Standardized Gross Motor Tests

The standardized tests of gross motor ability are mostly tests used in physical education and discussions of them appear mostly in P.E. Journals (notably, *The Research Quarterly*). To review all these tests would be outside the scope of this book, but some major tests having norms for elementary children will be briefly reviewed.

Rogers (1925) pioneered the measurement of gross motor strength by devising the Physical Capacity Tests derived by measuring lung capacity (on a spirometer), hand grip (on a manometer), strength in the back-lift and leg-lift (on a dynameter), and the number of pull-ups and dips. Franklin and Lehsten (1948) devised the Indiana Physical Fitness Tests normed on fourth through eighth grades yielding a score that is the sum of the child's performance on push-ups, squat thrusts in twenty seconds, straddle chins, and vertical jumps. The Indiana is much more manageable than Roger's tests and can be used to get a general idea of the motor strength and gross motor coordination of a child.

In 1954 Krauss and Hirschland created quite a stir by comparing muscular strength of elementary school children in Austria, Italy, Switzerland, and the United States. Their test of minimal muscular fitness, consisting of situps, leg lifted while lying down, and touching toes, was passed by at least ninety-two percent of the European children, and only forty-two percent of the American children. This test consists of six items that do not correlate with hand grip strength and has a reliability of .95. Norms and reliabilities for this test exist for the ages six through twelve (Phillips, et al, 1955).

The most widely used test of physical fitness is the AAHPER Youth Fitness Tests (AAHPER, 1958), which was standardized on 8,500 children in the fifth through twelfth grades. This test has extensive norms for pull-ups, shuttle-run, sit-ups, standing broad jump, softball throw, fifty-yard dash, and 600-yard run-walk. Unfortunately, this test has no norms for children younger than ten years of age and therefore is not very valuable in an LD diagnosis of younger children.

More recently, Cratty (1969) has designed a "Six-Category Gross Motor Test," normed on children between the ages of four and eleven. The six areas covered are body orientation, gross coordination, locomotor ability, balance, ball throwing, and ball tracking.

Cratty's test can be precisely defined, but has the drawback that it was standardized on only twenty children per age level and has no published retest reliabilities.

Another excellent source of norms for how well boys and girls between the ages of six and sixteen do on the isometric strength, running the thirty- and sixty-yard dash, horizontal jump, broad jump, softball throw, and brace test (a twenty-task test of motor coordination) can be found in Espanshade and Eckert's book, *Motor Development* (1967). Since these tasks correlate so poorly with each other, there simply is no standard measure of gross motor skill. These authors also include the norms of the AAHPER Youth Fitness tests to show the vast improvement in the overall performance of American children from 1958 to 1965, suggesting that practice and increased motivation may greatly influence a child's fitness.

For younger children the Denver Developmental Screening Test can be used as a measure of gross motor development. This test contains thirty gross motor items covering the age range of birth to six years of age. The Denver was normed on over one thousand children and does not require any special equipment. The gross motor test items, however, have fairly low retest reliabilities and should not be used for anything except for a screening test.

As the above review of standardized gross motor tests suggests, there are practically no good motor tests for the elementary school aged child. There is, however, one well-standardized test, the Lincoln-Oseretsky Motor Development Scale, which measures gross (and a number of fine) motor skills in children aged six to fourteen. The Oseretsky test was originally developed in Holland and was translated into English by Doll in 1946 who kept the European norms. Since then the test has been updated and restandardized on U.S. children (Sloan, 1955). The Lincoln-Oseretsky includes thirty-six items covering such diverse areas as jumping over a rope, winding a thread on a spool, balancing a rod on one's finger, jumping and turning about, tapping one's feet alternately as fast as possible, and balancing on tip-toe. These items are scored in terms of a total score with a split half reliability of .82 to .94. The Lincoln-Oseretsky is, therefore, recommended in a motor assessment of elementary children. Vandenberg (1964) in a factor analytic study found the items correlated very minimally with each other in a large sample of children, indicating that a child scoring low in one item would not usually score low on another item. Only one major factor was derived composed of nine mostly timed items requiring the rapid use of both hands. A much smaller factor composed of five tasks involving moving alternatively or simultaneously both sides of the body was also derived. All the other items did not form clear factors, suggesting that besides manual dexterity and body side integration, the gross motor skills do not form nice factors as suggested by Guilford — at least not for normal elementary age children. Pyfer and Carlson (1972) did not obtain any significant differences between LD and normal children on the Lincoln-Oseretsky, while Lewis, Bell, and Anderson (1970) did. Until more studies are done, the usefulness of the Lincoln-Oseretsky cannot be determined.

Fine Motor Development

Fine motor development refers to the use of the small muscles in the fingers and the hand. The causes for fine motor disabilities are many: there may be a disease of the muscles, the nerves that innervate the muscles may be damaged, the motor areas of the brain controlling hand and finger movements may be impaired, the child may have a maturational lag in the fine motor muscle development, or the muscles may be weak and uncoordinated because of lack of use.

There are twelve muscles located in the forearm innervated by the median, lateral, and ulnar nerves. Of these, only two move the forearm and the rest move the hand or the fingers. The hand itself has thirteen more muscles that control hand and finger movements. The physician by having the patient move his fingers in certain directions can determine which muscles or nerves are not functioning properly and whether the incoordination is due to damage to a particular muscle or one of the nerves. Damage to a specific muscle group or nerve is rare among LD children. The most common fine motor dysfunction among LD children is the result of incoordination of complex muscle movements.

When evaluating a fine motor problem, one should try first to test the child's coordination using a task that requires little or no visual ability. One such "pure" fine motor task is the finger opposition task. A child by the first grade would be able to touch his thumb and second finger, thumb and third finger, thumb and fourth finger, thumb and fifth finger in a period of ten seconds. The examiner demonstrates it with the child copying with his eyes open and then with his eyes closed. Surprisingly, the average child cannot do this task with his eyes closed until he is nine years old. Many books recommend observing for "motor spillover" in the other hand when doing this and other fine motor tasks. Motor spillover, or overflow, is the movement of the other hand when the dominant hand is peforming some complicated act. Many teachers have noticed that immature children and some older LD children will often have spillover with their tongues, characterized by making faces and moving the tongue around while doing a task. Forrest (1967), however, has compared normal and LD children and found no differences between these groups in the amount of overflow movements. A more precise test of overflow movements (sometimes also called inhibitory movements, because they involve inhibition of the contralateral muscle system) can be found in Fog and Fog's (1963) article on cerebral inhibition. This spillover is believed to occur because the neurological systems controlling hand movements have not completely matured in young children. After the age of about eight, however, there should be no spillover in fine motor movements.

A second form of fine motor coordination is hand-eye coordination, which comprises the skills to observe something and then move the hand in the direction indicated by the visual information. Rarely is anything done completely in the dark, so that most fine motor activities are actually hand-eye coordination tasks. When a child cannot perform a particular hand-eye coordination task, one must then decide whether this is due to (a) faulty visual perception (such as astigmatism), (b) improper integration of the visual image and motor movement (as experienced writing while using a mirror), (c) a lack of a motor plan (as occurs when a five-year-old tries to draw a diamond), or (d) poor muscle coordination. The two-year-old can only stack a few blocks on top of each other and cannot copy even the simplest square or triangle or draw a recognizable figure. This discrepancy between visual perception and motor coordination continues throughout the rest of the child's life. Even adults can tell the difference between very complicated drawings, but when handed a pencil will not be able to copy either figure unless they are a skilled artist.

The diagnosis of hand-eye coordination should begin with material requiring few motor plans. One of the easiest ways to measure this is to draw a "road" on a piece of paper and place the lines one-quarter or one-eighth inch apart. The child cannot lift his pencil or erase when he draws on the road and is counted off if he touches the sides.

There are several standardized tests of hand-eye coordination. The Hand-Eye Coordination subtest of the Developmental Test of Visual Perception by Frostig is a "road" test, but it contains only twelve items with a very low reliability. The Detroit has a Motor Speed and Precision subtest consisting of 371 circles covering an entire page. The circles at the beginning are one-half inch in diameter, and as the circles progress, they gradually shrink to one-eighth inch in diameter. The child's task is to put a cross or check mark in each circle without touching the edges. This test has norms for five to eighteen years of age, but no reliability data is available for this subtest. The author would guess, however, based on the large number of items and the fact that performance on motor tests is in general very consistent, that this test is a very reliable measure of pure hand-eye coordination.

The Southern California Test of Hand-Eye Coordination by Aryes consists of a road one-fourth inch wide. This test has been shown to be valid, to have fairly good norms, and is extremely reliable. In a study of one hundred LD children, Aryes (1965) obtained correlations between the motor test with the following measures: copying designs (.55), standing on one foot with eyes open (.47), standing on one foot eyes closed (.35), the Frostig Hand-Eye Coordination subtest (.57), right-left discrimination ability (.35), threading a grommet on a wire (.70), winding a string on a spool (.55), tapping out patterns (.61), distractibility and hyperactivity (.41), and chronological age (.08). With a group of normal children, these correlations were much lower with almost all being nonsignificant. Her investigation indicates that when a child has a significant perceptual problem or motor dysfunction, he is likely to have a much higher intercorrelation between these motor skills than a normal child.

Children who perform poorly on a hand-eye coordination test that requires a limited motor plan may have a visual problem or little experience with pencil and paper or a definite maturational lag in fine motor coordination. A child who does poorly on these hand-eye tests should be given the identical test using the other hand. There are occasional cases where children have begun using one hand when they are actually better with the other hand (Orton, 1937).

Another measure of fine motor coordination involves the copying of geometric designs or figures. Design copying involves a fair amount of intellectual ability as was dramatically illustrated by Slupinski (1955), who discovered that all the mentally retarded adults in his English institution with IQs below 38 were unable to copy a diamond, while all the adults with IQs above 57 could copy the diamond. Children with normal intelligence are able to visually discriminate between almost all types of geometric figures at the age of two, but normally a child cannot copy a circle until the age of three, a cross at the age of four, a square at five, a triangle at six, and a diamond at seven. The inability to copy more complicated designs is not a matter of visual perception or motor coordination, but one of not having the correct motor plan. This is hard for an adult to realize, but consider the copying of a diamond. To construct a diamond one must keep in mind there are only four lines, that the lines must be of equal length, that there are four imaginary corners or vertices to visualize, that when connecting these vertices one must slant the line at about 140 degrees, stop at the imaginary vertices, then slant the line to about 230 degrees, etc. A normal five-year-old simply cannot keep all these elements straight while copying the figure.

Is design copying a good measure of fine motor coordination if the child's mental age is taken into consideration? Aryes (1965) gave the design copying task and the Aryes Motor accuracy test to one hundred children with learning disabilities and fifty normal children and obtained a correlation of .24 between these measures for normal children and .54 for LD children. Clearly, design copying and fine motor skills were closely related in LD children, but not so much with normal children. In another extensive study, Townsend (1951) used a sample of 287 children aged six to nine years of age. Townsend administered an intelligence test (the Kuhlman-Anderson), seventeen figures which had to be copied (nine of them being the Bender-Gestalt), a visual discrimination task requiring the matching of thirty meaningless geometric forms, a fine motor tapping task in which the child had to tap as fast as he could, a motor coordination task involving putting marbles in small holes in a limited amount of time, a cancelling task in which the child must turn vertical dashes into plus signs. He obtained very good reliabilities for these tests and the experiment produced correlations between copying the designs and visual discrimination of .60, with motor ability of .52, with chronological age of .34, and with mental age (intelligence) of .58. These correlations would suggest visual perception, motor achievement, and intelligence are all related. However, when the crucial factor of intelligence was statistically removed, the correlation between copying and visual discrimination was .42, while the correlation between copying and motor ability was only .19, barely above chance level. Even though the motor tests were all fine motor tasks, the intercorrelations among these tests were only in the .30s.

Fine motor coordination can also be measured by the Lincoln-Oseretsky tasks of finger-thumb opposition, tapping of fingers and pencils, rapidly tapping right thumb with left index finger, making dots for fifteen seconds, making a ball with cigarette paper, putting matchsticks in a box and drawing perpendicular lines. In Vandenberg's factor analysis (1964) these fine motor tasks correlated well with each other, unlike the gross motor factors that did not seem to be related to each other. Bryant (1964) gave the Lincoln-Oseretsky to thirty-two LD boys and found that two-thirds of the LD children scored below the norms. A pediatric neurologist also examined these boys and found only one-third of them showed motor deficiencies on the standard neurological tests of motor impairment. Bryant then suggested that the Lincoln-Oseretsky might be more sensitive than informal neurological tests. Bryant's study, however, was done on a clinic population and when Forrest tried to replicate this study using a LD population in the schools, he did not obtain a difference.

In general, the research shows very low intercorrelations between various motor tasks. For example, Buxton (1938) correlated the performance on thirteen motor tests consisting of such tasks as pushing a stylus in a hole, tapping various cubes successively, packing blocks in a small box, tapping two bars alternatively with a stylus, and turning a handle, and found the average correlation to be .15, which is close to zero.

Apraxia

One of the more commonly encountered fine motor disorders is apraxia, which is the inability to form motor plans for precise and coordinated movements. There is oral apraxia, which is the inability to make all the lip and tongue movements to produce clear speech. These children, besides having slurred and slushy speech, cannot move their tongue from right to left or upwards to "touch the nose." One other test is to have the child say "pit ti ka" three times very fast, which can only be successfully accomplished if the child moves all his oral structures in a coordinated manner. Apraxia may extend to the eyes, and the child may be unable to close his eyes on command, or to move his eyes smoothly while following an object. The most common form of apraxia, however, is the child's inability to copy figures or form letters with any preciseness. Traditionally, hand apraxia is measured by neurologists having the patient copy a cross, a square, triangle, diamond, or a simple house with matchsticks. A more standardized method is to give the Beery Visual-Motor Integration test, which yields a visual motor copying age. Apraxia could then be defined as existing in an individual who is two or more standard deviations below on this task. The child with apraxia is practically unable to print the alphabet, and copying letters and words is so laborious because he must conscientiously think of each individual movement. Neurologists (Denny-Brown, 1958) also have a whole host of other apraxias, such as ideational apraxia (where the subject cannot pretend to do a motor sequence such as pouring water into an imaginary glass), apraxia of dressing (where the subject cannot dress himself), etc., which will not be discussed, because they involve spatial ability and other higher order concepts.

By carefully observing how a child copies designs or writes the alphabet one can get an idea of the child's problems. The child's grip on the pencil should be observed, whether he has the ability to make diagonals and other letter forms; whether his hand is shaking and shows other spasticity. From this one can separate poor coordination from the inability to make motor plans. In addition, the child can be given a motor-free visual perception test (such as the Detroit Motor-Free Perceptual Test), and this can be compared to a copying task to see if the disability is perceptual or the result of apraxia.

It has been the author's experience that most apraxic and clumsy children are usually between five and eight years of age, and by the age of eight almost all of these children outgrow these symptoms. It seems that mild apraxia and excessive clumsiness and poor coordination are some of the symptoms most often outgrown.

Handwriting

Handwriting is by far the most important fine motor skill in school. The research in handwriting was done to a large extent in the early 1920s, preceded by Gesell's study in 1906. Gesell was able to show that handwriting correlated well with IQ and with motor dexterity as judged on the child's ability to draw, cut, etc. Girls also had better handwriting than boys in this study. Within the next five years three scales were developed to measure handwriting, including the Aryes scale which is still used. Freeman (1914) investigated the speed and style of cursive writing and reported: (a) larger handwriting can be done faster, (b) that the beginning and ending letters of a word take much more time to form than the middle letters, (c) that letters requiring turns are more slowly completed, and this is the result of a perceptual decision, not just some mechanical factor, e.g., the combining of the parts of the letter, (d) there is no uniform rule of whether upward or downward strokes are faster, (e) the pressure in writing a letter is strongest at the beginning and end of a letter, (f) usually, but not always, downstrokes lead to greater pressure, (g) the way the pencil is held influences the pressure of the strokes, (h) children in constrast to adults have a more uniform rate of speed — adults move faster on straight lines and slow down more for curves, (i) children write with less pressure than adults. The results lead to the conclusion that beginning writers do not begin by learning individual strokes and then chain these together to make letters, but rather begin trying to make a whole letter, and as they become proficient, they increase the movement of the straight lines of the letters.

Another aspect of writing is the reversals of letters so common in first and second grade. Fildes (1923) noted that reversals of letters are common at this age and writing whole words in mirror writing is rare. One practically never finds a child who consistently writes in mirror writing, although it is much more common in left-hand children. Fildes did a set of seven experiments investigating reversals and found basically that: (a) reversals occur in copying and writing from memory, (b) letters and figures are often grasped as wholes, but without the extra cue of their position in space, (c) merely changing hands does not alter the number of reversals, and (d) when the child has learned to copy figures using right-hand movements (e.g., clockwise in drawing a circle), the child will continue this right-hand movement when asked to use his left hand.

Measures of Handwriting

As may be seen, the research and measurement of handwriting has not been oriented toward diagnosing the problems of LD children. A good diagnostician should not only look at the product, but also watch and time the child while he writes. Below are some causes of poor handwriting and their diagnostic significance.

1. The hand may be stiff and rigid. This could be due to emotional tenseness or the inability to hold the pencil properly. Children with mild agraphia or perceptual problems may also be tense, because they know they cannot do the task well.

2. The pencil slips out of the hand or is grasped with all fingers. This may be due to finger agnosia, and the child cannot feel when the pencil is slipping out of his hand.

3. The pencil is held incorrectly. This rarely leads to bad handwriting. Every teacher knows children with unusual ways of holding the pencil who write perfectly well.

4. The child writes with the opposite hand equally well. The child could be ambidextrous, or he has been forced to write with the wrong hand.

5. The child cannot copy accurately from the blackboard. This is almost always due to perceptual problems, although occasionally it may be due to poor motor control of the eyes. One should observe the child tracking visually.

6. Writing is large and malformed even when copying. The child's fine motor coordination is probably poor. He should have equal problems with, say, manipulating toothpicks or matchsticks.

7. The child is left handed and handwriting is poor or slant is wrong. The paper should slant in the same direction as the forearm and occasionally left-handers will slant their paper in the wrong direction.

8. Handwriting is perfect, but extremely slow. This is often a perfectionistic child or one who is afraid to do anything new. Sometimes it is a residual of a child who initially had great difficulty learning to write and developed a slow, deliberate pattern.

Intelligence, Academic Achievement, and Motor Skills

From the earliest days of special education there has been speculation that intelligence and academic skills grow out of motor patterns. Itard (1803, 1962) the first author to write a book on the education of the retarded child, hypothesized that every child must have certain sensory motor experiences such as touching, smelling, and tasting objects before he could learn more abstract concepts such as reading. Seguine (1868), often referred to as the "father of special education," took Itard's idea and developed it into a method of teaching exceptional children. For Seguine the evaluation of sensory and motor skills was essential before any remediation could begin. If the child did poorly academically, Seguin strongly recommended teaching motor activities first. <u>This practice of teaching primarily through sensori-motor experiences was also the keystone to the Montessori method of teaching.</u> Newall Kephart is usually credited with introducing the sensori-motor theory into the field of learning disabilities.

Kephart's theory, already discussed in Chapter IV, is explained clearly in his book, *The Slow Learner in the Classroom,* which first appeared in 1960. Kephart believes:

> In educating the slow learner, the problem is to determine where in the course of development the child has broken down and, through teaching and/or therapeutic procedures, restore the course of development. . . . When development is only *delayed* and is not complicated by the disruption resulting from neurological disturbance, the teaching problem is to supply experiences which will enhance development. . . .when development is *disrupted*, the child has either skipped a stage in development or one or more of the stages has been incompletely achieved. His behavior reflects the disruption. He is very good in some tasks, very poor in others. He reads difficult words and then stumbles over an easy one or one he has just read correctly in the line above. . . .He takes the most devious route to solve the problem or, on the other hand, he responds to a single stimulus as though it were all there was (Kephart, 1971, pp. 42-44).

Kephart's theory was carried a step further by Getman, Doman, and Delacato, who developed elaborate lists of the motor stages. Getman (1962) in his flamboyant book, *How to Develop Your Child's Intelligence*, postulated the child must go through five motor stages completely in order to develop normal academic and intellectual abilities. Glen Doman, of the Doman-Delacato System, specified the developmental motor stages in even greater detail, he lists at least fifty motor steps a child must go through in order to achieve normal academic ability. To review all these stages of development would be outside the scope of this book, but the theory of Doman is essentially that of Getman and Kephart.

The significance of these motor theories in a diagnosis is great. If Kephart, Getman, and Doman are correct, then the diagnosis of learning disabilities should be almost completely carried out with motor tests. Also, the diagnosis of an academic problem should lie not in analyzing the child's errors in reading and writing, but in trying to establish which stage of development the child missed.

The research in motor development has shown first of all that the correlation between intelligence and motor ability is very low for normal children. Correlations between IQ scores and motor proficiency tests are usually below .30 and often reach chance level. Singer and Brink (1967) obtained only a correlation of .27 with a nonverbal and .13 with a verbal intelligence test and a design copying task in third and fourth graders. Anderson (1939) has reviewed the relationship of the child's performance on infant tests, which are measures mostly of sensori-motor integration and later intelligence and found these two measures do not correlate with each other. Again this can be interpreted that sensori-motor development is probably not a precursors to higher intellectual functions.

With academic abilities and motor skills there is a similar low correlation for children with normal intelligence. Common sense would support this — we all know individuals who are clumsy and have poor motor abilities, but who are excellent in academic areas, and we also know very well-coordinated individuals who do poorly academically. Most of the research (Robbins and Glass, 1969) that has focused on whether motor training will improve academic or intellectual ability in children has revolved around the efficacy of the Doman-Delacato method. O'Donnell and Eisenson (1969), for example, gave Doman-Delacato exercises to poor readers aged seven to ten years old for thirty minutes a day for twenty weeks. All children were doing poorly academically, had at least normal intelligence, and most showed uncertain laterality. In spite of the extensive motor exercises, these LD children did no better than the control group on the Gray Oral Reading Test, the Stanford Achievement Test, or the Developmental Test of Visual-Motor Integration (a design copying test). Another line of evidence often mentioned in connection with motor abilities is that cerebral palsy children, who from birth have poor or no control over their leg and hand muscles and therefore have not been able to go through any of the motor stages, may still exhibit average or superior intellectual and academic abilities. One example is a man in England who has never been able to move any of his limbs and has never attended school, but has recently written a full-length novel typed entirely using the big toe of his left foot!

Laterality and Dominance

Whether an individual is left or right handed has been a preoccupation in our culture for many centuries. Left handedness has been mentioned in Homer and the Bible and has almost always been associated with deviousness or evil (Subirana, 1964). The Latin word for left is *sinister* from which we get the word sinister; the Latin word for right is *dexter* from which we get dexterity. This is incidentally not only a Western notion, for in the Far East the "left-handed path" in religion refers roughly to the Western equivalent of witchcraft. About eleven percent of the population is left handed (Enstrom, 1968) and about one to two percent is truly ambidextrous, that is equally skillful with both hands. Hecaen and Ajuriaguera (1964) have shown that left handedness follows the laws of Mendelian genetics very closely. Forty-two percent of all left-handed children had two parents who were left handed, while only seventeen percent of the lefties had one parent who was left handed. Only two percent of left-handed children came from a right-handed mother and father, which indicates rather strongly that left handedness is due to a single recessive gene. Levy and Reid (1976) have also made the observation that left (or right) handers who "hook," that is twist, the wrist over and hold the hand on top of the pencil behave differently than those who do not, and this may be related to lateralization of hemispheres of the brain.

When Broca made his discovery in 1865 that aphasia was the result of brain damage only on the left side of the brain with his right-handed patients, he assumed that the speech area lay in the right hemisphere of left-handed individuals. This was not an unreasonable assumption in view of the fact that the right side of the brain controls the left side of the body and vice versa. It was, however, proven wrong after World War II when Wada developed the sodium amytal test to determine the location of the speech area (Lansdell, 1964). When sodium amytal is injected into the left carotid artery in the neck, which runs from the heart to the left hemisphere of the brain and then to the right hemisphere, it numbs the left hemisphere first and after a few minutes the right hemisphere. Persons with the speech area in the left hemisphere then lose their ability to speak coherently a few seconds after the injection, while right hemisphere individuals lose the ability after several minutes. The Wada experiments demonstrated about ninety-seven percent of all persons have their speech area in the left hemisphere regardless of whether the person is right or left handed. There is also a fair amount of evidence that ambidextrous and some left-handed individuals have their speech area located in both hemispheres (Subirana, 1964).

Dominance and laterality are terms that are easily confused. Before World War II the dominant hemisphere was always considered the right hemisphere for left handers and the left hemisphere for right handers because of the incorrect notion that the speech area lay in the contralateral hemisphere. Today the dominant hemisphere is the area where the speech area lies, and this is almost always the left hemisphere. The phrase "mixed dominance," so popular in the LD literature, refers to something completely different. A number of early neurologists, particularly Orton, suggested that the dominant cerebral hemisphere could be found by evaluating which eye was dominant. Since it was believed that the image from the right field of vision went to the left hemisphere, then a dominant right eye would have the visual information going to the left hemisphere, which would hold the speech area. Eye dominance is the eye which a person naturally uses to look through a telescope or sight a gun with. If a person then had right-eye dominance and was left handed, he was said to have "mixed dominance," implying that information from the eye was going to the "wrong" hemisphere and therefore would cause such confusion as reading letters and words in reverse. Needless to say, this complicated theory is incorrect, because information from the right eye goes to both sides of the brain; all information received on the right side of the brain goes also to the left side of the brain via a group of fibers called the corpus collosum; and eye dominance is apparently unrelated to hand and speech dominance and most likely is the result of such a trivial matter as which eye has better acuity during the first few years of life.

Laterality refers to the sides of the body and how consistently the individual is right or left sided. A person with complete laterality would use his right side for writing, throwing a ball, sighting, standing on one foot, etc. Hand dominance and laterality is usually determined in children by observing which hand the child writes with and which hand he or she uses to do precise work, such as cutting, lacing the shoes, holding a pistol, throwing a ball. One also expects the dominant side to be better coordinated and to be a little stronger. The child will usually do these things with one side or the other over a period of time. The child who switches hands within a task such as writing with his right hand one day and the left the next is said to have confused laterality, which is different from ambidexterity where a child is proficient at say writing with the left, cutting with the right, throwing with the left, and the like. This distinction between ambidexterity and confused laterality should be carefully made, because the former indicates a normal condition while the latter is a neurological disability in children older than about seven.

A more formal measure of laterality is the Harris Lateral Dominance Test, which consists of ten items: (a) throwing a ball, (b) winding a watch, (c) hammering a nail, (d) brushing the teeth, (e) combing the hair, (f) turning a door knob, (g) using an eraser, (h) using the scissors, (i) cutting with a knife, and (j) writing. In addition the child must put dots in small one-eighth in squares, first with his right hand and then with his left hand. The child should do better in this cancellation task with his dominant hand.

Eye or ocular dominance is the eye that is preferred when viewing something through a telescope, peering in a paper roll, or the eye that does the leading as the eyes move across the page in reading. On the lateral dominance tests, the Harris ocular dominance is measured by asking the child to look in a tube (a kaleidoscope), having him sight down a yardstick pretending it is a gun, and looking through a hole at something. A more sophisticated test is the parallax test in which the person holds his finger about a foot from his nose while viewing something across the room. One then closes one eye and then closes the other; with one of these eyes the finger will appear to jump about an inch. The dominant eye is the one which does not jump when the eye closes. The nondominant eye does not cause a jump when closed, because when one views a scene the dominant eye determines the perspective of the image the brain receives. The neurological organization of eye dominance is more complicated than for handedness. When a person looks at an object, he looks at a particular point called the fixation point. On the right side of the fixation point is the right field of vision and on the left, the left field of vision for both eyes. The right field of vision goes to the left side of the brain and the left field to the right side. As with handedness the corpus colosum connects both sides of the brain, so that if there is damage to the left cerebral hemisphere, the individual will still have both visual fields.

There is one more form of dominance that appears on dominance tests and this is foot dominance. This is essentially the foot the child kicks with or stamps with or the foot that he stands on when standing on one foot. Often the preferred foot for kicking will be different from hand dominance because the child must stand on his strongest side and kick with the weaker side, because he cannot stand on one foot on his nondominant side.

The speculation that reading ability and other learning skills are related to hand and foot dominance began in the early twentieth century. Dearborn (1939) was one of the first to suggest that handedness was related to reading. He noticed one-third of his first twenty-five retarded readers were left handed and hypothesized:

> The outgoing movement of the left hand is from the center of the body towards the left. The left-handed person, possibly because he matches what his preferred hand does and this establishes the habit may show a preference for this same direction in his eye movements. . . .The confusion of letters which are the same form but different in position such as p, q, d, b, n, w, has been explained as due to the fact that our earliest perception of the letters may be quite as important as hand movements in fixing these memories.

This, then, was a clearly stated hypothesis of how hand and eye preference and reading were related.

Woody and Phillips (1934) combined the above two studies by matching right and left handers by age, sex, intelligence, and grade, and found that in their sample right handers made more reversals than left handers, suggesting that Dearborn's hypothesis about left handers was incorrect. Wilson, et al (1938) in an investigation of more complex variables studied 400 middle-class children with above average intelligence and found the correlation between reversals as measured by several means was not correlated with intelligence, physiological, or personality measures. They also found that the tendency to reverse is a persistent trait, with reversals in first grade correlating. .56 with reversals in the same children on a test administered two years later.

Orton (1937) hypothesized that reversals and a lack of sequencing led to learning disabilities and were the result of confused hand and eye dominance. Orton, it must be remembered, still believed that left-handed individuals had their speech area in the right hemisphere. To quote his own words:

> The existence of demonstrable mixtures between right and left motor preferences. . . implies that comparable integrating may exist between the critical areas of the various factions of language faculty in the two hemispheres of the brain, thus giving rise to a series of developmental disorders of language.

Today we can criticize Orton's theory on several neurological grounds: speech in left-handed individuals is in the same hemisphere as right-handed individuals thus not causing any contralateral confusion; the dominance of the eye is based on its acuity rather than some cerebral hemisphere activity; and half of the visual information from the dominant eye goes to the nondominant hemisphere.

In an experiment using nine year olds, Wolfe (1939) found no difference between normal children and LD children in copying geometric designs under normal conditions and when the designs were presented for only a few tenths of a second on a tachistoscope. This finding seems to negate the theory that LD children simply lack visual memory. When words were presented either as a whole or letter-by-letter from right to left and left to right tachistoscopically, the LD children did significantly more poorly even when the material was presented too fast for eye movements to occur. From this one may conclude that the perception of symbolic material is different from the perception of nonsymbolic material, and eye movements are probably not a significant factor in the reversals of poor readers.

Benton has been interested in right-left discrimination for many years. In 1951 Benton, Hutcheon, and Seymore found no support for the hypothesis that a relationship exists between arithmetic ability and right-left discrimination. In 1955, Swanson and Benton developed a twenty item right-left discrimination test, which was normed on six-to nine-year-olds. They found over eighty-five percent of the children seven years of age and older could correctly discriminate the right and left halves of their body when given unilateral and crossed commands. Six of the thirty nine-year-olds, however, performed all the tasks correctly except that they reversed their right and left in every case showing that they had the discrimination ability, but just could not remember which side was right. Right-left discrimination correlated well (.61) with chronological age, but there was a nonsignificant correlation with the child's ability to discriminate right and left on a doll facing the child. Discriminating directionality on one's own body then does not automatically lead to discrimination of right and left in the environment, contrary to the motor theorists.

Fisher (1959) found that children who had poor directionality also had a strong tendency to distort forms in their drawings. The drawing of a man or some other object requires a fair amount of spatial ability, because the person must visualize the head, arms, legs, etc. in correct proportion. Confused directionality may then be another sign of poor spatial ability. In another investigation by Silver (1962) 150 LD children from the ages eight to fourteen were compared with normal controls on a number of measures. While there were no differences in the percentages of left handers, eyeness, and mixed laterality, ninety-two percent of the LD children and none of the control group had problems in right-left discriminations. This finding indicates that poor directional orientation is extremely common among LD children who are in the third grade or above. This same percentage of children also showed abnormalities on a copying of design (the Bender) test, with eighty percent of the LD children showing significant abnormalities in drawing a man. Of interest are the more neurological tests, such as those for finger agnosia and the face-hand test, which were essentially normal for these LD children. Silver concluded that the eight percent of LD children who did not show any spatial abnormalities probably had emotional problems that interfered with their learning.

In 1961 Kimura developed a test for establishing cerebral dominance called the dicotic listening test, which involves presenting a subject digits over a set of headphones. The left and right ear receives a different set of digits simultaneously, and the individual repeats almost invariably those digits heard in the ear opposite of his speech area. Goodglass and Barton (1963) tried to do the visual equivalent to Kimura's experiment by presenting letters with a tachistoscope at a speed too fast for the eyes to move, to determine if letters in the right field of vision (which goes to the left hemisphere) are more accurately perceived than letters in the left field of vision. Even when the letters were presented in vertical columns to minimize any right to left reading habits, they found the right field to be more accurately perceived by both right and left handers.

Flescher (1962) did an exhaustive study of ocular-manual dominance and its relationship to the tendency to reverse words and letters while reading. He reviewed four different proposed theories of how laterality and reading were related. There was Orton's theory that one cerebral hemisphere (the dominant one) inhibits the other hemisphere and confused dominance causes reversals; Leavell's theory that it is the controlling eye in binocular vision that must be on the same side as the dominant hand for normal reading to occur; Barber, who felt that reading reversals were due to inadequate adjustment of the inversion of the retinal image; and the theory that only right-left discrimination is all that is related to reading (Benton, 1959). Flesher gave paragraphs that had been rotated either in mirror writing, inverted, or transformed using a clockwise-vertical rotation to 150 fourth graders and hypothesized that cross-dominant children would be more susceptible to one type of rotation than unilateral dominant children if any of these theories except the last one was correct. He found that certain kinds of rotations were more difficult than others for the children, but there was no difference between the unilateral and cross-dominant children when reading rotated texts. Even in this sophisticated experiment dominance was not related to reading.

Hecaen and Ajuriaguerra (1964) who have spent many years studying handedness, attempted to investigate its genetic aspects. They found that forty-two percent of all left-handed children had both parents who were left handed, seventeen percent had one left-handed parent, and two percent of the left handers had both parents who were right handed. These percentages follow very closely the percentages for Mendelian distribution of a single recessive gene. Hecien also suggests that the two percent of left handers with right-handed parents were probably "pathological" left handers who were left handed because of cerebral damage to the right hemisphere. Hicks and Kinsbourne (1976) also found genetic factors in handedness.

Critchley (1964) in his book on *Developmental Dyslexia* reports an investigation by Nesgaard and Hermann that tabulated the percentage of reversals made by both normal and LD Swedish children. They reasoned that if learning disabilities was a specific disorder, it should yield a definite pattern of reversals that would be different from those obtained by normal children just beginning to read. Contrary from what one would expect, the pattern of reversals for the LD children was almost identical to those of normal children (but, of course, the LD children made quantitatively more reversals), supporting the hypothesis that LD children are just slower to mature in reading processes needed to read words without reversing them.

One of the most careful and detailed studies of dominance and reading was performed on all the boys in Scotland born during a three-month period. When the children with IQs above 80 were tested at the ages of nine or ten (Belmont and Birch, 1965), the following percentages of dominance were found for a sample of 50 normal children and 150 LD children:

Types of Dominance	Hand Dominance Normal	LD	Eye Dominance Normal	LD	Hand-Eye Dominance Normal	LD
Totally right	70%	71%	66%	57%	50%	46%
Preponderately right	12%	17%	8%	9%	16%	17%
Mixed dominance	4%	2%	4%	7%	26%	31%
Preponderately left	8%	5%	2%	6%	4%	3%
Totally left	6%	5%	20%	22%	4%	3%

The figures speak for themselves — for every LD child with any kind of dominance there is an equal proportion of normal children with that type of dominance. Mixed dominance is just as common among normals as LD children regardless of whether it is hand dominance, eye dominance, or hand-eye dominance.

To summarize, the whole question of whether a child is right or left handed, right or left eyed, or right and left footed is irrelevant to a LD diagnosis, because these factors are not associated with learning problems. To avoid any inferences being made from these data, the author has always followed the practice of simply not mentioning the handedness of the child in his report. After all, one rarely describes the shape of the earlobe, or eye color, or number of fillings, or astrological sign of the child, because these variables are not relevant to a LD diagnosis; so why should dominance be added? There might be some validity to the theory that "pathological" left handers (e.g. left-handed child from an entirely right-handed family) may have some form of brain damage, but until this is shown by research to have a significance, it is best to lay this variable aside as one of those "scientific" myths that crop up from time to time.

Right-Left Discrimination

Hand-eye dominance relates entirely to which eye or hand is preferred, while directional awareness relates to whether the person can distinguish between his right and left. Right-left discrimination was first described by Obersteiner (1881) and has been of particular interest to neurologists who find that loss of this sense in adults is closely related to pathology in the right hemisphere, particularly the parietal lobe. Right-left discrimination is usually measured by giving the patient a series of commands such as "touch your right ear with your right hand" or "touch your left knee with your right hand," some of which are performed with the subject's eyes open, others with the eyes closed. The adult patient is expected to get all commands correct, including those involving crossing the sides of the body.

The interest in right-left discrimination began with Gerstmann's (1924) article on parietal lobe disorders in which he claimed that loss of right-left discrimination, finger agnosia, acalculia, and agraphia formed a definite syndrome now called Gerstmann's syndrome. Orton (1937) then suggested that lack of right-left discrimination was a major symptom of LD children, because these children reverse their letters and read words backwards. This coupled with Strauss and Werner's (1938) investigation finding that mentally retarded children with poor arithmetic skills failed right-left discrimination tasks firmly established the notation that directional discrimination was related to learning disabilities. Benton, Hutcheon, and Seymore (1951), however, repeated Strauss and Werner's study using a better research technique and found no relationship between arithmetic ability and directional discrimination in normal or mentally retarded children.

A test to measure right-left discrimination has been standardized on children by Swanson and Benton (1955), which involves giving twenty such directions. The first five require same side commands, next five crossed commands, then there are commands for eyes closed, and finally commands involved in placing one's right or left hand on the right, or left hand, eye, or foot of a picture of a person. There were no sex differences on this task. In a more detailed article Benton (1968) presented a test of thirty-two right-left discrimination items to children. He reports that orientation towards one's own body is much easier than making decisions about another's body or environment. Piaget (1926) has explained this by showing that making a judgement about another involves putting onself mentally in another person's place, and this is particularly hard for a child under the age of ten. Second, there was a difference between discriminating right and left and being able to correctly label right and left. For example, some children would correctly perform all the discrimination items on the test except that each time the examiner said "right," the child used his left. Benton considers that knowing the correct label for right and left is relatively unimportant compared to whether the direction is correctly discriminated. Third, the more often a child used the same hand on a series of activities such as cutting, writing, folding, using a screwdriver, etc., the better he did on the right-left discrimination test. This indicates that the more ambidextrous the child, or the more he switches hands between tasks, the less directional sense he has. Fourth, right-left discrimination also shows close correlation with intelligence as well as age. Finally, Benton reviewed four investigations that showed that lack of right-left discrimination was *not* related to learning disabilities.

There is a fair amount of controversy about whether right-left discrimination is related to learning disabilities. Many studies comparing various abilities of LD chidren and normal children matched in age and intelligence show the LD child to have significantly poor directional discrimination. The investigations reviewed by Benton showed no difference. This discrepancy is the result, the author believes, of first not taking the age of the child into account and confusing several kinds of directionality. There is right-left discrimination of one's body, then there is directional sense in the environment such as finding one's way around a building, there is spatial organization on paper of nonsymbolic material such as drawings, and finally there is orientation of symbolic material, namely letters and words. Kephart and Getman theorized that there is a logical progression of directional sense from one type to the next, and if the child cannot discriminate his right from his left, he will not be able to master the other directional skills and will obviously reverse his letters. It is true that the average child knows the right and left sides of his body by five, is able to locate his body in relation to the right and left side of things at six, and correctly distinguishes the right and left of other people at the age of seven or eight. The types of directionality are not, however, necessarily related to each other in LD children. Bannatyne (1971) points out that there are LD children who reverse their letters and have quite severe reading problems, but who have very high spatial abilities and are excellent artists and have no body or environmental directional problems. It is also obvious that a child can be taught his right and left fairly easily, as he can be taught letter orientation, so that a little training can remove the appearance of this "disability."

It has been the author's experience that some (about forty percent of the first and second grade) LD children have poor directionality in the environment, draw very poorly proportioned figures in free drawing, have poor gross and fine motor development, and are also fairly distractible and immature. These children may or may not know their right from their left depending on how carefully they have been drilled on this task, but clearly they have poor directionality. Along with these symptoms almost always comes the inability to sequence temporally, so that these children think they eat lunch at 10:00 a.m., that Christmas comes in April, fall follows spring, and the like. It appears as if the child is having a maturational lag and sequencing spatially and temporally is not developed. At the age of ten or eleven, poor directionality is very uncommon among LD children as is poor gross and fine motor development and distractibility, although temporal sequencing is still poor. Letters may still be occasionally reversed, but this is no longer a significant part of the picture of a learning disability. This is not to say that directionality problems do not crop up at later ages — the author remembers one colleague who had great difficulty learning to read and seemed to overcome his problem in adolescence until he was inducted into the Army. Whenever they were marching every man would turn one direction, and he would turn in the opposite direction. No matter how hard he tried, he was never able to master marching. He now incidentally has a college degree and is an LD teacher. To quote Critchley (1964):

> Although every child who is dyslexic writes very badly, he can copy printed or cursive texts slavishly and accurately. He may even be able to transcribe from print or script, or vice versa. But remarkable errors occur as soon as he writes spontaneously or to dictation. Occasionally they are so great as to preclude the patient from writing at all. In the case of a 'cured' dyslexic, defective writing and spelling may continue to appear long into adult life.

Body Image

The concept of body image is popular in the area of motor development and in the field of learning disabilities. All discussions of body image, the author has found to be based on Schilder's, *The Image and Appearance of the Human Body*, published in 1950. In this book he defines body image as: "The image of the human body means the picture of our own body which we form in our mind, that is to say the way in which the body appears to ourselves. . . .We call it a schema of our body or bodily schema. . . .The body schema is a tri-dimensional image everybody has about himself. We may call it 'body-image.'" Schilder reports that destruction of the cortex leads to the patient not knowing where he has been touched in an examination. He hypothesizes also that posture plays a role in building up the body image; that there is an "optic image' (i.e., location of body parts on a chart) and a tactile image; that localization of tactile image is independent of the sense of touch; that persons with a good body image have a good sense of direction; and that emotional problems will cause a change in the value and clearness of the body image. Schilder's conception of body image is one of a mental map of the physical body, and this map could be disturbed by either psychological problems (such as depersonalization, hypochondria, hysterical paralysis) or brain damage. This body image incidentally also goes beyond the body, and persons with problems with body image can have phantom limbs, and the image may include a hat, cosmetics, jewelry, and clothing.

Body image, then, is a very broad concept covering an individual's discrimination of his body parts (such as in finger agnosia), his discrimination of right and left, his body plane in relation to objects in the environment, realization of where the limbs are and how to move them, how a person represents his own body graphically (as in the Draw-a-Person task), and how a person feels about various body parts such as his sex organs. This concept is so broad that it is best broken into smaller units. First of all are very rare cases of individuals with cerebral disease who do not use part of their body because they do not believe it is theirs. Then there are individuals who are confused about discriminating directionality of their body and their environment, and this is fairly common among LD children, particularly those in the primary grades. This lack of directional sense is closely associated with poor visual discrimination and memory for letters and is due most likely to a delayed or immature perceptual system. Representations of the body parts graphically in a grossly distorted manner can be a lack of spatial ability and will show itself in the person not being able to copy designs without distorting them also. Distortion of the body in a drawing may also be due to a feeling of embarrassment or anxiety concerning a body part.

The diagnosis of motor functioning then begins with equal and integrated parts of the body. While evaluating gross and fine motor ability the clinician keeps a careful eye on the neurological basis of these movements and tries to relate these with the more cognitive areas of directionality and spatial reasoning. Finally, all these observations can be integrated into a more complex concept, that of body image, which is really how the person perceives his own body and its interaction with the environment.

Chapter IX

The Evaluation of Visual Perception

About seventy percent of the neurons reaching the brain are visual fibers, demonstrating how important the visual sense is in man. An inability to process visual stimuli because of a defect of the eye or the optic nerve is called an optical defect; while a failure to integrate information at a higher level is called a visual perceptual defect. This chapter will attempt to review the measurement of visual perception beginning with a discussion of how the eye functions and the various types of optical defects associated with learning problems.

Optical Functioning

Optical defects are usually diagnosed using one of three procedures: observing the child for symptoms of eye strain, using routine screening procedures such as eye charts, and employing the ophthalmological examination. Every clinician should be aware of symptoms that indicate optical problems. There are many checklists of varying quality, one published by the American Optometric Association is one of the better ones. Knox (1953) reviewed the literature and found ninety-four symptoms mentioned in association with visual problems. He then eliminated all but thirty of these and applied them to a group of 126 third graders. After having their eyes examined it became apparent that there were eleven symptoms that were closely associated with optical defects. These were: (a) losing place while reading, (b) avoiding close work, (c) poor sitting posture and position while reading, (d) holding reading closer than normal, (e) frowning, excessive blinking, scowling, or other facial distortions while reading, (f) excessive head movements while reading, (g) body rigidity while looking at distant objects, (h) tilting the head to one side, (i) tendency to rub eyes, (j) thrusting head forward, and (k) tension during close work. A list of the thirty symptoms can be obtained by writing the American Optometric Association (7000 Chippawa St., St. Louis, MO 63119). The clinician should be alert for these characteristics and should also keep in mind that they are only indications of visual problems, because perceptual problems, excess anxiety, and poor motivation can also cause some of these symptoms.

To understand the types of optical problems the anatomy of the eye must first be understood. There is the sclera, which is the white of the eye and blocks out the light. The sclera has the iris in front, which gives one one's eye color, and the pupil, which is the round hole in the iris. The pupil contracts and dilates with changing light, and the pupillary reflex is an important part of a neurological examination. Behind the cornea and the pupil is the lens — a clear flexible glass-like material. The lens is held in place by two fibers called the suspensory ligaments, which in turn are attached to the ciliary muscles. When the ciliary muscles expand and contract, they make the lens become longer and thinner or shorter and more rounded. This changing of the shape of the lens allows the lens to keep objects focused closer or farther from the lens. The image must be focused on the retina or it will appear blurred or fuzzy. The function of the lens and ciliary muscles, then, is to constantly adjust the image keeping it in focus. The part of the eye that does the actual "seeing" is the retina. This layer of cells is composed of one hundred million rod cells (called this because they look like rods under a microscope) that are sensitive only to black and white light and about seven million cone cells that are sensitive to colored light as well. The greatest concentration of these cells is in a point called the fovea, where the eye tries to focus the image. When one looks at something or "fixates" on the object, the eye focuses so this image will fall on the fovea and give the clearest image. This is why objects seen "in the corner" of the eye are not very sharp. There is a great deal of physiological evidence (Hubel and Wiesel, 1962) to show that the retina does not simply transmit the entire image to the brain to be interpreted as a TV camera transmits the picture to the station to be broadcasted. The image on the retina is upside down and reversed, but more importantly retinal cells react to different stimuli. Some cells transmit impulses to the brain only when the image is small and bright, others only when the image is moving, still others when the light goes out, and so on. So the brain receives each hundredth of a second, thousands of messages indicating such information as "a light went on," "it is moving," "it is a square," "it has a rounded side on top," "it is large," and by some unknown process the brain puts all this information together to make an image.

Eye movements are controlled by six eye muscles. The muscles (*rectus* in Latin) are in pairs with the lateral and medial (toward the nose) rectus muscles controlling the right and left movements of the eyes. The superior and inferior rectus muscles move the eyes up and down, while the superior and inferior oblique muscles move the eyes in a diagonal fashion. The physician typically examines a patient's eye movements by having him follow a penlight or the tip of a pencil with his eyes while keeping the head still. He moves the object back and forth, up and down, and along the diagonals while watching the patient's eyes to see if they follow smoothly and consistently. Eye movement control and scanning investigations are complex, because they are apparently related to the alpha rhythm of the brain (Leisman, 1976).

The anatomy of the visual system is, of course, much more complex than just described, but only the fundamentals of this system are necessary to understand various disorders that might be encountered in a clinical setting. The clinician must, however, be able to interpret the ophthalmological report to a teacher or parent and must, therefore, understand the fundamentals of visual functioning. Defects that occur to the eye include problems with visual acuity (how sharply one can see), visual accommodation (how well one can focus), and eye movements. These specific defects will be discussed separately with their implication to learning disabilities.

Visual Acuity

Visual acuity is how clearly a person can see an object. The shape of the cornea through which the image must pass, the shape and curvature of the lens in the eye, the flexibility of the lens and the ciliary muscles to focus the image exactly onto the retina, and the shape of the eyeball upon which the image is projected affect a person's acuity. Any imperfection in these four conditions will lead to either hypermetropia (far-sightedness), myopia (near-sightedness), or astigmatism, which can usually be corrected with glasses or contact lenses. Hypermetropia is the condition in which an individual can focus upon objects that are far away (by this is meant objects ten to fifteen feet or farther away), but cannot focus on objects that are held at reading distance (fourteen to eighteen inches). Objects that are close appear to be fuzzy or blurred, and if the condition is mild the person may see objects that are close up but must strain the lens and ciliary muscles to keep objects in focus. As a result, individuals with hypermetropia might be able to see the book adequately, but the resultant straining of the muscles may cause excessive fatigue, frustration, and such symptoms as headaches and watery eyes. Myopia is the condition in which an individual can see objects close up, but objects that are far away, such as on a blackboard across the room, would be blurred. Astigmatism is a condition where a portion of the person's visual field (such as the upper left-hand portion) is in focus, while the rest is out of focus. The child with astigmatism might be observed holding the book to one side or tilting his head when looking at something in an attempt to get the object into the portion of vision that is in focus.

Visual acuity is most commonly measured by the Snellen Eye Chart. Persons who can recognize the letters on the line marked 20 on the chart have normal 20/20 vision. If an individual can see the next line down which is made up of smaller letters, that persons with normal vision can see at only fifteen feet, he has 20/15 vision, which is better than normal vision. A person with poor vision who can see only the large "E" on the top line has 20/200 vision and can see at 20 feet what a normal person can see at 200 feet. There is a modified Snellen chart which uses "E"s that point in various directions, and the child points to the direction in which the "E" is pointing. These two charts are the most common devices for screening for optical defects. The problem with using them is that they are placed at fifteen or twenty feet away and, therefore, identify essentially only those children who are near-sighted. Since most school problems are associated with far-sightedness and not near-sightedness, these charts identify the wrong kind of visual defect. Spache (1939) pointed this out and found in a study that ninety-five percent of children who had visual difficulties as determined by an ophthalmologist were *not* identified by the Snellen Eye Chart. The reason that near-sightedness is not often measured in the schools is because the eye can accommodate for mild kinds of near-sightedness. Only when the vision is so poor that the accommodation must be made closer than reading distance does the child have difficulty seeing the page of a book.

Near-sightedness can be informally tested by showing the child a book that has small-face type and having him read from the book. Since a child can sometimes strain and overcome his visual handicap for brief periods, it is advisable to have him perform this task for a few minutes and to observe him for eye strain. If the child is too young to know his letters, he may be tested by presenting him with a set of lines with four types of "o"s and one "c", with the "c" being located in various locations in the line. The child with poor acuity will see the "c" as an "o" and will fail on this discrimination task. An inexpensive measure of near-sightedness is the Sloan letters, which consists of a chart held sixteen inches away with letters and words of decreasing size on it. This chart may be obtained from the Good Lite Company (7426 W. Madison St., Forrest Park, Illinois 60130) for twenty-five cents a card.

A more extensive measure of optical functioning can be obtained from vision testers that measure near-sightedness, far-sightedness, astigmatism, and binocular fusion. Vision testers resemble the machines used to check vision for driver's licenses. One of these is the School Vision Tester (a version of the Orthorater by Bausch and Lomb), which consists of a binocular viewer and a set of cards. Other vision screeners are the A O Sight Screener, the Keystone Telebinocular, and the Titmus Vision Tester, all of which cost more than $300.00. A much less expensive kit, which has approximately the same validity, is the Massachusetts Vision Test, which measures near- and far-sightedness, astigmatism, and color vision, but not binocular fusion.

Visual acuity depends upon the size and shape of the eyeball, and the eye continually grows from birth to the age of about fourteen. This means that the child may develop an optical defect any time while he is in elementary school. When he loses his visual acuity, it is usually a very gradual process with the child practically never being aware that his acuity is decreasing. When this problem is finally detected and he is fitted with glasses, the child is often amazed that he can now see such clear visual details as the individual leaves on trees. Since poor visual acuity can also be caused by fairly rare types of eye diseases or can be the result of side effects from some other disease such as diabetes, kidney ailments, or vitamin deficiencies, it is important to leave the final diagnosis of visual difficulty to the ophthalmologist (not optometrist).

Visual Acuity and Learning Disabilities

The research shows that newly born children have poor vision (in the neighborhood of 20/200), but by the time they are a few months old they have normal 20/20 vision (Maurer and Maurer, 1976). Eames (1935) did a careful study in which he compared the vision of 100 poor readers with a control group of 143 randomly selected school children. He found that fifty-three percent of the poor readers were far-sighted compared to twenty-eight percent for the normal readers. There was little difference in these groups in near-sightedness (poor readers 7.2%, controls 3%. Eames concluded that myopia was unrelated to reading, while hypermetropia was.

Spache (1940) reviewed twenty-six studies that had been conducted on the relationship between optical defects and reading achievement. Spache found some studies reported a definite link between vision and academic achievement and others reported no relationship. He attributed these discrepacies to the various methods of selecting samples, but it was clear that there were individual cases where retarded readers were fitted with glasses and then showed great improvements in reading. In the studies where large numbers of poor readers or spellers were compared to normal readers, there were only small differences in visual acuity, indicating that visual acuity is a problem for only a small number of children.

The ophthalmologists, Park and Burri (1943a), gave a standard ophthalmological examination to 225 school children who were six to thirteen years old without knowing how these children performed in the classroom. They found that the seriousness of the optical problem (both in acuity and eye convergence) correlated almost at chance level (.16) with reading performance. However, in a reanalysis of the data, Park and Burri (1943b) found that when they compared the reading levels of children when the child's intelligence was taken into account (with higher IQ children having a higher than grade level expectancy), there was a significant correlation (.46) between reading achievement and eye problems. They concluded that having optical difficulties in itself does not prevent children from reading at expected grade level, but the brighter children with optical problems did not read as much as they should, because they were easily fatigued by reading. This is not so surprising, because the eye can accommodate unless near-sightedness is so extreme that the eyes can focus only at a distance further than reading distance.

Allen (1977) has recently written a detailed article on the role of vision and learning disabilities, suggesting that eye movements and fusion do cause some reading problems. He presents a complex diagram of causation of reading difficulties (*Figure 18*). He also quotes Eberle (1974), who reviewed 134 textbooks on vision and found that of the forty most-quoted studies only fifteen were well designed. Concerning the fifteen studies he says:

> In terms of the number of visual defects per person, good vision appears to be associated with good reading and poor vision with poor reading. Those specific defects most often related to reading difficulties are hyperopia (farsightedness), lateral imbalances. . .especially if the child is also hyperopic, fusion problems and poor. . .ability. . .of the eyes to converge and diverge which is also closely related to fusion. Myopia does not seem to be related to poor reading and is frequently associated with better than average reading. . .The general impression from the good research in vision as it relates to reading in the elementary school child is that vision is important in determining whether children are successful in learning to read and whether they maintain a strong interest in reading (pp. 87-89).

Figure 18

Comparison of frequency distribution of refractive state at birth with that at ages 6 to 8 years.

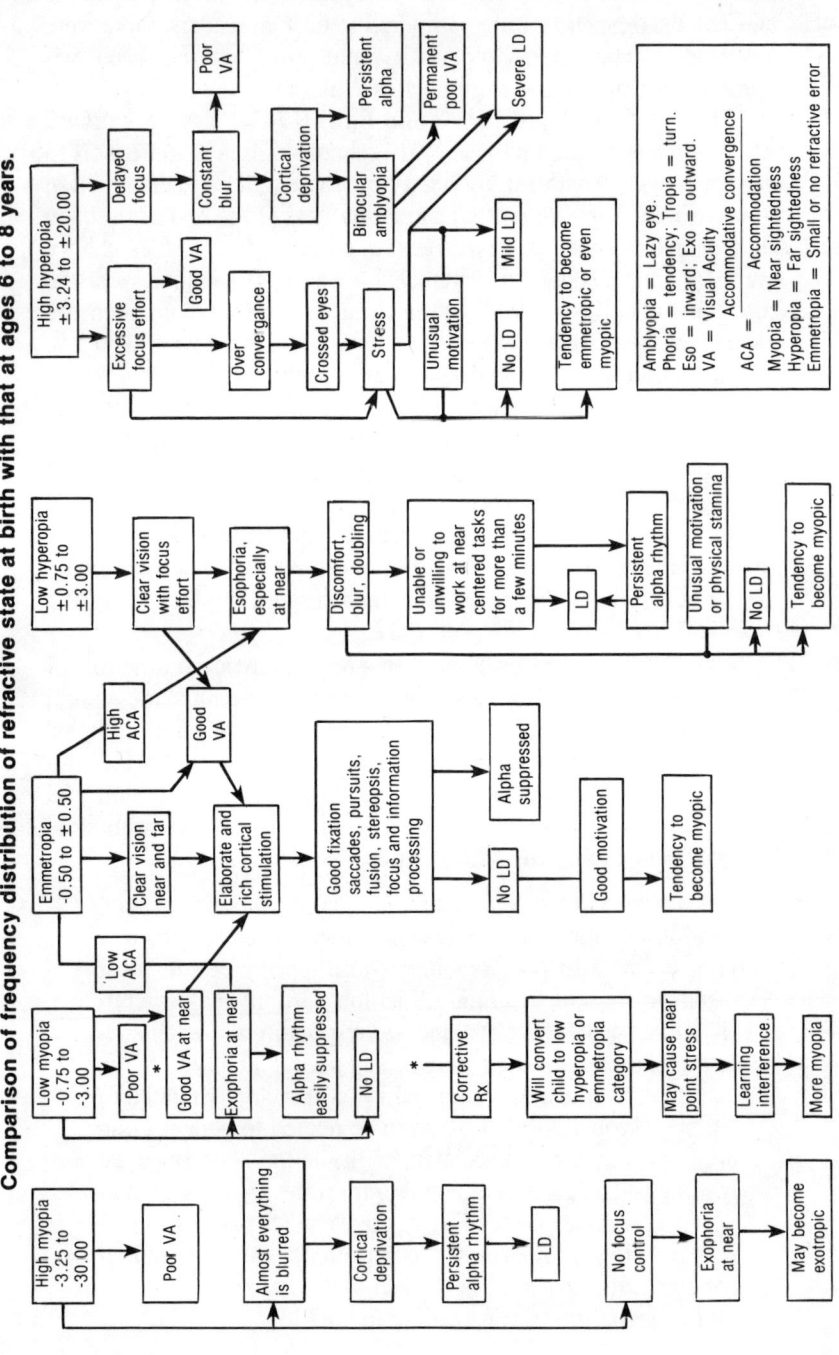

FROM Allen, J.M. The Role of Vision in Learning Disorders *Journal of Learning Disabilities*, 1977, 10, 411-415.

From these studies on optical characteristics of children, primarily with reading problems, it appears that:

1. There are a few children, perhaps a fraction of one percent of the school population, who read poorly because of a severe undetected visual acuity problem.

2. Undetected visual acuity deficits will, however, cause fatigue and sometimes headaches and make close work in school uncomfortable, thus decreasing some of their willingness to read.

3. Of the children with acuity problems, only those with extreme hypermetropia (far-sightedness) in the early years have problems that affect their academic work.

4. The traditional wall charts (such as the Snellen) do *not* pick up these cases of far-sightedness very well.

5. Most of the children (probably more than ninety-five percent) who have had serious learning problems have no optical defect.

These findings have been stressed again and again (Robinson, 1946; Vernon, 1971; Goldberg and Shiffrin, 1972) and have been aptly summarized by Money (1962) with: ". . .ocular and optical defects are of negligible dyslexic significance. Even when severe and undetected, such defects are usually sufficiently overcome to permit learning to read" (p. 29).

Binocular Coordination

For the brain to receive a single image from both the eyes, the eyes must be closely coordinated so that they are looking at the same place. This is done with the six eye muscles working very closely with each other. When the eyes are looking at something close they converge, that is, point more inward. Convergence may be crudely measured by having the child sit and watch a penlight or the tip of a pencil while it is moved from several feet away to a few inches from the nose. The eyes should converge in a smooth fashion without skipping or jerking, with both eyes coordinated so that they turn inward the same amount as the object approaches. If the eyes cross too much (cross-eyed) or one eye looks off (cast-eyed) the child has a strabismus. A strabismus by itself does not automatically mean a reading problem, because there are many cross-eyed and cast-eyed individuals who are perfectly good readers. When the lateral and medial rectus muscles do not balance each other off, they cause the eye to flick back and forth in small jumpy movements, and this is known as a nystagmus. When the eyes converge too much, that is, they turn inward too far for the image to fall properly on both foveas, the individual is said to have esphoria. The eyes turning too far outwards when focusing on an object is exophoria.

When there is good coordination between the muscles of the eye, the person's brain receives two images falling on the same part of the retina, and it fuses these images together to make a sharp three-dimensional image. When the muscles are not well balanced, the child might experience a blurred image, or he may in extreme cases (such as when one is very drunk) see double. If the person receives two widely differing images for long periods of time, the brain will cease to process information from one eye and the person will have amblyopia, which is the loss of sight of one eye. Exophoria and esophoria are usually mild cases of the eyes not converging. Low grades of these phorias can cause the letters to appear mixed and small words to be jumbled; as well as the child experiencing difficulty in following a line of print smoothly (Eames, 1935). Eames (1935), comparing 114 retarded readers and 143 unselected students, discovered esophoria occurred more commonly in the children with myopia, but this condition was not related to reading performance. However, children with exophoria of greater than three deltas (a measurement of convergence) had reading problems. Interestingly, these children with exophoria were not aware that anything was wrong with their vision and did not report seeing blurred images. Spache (1940) reviewed twenty studies and found: ". . .the preponderance of evidence favors the belief that muscle imbalance, particularly exophoria, and its concomitant fusional difficulties are associated with less than normal progress in reading and spelling." Later, Park and Burri (1943a, 1943b) were able to report a strong correlation of about .65 between reading achievement and exophoria in 225 school children when the child's IQ was taken into account. Park (1948) later examined 133 children with reading difficulties and found twenty percent had subnormal visual acuity in both eyes and fifty-five percent of these children had either exophoria or esophoria.

Eye Movements

As early as 1879, the French ophthalmologist Emile Joval noticed that the eyes do not move smoothly along a line of print while reading, but make sudden stops called fixations at every two or three words. These movements are called sciatic movements, and the fixations have been found to be about one-hundredth of a second in duration. The eye does not see while it is moving, so that word perception only occurs during the fixations (which take up about ninety-five percent of the time spent reading), and reading can be thought of as a series of successive stationary glimpses at words. The measurement of eyes while reading is now routinely performed in reading clinics by a "reading eye" machine, which records these movements by reflecting a light on the eye while the person is reading and recording the movements on film. Poor readers typically have many more fixations (they look at each part of the word rather than glancing at it and going on), and their movements are uneven (taking large and small jumps). They also have more regressions (going back and looking at a word again). Tinker (1939) showed that the Reading Eye could measure eye movements reliably (of about .80) only after twenty to forty lines were read, which is usually much longer than the typical reading passage on the reading eye machine.

With a fairly easy and accurate measurement of eye movements, many individuals in reading clinics have attempted to use these eye movement records as a means of diagnosing reading problems with the aim of recommending eye movement exercises for children showing abnormal fixations or regressions. Tinker, who has conducted numerous studies and reviewed hundreds of investigations in this area of eye movements (Tinker; 1936, 1939, 1958), has maintained that poor eye movements are simply the result of poor reading. When a child cannot recognize a word, he will look at it again and again, thus giving him a poor eye movement pattern. When the child is taught the words in the passage, his eye movements will dramatically change into normal eye movements. Tinker states: "All well-designed experiments which have attempted to evaluate the role of training eye movements to improve reading have failed to find such training is either necessary or desirable" (Tinker, 1965, p. 109).

There is only one optical defect that is clearly associated with learning disabilities, congenital oculomotor apraxia, which is the inability to move the eye muscles (Flam, 1970). This condition is easily diagnosed, because the person cannot move his gaze to a specific location when the head is held still. The clinician may want to observe less obvious optical conditions by having the child follow with his eyes the tip of an eraser when it is moved vertically, horizontally, diagonally, and then toward and away from him. This would tell him if the eye muscle movements might be hindering the child's reading by causing extreme eye strain or if the child is not able to move his eyes smoothly from left to right when he is reading. Diagnosing eye movement problems using a reading eye machine appears to be of little value, because children who cannot read the words in the passage will naturally have multiple fixations and regressions while reading those words.

Field of Vision

Some of the early reports on the vision of children with learning disabilities found that LD children had a narrowed field of vision.

This narrowing of the visual field was usually tested by having the child look at the examiner's nose while the examiner gradually moved a small white object from the side of his head to the front in a circular arc. The child was told to report when he could see the object in his peripheral vision. Although the checking of peripheral vision is still recommended by such authors as Kephart (1960), recent investigations have found that LD children, for the most part, do not have any narrowing of their visual field. It is now clear that the only time the field of vision is narrowed is when there is definite neurological damage. The neurologist can, with an analysis of how much the field is narrowed and in which eye it occurs, specify with great precision exactly where the lesion in the visual system must be. Should a clinician observe a narrowing of the visual field, he should have the child tested by a neurologist, because there is the possibility that the lesion is caused by a developing brain tumor.

Binocular Fusion

An individual perceives the world around him as a three-dimensional space with depth to it, even though the image of this world is a two-dimensional figure cast upon his retina. One is able to create a three-dimensional visual picture by many well-known visual-perceptual mechanisms. The first is binocular fusion, in which the brain takes the two images that it receives from each of the eyes and superimposes these images to make a single three-dimensional one, working much like a stereoscope or viewmaster. The eyes being a few inches apart will see two different images; the closer an object is, the more different the images of the two eyes. If one closes one eye or has a nonfunctioning eye such as in amblyopia, then one has to rely on some other mechanism such as the size of the object to judge its distance. Children are capable of judging depth at a very early age. When normal two-week-old babies were fitted with stereoglasses and given images that would appear to move toward them, all pulled back and tried to cover their faces with their hands (Bower, 1972). At six weeks, the infant is alert to many changes in position of objects in space and, since the child is at an age where he cannot even roll over by himself, it is unlikely that children develop binocular fusion from interacting with the environment. The ability of the brain to fuse two images is apparently due to some property of the nervous system that is complete in the first few weeks of life.

The exact relationship between fusion and reading achievement is not well understood. Robinson (1946, p. 24) has reviewed the investigations and reports a slightly greater number of poor readers with low fusion. This ability, per se, does not appear to be related to poor reading. He found that twenty-two percent of children who were poor readers had "extremely weak" stereovision, but eighteen percent were able to overcome their problems of stereovision with a little training and to see in three dimensions. This, however, did not "cure" the reading problem, because reading is vastly more complicated than simply seeing in three dimensions.

In summary, it appears that binocular fusion, like eye muscle movements, can be fairly accurately measured, but it appears to have little diagnostic significance to learning disabilities. Goldberg and Drosh (1968), eminent ophthalmologists, have summarized this with:

> While a certain minimal visual acuity is required to differentiate visual stimuli accurately, defective vision and muscle imbalance do not have a significant role in the etiology of a condition which is influenced primarily by cognitive learning. Reversals are not the result of poor vision, nor are they the result of weakness in near point acuity. The importance of low degrees of refractive error has been greatly exaggerated. It has been demonstrated that muscle imbalance and strabismus do not affect the interpretation of symbols. The effort to overcome phonics and to see binocularly may cause fatigue and discourage reading to some extent, but these difficulties are seldom of major etiological significance in extensive reading retardation.

Visual Perception

Visual perception is the integration and analysis of visual information after it leaves the retina. As already mentioned, there are about one hundred million retinal cells, and these cells are connected to only one million cells in the optic nerve. This means that about ten retinal cells are connected to one nerve cell, so that retinal cells do not simply "take a picture" of what falls on them. Rather some cells will transmit an impulse only when a dark image falls on them, others respond only with bright objects, still others only if the object is moving, or with large objects or triangular objects. There is, therefore, extensive coding of the image according to its size, shape, brightness, and motion at the retinal level.

This information goes along the optic nerve to a relay station called the thalamus at the base of the brain and then goes to the visual cortex of the brain. Since little is known of how information is processed beyond the retina, perceptual tests rely on what a person reports he sees, without making any reference to the anatomy involved. As a result, it is often difficult to decide exactly what a particular perceptual test is measuring.

Before describing the various kinds of perception and how they are measured, a general description of how perceptual learning occurs must be understood. Suppose one is from the city and goes to live on a farm. The first day one notices that twenty cows on the farm all look alike. When asked to describe these cows, one says they are brown and white, have four feet and are pretty much the same size. However, if one works with the cows and spends time with them, it gradually becomes apparent that all the cows are not alike. Without any careful observation or systematic viewing, one slowly develops a "sense" for various cows, and soon afterwards one can tell all the cows apart. If a friend from the city comes out to visit and asks how one can tell the cows apart, one might reply something like, "See this one here? It has white covering all its face, while this one here has a slightly different marking. Also that one there has smaller ears, and this one is just a little fatter than the other cows." Now what has happened? When one first came to the farm, all the cows looked alike because they all appeared to have the same characteristics — four legs, big, hair all over the body, white and brown, etc. However, with simple exposure to the cows, one gradually begins to notice differences in the characteristics of the cows so that the brown and white color of the cows becomes a particular white marking on the face. These various characteristics such as size, color, and shape are called perceptual features. The process of being able to distinguish finer and finer details is called differentiation. It should be noted that features can be taught, but in normal life, a person automatically distinguishes features without being told what they are.

Another example of feature learning is how a child learns to recognize faces. The learning of the differences between faces is of particular interest, because it shows that the child learns how to differentiate a very complex set of very similar objects before he is one year old, and that he has the capability to make very complex visual discriminations. This same child, however, cannot reliably differentiate various letters, because he has not learned the features for letters. The features needed to tell faces apart are such things as "coloring of hair," "very small differences of size," or slight differences in "roundness of face." None of these features help distinguish letters; for example, the "coloring" of the print, differences in size of the letters, and "roundness" are unimportant in telling letters apart. This visual discrimination of faces does not rely on being able to name the features and is generalized to strangers automatically without any teaching or consistent reinforcement.

Still another example is the fact that children with reading problems are usually able to discriminate an "O" from an "I," but become confused between a "b" and a "d." The reason they can make the first discrimination is that they are aware of the features of "straightness versus curveness," while they do not have the feature of "right-handedness versus left-handedness." To illustrate the features of letters, *Figure 19* presents a set of nonsense scribbles, which at first glance look very much alike. These scribbles are somewhat like what letters must look like to the child who has not yet learned to read and, therefore, has not learned the features of letters. When one examines the scribbles closer, one begins to realize that these figures are different: some have four coils, some have six coils, some spiral clockwise and others spiral counterclockwise, and some are stretched more than others. In other words, with experience with the scribbles, one becomes aware that there are three different perceptual features that can discriminate between them. These features are: (a) number of coils, (b) direction of spiral, and (c) compactness. Any person seeing just one or two coils would not receive enough feature information to reliably tell them apart. But with exposure to the whole gamut of them, their differences can be deduced. Similarly, the best way to teach a child the features necessary for letters of the alphabet is to expose him to all of them. This practice is sometimes not done where children learn how to make an "a," then a "b," and so on until they finally reach "z" many months later. For those wanting to learn about visual distinctive features, the following three books can be consulted (Chase, 1973; Reed, 1973; Sadanand, 1972).

With an understanding of visual perception and how a feature-analysis can be done, one can examine the various perceptual skills and discuss a child's disability in terms of how many and the types of features he can process. To begin, the aspects of perceiving something in space will be discussed. There are four perceptual mechanisms that help to form a three-dimensional image. Binocular fusion already discussed is the first with the second being interposition.

Interposition

An object appears closer to a second object if part of it is in front of the object. This is fairly apparent by simply looking around the room; the furniture interposed on the lines of the wall make it seem closer. A number of texts (e.g. Kroth, 1971; Lerner, 1971) suggest that children with learning disabilities may not have visual interposition. Their evidence is when a child is given an overlapping figure, such as a triangle and circle, the child sometimes outlines both figures when asked to outline just the triangle. Two of the Frostig subtests consist almost entirely of tracing overlapping figures along with the Position in Space subtest, which is specifically such a test. The accuracy of this claim is in question. Bower (1966) in a set of ingenious experiments demonstrated that even infant children had the ability to interpose.

It seems that the test of interposition using two-dimensional overlapping drawings is not measuring any type of depth perception anyway, because it is not using any three-dimensional stimuli. It seems more accurate to say that when a child does not outline a figure in an overlapping figures task, he does so because he is confused by the visual stimuli. Until more evidence can be marshalled to support Kroth's and Lerner's claim, it appears much wiser to ignore this perceptual measure and not to use any tests of interposition.

**Figure 19
Nonsense Scribbles Used by Gibson**

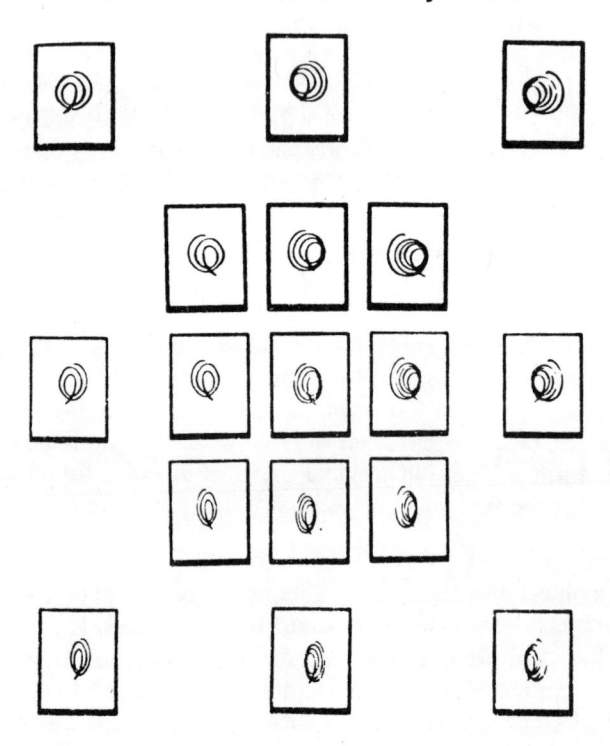

From Gibson, J.J. and Gibson, E.J., "Perceptual learning: Differential or Enrichment?" *Psychological Review*, 1955, 62, 36.

Size Constancy

The third mechanism whereby depth is perceived is by the size of the object. For example, one can tell approximately how far away a football is by simply noticing how small the football appears. The farther away the object, the smaller its image, or more precisely, if the object is twice as far away, it will be half as large. Under normal circumstances of close distances, objects do not appear to shrink or enlarge in size as one moves closer or farther away from them. A pencil appears to be the same size whether it is a foot away or a yard away even though the image on the eye is three times larger when it is a foot away. The phenomenon by which objects appear to be the same size, regardless of how far away they actually are, is called size constancy. Experiments by Bower (1972) have shown that infants, besides having interposition, will show size constancy at the age of six weeks. Since six-week-old infants have had little experience with moving around in the environment, it appears that this mechanism, like those of binocular fusion and interposition, is physiologically determined.

A number of authors in the field of learning disabilities (Frostig, Aryes, Lerner, Cruickshank, Kephart, etc.) have indicated that LD children have problems in size constancy. If one, however, examines the size constancy tests that are typically used to support this contention (such as the Size Constancy subtest of the Frostig), one finds that the tests are two-dimensional and involve working with overlapping figures. The author has been unable to find a single instance in his own experience, or in a report in the literature, that deals with an LD child who noted that objects shrunk as they moved away for distances up to about twenty feet. In fact, the author seriously doubts that the experts in the field of learning disabilities believe that LD children have this serious impairment of perception. Rather they are referring to the performance of children on overlapping figures tests. These tests will be reviewed later in this chapter, because the discrimination of overlapping figures requires a number of skills such as attention, the coding of relevant features, and the perception of Gestalts.

Form Constancy

A fourth mechanism involved in the perception of three-dimensional objects is form constancy. When a round plate is viewed laying on a table, the plate forms an oval image on the eye, yet it appears to be round. Form constancy is the perceptual mechanism whereby objects appear to have the same shape regardless of what position they occupy in space. This perceptual mechanism appears to be physiological and can be demonstrated in children as young as a few months old. As with the other mechanisms involving the perception of three-dimensional shapes, form constancy does not seem to have any relation to learning disabilities. The research on form constancy is reviewed in detail by Epstein and Park (1963), and one subtest of the Frostig Developmental Test of Visual Perception has a form constancy test. This subtest has, however, such a low reliability that it should not be used for diagnostic purposes.

Visual Discrimination

Visual discrimination is the ability to distinguish between two objects. Visual discrimination involves three different skills — simultaneous discrimination, successive discrimination, and recognition. Simultaneous discrimination involves presenting a person with a set of objects at one time and having him decide if they are alike or different. Same-different judgments can be made without knowing the names of the objects. For example, the child may be given the word "can" followed by a row of words "and, cat, could, can, cap" and must circle all the words that look like the word "can." Successive discrimination involves showing the person a stimulus, then removing it, and having him choose the object he has just seen from a set of objects. The child may be shown the word "can" on the board; it is erased, and then he must point the word out from the words "can, cap, etc." This latter process is more difficult, because it involves memory as well as discrimination. Finally, in visual recognition, the child is shown a set of objects and asked to simply point out a particular object. One may write four words on the board and say, "Which word is 'can'?" Recognition is still harder than the other two tasks, because it involves past learning. The most complicated examples of visual discrimination tasks can be found on reading readiness tests such as the Lee-Clark Reading Readiness test, which begins with discrimination of animals, then individual letters, and finally words. The research has shown that when the standard is located in the middle of the four alternatives, the task is easier than placing all the alternatives in a row, because the child must look back and forth traveling much farther distances. Many alternatives make this task much more difficult, because children have problems in systematically going from one alternative to the next and back to the standard.

Unlike depth perception, form and size constancy, the ability to make visual discriminations is learned with experience and is not "wired into" the brain. The child learns the features of his mother's face at the age of about six months; by eighteen months he can discriminate objects from each other and has trouble only with objects that he has little experience with. The child of three or four will know that a toy truck viewed from the right side is the same truck that is viewed from the left side, so that when he is shown a "b" and "d," he assumes that this must be the same letter. The learning of visual features goes on throughout life, so that one may learn at the age of sixty, for example, to diagnose various types of cancer cells from microscopic specimens that to the layman look alike.

Some LD children have visual perceptual problems in discriminating all visual stimuli, but a great number have only problems in discriminating letters and words. Gibson (1970) gave seven-year-old children a series of discrimination tasks using nonsense words and had them mark the words that were the same as the standard. In analyzing the mistakes the children made, she found that all letters were not confused equally. Of the letters "C, G, P, R, E, F, M, N, W" there was the most confusion between "C" and "G," "P" and "R," "M" and "N." If one looks at a feature chart of these letters, it becomes apparent that the more features a letter has in common, the more likely the letters will be confused. One common diagnostic mistake is to assume that if a child confused two letters on a discrimination test, the child will make this mistake every time. Actually, the errors are *not* consistent and a large number of mistakes tells one only how efficiently the individual's feature system is working.

Barrett (1965) has reviewed twenty-three investigations concerning the relation between visual discrimination abilities of entering first graders and their subsequent reading achievement level at the end of the first grade. These studies found that the performance on the visual discrimination task for matching letters or words correlated about .50 with subsequent reading. This strong relationship was as high as any other factor in reading, including intelligence. The investigations that compared discrimination using individual letters and those using words correlated the same amount with reading achievement. The correlations between reading and visual discrimination of nonverbal materials were found to be much lower (in the .20s and .30s), indicating that discrimination tasks using pictures and geometric figures and the like are not good predictors of reading success. This makes sense in terms of feature theory, because the features of designs are not the same as those found on letters (Stroud, 1945). In the higher grades very similar findings have been made. Gates (1926) gave a detailed set of tests to 310 children in grades one through six. He found that matching geometrical figures in a visual discrimination task correlated .01 with reading individual words, .10 with reading comprehension, and .08 with spelling. The same discrimination task using words correlated .55 with word recognition, .64 with reading comprehension, and .54 with spelling. Visual discrimination correlated only slightly with intelligence (.21), and when IQ was statistically factored out, the correlations between reading and visual discrimination of letters were even a little higher.

Several researchers have tabulated the number of visual confusions of beginning readers starting with Goldscheider and Muller (1893), who first reported the "b-d" and "p-q" reversals. Davidson (1935) analyzed the errors of first graders and found the following centages of errors: d-b = 65%, q-p = 62%, d-p = 19%, b-p = 19%, b-q = 15%, and d-q = 13%. The percentages for kindergarten children were much higher, ranging from ninety-three percent to thirty-five percent in the above series. More recently Popp (1964) found the letters with the greatest discrimination mistakes were in order of most to least: p-q, b-d, b-q, d-p, b-g, h-u, i-l, k-y, t-u, c-e, d-h, h-n, k-y, j-k. As may be seen from these studies, the most common type of error is reversals, followed by inversions, with confusion of broken versus solid lines being the least common error. If we think of children with visual dyslexia as having a weakness of visual processing or developmental lag in visual skills, then it would make sense that these children would reverse their "b"s and "d"s in the second and third grades. Since letter discrimination correlates so highly with reading, one would expect children with poor visual discrimination to be poor in reading. This, of course, is well known and is the basis of a majority of reading readiness tests, most of which contain a section on visual discrimination.

Figure-Ground Perception

A number of authors (Strauss and Werner, Kephart, Learner, Vernon) have stated that children with learning disabilities have difficulties learning to read, because they have a deficit in visual figure-ground perception. Figure-ground is the ability to distinguish an object (the figure) from its background (the ground). Kephart (1960, p. 136), for example, states that children have difficulty reading because they focus on "flaws or spots in the paper" rather than concentrating on the type. This rather unbelievable suggestion that LD children do not perceive the print the same way as other children originates from a long series of misinterpretations of perceptual experiments done over the last half century. They may be traced back to Rubin, the German psychologist, who described the first reversible optical illusion.

In 1922, Rubin noted the famous face-vase illusion, showing that perception is not always constant. A few years later, Gottschaldt (1926) presented adults with a series of designs, some of which are shown in *Figure 20*. He simply asked his subjects what they saw to determine if they would see the complex design or its parts. He repeatedly presented these figures to his subjects and reported that frequent exposure to them did not cause his subjects to begin to see the designs as small units. These figures are now known as embedded figures, and his study was translated into English by Ellis (1938), causing many psychologists to interpret the results to mean that the inability to see the simpler designs in more complex ones is a lack of figure-ground perception (with the simple designs being the figure and the complex ones the ground).

In the United States, Munn and Stiening (1931) examined the development of figure-ground by presenting fifteen-month-old children with either a cross or another geometric figure in a two-choice situation. If the child chose the cross, he received a piece of chocolate. In a series of varying conditions, they were able to show that children, after they had acquired the habit of choosing the cross, chose this figure regardless of how confusing the background accompanying the cross. This study, which has been repeated under many conditions, shows that normal children at a very young age can discriminate figure-ground.

The first experiment to try to tie figure-ground perception to exceptional children was done by Werner and Strauss (1941), who presented figures of common objects with distracting background to "familial" and "organic" retardates. The brain-injured children did worse, and they concluded that brain-injury causes a deficit in figure-ground perception. These drawings (particularly the hat with the zagged lines through it) were to become very popular and appear today in many books as tests of brain-injury. There are, however, some questions about the experiment, principally that the figures were exposed to the subjects one one-fifth of a second, with one of the criterion for the organic group being that the were distractible. The two groups were also not adequately matched for intelligence. Rubin (1969-1970) replicated this experiment controlling for these variables and discovered no difference between brain-injured and familial retardates on this task.

Strauss and Lehtinen (1947) in their book also introduced the Marble Board Test (already reviewed) as a measure of figure-ground perception. Strauss believed the child without figure-ground perception could not distinguish the marbles from the holes in the board. In

Figure 20
Examples of Embedded and Overlapping Figures

Embedded figures, similar to those of Gottschaldt, used by Ghent.

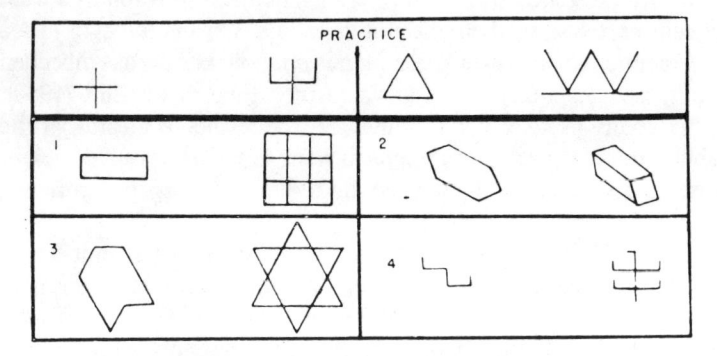

Task is to find the figure at the left which is in the figure on the right.

Overlapping geometric figures used by Ghent.

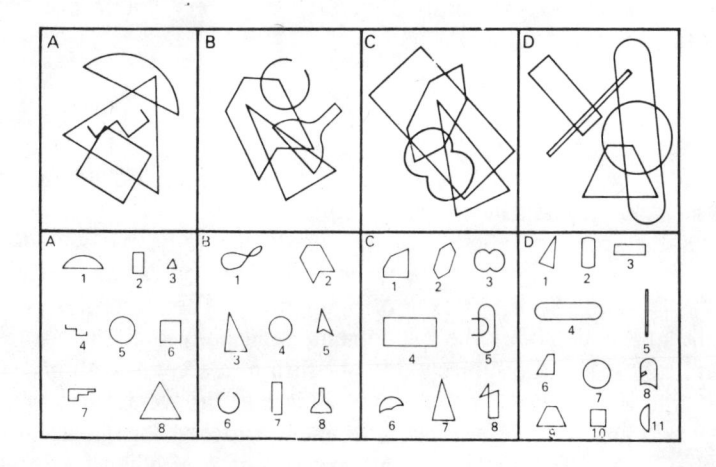

Task is to find which of the eight figures in the lower half are located in the upper half.

From Ghent, L., *American Journal of Psychology*, 1956, 69, 575-587.

a replication study Craine and Werner (1950) gave this Marble Board test to normal and mentally retarded children matched in mental age and found, surprisingly, that the mentally retarded actually did better on the task.

Ghent (1956) decided to study the differences between the perception of embedded and overlapping figures by presenting both types to children aged four to thirteen. She found that at all ages children found the overlapping task much easier than embedded figures. Both tasks require careful scanning of the material and ignoring irrelevant details, but the embedded figures task requires a kind of mental construction that young children simply cannot do. As a result, they do not understand the embedded figures task unless it is extremely simple.

In 1960 Goetzinger, Dirks, and Baer gave the Gottschaldt embedded figures test to normal and dyslexic children and found no difference in the perception of these figures. Walters, Loan, and Crofts (1961) in another study gave the Steer-Allen Figure-Ground Confusion test and found no difference between normal and dyslexic boys in the third to sixth grades. Ritter and Yesseldyke (1976) have reviewed this area and in an experiment showed basically that figure-ground perception was closely related to object recognition, but more difficult. Soon after these studies were conducted, Karp and Karnstog developed the first standardized Children's Embedded Figures Test. This test consists of thirty-eight plates of embedded figures in which the child must pick triangles and squares out of drawings and designs with these simpler figures embedded in them. The test was normed on 160 children aged five to twelve and has a good retest reliability (.87 for five-year-olds). There is also an Embedded Figures Test that can be used with older children and adults, which is equally reliable. Stuart (1967) did find this task significantly related to reading in eighth graders.

Aryes has also published the Southern California Figure-Ground Visual Perceptual Test, which consists of a multiple choice set of eight overlapping figures and nine embedded figures. This test has a reliability below .40, which is much too low to make an individual diagnosis.

Finally, Kaufman (1969) has reviewed the whole concept of figure-ground and its relation to academic skills, particularly reading, and concluded the concept of "figure-ground" is too broad to be of any meaningful use. He found figure-ground to mean:

1. The leveling of differences between figure and ground (as in perception of objects in depth),

2. The lack of precision of a figure (as in overlapping figures),
3. Uncertainty as to which is figure and which is ground (as in seeing spots on the paper),
4. Formation of simpler figures impoverished in content (as in an embedded figures test),
5. Instability of the figure and tendency for the figure and ground to alternate (as in the Rubin figure),
6. Excessive lines of a perception to consolidate (as in Strauss' figure-ground task), and
7. Upon accomplishing a figure formation, an inability to form a new figure (as in Gottschaldt's experiment).

He concluded, ". . .we can see that figure-ground, as used in educational studies, is a broader concept than the classical concept found in perception theory. Unfortunately, it may become too broad to be useful." It is also of note that one of the best controlled studies (Carter and Diaz, 1971) did not find that placing either normal or brain-injured children in a situation with confusing visual figure-ground affected their reading comprehension as measured by the Stanford Reading Test.

To summarize, visual figure-ground is a concept too broad to be useful. Children from a very early age are capable of distinguishing figures from their background. It is highly unlikely that LD children lack this perceptual ability. The research also shows that children of the age of four or five will do poorly on a task of picking out drawings or designs that overlap. This can be performed by children if there are only two overlapping designs, but is difficult when three overlapping designs are present. From this, one may conclude young children do not do well in tasks where they have to systematically scan, isolate, and recognize figures with a confusing background. This task of picking out overlapping figures is fairly easy for children with normal intelligence who are of school age. From the limited studies, LD children do not have figure-ground problems as measured by overlapping or embedded figures.

Visual Closure

Visual closure is another perceptual ability that has been said by several authors (e.g., Kephart, Kirk, Lerner) to be linked with learning disabilities and are part of many informal and formal LD tests. Visual closure, like figure-ground, has been used to describe several different types of perceptual abilities. Visual closure generally, however, refers to the ability to see parts of objects as wholes. For example, one can look at an "M," which has a portion of the center lines erased or covered up with a smudge, and still recognize it. Visual closure was first described by the Gestalt psychologists (Koehler, 1929) and became of interest to LD specialists when Goldstein reported that some World War I soldiers who had sustained brain damage were unable to recognize drawings of simple objects that had portions of the pictures erased. These brain-injured soldiers could only recognize pictures or simple line drawings by tracing over the missing portions with their fingers.

The first experiment of visual closure using children was done by Street (1931), who gave a series of incomplete figures to children and asked them to identify the object. He found that the ability to recognize these figures increased dramatically from the age of two to twelve. Street's test consisted of thirteen figures and was normed on 754 children in third through sixth grade. He found this test did not correlate with intelligence when age was statistically partialled out and has a good reliability. Very little was done in this area until 1960, when Gollin gave a series of incomplete figures to children aged two-and-one-half to five-and-one-half years old with varying amounts of the lines erased. He reported that these children could recognize the objects if only a few lines were missing, indicating that normal children can recognize incomplete drawings. This is not surprising when one realizes that children recognize their toys, for example, when they are piled in a heap with many distracting objects in front of them obstructing their whole view. Gollin's experiment also suggested that the young child's inability to recognize incomplete pictures was due to their inability to recognize objects when the number of visual features had been reduced. Walters, Loan, and Crofts (1961) gave a visual closure task to normal and dyslexic third graders and reported that the LD children did significantly more poorly on this task. Goins (1958) found that the Street test correlated only .30 with first-grade reading in December and .16 with reading in May. The Street test was also found to correlate .38 with intelligence for this age range.

Another measure of closure is the Visual Closure subtest of the ITPA. This is a rather unusual test of visual closure and is timed. It appears also to be a test of systematic scanning and picking up relevant details from a confusing background (e.g., also a figure-ground task). The reliability of this test is low, probably because it involves only four items. One wonders, as with the Street test, how relevant this skill is to the learning problems of children.

Kephart (1960) has suggested that LD children have visual closure difficulties because they do not see words as wholes. He suggests that LD children might see the sentence, "See Spot run.", as "Se eSpo trun.", because they do not have any visual closure. The author has not been able to find any evidence to confirm this theory, although he suspects that LD children can see word boundaries. The author has, however, come across one LD child in several hundred who appeared to have a specific visual closure difficulty. This child could not, for example, copy a circle of dots (as on the Beery) that were arranged in a circle because he kept beginning and ending at a different place. He would read half a word and miss the other half completely. His written spelling was fragmented and showed no attack of the word as a whole. He also could not do simple calculations because the spacing was all confused, and in spite of this, he had a high average intellectual level and on the PIAT, which is a multiple choice test requiring little output other than pointing, he was at grade level in all areas except General Information (which was two years above grade level). Incidentally, he overcame his visual closure problem in about a half year with an hour a day in an LD lab.

In summary, there are many problems with visual closure measures, and so it would probably be advisable to be concerned with visual closure only when it is clear that the child is seeing words and numbers as fragmented parts. In the author's experience, children with overall visual perceptual problems will do poorly on closure tasks, as they will on figure-ground tasks, and children with a "pure" visual closure problem are exceedingly rare (perhaps less than one percent of all LD children).

Visual Memory

Visual memory has been of great interest to diagnosticians since Hinshelwood (1917) hypothesized that the LD child may see the simple service words dozens of times and still not be able to recognize them. LD children also often reverse their letters or take much longer to learn manuscript and cursive, because they cannot remember "how the letters should look." Hinshelwood observed that a number of children who could not read got by in the first grade by listening to other children and memorizing the book from the other children's reading. This led him to assume that material perceived auditorialy was stored in a different area of the brain than material perceived visually.

The above observations suggest that there is an independent memory for each of the three sensory modalities. An alternative hypothesis is that there is only one memory store which is intermodal, that is, neither coded in the auditory or visual sense, and that problems in visual or auditory memory occur in the process of "revisualization" or "reauditorization" of the event. This process of changing an intermodal representation (often called inner language) has been extensively discussed by Johnson and Mykelbust (1964) and has been supported by experiments in which a person is presented material visually (such as on a screen before him) and auditorily (on earphones) and later the subject can remember the information but cannot tell whether he had heard or seen it. The issue of whether memory is coded in one or two separate stores is also clouded, because remembering which letters belong in a word (as in spelling the word) is more than simply visual memory, as this process also involves associating the visual symbols (e.g., c-a-t) with the auditory equivalent (e.g., /kat/). Reading is clearly a mixture of these, because the child does not remember every word at first glance and has to sound words out and, clearly, he does not sound out every word he reads. LD children may often be much stronger visually or auditorially, and this can be readily recognized by observing their errors in reading and spelling.

The experimental evidence that there are different auditory and visual memories is scant. Jensen (1971) reviewed a half dozen or so studies that presented material visually and auditorially and found that some individuals learned better visually or auditorially. Kay (1958), for example, presented noun pairs to college students, finding that twelve percent did signficantly better visually, four percent did significantly better auditorially, with the majority doing equally well in both modalities. Jensen criticized the methodology of Kay's experiment on the ground that these differences could have been statistical and redid this study with the proper controls, finding no significant differences between the two modalities. He points out that these were college students, and had they any significant modality deficits, they probably would not have made it to the university. Using younger subjects, Dornbush and Baslow (1970) matched nine good and nine poor readers in the first, third, fifth, and ninth grades and gave them a visual and auditory memory for digits task. The children were superior in recall of the auditory presentation in almost all cases, and no differences could be found between these two kinds of memory and the reading achievement level of the children.

The general question of the difference between auditory and visual memory becomes more and more complex the more closely it is examined. When we ask a child what he had for breakfast this morning, are we tapping his visual or auditory memory? Is there a separate visual memory and another auditory one with a multitude of links between them so that auditory and visual events are remembered simultaneously, or is there one memory store with visual and auditory events simply employing a special code in this store? There are to date no definite answers, but there is some preliminary evidence that may shed some light on this issue. From neurology we know that there is definitely one area of the brain that processes auditory and another area that processes visual information. At the auditory and visual cortex closure, discrimination and recognition occurs. When, however, electrodes stimulate the lower temporal area of the brain (Penfield and Roberts, 1959), the person will be transported back to some event in the past such as being at a concert. The individual not only sees the event as if he were at a movie during the stimulation, but he can hear the event so clearly that he could, for example, hum the tune of the concert as it is played. In addition to perfect recall of the event, which could have occurred five or ten years before, the person will experience the original emotions that accompanied the event.

This leads to the hypothesis that all events in one's life are recorded in complete sensory detail in a central area of the brain, and that memory of an event is actually a partial recall of this perfect record. Certain persons with photographic memory apparently have complete access to this perfect record. One can often greatly improve the person's recall of an event through the use of hyponosis, which is now done in some police investigations. This event memory, however, is apparently coded much differently than memory for symbolic material. It is not uncommon for subjects in experimental memory studies to be able to describe the room they did the experiment in and what the experimenter looked like several months later, without being able to recall a single word or letter used in the actual experiment even though they had learned the list of words perfectly. Similarly, LD children may remember a great deal of what went on in class, as can be demonstrated on the general information sections of tests, and still forget how to spell the simplest word that they have seen thousands of times.

While event memory is apparently stored as a sound motion picture, the method in which symbolic material is stored is not well understood. We know that excellent spellers and chess players who usually have excellent visual memories do not store information as it was originally perceived. When a speller "sees" a word he is to spell, the word is in a standard face type idiosyncratic to him and not in the face type in which he originally saw the word, and the master chess player will see the chess pieces move across his imaginary board in the correct sequence even though he might have read the game in the newspaper in chess notation (which involves numbers and letters such as P-K4). In a like manner, when one reads *War and Peace*, for example, one can describe in great detail what happened, who was thinking what, various scenes without remembering more than a few sentences of the actual text. The brain has somehow transformed all these words, which are almost completely forgotten, into a completely different code that may persist for years. It seems, then, that symbolic material (which includes verbal material, visual systems such as chess, music, and other complex systems such as geometry and math) is coded in what the author has called an intersensory code and is closely related to meaning and greatly removed from the actual sensory experience. This intersensory code does not necessarily record the modality in which the information was received, so that one often cannot remember whether one learned a fact on TV, read it, or was told it. This information being so removed from the senses forms complex analytical systems and categories (or schemas in Piaget's terms), so that the information cannot be characterized as being either something in visual or auditory memory. For example, is the concept of time; or larger and smaller; or country, nation, and state; something you remember in visual or in auditory memory? Similarly, when the reader is asked to describe how a good speller recalls words, is he using his visual or auditory memory to do so?

There are many types of visual memory and several ways to measure this ability. The basic dimensions of visual memory are:

1. Recognition versus recall memory,
2. Long-term versus short-term memory,
3. Static versus sequential memory, and
4. Symbolic versus nonsymbolic memory.

The first dimension refers to whether the person must report whether he has seen the material before or if he must reproduce it without any cues. A fill-in-the-blank question measures recall memory, while a multiple choice item measures recognition memory. As might be expected, recognition memory is vastly superior. Shephard (1967) demonstrated this dramatically in an experiment in which he presented 600 words, 1,360 short sentences, and 748 colored pictures to adults in three experiments. The subject's task was to read the words or look at the pictures, and when finished they were tested for recognition of the material. Recognition for the words was ninety percent correct for words, eighty-eight percent for the sentences, and ninety-eight percent for the pictures. This was not an easy task, with half of the words being very rare ("ferule," "wattled") and the sentences being complex ("A dead dog is of no use for hunting ducks."). Had the subjects been given a recall task, they would perhaps have gotten a few dozen words or a few sentences. Recognition memory for nonsymbolic memory was incredible; the subjects correctly recognized 1,500 landscape slides at eighty-seven percent accuracy after seven days. The author has done a similar experiment having kindergarten children recognize fifty drawings of common objects. In this case, the children's performance was essentially perfect. Bahrick, Bahrick, and Wittlinger (1974) also showed that people in their fifties still remembered seventy-five percent of the faces of their graduating class, regardless of its size.

Samuels and Anderson (1973) gave a visual recognition and recall task using letter-like figures to normal second-grade children. They used letter-like figures (Gibson figures), because most of the children knew their letters and would have said the names of the letters or words to themselves — thus making it an auditory task as well. Visual recognition correlated nonsignificantly with intelligence, but significantly with reading (.31) and spelling (.33). The visual recall task, where these figures were paired with three letter words, correlated slightly with intelligence (.25) and fairly strongly with reading and spelling (.58 and .57), with the two tasks correlating .43 with each other. When good and poor readers were equated on intelligence, the poor readers did significantly more poorly than the good readers on both tasks.

The second dimension of memory refers to short-term memory, which is memory for tasks lasting roughly for less than half a minute, and long-term memory is any interval longer than this. Most LD tests measure only short-term memory (digit span, the ITPA and Detroit memory subtests, the Graham-Kendall), while most schoolwork requires the child to recognize or recall something seen or heard hours, days, or even weeks later.

There is one aditional type of visual memory, which is actually very short-term memory, called iconic memory, and it lasts only a few tenths of a second. This type of memory has been extensively studied (e.g., Aaronson, 1967) in relation to learning disabilities, because it is directly related to reading. When a child is reading, he is only seeing the words when his eyes are at rest. Typically, the child's eyes stop only for one-tenth second (that is 100 milliseconds) to perceive the word before moving farther down the line. One can duplicate this process experimentally using a tachistoscope on which words can be flashed from one to 1,000 milliseconds. When this is done at 100 milliseconds, one finds children and college students can report correctly only one to four random letters, with four or five letters being their "span of apprehension" or the upper limit of their iconic memory for letters. However, when the letters are organized into complicated words such as the word "sophistication," adults can read the word and the beginning reader reports only four letters. Adults in the process of extensive reading apparently develop some memory process for the word, so that they can see the word as a whole unit. How the brain can see this as a whole unit is not well known (Smith, 1971), but it would appear that LD children have a real deficiency in this type of memory, because they are constantly breaking words up into small units and, as a result, read very slowly and hesitantly.

With adults, the question of what happens within the one hundred milliseconds when the eyes are stationary has been studied by masking the letters within this interval. In general, it takes the brain about ten milliseconds to recognize a letter, so four-letter words would take forty milliseconds to be perceived (Kahneman, 1968). These experiments have not yet been performed to any extent with children (Boswell, 1971), so little can be said about basic visual processing of LD children. Goins (1958), however, has reported that training children tachistoscopically, gradually increasing digits with fast exposures, does not improve their reading ability. Crovitz and Schiffman (1965) have also presented evidence that this span of perception for letters at one hundred milliseconds follows typical memory curves, indicating that tachistoscopic tasks are memory tasks. By presenting fifth graders with nonsense syllables tachistoscopically, Wallach (1963) obtained correlations between memory span and spelling of .47, memory and reading of .37, and .30 with arithmetic achievement.

The third dimension of memory is that of static memory versus sequential memory. The difference between static and sequential memory is of interest because quite a few LD children have difficulties in remembering the order of the letters in words. Such children will write words such as "wish" as "wihs," or "such" and "scuh," and the like. Sequential memory is usually measured by showing the subject a set of cards laid out in a row in a particular order, then scrambling up the order and having him put the cards in correct order again. In a large investigation of 310 children in second through twelfth grades, Rizzo (1939) presented the children nine-letter nonsense words that were flashed on a screen either successively or at once. He found that this measure of static and sequential memory correlated moderately well with each other (.49) and was related to reading only in the second-grade children. Weiner, Bosley, and Rabinovitch (1970) compared normal and LD children on a visual sequential task using arrays of lights. They found no relationship between performance on the sequencing task and reading. One position is that of Orton, who maintained that LD children have a specific deficit in sequencing material both temporally or visually. He linked this inability to faulty spatial organization and lack of right-left discrimination. Poppen, et al. (1969) have developed this into a theory that one type of learning disability is due to a general sequencing disability.

As already reviewed, many researchers do not report these variables as being related to learning disabilities, except in the early primary grades, suggesting that the lack of right-left discrimination is just part of a general maturational lag. The other position taken is that sequencing of memory items is just one more feature of memory. Not only is it another feature such as straight-curvedness, but it is one of the most difficult features to master. The most common mistake made on the digit span task by normal subjects is to reverse the order of a number pair. In real life, we only have to think of how many times we have reversed a telephone number to realize how easy it is to get this feature wrong. Since two studies found no relationship between visual sequential memory and reading, except in the early grades, visual sequential memory may not be a special defect of LD children.

The fourth dimension of memory is the type of material used. One finds that LD children who cannot remember words do not necessarily have deficient memories for people's faces or objects around them. This is evident from the examples of visual discrimination research already reviewed, which show that tasks involving geometric figures and pictures do not correlate with reading, while letters and letter-like forms do. Visual tests requiring the remembering of pictures, which have no verbal component to them (i.e., pictures that subjects cannot label), would not involve intermodal processing, and therefore, would most likely not use the same processes as reading. These visual processes, therefore, could be normal with the child being a poor reader. If the visual processes were very poor, however, the intermodal processes would also be poor, and the child would most likely be a poor reader. In this connection, McGrady and Olson (1970) did an extensive experimental study comparing the performance of normal and LD eight- and nine-year-olds on four modalities (auditory, visual, auditory-visual, and visual-auditory) and two content areas (verbal and nonverbal). The LD children did much more poorly on verbal materials than nonverbal materials with no differences in the modality in which the information was presented. In other words, the type of material used was far more significant than the modality.

High visual memory for symbolic material differs greatly from high visual memory for nonsymbolic memory, which is often called having a "photographic memory." Persons with photographic memory can recall in photographic detail events that happened many years previously. A few individuals, such as Luria's mnemonists (Luria, 1968), have perfect visual memories, which means that they can recall visually everything that they have ever seen in their lives with such clarity that they can read back, for example, pages of books seen years previously. Persons with partial photographic memory will remember events in which they were emotionally involved, but not remember in perfect detail other events. These individuals will see pages of books, but often they cannot "read" them because their detail is not clear. There is a fairly foolproof test of photographic memory called the Julez test (to be described later). Persons with partial photographic memory are not particularly good spellers in the author's experience.

There are a number of standardized tests of visual memory. The major ones are:

1. The Visual Sequential Memory of the ITPA. While this test is good in that it uses symbolic material, the retest reliability is close to chance level, so that it cannot be used for diagnostic purposes.

2. The Visual Attention Span for Objects subtest of the Detroit. This task is not purely visual because there is nothing to prevent the child from saying the name of the object when it is presented, thus making it an auditory task as well. One can reduce the auditorization of the task by having the child hold a pencil or his tongue between his teeth, but this procedure would invalidate the norms.

3. The Visual Attention Span for Letters of the Detroit. This test has the same failings as the other Detroit subtests in that the letters can be auditorized. The two Detroit tests also do not have any published reliabilities, so little can be said about their test characteristics. It has been the author's experience that LD children do much more poorly on the span for letters and many do fairly well on the span for objects.

4. The Revised Visual Retention Test by Benton. The test has good reliability and norming. In one study fifty-four percent of normal and fifty-two percent of brain-injured children were correctly identified with this test. How accurate this test is in identifying LD children has not been established.

5. The Memory-For-Designs (MFD) test by Graham and Kendall. Graham and Kendall (1960) report that this test is unreliable for children below the age of eight. They also found that a group of children with reading difficulty did not differ from normal children on this test. The MFD correlated .34 with intelligence, and the authors of the test suggest that this test measures more complex variables than just visual memory.

6. Another test for visual memory is the Print-the-Alphabet (PTA) test (Johnson, 1977) which consists of simply asking the child to print all the small letters from a to z and then all the capital letters from A to Z. The letters are then scored for reversals, incorrect case (the child uses a capital for lower case letter) and omissions. LD children do particularly poorly on this test because they cannot remember the letter forms though almost all can say the alphabet orally.

7. Another test of visual memory is one developed by Julez, which is used to screen children for a photographic memory (Julez, 1971). This test consists of one hundred dots randomly placed in two squares. The individual stares at one square and tries to place all the dots in his mind's eye, and then he looks at the second square, and if he superimposes the dots will see a number. There is also a version using 10,000 dots and individuals with partial photographic memory can correctly do this task.

The research into whether LD children have specific visual skill deficits or have just a weak visual perceptual functioning is singularly lacking. To demonstrate a specific visual skill deficit, one would have to have fairly reliable and valid measures of subskills and test children over a period of time to show these are rather consistent individual differences. As far as this author is aware, such research has not been done except for a few isolated visual traits. Design copying tasks probably come closest to this, although they do not measure visual memory and are contaminated by motor coordination variables.

Tests of Visual Perception

In the foregoing discussion many tests measuring specific visual abilities were described. The ideal psychometric test in visual perception would be a single test made up of a series of highly reliable subtests, which would measure acuity, color blindness, interposition, binocular fusion, ocular dominance, size constancy, shape constancy, visual discrimination, closure, figure-ground, and the various types of visual memory. Such a test would take hours to administer and would be testing a number of skills that are only peripherally related to learning problems. A better strategy is to give the child a complex visual task that involves many subskills so that these abilities can be tested simultaneously. For example, when one asks a child to examine a set of overlapping figures and outline all the diamonds, one is testing his acuity, discrimination, figure-ground, and motor coordination.

Copying Tasks

The copying of designs is one of the most common of visual perceptual tests. The copying of a design as mentioned in Chapter VIII involves: (a) adequate mental age to use a motor plan, (b) normal visual perception of the design to be copied, and (c) the motor coordination to execute the design. These tasks are quite old, and the copying of geometric designs appeared on the first Binet Intelligence scales and are still used to assess for mental ability on the Kuhlmann-Binet, the Merrill-Palmer, and the Stanford-Binet intelligence tests. Gesell was particularly interested in the drawing of geometric figures as a measure of mental maturation that was relatively free from verbal influence. Below is a list of the Gesell figures and the average age at which the copying of the figures is mastered (Silver, 1950 and Ilg and Ames, 1965).

At the age of:	The child can:
18 months	scribble spontaneously
2 years	imitate a vertical or circular stroke
3 years	copy a circle
4 years	copy a cross
5 years	copy a square
6 years	copy a triangle
7 years	copy a diamond
11 years	copy a British flag, cylinder, and cube

These Gesell figures also appear on the Denver Developmental Screeing test and the Purdue Perceptual-Motor test as motor tasks.

Goldberg and Schiffman (1972, pp. 90-93) have done extensive correlations of the Gesell figures and other measures using 157 children aged six and seven. They found that each of the eight Gesell figures correlated between .45 and .70 with a total perceptual score. The total drawing score correlated .41 with intelligence (on the WISC), .33 with the WRAT, and .22 with the Gray Oral Reading test. This would indicate that this visual-motor skill is related to academic achievement.

Maccoby and Bee (1965) have discussed the difference between being able to perceive a figure accurately and being able to copy it.

They point out that normal children can discriminate between a square, circle, and triangle before the age of one; at the age of two a child can fit various geometric shapes into the correct cutout patterns on a board, but the normal child cannot copy a circle until the age of three and a square at five, showing that for normal children, at least, the copying of designs is not one of visual perception.

Besides the Gesell figures, which are not really standardized, there are a number of figure drawing tests. The Ellis Designs test is a set of seven designs to be copied on a plain sheet of paper. This test first appeared in Bonner and Healey's (1929) textbook on psychological testing and was normed by Wood and Schulman (1940). The Ellis test is still occasionally used, because Strauss and Kephart (1955) included this test as the measure of visual perception in their book, even though it is poorly normed and has no reliabilities.

The Bender-Gestalt test, already discussed in the section on brain-injury tests, has been used to diagnose visual perceptual problems. Koppitz (1960) compared the Bender on normal and LD children from first through fourth grades and obtained a significant difference between these groups. The LD children had more distortions, rotations, substitutions of circles for dots, perseverations, parts not joined, or incorrect angles. Lachmann confirmed these results in a different study, and Smith and Keogh (1962) obtained a correlation of .39 between the Bender administered to kindergartners and reading achievement in first grade. Interestingly, the Bender correlated .54 with the kindergarten teachers' predictions of child's reading ability and .51 with a reading readiness test. Silver and Hagin (1964) found rotations on the Bender was only one of two in eight measures that separated normals from dyslexics as children and also as adults. Culbertson and Gann (1966) and O'Conner (1969) both found the Bender to correlate about .50 with the Frostig. Chang and Chang (1967) found the Bender to differentiate low and high readers in second grade, but not in the fifth grade. Finally, Duffey and Clair (1972) found the Bender given in first grade differentiated good and poor readers in fourth grade better than an intelligence test.

There is also much negative evidence that the Bender predicts learning problems (Ackerman, Peters, and Dykman, 1971; Ferinden and Jacobson, 1970; Hartlage and Lucas, 1976; Robinson and Schwartz, 1973 to cite a few).

To summarize, the Bender seems effective in diagnosing LD problems in the first few grades, but not so after about the third grade. This test correlates well with reading readiness measures. It should be used with an IQ test, because of the intellectual nature of the task, and it has been reported in some but not other cases, to add some additional information beyond the IQ test.

The Developmental Test of Visual Perception (DTVP) by Frostig is a general visual perceptual test for children four to seven years of age. This test is normed on about 1,000 middle-class white children. The test has five subtests consisting of a fine motor task, outline various shapes with confusing backgrounds, and copying matrices of evenly spaced dots. Boyd and Randall (1970), in a factor analytic investigation, report that the Frostig measures one general perceptual factor, not five isolated abilities. Sabatino, Abbot, and Bechner (1974) obtained a retest reliability of .78 for the total score for kindergartners, which was considerably higher than the Bender (.46) and equivalent to the Metropolitan Readiness test (.81). All subtests, however, had reliabilities too low for individual diagnosis. In a review of the Frostig, Meyers and Hammil (1969) concluded, "The DTVP adequately predicts reading readiness at the first-grade level, but not the level of achievement allowed in the first grade. . .it is related to a 'small degree' with second- and third-grade reading ability. The predictive value of the DTVP at these levels is not as high as that of intelligence, however." Even this conclusion has been challenged by two investigations (Liebert and Sherk, 1970; Colarusso, Martin, and Harting, 1970).

The Motor-Free Visual Perception Test (MVPT) is a visual perceptual test that does not require the child to draw or copy. The test was normed on 881 children in twenty-two states and consists of thirty-six plates covering the visual tasks of matching designs and letters, recognizing embedded and overlapping figures, visual closure, correct orientation, and memory for letters and designs. The test correlates well with other visual perceptual tests and has a reliability of .81. This test has norms for children aged four to eight. When compared to other tests, the MVPT has much better test characteristics and is the test of choice for determining if the child has a "pure" visual perceptual problem.

The best standardized figure copying test is the Developmental Test of Visual-Motor Integration (VMI) developed by Beery and Buktenika. This test consists of twenty designs to be copied in a booklet. The test was standardized on 1,039 children aged four to eight years old. The test has a reliability of .93. The VMI has the advantage over the Bender in that it does not take special clinical training to administer the test. The manual is fairly complete and gives examples of designs drawn by children that are scored as passing or failing. Berry and Buktenika found that the interscorer reliability was high and this test correlates .50 with reading in first grade and about .45 with IQ.

Another common visual perceptual task is the Draw-A-Man (DAM) test, which has many forms. The best standardization is by Harris (1963), who asks the child to draw a man, a woman, and then himself. The test is scored for the absence or presence of ninety-three characteristics (e.g., eyebrow, neck, nostrils, etc.) and yields an IQ score that gives a fair indication of the child's visual perceptual development if he has normal intelligence. If the DAM IQ is 15 points (i.e., one standard deviation) below the intellectual level (as determined by a verbal test), the child can be said to be significantly below in perceptual development. This test differs from the VMI in that the child must reproduce an abstraction from memory. The DAM, therefore, is a composite task involving: (a) motor coordination, (b) intellectual development of how to form the parts of the body, (c) experience with drawing persons, and (d) spatial ability. This last aspect is of interest, because often grossly distorted body proportions will indicate spatial problems. Swensen (1968) and Roback (1968) can be consulted for reviews of the figure drawing literature.

Diagnosing a Visual Perceptual Problem

Learning disabilities are often considered perceptual problems, but actually the LD child's disability may be much broader than this. One must first consider whether the child has any significant sensory, biological, or neurological disability. In the case of children with cerebral palsy, spina bifida, and epilepsy, the child may well have both abnormal neurological signs and perceptual problems. The next level of analysis revolves around the child's motivation, previous learning, and concentration. If these are fairly good, one may begin to make a decision as to whether the child has a general verbal deficit. Children who score significantly lower on tests when the content is verbal or auditory in nature, will also very likely have a low Verbal IQ on the WISC and a low IQ on verbal-oriented tests such as the Stanford-Binet and Slosson. Since this ability correlates highly with general academic performance, children low in the area will usually also do poorly in school.

The third level of analysis comes with a decision of whether there is a difference in the way visual and auditory information is processed. There have been a number of investigations into this area, two relevant studies being: Goetzinger, Dirks, and Baer (1960), who found differences between LD and normal readers in auditory but not visual tasks; and Bruininks (1969), who gave six auditory and six visual tasks to normal and poor lower-class readers and found the good readers did significantly better on four auditory and only two visual tasks when IQ was held constant. If a definite modality difference is obtained (and often it is not), the clinician can then make recommendations as to which sensory channel to teach the child. If the deficient channel is visual, the clinician can then begin to establish if the child has a specific visual perceptual deficiency. Here, the child's figure-ground, closure, discrimination, and memory can be tested. Children with learning disabilities with one specific visual perceptual ability that is extremely poor, with other visual abilities being normal, are fairly rare. In fact, common sense would suggest that a child with such a specific disability might well develop coping mechanisms and, therefore, not be low enough in academics to be considered for an LD program. In the author's experience, most specific examples of a limited deficit have been essentially the result of one subtest being low because of testing error.

Chapter X

The Evaluation of Auditory Perception

Reading is actually a visual symbolic system used to represent oral language or, as some have said, a language based on a language. Referring to *Appendix A* one can see that it is convenient to think of six auditory processes feeding into Auditory Word Perception, which is simply the ability to perceive words accurately. This ability interacts closely with Auditory Long-Term Memory, which goes into Reading Comprehension along with the skills of Verbal Reasoning, Syntax, and Isolated Word Recognition. The processes that go into word recognition and the various kinds of auditory memory will be discussed in this chapter, while the syntax and language skills will be discussed in the next chapter. Before going into the individual processes, a fundamental difference between auditory and visual processes should be noted. Visual stimuli can be presented simultaneously so that the individual can look back and forth to make comparisons to differentiate between the stimuli. They involve directionality, spatial reasoning, and the ability to move the eyes to the desired location, while all auditory processes are time dependent, because as soon as something is heard it is gone.

Auditory Acuity

Auditory acuity is measured in decibels (dB), which is simply a measure of sound pressure on the ear drum. The decibel scale is a logarithmic one, so that each increase of 20 dB is actually ten, not two times louder. A 20 dB noise cannot be heard unless the background is completely quite; a whisper is about 40 dBs loud; the average classroom functions at 65 dB; a noisy truck or motorcycle makes a sound of 85 dB, and a 120 dB noise made by an airplane taking off is painful to the ears. A hearing loss is measured in terms of the loudness in decibels of the softest sound a person can hear fifty percent of the time. But it is not so simple, because hearing varies with frequency (or pitch) of the tone. The human ear can hear approximately between 20 cycles per second (Hertz) and 20,000 Hz.

Low frequencies, such as a 50 or 100 Hz, are equivalent to the low notes of a piano; middle C on the piano is 256 Hz; and 5,000 Hz is produced by high pitched instruments such as the piccolo. The human voice ranges between 100 and 10,000 Hz with the n, m, d, and p sounds, for example, being produced at about 300 Hz, while the sh, ch, s, and th sounds are produced at 6,000 Hz.

In the schools, a child's hearing is normally tested with a pure tone audiometer, which presents five different pitched tones through earphones at various intensities. The child usually indicates that he or she has heard the tone by raising a finger, and overall hearing is the average of the five frequencies. Hearing loss is usually classified into five levels, and since the clinician is sometimes asked to make the decision of whether a child with a mild hearing loss also has auditory perceptual problems, the five levels will be presented.

Loss	Amount of Loss
0 to 25 dB	*Normal Hearing.*
25 to 40 dB	*Mild Loss.* Student will have slight difficulty in hearing conversational speech at distances of three to five feet. May miss half of class discussion if face is not visible or classroom noise is present.
40 to 55 dB	*Moderate Loss.* Conversational speech must be loud to be understood. Classroom discussion will be difficult to follow and student will probably have speech and language difficulties.
55 to 70 dB	*Severe Loss.* Student may hear a moderately loud voice if it is very close to the ear. Speech and language will not be learned without hearing aid and special instruction.
70 to 90 dB	*Profound Loss.* Child will not be aware of sound in the environment.

There are two different kinds of hearing losses. To understand these one must know how the ear functions. The outside ear (the pinna) leads into the ear canal, which ends up at the ear drum (tympanic membrane). Beyond the tympanic membrane begins the middle ear, made up of three bones (ossicles) called the hammer, anvil, and stirrup. These bones are connected to a snail-shaped ball (cochlea), which contains fluid and thousands of sensory hairs that transmit electrical messages to the brain via the auditory nerve. The sound comes into the external ear, hits the tympanic membrane, and causes it to vibrate. These vibrations move the three ossicles, which mechanically amplify the sound thirty times and set the fluid of the cochlea moving. The vibrating fluid causes the hairs to bend; whenever a hair bends it transmits an electrical impulse to the auditory nerve, which goes up the spinal cord and to the primary auditory cortex of the brain.

Children with a hearing loss have either a conduction or a sensory-neural loss. Conduction losses are due to a blockage in the outer ear or a defect in the middle ear. The most common cause of reduced conduction is wax or a small object blocking the ear canal or the person may have had a ruptured ear drum, which usually heals with a scar that reduces auditory acuity. Another common conduction loss is due to reduced mobility of the ossicles from inner ear infections called otis media. In school-age children, eighty percent of hearing impairments are due to allergies, infections, or blockages in the ear canal. Other causes are hearing defects due to adverse side reactions to medications, a calcification of the ossicles, and genetically inherited disorders (Hardy and Bordley, 1959; Konigsmark, 1972).

The second major type of deafness is sensory deafness, which is due to the hairs of the cochlea not working properly. This type of deafness can be diagnosed because the air conduction loss will be as low as the bone conduction loss. The sensory hairs cannot be replaced, so nothing can be done for sensory deafness except to amplify the sound with a hearing aid so that the residual hairs will pick up some sound. Nerve deafness results from auditory nerves being damaged, and nerve damage will appear on an audiogram in the same manner as sensory deafness.

These two different kinds of hearing losses can be diagnosed from an audiogram. The audiologist first presents through earphones varying intensities of sound, which are perceived via the ossicles, and a measurement of "air conduction" is made. Then a small speaker is placed over the ear and the sound is conducted through the temporal bone of the skull bypassing the ossicles and going directly to the cochlea, yielding a "bone conduction" measure. If air conduction acuity is lower than bone conduction, then there is a strong indication that the eardrum or ossicles are not functioning properly. If both air and bone conduction are low, then there is sensori-neural damage. *Figure 21* shows an audiogram, and one can see that the two types of losses are represented. The actual decibel losses in the right-hand side were obtained by averaging the 500, 1,000, and 2,000 Hz reception,

Figure 21
Audiometric Evaluation

Name: __Nikki J.__ Birthdate: __1-11-75__ Age: __6-1__ Sex: __F__ Date: __2-11-81__

School: __Naropa Elem__ Grade: __1__ Ref. By: __School Nurse__ Examiner: __Hughs__

Code:	Air	Air Masked	Bone	Bone Masked
Right (red)	o	[o]	>	▷
Left (blue)	x	[x]	<	◁

Test Conditions: __Good - Cooperative__

Tuning Forks __Not Used__

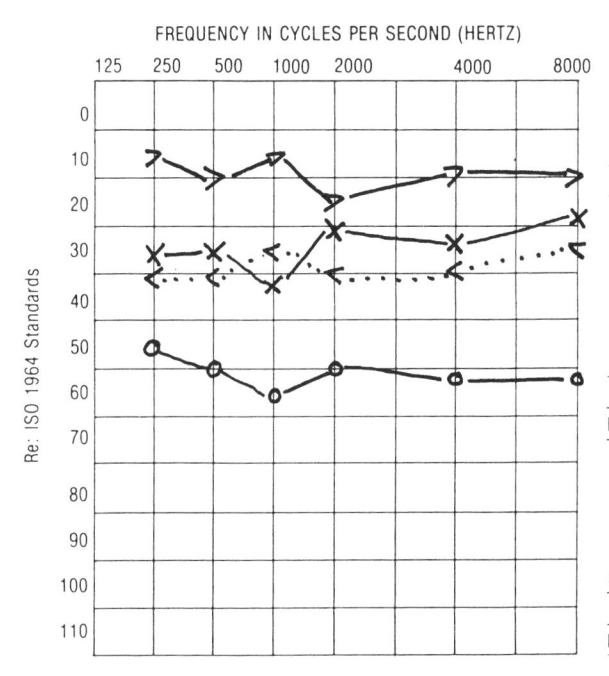

Pure Tone Average 500-2000 cps.

	Air	Bone
R	53 db	15 db
L	35 db	33 db

Speech Reception Threshold

R-Ear	55 db
L-Ear	40 db
Freefield (Both)	50 db

Speech Discrimination

S.L. __40__ db

R-Ear	50 %
L-Ear	30 %
Freefield (R & L)	35 %

History: Student failed first grade screening test by school nurse twice. Having academic problems, but speech appears normal.

Comments and recommendations: Appears to have neurosensory loss in left ear and conduction loss in right ear. Student should see a physician. For other recommendations see enclosed sheet.

while the speech reception threshold was obtained by using words instead of tones at various intensities.

The research on the relationship between auditory acuity and learning is relatively sparse. Fiedler (1949) reported seven percent of the school population he studied had a 20 dB loss or more. Kennedy (1942) found little relationship between auditory acuity and reading, while Bond (1942) did find a relationship. Reynolds (1953) reports that auditory acuity correlated significantly with reading comprehension, but not word recognition. However, when intelligence was statistically partialled out, there was no longer a relationship, suggesting children with lower IQs also performed more poorly on the hearing test. In a more relevant investigation Roach and Rosecrans (1972) compared verbal and nonverbal IQ scores with hearing loss. The WISC verbal, which measures verbal comprehension as well as intelligence, correlated significantly (.51) with a hearing loss, while nonverbal IQ did not. They then compared this correlation at various frequencies and discovered that the 250 to 4,000 Hz range correlated highest with verbal intelligence, suggesting this is the range of frequencies most sensitive to auditory comprehension.

In modern school systems, screening for hearing problems using a portable audiometer to measure pure-tone air conduction is routine. Since hearing is closely related to language, all LD children should be screened for hearing problems. Farrald and Schumber (1973) have suggested that children with auditory acuity problems might be identified also by observing them for: (a) facial contortions and body strain, (b) strong eye contact and visual focus, (c) inattention when spoken to or little response to loud noises, (d) inability to identify sounds, poor auditory discrimination, and misinterpreting simple sounds, (e) asking "What?" all the time, (f) having a speech defect or inappropriate voice quality, (g) complaining of ringing in the ears (titinis), (h) speaking very loudly or softly, or (i) having chronic ear infections.

Auditory Perception

Very little is understood of how the thousands of sounds varying in hundreds of pitches and intensities that bombard the ear each minute are translated into meaningful information. An example of the complexity of this task was demonstrated in the 1950s when Bell Laboratories developed a voice spectrogram for visually recording speech sounds. The Bell scientists wanted to isolate the various words in speech and then determine which sounds were involved in making these words. To their surprise, there were often longer pauses within a single word than between words. Considering that words are recognized in a few hundredths of a second, it is clear that the brain does not simply listen to a set of sounds and then match them with previously known words. The only way in which the brain could possibly process auditory information as rapidly as it does is to ignore a great deal of irrelevant sounds, to fuse the individual sounds into higher units, and to employ a distinctive feature strategy to recognize these higher units (Mattingly, 1972). For example, when we are listening to a lecture, we must filter out the air conditioner or fan, the outside street noises, the rustling of clothing, etc. These noises are, however, registered, because if the noise suddenly stops, it is noticed. Figure-ground perception must occur to reduce the auditory stimuli to a manageable number of units. On the other side of the coin, the brain must also fuse a multitude of different sounds into a whole. If we are listening to an orchestra, twenty different instruments may be playing, yet we hear it as a pleasing whole and respond to the combined sound. Only when we try to listen to a particular instrument do we realize that we are not hearing the individual instruments.

Finally, we hear by distinctive features, which is readily noticeable when learning a foreign language. We begin by hearing only those sounds in our own language and grasp only a global idea of what is said in each sentence. With time, the more subtle features of grammar, tone, inflection are gradually noticed, and when these features become automatic, we become a "fluent" speaker. In fact the whole notion of distinctive features described in the chapter on visual perception originated in the 1950s in an analysis of spoken language (Jakobson and Halle, 1956). Not only are individual words recognized by distinctive features, but there is evidence to suggest that whole sentences are stored by their simple structure (subject, verb, object) with distinctive features to suggest syntactical markers such as passives, future tense, questions, etc.

Before discussing the individual auditory subskills, another set of experiments by Warren and Warren (1970) will be described to give the reader an overall idea of how auditory perception works. These researchers investigated auditory illusions by taping a few sentences in which a part of a word had been spliced out and replaced with a cough or other extraneous sound. Even when the adult subjects were told what had been done, they could not locate the word that had a missing part. The words were perceived as wholes, and the location of the cough even after repeated listening could not be located. Another interesting illusion occurs when a word is repeated over and over again with no other words to give it context; the subjects hear the word change, so "dress" becomes "Esther," "stress," "Joyce," etc.

When the word is heard twice a second, the average college student hears thirty changes and does not believe the experimenter when told the word has not been changed. Children at age five hear few or no transformations, by the age of eight all children tested heard transformations. Apparently, a vast amount of auditory decoding involves hearing the correct word based on anticipation of its context in the sentence. When the context is broken, the brain still continues to guess, suggest sounds, and so on.

Figure-Ground Perception

The ears, unlike the eyes, cannot cut off stimuli. From the day a child is born he is bombarded with sounds and in the first few years of life begins to make finer and finer discriminations and unconscious categorizations of sounds. When the child begins verbal communication, he or she begins to separate the speech sounds from other background noises. One can see this with preschoolers, who at the age of three and four will interrupt an adult to point out the faint droning of an airplane or a truck moving outside the building. By school age, the child hardly notices these noises. The author remembers one case where an eight-year-old boy was thought to have poor attending behavior until the teacher heard him say to himself in class, "Well, there goes Charlie." She questioned him, and he told her that the sound outside was his neighbor Charlie starting his car about a block away. The teacher concluded from this that he must have "super" awareness of sounds and therefore good attention. Actually, it appeared to the author that the teacher had missed the point, because the boy was tuned into such irrelevant noises that he had a severe figure-ground problem.

Figure-ground perception is based on a very complex neurological system that operates at several levels of the nervous system. First, there is general masking, which is an automatic process involving the brain stem and some neuropathways going from the brain to the cochlea (called efferent pathways). When an individual hears a pattern of sound against a steady or regular background, the signal is sharpened and amplified while the background noise is diminished. This mechanism, also found in the visual system, works on all simultaneously perceived sounds, not just sounds with meaning. Experimentally this can be demonstrated by presenting through one earphone random noise and adding to it a particular tone so that the tone can barely be heard over the background noise. When this background noise is presented to the other ear as well, however, the signal suddenly jumps out because the hearing mechanism takes the noise from one ear and cancels out the noise from the other ear (Jeffress, 1965).

A second mechanism to eliminate extraneous noise is called habituation (Groves and Sharpless, 1970). Basically when there is a repetitive sound such as a fan whirring, the person is aware of the sound first, but his awareness of it fades until the signal changes (i.e. misses a beat, gets louder or softer). This fading can be shown to cause a reduction of the firing of neurons in the auditory pathways. The reticular formation is intimately involved in habituation, and this is of particular interest because this is the area of the brain that is also apparently involved with arousal level, which has been found to be abnormal with most hyperactive children.

Third, there is the "cocktail effect," which is best illustrated by an example; suppose you are at a cocktail party in a circle of friends listening to someone speak. When you are interested in what the person is saying, you can hear his voice with the other voices being more-or-less background buzzing. However, when you become bored, you can "tune in" another conversation outside the group. When you are listening to the other person's conversation, you do not hear what you friend is saying unless he mentions your name; when you suddenly "tune in" again. The cocktail effect is the ability to tune in and tune out various simultaneous conversations. Under controlled conditions, in which the conversations are taped and played over earphones, it has been discovered that a person can only pay attention to one conversation at a time (Moray, 1969). When a person is listening to two things at once, he or she is tuning into one conversation for a few seconds and then shifting the attention to the next conversation. The cocktail effect relies on being able to use selective attention to the voice quality (is it a male or female voice) in conjunction with auditory depth perception.

One would expect that the child who cannot pay attention to the teacher (and is not just bored with what the teacher is saying) probably does not have adequate figure-ground mechanisms. In spite of this, there is very little research into how figure-ground is related to school achievement. Flowers (1968) gave a competing messages test to deficient and proficient readers in third grade. The students were given a different message in each ear and had to pick out one of them. This task was unrelated to intelligence, and poor readers did significantly less well than good readers. The correlation of this figure-ground task and reading, as measured in the Gates word and paragraph reading, was .50 for first and .58 for second graders. The correlation of this task measured in kindergarten with first- and second-grade spelling, vocabulary, word study skills, and language ability ranged between .41 and .48. The correlations between figure-ground and total phonics ability (naming letters, identifying letter and word sounds) was .44. As may be seen, this task does almost as well in predicting reading ability as many reading readiness tests. Conners, Kramer, and Guerra (1969) have given a similar figure-ground task in which the child hears two different sets of digits in each ear who must report all the digits heard. Both normal and LD children reported those heard in one ear first and then those heard in the other ear, because the brain cannot switch back and forth from one ear to the next in the short time the digits are presented. They found, however, that the LD children did significantly more poorly on the first set of digits from the dominant ear, but not on the second half of the digits presented to the nondominant ear. This interesting finding, if repeated, would suggest that LD children may be more "right-brained" than "left-brained."

There are only a few standardized measures of figure-ground perception generally available. One is the Woodcock-Goldman-Fristoe Auditory Discrimination Test, consisting of a tape and a book with four pictures on a page. During the "quiet" test various words are read off and the subject points to the appropriate picture. the second half, the noise test, is identical except that there is an extremely noisy cafeteria scene added to the tape. This is a very hard test, and most LD children do extremely poorly on this test, which has a reliability of about .65. Very similar to this is the Goldman-Fristoe-Woodcock Auditory Selective Attention test, which is more detailed, has much better reliability, and is made up of three different discrimination tests.

Auditory Discrimination

Auditory discrimination is the ability to distinguish between two different sounds. It is usually measured by presenting two words that are identical or different by one phoneme. The examiner may say "pin" and "pen" and the child says "different," and then the examiner says "rock" and "rock" and the child says "same." Poor discrimination can be due to unfamiliarity with the distinctive features of the language or a deficiency in processing these features. Wepman (1968) has pointed out that auditory discrimination for words gradually increases to the age of nine and then levels off with about one-fifth of first graders still making inadequate discriminations. Dystra (1966) has done an extensive review of auditory discrimination and reports that the discrimination aspects of reading have been examined only infrequently. He concluded from twenty separate studies:

> When comparisons are made between matched groups of 'good' and 'poor' readers, skill in auditory discrimination appears to be significantly related to achievement in

reading. . . .When the auditory discrimination skills of disabled readers are examined, research is in general agreement that disabled readers are markedly deficient in these skills. However, examining relationships between auditory discrimination and reading achievement of unselected populations of elementary and secondary students results in inconclusive findings. . . .Furthermore, age does not seem to be a factor in determining whether or not skills in auditory discrimination are related to reading achievement. Studies involving pupils from grades two through 12 appear to be equally inconclusive in trying to establish the extent of the relationship. . . .Studies which have attempted to assess the relationship of auditory discrimination ability during the pre-reading period and future success in learning to read have generally reported small positive correlational relationships ranging from approximately .20 to .40.

Another interesting finding was that the correlation between auditory discrimination and reading was higher for pupils learning to read using intensive phonics programs. In many investigations auditory discrimination would correlate with reading, while auditory blending and rhyming did not. After summarizing the data, Dystra engaged in his own investigation using a multiple regression technique to predict word recognition at the end of first grade from tests administered in September. The single highest variable that predicted reading was intelligence, which accounted for twenty-one percent of the variance. The addition of the Harrison-Stroud, a test of auditory skills without any discrimination subtests only added eight percent more variance, and two auditory discrimination tests brought the variance up to thirty-six percent. For paragraph recognition, however, auditory discrimination accounted for twenty-two percent. Why discrimination would be a better predictor of paragraph reading is not clear, except that word recognition is more of a visual task. Other studies since then (Benger, 1968; Blank, 1968) have also obtained small but significant correlations between reading and auditory discrimination.

Auditory discrimination is part of overall auditory processing, and Templin (1957), for example, has shown this measure also to relate to length of sentences used, complexity of sentences, number of different words used in oral language tasks, as well as correlating significantly with two picture vocabulary measures. Rechner and Wilson (1967), however, found three studies that support and three studies that fail to support a relationship between auditory discrimination and articulation problems.

There are several measures of auditory discrimination:

1. The most frequently used is Wepman's Auditory Discrimination Test consisting of forty word pairs, thirty that are different and ten that are the same. The Wepman has a retest reliability of .91 and has been found to correlate .32 with general intelligence. There has been a fair amount of literature criticizing the Wepman. Katz and Illmer (1972) suggest the same-different concept is difficult for some children. Vellurtina, DeSetto, and Sleger (1972) also suggest that the 30/10 split between same and different words leads to unnecessary misses, because the child expects a 20/20 split. Neville and Bucke (1968) compared performance on a Wepman-like task using thirty-seven real and nonsense words. The list that was presented first — whether real or nonsense — was discriminated better, implying that fatigue is an important variable in this type of task. The nonsense words overall, however, were more poorly discriminated. Since the nonsense words contained the same sounds as the real words, this task apparently does not measure just the ability to hear the differences between sounds. Rather the task involves a fair amount of memory, because the child must hold the first word of the pair in memory and then make the comparison (*see* Flowers, 1968). Finally, Goetzinger, Dirks, and Baer (1960) compared good and poor readers on three auditory discrimination tasks (the Wepman, the W-22 used by audiologists, and the Rush-Hughs), and they report that the Wepman did not correlate with the other two discrimination measures, which correlated well with each other.

2. The Goldman-Fristoe-Woodcock Test of Auditory Discrimination is a screening test that consists of a tape with words being read, and the student must point to one of four pictures that represent the words. There is a training procedure to make sure the child knows the picture names. This test is fairly well standardized, but the four-choice situation apparently leads to low reliability (.60s). The other half of the test is the figure-ground task already described.

3. The Goldman-Fristoe-Woodcock Auditory Skills Test Battery has a much more reliable discrimination test that has three parts. The first part screens for difficult sounds, while parts II and III give a detailed feature analysis of which sounds are poorly discriminated. This test is very reliable and well standardized and is the test of choice.

Auditory Closure (Phonemic Synthesis)

Auditory closure or sound blending is the ability to take separate sounds and put them together to make complete words. The interest in blending goes back to Monroe's (1932) study comparing 269 poor and 126 normal readers. Monroe devised a test in which the experimenter said isolated sounds such as "d — ee — p," and the LD children were able to put significantly fewer of these sounds together to make a word. Most commonly, blending tests are administered at one sound per second with a distinct pause between the sounds. Mulder and Curtin (1955) obtained a correlation of .44 between reading and auditory blending in a sample of fourth-grade students. Conners, Kramer, and Guerra (1969) compared seventy-five LD and seventy-five normal children in grades one through six using a task blending two to ten different sounds. The LD children did significantly more poorly, but the number of sounds did not seem to be a significant factor. Chall, Roswell, and Blumenthal (1963) and Bannatyne and Wickearajate (1969) also obtained similar results.

Flowers and Crandall (1967) in a rather unique experiment presented twenty-five sentences through stereoscopic headphones to 212 children with speech delays. The left ear had all the frequencies except 2,400 to 2,880 Hz filtered out, while the right ear had all frequencies except 420 to 540 Hz filtered out. The subjects had to fuse the high frequencies of the left ear with the low frequencies of the right ear to recognize the sentence. The scores on this biaural synthesis experiment administered in kindergarten correlated .22 with PPVT scores, .50 with first- and second-grade reading scores, and about .40 with science, social studies, and arithmetic achievement scores. Tapes for these experiments are available (Flowers-Castello Tests of Central Auditory Abilities).

Tests of sound blending are:

1. Most of the oral reading tests have a sound blending section to them, but these are not standardized and have unknown reliabilities.

2. The Sound Blending test of the ITPA includes twenty-five words, but it has only a retest reliability of .50.

3. The Rosewell-Chall Auditory Blending Test (Chall, Rosewell, and Blumenthal, 1963) is not readily available but has a good reliability over age. Sound blending in first grade correlated .51 with silent reading, while correlated only .03 with intelligence, showing this is a good independent predictor of reading.

4. The Goldman-Fristoe-Woodcock Auditory Skills Battery has a Sound Recognition test of thirty items in which the administrator says a word like "t. . .ee," and the child must say "tea." This battery also has a sound blending test of thirty-three items. These tests are

well standardized, are easy to administer, and have good reliability making them the tests of choice.

Auditory Memory

Memory is by far the most extensively studied psychological process. There are presently a dozen well-known methods for measuring memory experimentally, one-half dozen well-respected theories, and literally thousands of experiments to support or refute some aspect of these theories. Those wishing to explore this area in more depth should consider several recent books on the subject (Baddeley, 1976; Crowder, 1976; Deutsch and Deutsch, 1975; Tulving and Donaldson, 1972). In order to try to organize this vast literature so that it can be applied to diagnosing learning problems, auditory memory shall arbitrarily be divided into five areas with the full realization that memory may in fact be just one process (Wickelgren, 1973).

First, Deutsch (1972) in an interesting set of experiments has reported that memory for musical notes and tunes follows the same characteristics as verbal learning. In one experiment (Deutsch, 1975) subjects were presented a tone and six seconds later a second tone was presented, with the subject's task being to decide whether the two tones were identical or not. Between the tones the subjects were presented with either intervening tones or digits. Deutsch was able to demonstrate that there was apparently one memory, a nonsymbolic memory for sounds in the environment, tunes, rhythms, and it is usually measured by the Seashore Tests of Musical Talent. Wolf (1967) found LD children did more poorly than normals on the rhythm, time duration, and tonal memory of the Seashore. The other memory is for verbal material, which is discussed below and is represented as a separate process in *Appendix A*.

Second, there is a primary memory for words often called echoic memory, which is the auditory equivalent to iconic memory. This memory is purely acoustic, and Norman (1969) has presented evidence that it can hold information up to two seconds. Its capacity is somewhere in the order of six sounds per second, which is the maximum rate of sounds one can listen to and still hear each sound, but is considerably smaller in capacity than the one hundred characters per second for visual iconic memory. Watkins (1972) found that this memory is not sensitive to the number of syllables in words, indicating it codes for words, and Crowder (1971) reports that it is sensitive to changes in vowel, but not consonant sounds. The purpose of this memory is not clear, but Crowder (1976) notes that all the prosodic features of speech, that is the pitch, stress, and intonation that we give words to convey subtle meaning are conveyed only in the vowels. This memory system may then perhaps be equivalent to what is called Auditory Word Perception in *Appendix A*, and deficiencies in this lead to failure to identify words quickly and accurately along with the intonation.

Third, there is span of attention that is the area most commonly measured by tests used by LD clinicians. Span of attention is usually measured by presenting digits in a task originally designed by Jacobs in 1887. It has been considered for years as a measure of short-term memory (STM), but in the last ten years the evidence has been growing against this view. Milner (1970) and others (Warrington, Langue, and Pratte, 1971) have reported cases of individuals with the temporal lobe of the brain damaged or with severe amnesia who retain normal intelligence as measured on standard IQ tests, have seemingly unchanged personality, normal long-term memory (LTM), but cannot remember such simple things as what they were doing ten minutes ago. Furthermore, these subjects could not learn new material. For example, when normals were given a digit-span test, they could hold six digits in memory, and after they had learned these, they could learn more until they finally could repeat back a twenty-digit sequence. Persons with temporal lobe damage, however, could hold the normal capacity of six digits, showing normal span of attention, but were unable to learn any more digits even after dozens of trials. This, then, shows that span of attention, which is the most common measure of memory of LD tests, is not related to STM, which is involved in learning new material.

Incidentally, other patients with parietal damage have just the opposite — defective LTM and normal STM and a measured span of attention of only one digit (Shallice and Warrington, 1970). While span of attention is typically seven chunks (Miller, 1956), experimental evidence is that STM has a capacity of only 2.5 to 3.5 items, depending upon which kind of complex measure of STM is being used (Craik, 1971). It has also been reported that intelligence and the meaningfulness of the material affect span of attention, but not STM as measured by other tasks (Crowder, 1976, p. 150). Finally, Craik has reported that memory span correlates .49 with STM and .72 with LTM. Putting all this information together it appears that span of attention is a measure of a combination of STM and LTM, with the LTM component being more significant.

Fourth, short-term memory is the memory that lasts only a few seconds and is the memory for what is in one's present awareness in contrast to memory for items that one must retrieve from the past. It was thought in the 1960s that there were biological differences between STM and LTM, with STM electrically and LTM chemically coded. This theory has not held up very well (Squire, 1975), so that it is best to describe these memories in terms of their characteristics as determined in learning experiments. If one gives a list of words to be memorized in which the subject must anticipate the next word on a memory drum or anticipate the second word in a word pair, one is essentially giving a STM task, which corresponds to giving the student a spelling list or table of math facts to learn. STM tasks require working with new material in the present awareness, which is a lot like what a student does when he or she is learning to read and must continuously search his or her memory for words, remember decoding rules, and retain previous decoded words to use context cues.

Fifth, LTM is usually considered memory for events that have happened more than about two minutes prior to input, provided there has not been any rehearsal of the information. LTM differs from STM in many respects in that it codes information primarily by meaning. For example, material in STM is forgotten according to the familiar learning curve found in almost any psychology text, while memory for passages decays practically not at all between one hour after it has been learned and two weeks later. The individual abstracts basic facts and meaning from the passage, and this is retained for long periods of time. Organizing material into logical categories helps recall of material particularly in LTM tasks. Bower et al. (1969) in a set of experiments showed that adults could learn perhaps ten to twenty random word pairs with several trials, but could learn 112 words in three trials if they knew the words were all minerals or some other category. These types of experiments have been repeated with children (Keppel, 1968) and can explain why children with a memory store of only about six units can in the course of a school year learn thousands of new items of meaningful information.

Short-term memory differs from long-term memory in that STM has a greater input capacity (Baddeley, et al., 1969), the material can be retrieved out of it faster (Waugh, 1970), it is coded more by the phonological similarity (word sounds) than by semantic similarity (word meaning), and has a very limited capacity (Baddeley, 1972). These facts have lead a number of authors to propose a memory model in which one assumes that sensory information enters "consciousness" and there goes to STM where it is held and processed. From STM it then goes to LTM and is coded for meaning. The information that does not get into the attention span or is not coded into

LTM is then considered "forgotten" or not retrievable. This theory (Waugh and Norman, 1965), however, has two serious defects: it cannot explain how individuals with temporal lobe amnesia have defective STM and unimpaired LTM, and it cannot explain why rehearsal of material does not improve its retrieval from LTM (Craik and Watkins, 1973). To account for these facts and much more evidence (Baddeley, 1976; Crowder, 1976) one must conclude that instead sensory information is constantly entering STM and LTM simultaneously, with STM coding more literally for words, while LTM is coding for meaning. Span of attention, then, is a mechanical rehearsal loop that draws on STM and LTM and is a very poor measure of STM. In fact, it has been proposed that of the six digits in an adult's span of attention, only the last two are held in STM (Baddeley and Levy, 1971).

We now have a new way of looking at the area of learning. A great deal of basic school learning such as "ph" makes an "f" sound or "door" is not spelled "dore" or "6 times 7 equals 42" are all basically meaningless information that cannot be coded very well by multiple features or semantic attributes and therefore must be learned by continuous learning and overlearning in a STM situation. Other information, which is the kind asked on IQ tests, such as "How many legs does a dog have?" "Why does oil float on water?" "How are a bicycle and a car the same and different?" "What does regulate mean?" can be retrieved by the cuing in on distinctive attributes, searching relevant semantic categories, and requires relatively little idiosyncratic, meaningless information. One can now describe the LD child as a student who has relatively poor STM and normal LTM. In other words, some LD students are children deficient in the STM processes, while the student who is a "slow learner" or "retarded" is more of a student with deficiencies in LTM coding.

Measures of Memory

The oldest measure of memory, except for Ebbinghouse's nonsense syllables, is the digit-span test going back to Reuther (1909) who published the rules for constructing a digit-span test: (a) do not repeat a digit in a series, (b) do not begin the series with the number one, (c) do not use the number zero, (d) do not place consecutive numbers together or form suggested historical dates, and (e) do not use two series with the same digit in the same place. The digit span appears on the Stanford-Binet, WISC, Slosson, ITPA, and Wepman from which one can derive the following norms:

Age of Child (years)	No. Digits Forwards	No. Digits Backwards	No. Related Syllables
2½	2		
3	3		12-15
4			25-27
4½	4		31-33
6			44-45
7	5		50-51
8		3	56-57
9			62-73
10½		4	71-72
11½	6		77-78
12		5	80-81
18		6	116-117

If a digit-span task is desired, the auditory sequential memory test of the ITPA or the Wepman are reliable. For a test of unrelated words, the Wepman Auditory Memory Span Test, employing two to six words can be used. The auditory memory test for unrelated syllables on the Detroit correlates about .60 with digit span. Memory for sentences, which is the task closest to school learning, has been standardized only on the Detroit, although many LD diagnosticians have used the Spencer sentences. Spencer has publicly asked that his sentences not be used because of their low reliability. Unfortunately the reliability and norming information of the Detroit is not available.

The Auditory Sequential Memory Test is a digit-span test that is normed on 1,000 children aged five to eight years. It has a good reliability, and LD children do much more poorly on this test than normal children. The Auditory Memory Span Test is almost identical, except that it consists of two to six random, one-syllable words. These two tests correlate about .60 with each other.

The Goldman-Fristoe-Woodcock Auditory Skills Test Battery has three memory tests. Recognition Memory consists of reading 110 words to the student, and he or she must respond by saying if the word has been said before in a previous sequence. In the Memory for Content test the student is first taught the names of thirty-two pictures. Then the student is read a set of words and the page is turned showing four to eleven pictures of which two pictures of words were not read. The student must point to these two pictures, thus yielding an auditory memory score not involving any verbalization by the student. In the Memory for Sequence test the student is read a set of words and must place a set of pictures in the exact order in which the words have been read. These three tests have adequate reliabilities and are well normed.

What is rather remarkable about this area is that with the thousands of investigations in memory, the number of standardized tests available to the clinician is so limited. Since digit span is probably a measure of span of attention rather than short-term memory, as most likely are the tests using unrelated words, it is probably best to rely on such observations as how long it takes a student to learn a set of letter sounds or a set of spelling words or some math facts for a measure of short-term memory. Even more surprising is that schoolwork involves a large amount of long-term memory, and the author could find no standardized measures of this ability. He had, therefore, developed the Oral Language Test (1980), which involves reading the student three, 225-word original meaningful stories that contain fifteen items of information. The student's task is to repeat the story, and he is scored on how well the story is sequenced and how many items are recalled. There is also a measure of comprehension, similar to listening comprehension questions on reading tests, and a measure of the ability to abstract from the story. One reason for the lack of long-term memory tests, which require the recall of meaning rather than literally repeating the words, is probably because many clinicians make the assumption that poor STM will also result in poor LTM. Judging from the research in this area and the observations of how well so many LD children do on general information tasks in contrast to digit- and word-span tasks, it is very likely this assumption is not valid.

There has been some research that bares on the diagnosis of memory problems in LD children. Stauffer (1947) did an extensive study of the various types of memory of fifty-one LD students aged nine to eleven. He reported that the LD subjects: (a) scored higher on the Detroit Visual Span of Objects than on the auditory memory tests, (b) there was no significant difference in the visual and auditory presentation of letters on the Detroit, (c) did better on the related (sentences), than unrelated words, and (d) did best on the visual memory for pictures as compared to other auditory measures. Sabintino (1972) found the relationship between memory for sentences for thirty LD children to be .61 with their recall of digits, .62 for memory for tapped patterns, and .40 for their comprehension of oral stories. These are relatively high correlations and correspond to the

Goldman-Fristoe-Woodcock, where the manual reports Recognition Memory correlated .45 with Memory for Content and .56 with Memory for Sequence, and only .14 with Sound Blending. Bryant (1934), in a very elaborate investigation into the types of memory of 200 four- and five-year-old children, found that a task where the child must remember a name with a photograph of a face did not correlate with other kinds of memory. Visual memory for common objects correlated with other visual memory tasks, but not with memory for a visual sequential task, digit span, or sentence memory. A paired associate task, which is the classic method for measuring STM, correlated only moderately with digit span and sentence memory. Digit span correlated in the .30s with memory for faces paired with names, visual memory for objects, visual sequences of cubes, a vocabulary test (presumably a long-term auditory memory task), and .50 with sentence memory. Memory for sentences correlated highest of twelve tests with a composite memory score and very well with the Stanford-Binet IQ (.65), suggesting this to be the best overall memory measure.

The Auditory Diagnosis

Reading, spelling, social studies, and language arts all obviously involve a great deal of auditory processing. In fact, math and its allied subject science also involve many auditory skills. If one identifies auditory problems in a child, it is not enough to simply label him or her as having "auditory dyslexia" or as being a "visual learner," because this does not suggest any remediation. To begin a remedial program, one must know what kind of auditory problems the child is having and if it is at the level of acuity, sequencing, blending and discrimination, recognition, memory, or comprehension. Below are some patterns the clinician should look for, although this chapter has tried to suggest dozens of combinations.

1. The student may have poor auditory acuity or have had poor acuity at the ages of two to five when language was developing.

2. The student aged five to eight simply may be neurologically immature and essentially that student who develops auditory discrimination, blending, etc., later than most children. This student will often have fine motor problems and a short attention span.

3. The student may have poor sequencing and will have difficulties organizing his or her work, retelling stories and ideas in order. The student will often reverse printed letters and have an extremely poor concept of time.

4. The student may have a specific disability in discriminating speech sounds. This can be due to a hearing loss, having a different

accent, and having delayed speech development. Phonics will be especially difficult for the student.

5. The student may have a specific sound blending problem, which may be due to using very poor strategies in decoding words or being unable to fuse isolated parts into a whole. These students also often have short attention spans and have a poor span of attention as measured by digit span.

6. The student may have a limited vocabulary or exposure to the words used in school, giving him or her a poor word recognition. As a result, the discrimination and blending of words is very difficult and this shows up in the student's speech, which is also very limited.

7. The student may have a poor short-term memory, which means his skills in discrimination and blending are adequate, but it takes the student a very long time to learn and retain new material. Since most discrimination and blending tasks involve some memory, the student may also score low on these tests. However, when he or she receives instruction in blending and discrimination, the learning of auditory material remains very slow.

8. A student may have all the above skills, but have great difficulty in making analogies, extracting the main idea from a paragraph, making inferences, defining words, and the like. The student will also usually have a low verbal IQ, and the greatest school problem will be in following directions and reading comprehension. The distinction between coding for events and for meaning in STM and LTM is important in defining these kinds of students.

9. Finally, a student may have normal auditory abilities, but their expressive abilities are very poor. These will be discussed in the next chapter.

LD children with a specific auditory deficiency are relatively rare, because a narrow deficit is much easier to compensate for. The most common auditory problem of LD children after the age of eight or nine, when maturation has taken place, is the lack of adequate STM. The treatment for this disorder is continuous repetition and overlearning, which is probably the most common remedial technique in the LD lab. These children forget directions, oral sentences, sounds of letters, addition and subtraction facts, even though they have mastered the other basic auditory perceptual skills. The author is unaware of any investigations using LD children that control for testing error that have tried to establish the percentages of children with just a "pure" visual or "pure" auditory memory deficit. In the hundreds of cases of LD children the author has encountered, only a half dozen clear-cut cases of a pure auditory or visual memory deficit that could be remediated by teaching the child to use another channel have been encountered. It seems that in the symbolic mode this visual-auditory memory distinction may not exist, except in very rare circumstances. In fact, when one can establish that one modality is far superior to another, it may be a sign that the child has some specific brain damage.

Chapter XI

The Speech and Language Evaluation

In contrast to primitive societies where most learning occurs by observation and imitation, modern societies rely almost completely on language for learning. The child begins at the age of two learning his first symbolic system, which is oral language. By first grade the average child has mastered all the basic construction — passives, subjunctives, conditionals, etc. (Brown and Fraser, 1964) — and has a speaking vocabulary of at least 2,500 words (Strang, 1968). He must then learn to read, which will become his second symbolic system, or as Morency (1968) has stated: "In fact...there are two distinct stages specific to the early reading process. The child first learns that the symbols which appear on a printed page represent and correspond to his spoken language. In other words, the initial stage of reading consists of decoding orthography into previously learned speech patterns. The second stage involves comprehension through arousal of sounds to effect a meaningful state derived from past verbal learning." The student must also master a third symbolic system — punctuation — which is even more difficult, because it uses arbitrary marks to represent such abstract ideas as subordination (commas), direct and indirect ideas (quotation marks), and beginning and ending of ideas (capitals and periods). Much later specialized symbolic systems such as musical notation, algebra, chemical notation, calculus, and computer programming may be introduced.

The LD child may be described in terms of which symbolic system he has mastered, so that the sixth-grade student, for example, who scores above average on oral tests, can read close to grade level, but is several years behind in writing, spelling, punctuating, and "putting his ideas on paper," can be identified as having mastered the first and second language systems, but as still being weak in the third system. The evaluation of this first system, the subject of this chapter, is very important to academics and should actually be done before any of the others. Hollingworth (1969) and Mae (1966) have reported good correlations between listening comprehension and reading, while Haring and Ridgeway (1967) found twenty percent of the variance in reading can be accounted for by a general language factor. This has been confirmed by Werner, Simonian, and Smith (1967), and Fry, Johnson, and Muehl (1970) demonstrated that average readers compared with LD students matched on IQ had significantly less contractions, made less subject-verb agreement errors, and made more normal compounds on a language task. Stark (1975) has more recently reviewed the literature linking language and reading and concludes, "We believe that there is a significant amount of evidence to indicate that speech and language pathologists can make a very important contribution to the prevention and treatment of reading problems."

The diagnosis of oral language is traditionally divided into: (a) the quality of the voice including pitch, amplitude, and rate; (b) the articulation of the sounds in speech; (c) the fluency of speech; (d) the syntax and vocabulary used by the child; and (e) the abstractness of the speech and verbal reasoning. Since the clinician will inevitably come across cases involving deficiencies in each of these areas, they will be briefly covered, although the quality, articulation, and fluency of speech have only marginal connection with learning disabilities.

Diagnosis of Voice Disorders

Voice disorders are perhaps the most ignored and untreated type of speech problem, because speech and language specialists receive sparse training in this area, which often involves medical and psychiatric expertise (Schearer, 1972).

The sounds used to make words are made by the lungs producing a stream of air that leaves the trachea and enters the larynx of the throat. The larynx, sometimes called the voice box, is made of a hard cartilage material that houses two tough bands known as the voice bands or vocal cords. When the air passes through the voice bands, the bands vibrate and cause the basic tone of speech. The air then passes to the back of the throat into the pharynx where the air disperses into the nasal cavity, which causes the sound to resonate before leaving the mouth. In the mouth the distinct sounds of the words are made using the tongue, lips, and the teeth. Voice disorders involve the sound of the speech as it is made by the vocal cords and the pharynx (particularly the nasal cavity), while articulation disorders involve the tongue, lips, and teeth. Voice disorders are usually divided into the loudness of the speech, the quality of speech, such as it being too husky or nasal, the pitch of the speech, and the rate of speech.

One of the first things that should be examined with a loudness disorder is the child's hearing. The most common cause of a loud speaking voice, however, is emotional in nature. The child with loud speech might come from a family where one has to shout to "be heard" or may have a feeling of inadequacy that is compensated for by talking too loud. After a few years of talking loud, the loud speech may become a habit. Another cause of a loud voice might be the inability to generalize to a particular social situation. For example, children on the playground are much louder than in class, and the child who cannot generalize from the playground to the class may simply continue talking loudly. A child with a loud voice will sometimes, but now always, have an increased pitch in his voice. Sometimes teaching him to lower this pitch will decrease the loudness.

The child with a voice that is too soft could have a weakness of the larynx or the muscles that control breathing, but most likely he has an inhibited personality. A child who is not sure of what he is saying may say it softly hoping no one will catch it and contradict him. To ask such a child to talk louder (as teachers invariably do) may just intimidate him more. Sometimes a soft voice or little speech may be an attempt to hide an articulation defect. Shy children with weak voices may sit in a slumped position with chest caved and actually breathe in when talking so that their weak speech appears to be physiologically based. This posture and incorrect breathing may be due to the child's anxiety of the test situation rather than a physical problem.

Excessive nasality is a voice disorder that makes the person's voice sound as if he were "talking through his nose" or sound very "tangy." The most common cause of temporary nasality is the congestion of a cold. Nasality occurs when the palate is relaxed, which opens the nasal cavity. Since nasality is normal, excessive nasality may be learned by imitating models. Nasality may also be caused by the physical defect of a soft palate. The absence of appropriate nasal resonance is called denasality, which is the result of the nasal cavities being blocked with fluid or by a swelling of the nasal cavities due to an allergy. A change in nasality can also occur after the adenoids have been removed.

Finally, there is breathiness, which gives a person a "husky" voice. This may be the result of the voice being pitched too low (thus relaxing the muscles too much), from laryngitis or other physical ailments, or from excessive shyness. Hoarseness is also a voice disorder that is of interest to the clinician, because some children with hoarse voices have nodules on their vocal cords. Dice and Shearer (1973) have shown that one cannot tell the presence of nodules by simply listening to the child, so all children with chronic hoarseness should be referred to a physician for a larynogoscopic examination.

Voice disorders apparently are not related to learning disabilities directly, except that a voice disorder might signal some other problem. The voice disorder should be treated seriously because it might be due to a tumor of the vocal mechanism. More commonly the voice disorder is an indication of an emotional problem or abuse of the vocal cords by excessive yelling. For more information on voice disorders the clinician may want to consult Greene's (1972) *The Voice and Its Disorders*, or Lerman's (1972) "Voice Disorders," or Wilson's (1972) *Voice Problems of Children*, or Murphy's (1964) *Functional Voice Disorders*.

Diagnosing Articulation Disorders

English has about forty-four individual sounds and, of course, only twenty-six letters to represent these. These sounds are usually represented by the International Phonetic Alphabet (IPA) found on most articulation tests. Proper articulation gradually increases from the age of two to eight. Some sounds such as /p/, /b/, and /m/ are easily pronounced and can be said by the average three-year-old child, while /hw/, /z/, and /zh/ are still not correctly pronounced by many first graders. Early investigations (Wellman, et al., 1931; Poole, 1934) asked the child to repeat various words, each of which contained a different sound. Templin (1957) refined this method by using words with the sounds in the beginning, middle, and end of the words, because she observed that beginning sounds were often easier to pronounce than ending sounds. Sander (1972) has recently pointed out that using Templin's scoring method (failing an individual if he did pass a word at the age at which seventy-five percent of the children gave the correct response) obscured some of the data, because children show great variability in articulation. *Figure 22* shows the age at which fifty percent and at which ninety percent of the children master various sounds and, as may be seen, there may be as much as a five-year spread. This information would support the view held by many speech and language therapists that many articulation defects in young children are simply maturational — they are merely the children between the fifty and ninety percent level.

The sounds in words are classified as voiced and voiceless, stops, fricatives, nasals, and glides. This system is based on where the sound is made in the mouth and how the air passes through the mouth and nose. Any standard text on speech and language therapy will describe these in detail.

Figure 22
Normal Age Range of the Articulation of Certain Sounds

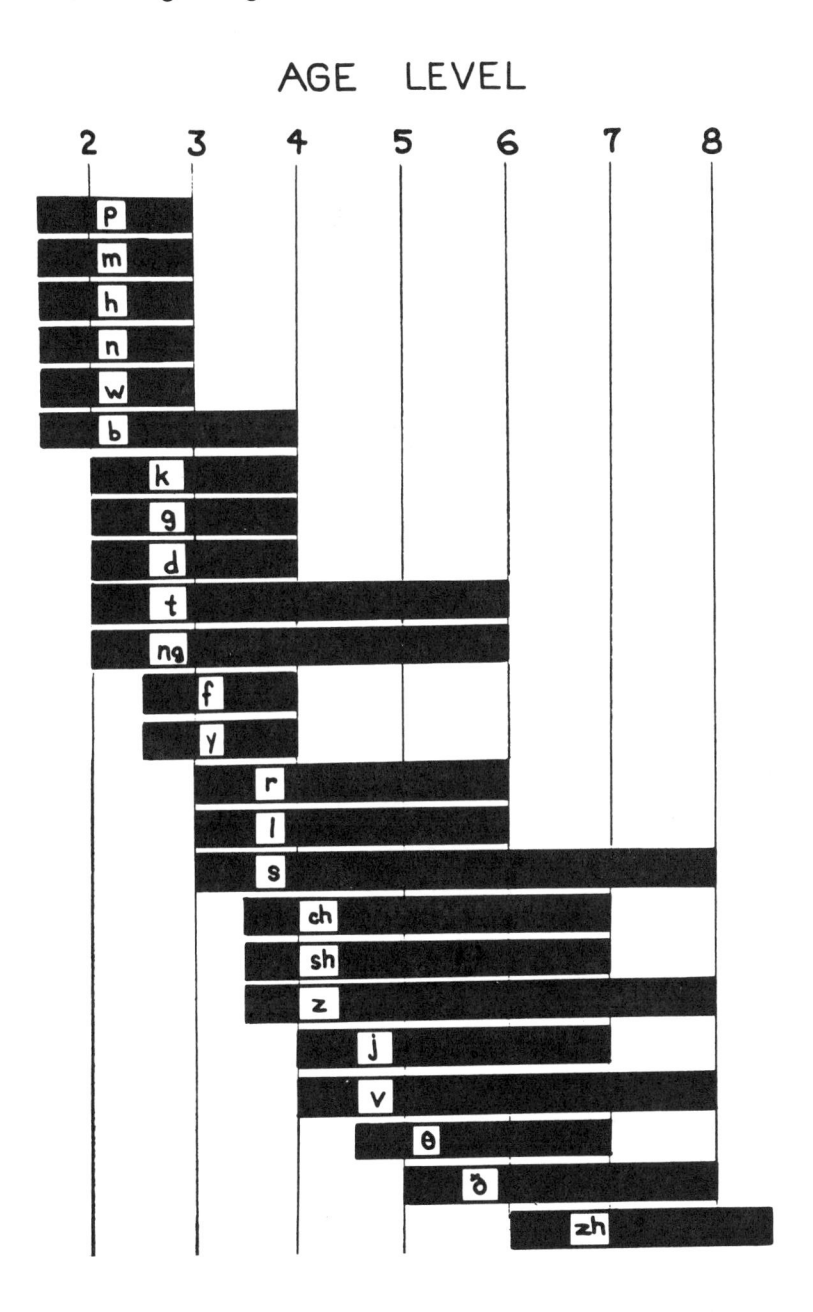

AGE LEVEL

Average age estimates and upper age limits of customary consonant production. The solid bar corresponding to each sound starts at the median age of customary articulation; it stops at an age level at which 90% of all children are customarily producing the sound. (From Templlin, 1957; Wellman et al., 1931).

Before discussing the actual tests of articulation, some of the literature regarding the testing for articulation should be examined. Templin (1957) in her detailed study of the development of articulation skills in 480 children found articulation gradually increases until the age of eight; there were no sex differences in sound discrimination, but girls were a year ahead in articulation; that the order of difficulty from least to most was diphthongs, vowels, consonant blends, double consonant and then triple consonant blends; and that final consonants were the most difficult. Morley (1972) tried to fit speech problems into distinct syndromes and found five causes of articulation problems:

1. Developmental dysarthria is characterized by poor control of the muscles for articulation. The child has poor muscle tone, poor control of muscle groups, and may have sucking and swallowing difficulties. Of her sample of this type, about half had dyslexia and all had words before the age of two and phrases before three-and-one-half.

Dysarthria has been carefully defined by Peacher (1950), who points out the original meaning of this condition was "a defect of articulation when due to a lesion in the central or peripheral nervous systems in which sound substitutions, dislocations, and omissions occur using vowels, constants. . . ." It is now used to cover all motor disabilities of speech except the highly symbolic aspects. Dysarthria or the disturbance of rhythm and articulation speech can be caused by cerebral palsy, accidents to the head, which often result in facial paralyses, edema (water) and hematomas (blood) pressure on the speech area of the brain, reaction to infections (both viral and bacterial), vascular accidents, and developing tumors. Developmental dysarthria is a condition that occurs when the child begins to speak and is associated with a developmental lag and not a specific brain trauma. Peacher notes that dysarthria results in disturbances in rhythm (i.e., dysprosody) and articulation, while simple articulation defects are simple sound substitution defects.

2. Developmental articulatory apraxia (dyspraxia) is the poor control of voluntary muscle movements while involuntary muscle movements are normal. The children usually have normal comprehension and writing, do not lack fluency in speech or have delayed speech, but cannot recognize different tones and make irratic consonant sounds. Of her sample, one-third had learning disorders and none had significant emotional problems.

3. Dyslalia is poor articulation with no abnormalities of lips or tongue movements, and speech is not delayed. It results from the

development of faulty patterns of articulation of imitation of a model with poor articulation. This disorder is also relatively easy to remediate.

4. Articulation disorders due to faulty hearing. These children have significant hearing losses or had severe ear infections at the age of acquiring sounds.

5. Articulation due to faulty structure in mouth or tongue, including such disorders as cleft palates.

In an investigation to determine the validity of articulation tests in kindergarten, Steer and Drexler (1960) report that one study of 2,000 pupils discovered a marked decrease in articulation from grades one to four, with none of the children being treated. Clearly articulation, like so many other abilities, develops at different rates for different children with almost all children maturing by the age of ten. These investigations followed ninety-three untreated pupils tested in kindergarten and evaluated their speech five years later. They found that children with low tested IQ, poor social maturity, or those who had articulation errors in initial and medial places and error in all sounds except /f/ and /l/ were outgrown with no remediation. Only the children with final position errors, with a large number of total errors, or who had errors in the /f/ and /l/ sounds continued to have articulation problems lasting more than five years. This valuable study, if replicated, could point the way to distinguishing those children who outgrow their disability and those who will have long-term disability.

There are a number of articulation tests, and they rely on the same general principle and all have the same general validity. The child is shown a picture, and he must name the picture and the incorrect sounds are recorded. Fristoe and Goldman (1968) have shown that one can include several different sounds in a single word without losing any significant accuracy. The main articulation tests are:

1. The Arizona Articulation Proficiency Scale: Revised. This test takes ten to fifteen minutes to administer and has norms for children three to eleven years of age. It was normed on about fifty children per age and has an unusual feature in that it weights the sounds by their occurrence in speech, so one can obtain a measure of the intelligibility of speech.

2. A Deep Test of Articulation. This test has no norms but examines the sounds in depth, so that it is more a test geared for planning therapy rather than screening for a disorder.

3. The Denver Articulation Screening Examination. This test was designed to screen culturally disadvantaged children and was

normed on 1,455 minority children, ages two-and-one-half to six, who lived in Denver, Colorado. It has good retest reliability.

4. The Fisher-Logemann Test of Articulation Competency. This test consists of 109 pictures and employs a distinctive feature analysis to the articulation errors. It has no norms, but does discuss dialectic differences in the manual.

5. The Goldman-Fristoe Test of Articulation. This twenty-minute test measures articulation errors for all ages in two different situations: with individual words and then with the child repeating a story he has been told so that articulation in the context of talking can be measured.

6. The Laradon Articulation Scale: Revised. This is a screening test that takes ten to forth minutes to give and yields a score for articulation and intelligibility.

7. The Photo Articulation Test. This test has norms for three- to eleven-year-olds and uses seventy-two color photographs. There were about fifty children per age level in the norming sample, and the test yields a score for tongue sounds, lip sounds, vowel sounds, and a total score.

8. Predictive Screening Test of Articulation. This test is an attempt to separate those children who need speech therapy and those who will outgrow their articulation problem. In an elaborate investigation, 111 items were given and these were reduced to 47 that discriminated between these groups. This 47-item test, which is normed for first graders, will, however, misclassify thirty-three percent of the children.

9. The Riley Articulation and Language Test: Revised. This test is primarily a language test, although it does contain some articulation items. It is very brief, taking only five minutes and should be used only for screening.

10. A Screening Deep Test of Articulation. This is a shortened version of the Deep Test and has been normed on 700 kindergarten children. It takes only five minutes to give.

11. The Templin-Darley Tests of Articulation. This test has 141 items and was normed on three- to eight-year-olds. The test takes five to fifteen minutes to administer and is considered by many as the most comprehensive articulation test available. It yields ten different articulation scores.

In a comparison of the Arizona, Templin-Darley, and Photo Articulation Test, Shanks, Sharpe, and Jackson (1970) report that middle-class children received significantly higher scores than lower-class children, and that the Photo Articulation Test, which uses color photographs, elicited more responses than the other tests.

The relationship between overall language ability and academic skills is fairly well established, but with academics and articulation this relationship is not very clear. In a comparison of over one hundred second graders with articulation problems and a matched control group, Yedinack (1949) found the children with articulation problems had normal silent and oral reading vocabulary and comprehension. There was, however, a group which had both a reading and articulation problem and this group scored no lower in reading than LD children with no articulation problems. This would suggest poor articulation per se does not affect reading.

Fluency Disorders

Incidences of stammering, stuttering, and cluttering have been reported for centuries, including the famous example of Demosthenes the Greek orator who by legend was cured by placing stones in his mouth. Today the literature on this subject is vast, with many volumes devoted to describing and attempting to find the origin of this disorder. Traditionally, stammering refers to the condition in which the person's speech contains excessive pauses and interruptions that interrupt the flow of his speech so that it impedes his communication. All of us experience movements in the middle of sentences, usually at grammatical boundaries, where we "cannot think of the word," or hesitate to "try to think what we are going to say," or fill a lot of spaces when we are nervous with "ah" or "uh's;" the true stammerer does this consistently and frequently until he or she is embarrassed about it. Stuttering traditionally refers to a condition in which the person repeats syllables, words, or phrases to a significant degree until the person is aware of it and often tries to hide it. Today, stuttering and stammering are often used interchangeably because many clinicians believe they are just an expression of the same dysfluency disorder. Cluttering, on the other hand, refers to the disruption of fluency of speech by involuntary repetitions of sounds, syllables, or words that the person is unaware of. The speech is often very rapid and, therefore, not very intelligible, and the person does not slow down or hide his condition.

The measurement of fluency disorders is controversial, because unlike articulation or language disorders there are no objective tests for fluency. Speech and language therapists often simply ask the child to tell what he or she did over the summer or the weekend, or to talk about a hobby or interest and judge his speech based on this sample. This technique works well in severe cases, but does not work well overall because stuttering (in the broad sense) varies from situation to situation and depends a lot on how relaxed the child is. This is why

Wendell Johnson, a most eminent authority on stuttering, suggests a self-report as part of an evaluation for a fluency disorder.

A widely used scale for evaluating a fluency disorder is the Iowa Scale (Johnson, Darley, and Spieslershack, 1963, p. 281) that has eight categories on which individuals are rated. These are: (a) the interjection of irrelevant sounds, words, or phrases; (b) the repetition of part of a word; (c) the repetition of a whole word; (d) the repetition of a whole phrase; (e) the revision of the pronounciation of a word; (f) the use of incomplete phrases; (g) the use of broken words; and (h) the prolonging of sounds in a word. The main advantage of the Iowa scale is that it has the child or adult read passages and has norms for these eight categories for both stutterers and nonstutterers.

Another scale that was developed and normed was Bronscom, Huges, and Oxtalby's (1955) investigation in which they obtained a speech sample from preschoolers by: (a) showing pictures and asking questions about them; (b) playing "store" using no props; (c) giving the child four puppets and having the child make up dinner conversation; (d) having the child discuss the colors he likes and dislikes using a color chart; and (e) having a telephone conversation with the child using a play telephone. These methods are listed because they show some creative ways to sample a child's speech. The researchers then scored the speech sample for number of repetitions, total word count, stallers such as "ah" or "uh" and nonsense syllables. Syllable repetitions had a retest reliability of only .67, word repetitions a reliability of .95, and phrase repetitions of .61. Total word count was very reliable (.98), as was total repetitions per one hundred words (.93), illustrating that reliable quantitative data on stuttering can be obtained. Norms and typical indexes for several other language measures are also given in this article.

The third kind of fluency disorder, cluttering, has been defined by Weiss (1964) in his book on the subject: "Cluttering is a speech disorder characterized by the clutterer's unawareness of his disorder, by a short attention span, by distortions in perception, articulation and formulation of speech and often excessive speed of delivery. . .; cluttering is the verbal manifestation of Central Language Imbalance, which affects all channels of communication (e.g., reading, writing, rhythm and musicality) and behavior in general" (p. 1). Unlike stuttering, it improves with concentration, is characterized by pauses before vowels, is usually accompanied by reading problems, and the clutterer usually has poor "smudgy" handwriting, no sense of rhythm, and "jerky respiration." Weiss takes an extreme view that cluttering precedes all stammering, while most researchers believe that some stammering develops from cluttering, and he suggests the etiology of this disorder to be the result of maturational lag with a strong hereditary component.

The proposed causes for stuttering are numerous. They range from those who believe it to be emotional (e.g., Sheehan, 1970; Johnson et al., 1967) to theorists who believe it is due to the density of the bone and tissue of the skull (Timmons and Boudreau, 1972). One example of research into this was done by Wendell Johnson (1959), who asked 1,650 questions of stutterers, their parents, and normal controls to establish the cause of stuttering. In reviewing these replies, one gets the same impression that one gets with the LD literature — that there must be dozens of kinds of stutterers, and the condition is caused by many factors. What is of note is that in an investigation of 8,000 school children, Nelisen and Johnson (1936) found that forty-two percent of the stutterers outgrew their disorder by third grade without any intervention. In other words, it appears that about half of all stuttering is closely associated with a developmental lag, while the other half is an important long-term condition.

Language Development and Delayed Speech

Studies before the 1950s concentrated most of their efforts toward developing norms on how many words a child learned, and they counted such things as nouns and verbs and the length of memory span for sentences. Some examples of this type of research are Woodward and Lowell's (1916) collection of children's associative frequency tables showing children and adults have different association values; Piaget's (1926) report of the percentages of various types of speech for six-year-olds (e.g., forty percent monologues, fourteen percent questioning, etc.) and Murphy's (1957) list of one million words in the spontaneous speaking vocabulary of primary children updated in 1969 by Wepman and Haas.

In the year 1957, however, a major revolution in linguistics occurred with Chomsky's *Syntactic Structures*, which began the mapping out of language with such boldness and intuition that many suggestions about how the mind works come directly out of this field. Chomsky showed that children's language is not a simple process of imitation, but follows a complex set of rules that progressed in a definite order. For example, the child of three will suddenly begin to use the plural form and will be heard to say words such as two "shoeses," "bootses," "scissorses," which he has never heard an adult say. The child, without ever being told the "rule," had developed an internal syntactical regularity that he applies to everything until he learns the qualifying rules and exceptions. By following a child's mistakes carefully, one can pinpoint the exact week that the child acquires and begins to use possessives (dad's shoes), negatives (I don't want it), self reference (me, mine, I), polite commands (Would you please close the door?), and so on.

One brief illustration is the development of negatives, which seems to go through three stages that parallel three cognitive stages (Comer, 1976). When the child first uses a negative, he uses it in terms of nonexistence, so that he says "no pocket" when he finds there is not a pocket in his shirt. Next he will begin to say "no wanna apple," and the like, to express rejection of something. In the last stage, which comes many months later, he will use negatives as denial to contradict what another has said with something like, "Daddy not small like baby." Interestingly, young children will use three different forms of the negative to denote these three different meanings, so the child may always use nonexistence in the form of "X no more," rejections with the word "don't," while reserving the word "not" to denote denial. In other words, the child adds extra meaning in his language that parallels his understanding, and it takes a while before he generalizes and begins to use the words as adults do.

In the space of about three years, the child develops thousands of complex syntactical (grammatical) structures. This development of so much in such a short span of time is nothing short of incredible. The early studies in this area in the 1960s discovered that the child between the age of one and two used essentially one-word sentences to describe a whole event. The child might point at his father's shoes and say "daddy" to mean "those are daddy's shoes." When two-word sentences begin at about the age of two, the child might use a pivot word and then a whole list of words after it. For example, Bowerman (1976) observed that at the age of twenty-three months her daughter in two days used a normative plus an agent 102 times, saying such things as daddy *sit*, *more* lights, *taste* cereal, daddy *here*, where the italicized word was the action and functioned as a verb, although the word "here" in "daddy here" was apparently shortened for "is here" or "go here." Each child develops his own idiosyncratic understanding at first and constantly either under- or overextends concepts. Underextension is where a child may call automobiles "cars" only when they are moving in the street or the word "off" for taking things off one's body but not for taking things off furniture. Overextension is calling all adult males "daddy" or calling all round objects a "button." The reason for extensions is that when a child hears a word such as "dog," he does not know if the important distinctive features for dog is "it barks," "has four legs," "has fur," "licks with his tongue," or "is on a leash," so he centers on one aspect and learns from later contexts which of these is the relevant feature.

Having a working knowledge of how language is learned is of great importance to the clinician, because with this basic framework the clinician can evaluate how the LD student is processing information. Taking just one example: the under- and overextension concept is essentially the basis of scoring the verbal parts of language and intelligence tests. When the child says a stomach "growls" or a car and wagon are alike because "they go," the definition of a donkey is "you ride it" or "God" discovered America, one must query the student further to establish if he has over- or underextended the concept.

It would be impossible to describe in detail language development here; however, this can be found in almost any book on language (Bowerman, 1976, is an excellent example). The field of linguistics has contributed a great deal to the diagnosis of learning disabilities. Chomsky proposed that there was a LAD (language acquisition device) that generates correct grammar (Process 38 in *Appendix A*) according to a very complicated set of rules based on "semantic markers" and regularities in "deep structure." Semantic markers are distinctive features such as plurals, past tenses, negation, and one can code any simple sentence with markers to make a complex sentence (Wardhaugh, 1971).

Some investigations attempting to test the validity of Chomsky's LAD have lead to the development of language processing tests. Berko (1958) developed a set of twenty-seven cartoon figures and gave them nonsense names such as a "wug" and showed them to the preschool child saying, "Here is a wug. Now there is another one. Now there are two. . . ." and the child was expected to insert the correct grammatical construction. This became the basis of the ITPA Verbal Association and Northwestern Syntax tests. Berko was able to demonstrate that one could test for linguistic constructions independent of previous experience, and that children as young as three were indeed formulating grammatical rules without any training. Fraser, Bellugi, and Brown (1963) tried to tease apart the child's comprehension of languge (what he understands after hearing something), his imitation of language (what he can repeat), and his production of language (what he can spontaneously say about a situation). The child was shown a picture of two different events such as one or two sheep jumping over a fence, and he must point to the correct picture for the comprehension test; he had to repeat a sentence that was grammatically similar to the picture for the imitation task; and he had to make up a sentence after being shown two pictures and given the names of the objects in them for the production task. What the investigation revealed was that the difficulty of the task in terms of grammatical constructions followed standard linguistic theory, just as Chomsky's LAD would predict. Secondly, the comprehension task was much easier than the production task, confirming the notion that children understand grammatical constructions long before they can actually use them. Finally, and most interestingly, they were able to convincingly show "...that imitation is a perceptual-motor skill not dependent on comprehension.... It seems reasonable to conclude that the imitation performance did not work through the meaning system." In other words, the use of imitation of sentences as is done in the Menyuk and the Carrow Elicited Language Inventory is probably a poor measure of language processing and may be tapping span of attention. This fits well with the information on span of attention and short-term memory in the previous chapter.

Children with delayed language are of interest, because if we accept the primacy of oral language over other symbolic systems, the LD pupil who has delayed language will probably benefit more from an oral language program than from a reading-spelling-written language program. There are numerous causes for delayed language, and these will be briefly enumerated:

1. Emotional reasons. In mild cases one finds that some LD students have had a history of delayed speech because of a traumatic even that occurred between the ages of two and five. The author knows of one child who stopped talking for half a year and never caught up after a pop bottle exploded in his face; another child who stopped talking for over a year because his father deserted the family. Sometimes unrealistic parents will put so much pressure on their children that they will have infantile speech (Eisenson and Oglive, 1971). The author recalls one girl with learning problems, a low verbal IQ, many language problems, whose mother reported that they entertained constantly, and whenever company came over they sent her daughter to her room so she "wouldn't interfere." In more extreme cases, there is a large literature on the language of schizophrenics and autism (Rutter, 1971), who are children who have very bizarre language and also shun almost all emotional contact. There is also a condition known as selective mutism in which the child will talk at home, but refuse to talk anywhere else. These children, incidentally, usually also have IQs in the low 80s.

2. Mental retardation. In one examination of 134 cases of delayed language referred to a clinic in New York City, fifty-two per-

cent of the cases were children who were mentally retarded and an additional twelve percent had IQs in the 80s (Luchsinger and Arnold, 1967, pp. 513-544). Mentally retarded children can be identified, because they do score low on the nonverbal portions of the IQ test and also have poor adaptive behavior.

3. Deficient early language experience. There seems to be a critical period between the age of one-and-one-half and four in which the child learns a tremendous number of features of language. Some children who have been institutionalized or have had a hearing loss or a cold, disinterested (often very depressed and suicidal) mother during this period may have poor language skills and learning problems. Cazden (1972) has reviewed a number of studies on parent-child interactions during the age of language acquisition, including her own experiments to modify this environment by visiting minority homes and teaching parents to interact with their children.

4. Cultural influences. Cultural influences on language have been extensively studied in relation to minority children. Labov (1971) has presented the thesis that Negro children from lower-class environments are typically several years behind on standardized skills, because they speak essentially a different language from middle-class white children. He says a careful analysis of this NNE (nonstandard Negro English) will reveal why these children appear to be so "nonverbal" and have such problems comprehending passages in books. This cuts much deeper than the child not simply understanding the vocabulary in English. First, Labov in a beautiful example shows that standard middle-class English (the kind used in text books) is extremely verbose with long phrases and extraneous words that often conveys something a ghetto child can say in two or three words. He then goes on to show that language like "they mine" and "me got juice," actually follows elaborate linguistic rules as complex as standard English, but sounds incorrect to the middle-class speaker. When a lower-class student reads a sentence incorrectly, often his reading errors conform to his native grammatical structure, showing again that reading is a complex process of verbal processing and not simply a problem of decoding the visual image. Negro ghetto children will often read the sentence, "John asked if Mary wore a coat" as "John asked if Mary wear a coat," because the latter is the correct way of saying this in NNE (Shuy, 1969).

Another cultural influence — that of the difference between lower- and middle-class language has been investigated by Bernstein. Bernstein (1966) has classified language along two poles: restrictive language, which is very pragmatic, assures that the hearer understands the context and presupposes a lot, and elaborated language, which is highly explicit and is so elaborate that its meaning is clear without any prior knowledge or information on the context. Bernstein observed that lower-class children (in England) used restricted language and not elaborated language; while middle-class children could use both, depending on the situation. Both, however, communicated equally well in informal situations, except that all the school material was in elaborated language, and the school required its students to use elaborated language. These studies have been expanded (Brandis and Henderson, 1970) and report low correlations (.20s) between social class and IQ and language tests. Tulkin and Kagan (1970) were able to show that maternal attitudes toward talking with their children correlated slightly better with achievement scores. Bernstein's distinction between the two kinds of language seems to be an important point, because one often encounters the pupil who is "vague," "can't explain himself well," and who does not have a low IQ or any obvious language deficiencies. These students are often children who use restrictive language.

Linguists and others interested in minority testing and social class differences (Bartel, Grill, and Bryen, 1973; Bryen, 1974; Dillard, 1972; Gonzales, 1974; Harber and Bryen, 1976; Williams, 1970) have made a strong case that cultural influences on language are much deeper than the ghetto child simply not knowing middle-class words. It affects the structure of the child's language and his basic mode of expressing himself. It also should be noted that how to overcome culturally based language deficiencies is not clear: Rystrom (1970) trained first-grade Black children in standard English with no effect, and Cagney (1977) found that first-grade speakers of Black dialect could understand stories in standard English better than when they were told in NNE.

5. Physical trauma to the nervous system. The term aphasia in its narrow sense has been restricted to those disorders of language due to a cerebral accident, such as a head injury, cerebral palsy, or a central nervous system disease. This topic has been covered in the chapter on neurology, and it should be noted that the nervous system of children under twelve is so plastic that aphasia is by no means a clear-cut syndrome at this age.

6. Congenital dysphasia. When there has not been a clearly defined trauma to the brain, but the child exhibits a marked language retardation that closely resembles aphasia, he can be thought of as having "congenital" aphasia, or more correctly "dysphasia." This condition may be due to the slow maturation of the language area of the brain.

Morehead and Ingram (1973), who are two noted linguists, compared the syntactical ability of fifteen children (average age seven) attending the Institute of Childhood Aphasia with fifteen much younger normals (average age two-and-one-half years) by scoring their free speech. The normals used more common transformations, more transformations per utterance, and lexographic categories, but the aphasic children did not develop deviant language or unusual linguistic systems that were qualitatively different from the normal children. Rather they developed quite similar linguistic systems with a marked delay in the onset and acquisition time. Moreover, once the linguistic systems are developed, deviant children do not use them as creatively as normal children for producing highly varied utterances. In other words, those long lists of characteristics of aphasic language that one finds in many language books are merely the descriptions of speech of young children.

There have been few investigations into whether LD students also have deficient grammatical skills. Vogel (1974) and Semel and Wiig (1975) report that elementary age LD students were significantly below normal readers in expressiveness and comprehension of syntax. Wiig, Lapointe, and Semel (1977) compared thirty-two LD children, with verbal IQs controlled for, and found LD students were significantly poorer on language tests. They were able to distinguish two diagnostic groups: those who were low in morphology and syntax and comprehension of linguistic concepts, and those who exhibited word finding and retrieval problems. The former appear to have syntactic disorders, the latter more of a vocabulary disorder. More research in this area will hopefully elucidate exactly what language disorders result in what kind of learning disabilities.

Language Tests

Language is very complex and the diagnostician should always try to obtain information on four basic areas: (a) language productivity and quality of speech in terms of how much the child speaks and if he has articulation or voice problems; (b) the vocabulary of the child in terms of the number and kinds of words he knows; (c) the verbal reasoning of the child and how well he is able to abstract using verbal information and apply these to new situations; and (d) the syntactical quality of the language. In addition to this, a knowledge of when the child began speaking and a history of his hearing during the first five years is often important.

The child's productivity and quality of speech can be obtained from interviewing adults who are familiar with the child. This is particularly helpful with children who may have fluency, voice, or mild articulation disorders, because these conditions may vary so much from situation to situation.

Vocabulary tests are of two different types — one measures simply how many words a child knows (receptive vocabulary), and the other requires the child to define the word, which is a much more complex task (expressive vocabulary). There are five commonly used measures of vocabulary:

1. The Peabody Picture Vocabulary Test (PPVT) comprises 150 four-picture plates with the examiner saying a word such as "bronco" or "hovering," and the examinee must point to the appropriate picture. This test yields a mental age and IQ score, but the test clearly does not measure what is normally thought of as being intelligence. It was standardized on 4,000 white children from Nashville, Tennessee, and has a reputation of scoring "high." One investigation (Fitzgerald, Pasework, and Gloecker, 1970) reports that the PPVT scores of one hundred educationally handicapped children were an average of nine points higher than the Verbal IQ on the WISC and five points higher than the Performance IQ of the WISC. Anyone testing a child with low intelligence or a child of a different background should consult Matheny (1971) and Hickey (1972) first. The PPVT is usually used as a measure of receptive vocabulary (because it requires only a pointing response), but the author has found that when it is compared to other language tests it varies so much from these, possibly because it is so sensitive to social class, that one has to be cautious in interpreting its results. It has a low split reliability of .85 in spite of the large number of items, probably because it is so easy to guess on the four choices.

2. The Full Range Picture Vocabulary test by Ammons is a test very similar to the PPVT, except that the words are arranged by mental age. This test is rarely used because it was standardized in 1948.

3. A much more up-to-date test is the picture vocabulary test of Hammill's Test of Language Development. This subtest is shorter, better standardized than the PPVT or Ammons, and has the same approximate reliability as the PPVT.

4. The Stanford-Binet Intelligence Test has a separate vocabulary test, which arranges words in order of difficulty by mental age. The child receives one point for each correctly defined word. This test has been recently standardized (1972), but the reliability of this particular subtest is not reported. It should also be noted that since the Binet has been restandardized, the mental ages on the vocabulary scale are no longer correct and may be as much as a year off due to the peculiar restandardization procedure.

5. The Wechsler Intelligence Scale for Children (WISC-R) has a vocabulary scale of thirty-two words that the pupil must orally define. The child is given a score of one point for a concrete response (e.g., diamond as "wear it in a ring") and a two-point response for a more abstract response (diamond as "a jewel or hard rock"). Graham (1963) has reported that the one-two point technique correlates much higher with basic vocabulary than simply giving one point for each correct word as is done on the Stanford-Binet. The retest reliability of this subtest is .85 for eight- to sixteen-year-olds, showing that this is more reliable than the PPVT (because retest reliabilities are usually lower than split half reliabilities). The WISC-R, often given to LD children as part of the IQ determination, appears to be the best measure of expressive vocabulary. There are a number of tests that measure the student's syntactical development:

1. The Carrow Elicited Language Inventory. This test comprises fifty-one sentences that are read to the child, and his responses are taped. The sentences have a maximum length of ten words to reduce the memory load on the child (although the author suspects that even ten words would be difficult for an LD child) and are scored for about fifty grammatical categories. This is an excellent test if one wants to employ an imitation task, which is a less desirable method for measuring language. The test will, however, pick up children with severe auditory or syntactical problems. Similar to the Carrow is the twenty-seven Menyuk sentences (Menyuk, 1969) which ninety-five percent of five-year-old children can repeat correctly, and it is often used as an informal test.

2. The Developmental Sentence Scoring by Lee and Canter (1971) is a method for scoring the child's spontaneous speech for sentence complexity. The clinician takes a fifty-sentence sample and scores it for eight categories of complexity. There is a scale for various kinds of pronouns, verbs, and questions. This measure has a retest reliability of .71 and was normed on 200 children aged two to seven. It is difficult to score, but is valuable to those wanting an overall score for sentence complexity, a score not found on any other test.

3. The Northwestern Syntax Screening Test. This test for three- to seven-year-olds involves imitating twenty sentences and a task in which the child must point to the appropriate picture while being read a sentence. The test is normed on 344 middle-class children, but has no data on reliability.

4. The Test for Auditory Comprehension of Language by Carrow. In this test the administrator reads a sentence and the subject points to one of three pictures that illustrates the sentence. There are

101 items representing most forms of speech, and this test comes with a Spanish version that allows one to decide whether English or Spanish is the dominant language of a Spanish-American child. There is also a screening test composed of twenty-five items that is designed for group administration.

Finally, there are fourteen commercially available language tests to measure the language ability of bilingual children to see which is their dominant language. These are reviewed by Young (1976). The most promising of these are the Bilingual Syntax Measure normed on 2,000 Anglo and Spanish-American students; the Del Rio Language Screening Test measuring listening vocabulary, semantics, and syntax; the Language Facility Test normed on 4,000 children three to fifteen years of age; and the Pictorial Test of Bilingualism measuring listening and speaking grammar and semantics in both languages.

Another language skill is general verbal reasoning described in detail in the previous chapter on intelligence. Verbal reasoning (process 35 in *Appendix A*) is most often measured by having the individual express in his own words a solution to a predominantly verbal problem. The most common measures of verbal reasoning include questions about general information, similarities, opposites, verbal absurdities, and defining words. The better the child's verbal reasoning, provided he has had an adequate cultural background, the better he will be able to comprehend and code and remember information in his environment.

The PIAT and the WISC-R have specific general information scales and the Stanford-Binet and Slosson also have a large number of general information questions such as "Who discovered America?" or "How many inches in a foot?" Similarities and differences or opposites (although opposites are more culturally loaded) are good measures of how well children can abstract features from words and can be found on the WISC-R, Slosson, Stanford-Binet, and Detroit. Since verbal reasoning involves all these skills and much more, and single subtests generally have poor reliability, the best measure is an average of the student's performance on a number of these scales. The best standardized and reliable measure is the WISC-R Verbal IQ, with the Arithmetic subtest prorated out (prorating procedures are found in the manual) because this latter subtest measures essentially a different process. The Stanford-Binet and Slosson are poorer measures, because they contain memory, arithmetic, and nonverbal items. One can also average the Auditory Reception, Auditory Association, and Grammatic Closure of the ITPA or the Verbal Absurdities, Verbal Opposites, and Likenesses and Differences of the

Detroit. One also should not forget that the listening comprehension portions of many oral reading tests can also be a good measure of verbal comprehension.

Evaluating Language Abilities

The evaluation of oral language ability is vital to a learning disabilities diagnosis, because language is so much an integral part of learning. There is a fair amount of evidence that "thinking," that is, problem solving in its broadest sense, is not necessarily a verbal process. One can solve complex spatial problems without being able to verbalize them; solutions to problems often come in intuitive "flashes" to which we only later attach words; there are intermodal processes discussed throughout this book that are clearly neither auditory nor visual; and deaf individuals can solve difficult problems without any language (Furth and Milgren, 1965). Information processing at this nonsensory level is basically what we call intelligence and may be thought of as having at least two major subcomponents: visual and auditory. The auditory aspect is being able to receive words correctly, which in turn involves auditory acuity, discrimination, closure, figure-ground, and recognition. After auditory reception has occurred, there is auditory integration with other previously learned information, and finally auditory reasoning involving the manipulation of words to form the correct pattern to the solution of a problem. For example, when we use the analogy "Man is to boy as a goose is to ---," we are employing a very simple intellectual transformation of big is to small and big is to small, but we are also requiring a very complicated language retrieval problem. The clinician in doing the evaluation should be aware of the subtleties of language development, the coding of features, and the following conditions:

1. The child may have a hearing impairment during the age of language development, so that he may not have picked up the subtleties of language. Often the hearing impaired student will have slight articulation problems, will leave off endings of words, and will misuse pronouns and the like; but his major problems in school are usually the comprehension and expression of language ideas.

2. The child may come from an environment where he was not exposed to the language used in school. This includes minority children and lower-class white children, where the child may not have ever had his language expanded or elaborated while he was learning it. These students, besides scoring low on verbal reasoning tests, will also score relatively poorly on vocabulary tests such as the PPVT.

3. If the child is below the age of seven or eight and has poor ver-

bal reasoning, it may be due to delayed language, which is apparently due to the slow maturation of the neural pathways of the language mechanism. These children will exhibit many other immature language patterns such as poor articulation and may also have poor motor development and be very distractible.

4. An extremely rare condition for children that depresses verbal reasoning is traumatic aphasia. This is due to some insult to the brain, which may have occurred at birth or later in life by tumor or head concussion. The diagnosis of this condition lies in seeing if the child has suddenly developed concomitant neurological signs.

5. If the child is above eight years of age and is normal in nonverbal areas, but has a specific disability in language reasoning, he then has congenital aphasia or a permanent verbal processing disability. This is apparently due to the poor functioning of the left side of the brain. These students do particularly poorly in reading, spelling, and writing, and they are so poor linguistically that their teachers often feel the pupil is mentally retarded.

6. Lastly, emotional factors can cause the child to score low on language tests. The student who is hostile and does not want to be tested, the student who is depressed, or the student who is frightened and feels he may make a mistake will often do poorly on verbal tests.

The evaluation of language is complex, and the clinician must keep differences in cultural background, receptive-expressive abilities, emotional factors, and syntax-reasoning in mind. If the student has articulation problems, then a picture articulation test would be in order. If there are stuttering or cluttering problems, the clinician should begin to investigate under what situations and how frequently it occurs. Next, the continuity of speech may be examined — is there a beginning, middle, and end to the student's stories? This is done informally, usually by showing the student a picture for which he must make up a story or by having him retell a story. As the student retells the story or describes a show he just saw on TV, his grammar in terms of subject-verb agreement, verb tenses, noun plurals, and complexity of structure can be estimated. Should the student use very simple sentences or make many grammatical mistakes, this can be further examined with a sentence scoring technique or one of the syntax tests (preferably one not using imitation).

At this point clinicians also look for various aphasia symptoms, such as "word finding," although these are basically just characteristics of immature speech and not special neurological symptoms. After this, the clinician may want to examine the student's verbal reasoning by listening carefully while he describes some complex event, such as how one plays baseball or makes pizza. One can then make this task much more difficult by asking questions such as, "What do you mean by inning?" and see if he can explain this abstraction without trying to use an example or draw a picture. Often one will also have IQ, Detroit, ITPA, or Woodcock-Johnson scores that can be analyzed for concreteness. Often clinicians have their own reasoning items such as, "What would you do if you found a letter (or lost child) in the street?" or "What does 'people in glass houses shouldn't throw stones' mean?" If the clinician is perceptive and evaluates these areas, he or she should be able to determine if the LD student has problems because he has a weak first symbolic system or if the cause of the learning problems is due to something else. The clinician should also be able to make a good guess as to whether the deficient language is due to a cultural, experimental, emotional, or neurological cause.

Chapter XII

The Intellectual and Emotional Evaluation

The most common definition of learning disabilities is that which applies to children with "normal" intellectual ability who are achieving a certain amount below their "intellectual potential." This raises the whole issue of what is intellectual ability, how many kinds of intellectual ability are there, and how does one go about assessing the different kinds of ability. The second issue is how does one determine if emotional factors are keeping the child from achieving his fullest potential.

What is Intelligence?

Spearman (1927) in his *The Abilities of Man* suggested four general kinds of definitions of intelligence. Intelligence can be defined as a "conscious adaptation to new situations" which has the problem of how one defines adaptation. A pedagogical definition is "the ability to act effectively under given conditions," where the conditions are usually defined as school or life situations. The scholastic definition championed by Binet defines intelligence as the ability to abstract, where abstract means to use and manipulate symbols that are removed from the immediate stimulus property of the object. Finally, one can define intelligence as a global problem-solving ability as measured on IQ tests. Most experts agree that intelligence is a combination of the above, but the easiest way to define intelligence is in terms of what it is not.

First, intelligence is not simply knowledge. Knowledge is what one has been taught and remembers; intelligence is the ability to manipulate familiar material into new combinations. When we ask a child how a car and a bicycle are alike, the child must think of all the characteristics of a bicycle, then all the characteristics of a car, and then abstract their common characteristics. A four-year-old may visualize the family car as a large object you ride in, and then visualize his bicycle seeing himself riding it, and then will tell you that a car and bicycle are not alike because one is bigger than the other. A six-year-old usually goes beyond looking for simple physical similarities and will say they are the same because they move. A ten-year-old may abstract even beyond the quality and function and say they are both transportation. When he says they are both transportation, he has revealed that he is aware of characteristics that are beyond what can be visualized and is thinking in terms of classes and categories.

This ability to abstract is measured most frequently by intelligence tests by testing the child's vocabulary and general information. Both of these items, of course, are very sensitive to the cultural background and should not be used with lower-class children (whatever the race or ethnic origin). For middle-class children, however, these two items correlate very highly with intelligence as measured by the rest of the test and with school performance. On the surface one would assume that asking vocabulary items is really a test of knowledge rather than intelligence, but investigations into speech development reveal that thousands of words in the average six-year-old's vocabulary are learned from context without anyone telling the child the meaning of the words. The normal child stores each new word along with its context, and after he has heard it a few times deciphers its meaning. A child's vocabulary then is a measure of his manipulation of verbal symbols. For example, the middle-class sixth grader who can define "regulate" only by saying "regulate the heat" and other similar words is revealing that he does not have the fluidity of thought in the most pervasive symbolic system of his culture. In the same vein asking this child general information such as "What does the heart do?" or "Who discovered America?" is really asking him if he has been able to sort out basic information he has received in his school experience. If he does not know, he either has an unusual cultural background, or an extremely poor memory, or does not have the mental capacity to have abstracted any meaning from his school experience, so he cannot retrieve this information in this new context.

Intelligence also should not be confused with language proficiency. Furth (1971, 1964) has done an extensive review of how deaf children perform on intellectual tasks and IQ tests. He has found that deaf children solve nonverbal items on intelligence tests at the same age as hearing children. These children who have had no spoken language could reason out pictures that belong together because of some characteristic, could reason out pictures involving sameness and symmetry, could classify objects along several dimensions, and could manipulate symbols by matching them. They did more poorly on pictorial opposites, and Furth suggests that this is a linguistic concept.

While philosophers debate the question of whether we think in words, the research mentioned throughout this book postulates that thinking is in an abstract mode that is neither visual or auditory. If this is true, we can see how it is possible to have high intelligence and still have severe auditory or visual processing disabilities. Furth, for example, has shown that deaf children can solve without verbal instructions a problem like: a small black triangle is to a big black triangle as a small white triangle is to (blank). The verbal analogy to this nonverbal IQ item would be: a pony is to a horse as a lamb is to a (blank). One could, incidentally, make this into a highly culturally biased item with: a stallion is to a mare as a ram is to a (blank), with only a well educated child knowing the word ewe.

The Measurement of Intelligence

In the nineteenth century there were already special provisions for the mentally retarded in the law. If a person suspected of being retarded committed a crime, the court would usually ask a physician to testify on his mental competence. The doctor would typically ask the individual what day it was, have him read a section of the newspaper aloud, ask him about current events, or ask him some riddles. From this the doctor would decide if the patient was normal, a moron, an imbecile, or an idiot. This procedure continued until 1890 when the French government offered a research grant to anyone who could come up with an objective method for separating the children who would do well in school from those who would do poorly. Alfred Binet won the grant by developing the first standardized intelligence test. The Binet test is still essentially a collection of puzzles, riddles, and games used by French children at the turn of the century arranged by mental age (MA), which was basically the age at which two-thirds of a randomly selected population of normal children passed the task. It was not until twenty years later that Terman at Stanford realized that the ratio of mental age divided by chronological age yielded a number that he called the child's intelligence quotient (IQ). While most tests still have charts for converting a child's IQ into a MA, all modern IQ tests (except the Slosson and PPVT) use the normal curve to derive intelligence.

The most common measures of intelligence for school-age children are:

1. The Wechsler Intelligence Scale for Children — Revised (WISC-R) yields a Verbal Intelligence score based on five verbal reasoning subtests. In factor analytic studies (Cohen, 1959) four of these tests correlated highly with each other, with the Arithmetic subtest loading on a different factor. The Arithmetic subtest is the on-

ly timed verbal test, and it is the only subtest that measures a skill directly taught in school. It is suggested that this subtest be prorated out (the procedure is given in the manual) if one wants to obtain a verbal reasoning score approaching "academic potential" uncontaminated by skills taught in school. The optional subtest, the Digit Span, has also been shown to correlate poorly with Verbal Reasoning and should not be included in a Verbal IQ score. The Verbal IQ has high reliability, and since the Binet is a combination of nonverbal and verbal items, this is the test of choice for measuring verbal reasoning. Although the WISC-R Verbal IQ is considered an intelligence test, this test can also be considered one of the most reliable and best standardized measures of what speech and language therapists call receptive and expressive language. In fact, if the Verbal IQ is over 20 points lower than the Performance IQ, many specialists would consider this as clear a case for aphasia as can be made.

The second IQ score is the Performance IQ obtained from five nonverbal subtests. Four subtests, excluding Coding, correlate well with each other. The Coding subtest is the only Performance subtest that requires manipulating symbolic material, and in the author's experience this subtest is often the lowest of the performance subtests for LD children, because it is more of a visual-motor and visual memory than intellectual test. The Performance IQ is highly reliable and correlates well with the visual items of the ITPA. It should be noted that all the performance subtests are timed, and this should be taken into account if the child has a problem with speed. The Performance section of the WISC-R is valuable because it is one of the only reliable, diverse nonverbal measures that can be used to decide if the student with verbal problems has normal intellectual ability. The optional subtest, the Mazes, has low reliability and does not correlate well with Performance IQ.

The third score of the WISC-R is the Full-Scale IQ, which is approximately the average of the Verbal and Performance IQ. Since both these scores are reliable, the Full-Scale IQ is not very useful in a diagnosis. The standardization of the WISC-R is excellent.

A large number of studies exist that have attempted to correlate WISC subtests with learning disabilities. All the Verbal subtests of the WISC-R, except for the optional Digit Span subtest, have reliabilities above .80. Except for the Block Design subtest, which is very reliable, all the Performance subtests have reliabilities between .69 and .77 (for ten-year-olds). Covin (1977) has also been able to show that these reliabilities apply to the LD population as well as to normals.

The first question that arises is what do the subtests measure besides verbal and nonverbal reasoning. Kaufman (1979) in his book on the WISC-R describes several systems that have been proposed. Along one dimension are Information, Similarities, Vocabulary, and Comprehension subtests representing verbal reasoning versus Digit Span and Arithmetic (and possibly Coding) representing attention and concentration. Another system has the Information, Arithmetic, and Vocabulary subtests representing acquired knowledge while Similarities, Comprehension, and Digit Span represent more basic inherent reasoning ability. On the Performance scale, Kaufman (p. 153) suggests that "of all the WISC-R subtests Picture Completion, Block Design, and Object Assembly tend to be among the least dependent on specific cultural and educational opportunities." He believes also that Picture Arrangement, Coding, and Mazes measure a separate ability to solve sequential problems.

Lutey (1977) is a review of 26 LD WISC studies reports that eighty-six percent had Performance IQs equal to or greater than their Verbal IQ. But the Performance IQ was only an average of two points higher than the Verbal IQ, suggesting that this difference is small. In thirty-one WISC and seven WISC-R studies involving over 1,500 children, Lutey reports the following subtest patterns for LD students:

Highest (WISC)	Highest (WISC-R)	Lowest (WISC)	Lowest (WISC-R)
Similarities	Obj. Ass.	Information	Arithmetic
Pic. Compl.	Pict. Compl.	Coding	Vocabulary
Obj. Ass.	Pict. Arr.	Arithmetic	Coding
Pict. Arr.	Comprehen.	Digit Span	Information

On the WISC the lowest four subtests make up the ACID (*A*rithmetic, *C*oding, *I*nformation, *D*igit Span) pattern, with the WISC-R becoming the ACIV pattern. The low Arithmetic and Coding subtests make sense, since LD students are referred for academic problems (and the Arithmetic subtest is nothing other than solving math problems and Coding is the only subtest using symbol manipulation). The low Information and Vocabulary subtests suggest that LD students have difficulty in the acquired knowledge dimension just described.

The most important point about WISC-R subtest profiles is that one cannot make a LD diagnosis based upon these scores, because there is a difference of four scale score points on the Verbal and five scale score points on the Performance subtests for two-thirds of normal children. The WISC-R, then, can be used as an instrument to obtain an accurate measure of basic verbal and nonverbal reasoning (especially if the Arithmetic and Coding subtests have been prorated out).

2. The Stanford-Binet Intelligence test is a collection of verbal and nonverbal tasks arranged with six tasks per each mental age. The same tasks are not presented at each age level, so some age levels may have three nonverbal tasks, and the next age level may have none. Because of this there is no reliable way to judge verbal and nonverbal reasoning, although several informal, unvalidated checklists exist. It should also be noted that because of the peculiar norming procedure of the Binet, the items listed under a particular mental age may actually be one-half to one year off. The Stanford-Binet correlates .71 with the WISC-R Verbal, .60 with the WISC-R Performance, and .73 with the WISC-R Full-Scale IQ. One reason the Stanford-Binet and WISC-R do not correlate very well is that the Stanford-Binet is heavily verbal and the performance items of the WISC-R do not correlate well with it (Wechsler, 1974). The Binet, however, yields a reliable overall IQ score and is very well standardized.

3. The Slosson Intelligence Test is a brief individual test taking about fifteen minutes compared to the hour for the WISC-R. This test has good reliability and correlates very well with the Stanford-Binet. This test is a collection of verbal and nonverbal items with six items per mental age. Unlike the Binet, the Slosson takes no special training to learn to administer. Between the ages of six and eighteen, the Slosson contains one nonverbal item, eight likenesses and differences items, twenty-three definitions of words, thirteen general information, seventeen mental arithmetic, and one memory item. As may be seen the Slosson is almost completely verbal and contains a heavy dose of arithmetic problems, which is a school-taught subject not correlating very well with intelligence. This test also uses the old CA divided by MA formula, which can skew IQ scores. Hammill (1968-69) had teachers administer and score the Slossen two months apart on 155 children aged four to sixteen. He found that the teachers agreed well with each other on the scoring, and the retest reliability was excellent (.95).

4. The Peabody Picture Vocabulary Test (PPVT) is a test used by psychologists and language specialists for different purposes. Speech and language therapists use it as a measure of "receptive vocabulary," but this test yields an IQ score that correlates well (.60 to .80) with other IQ measures. The test is fairly reliable but was normed on the unusual population of 4,000 white children living in

Nashville, Tennessee, in 1956. Since there are only four choices and children are encouraged to guess, there can be some large variations from one administration to another. Most persons using the test also report that children typically obtain a PPVT IQ which is 6 to 10 points higher than that obtained on other standardized individual measures. This is probably because of the unusual norming population and the fact that the PPVT still uses the old CA divided by MA method of determining IQ. Jensen (1968) has shown the PPVT to be very sensitive to cultural variations, and minority groups do poorly on this test. Since the Slosson takes just as long to administer and contains a variety of items, it is recommended that this test be given instead for screening measures of intelligence.

5. The Raven's Progressive Matrices is one of the few nonverbal cross-cultural tests available that is well standardized. It was standardized on 1,400 English children with American children matching the British norms almost exactly and oriental children actually doing slightly better than these two groups of children. The reliability of the test is good, and it may be administered in ten to fifteen minutes either individually or to groups of children. One study (Martin and Welchers, 1954) gave the Stanford-Binet and Raven's to 789 seven-, eight-, and nine-year-old children in a low-economic area of New York City. For the 435 white children the mean on the Binet and the Raven's was 90, but for Black children the mean on the Binet was 90 while the Raven's was 80. There were no significant sex differences, and these researchers concluded that although the matrices seem intuitively "culture fair," the Raven's may not necessarily be so.

6. The Cattell Culture Fair test is sometimes used because it is an intelligence test that claims to measure intelligence without cultural biases. This test consists of a number of nonverbal items including matrices, and when middle-class children from various countries are compared, they come out about the same. However, in a number of investigations comparing different social and ethnic groups within the United States, the Cattell scores for lower class children and minorities come out lower (Willard, 1968).

7. The Porteus Maze test has been described in the section on brain-injury testing, and this test has no description of the norming population or any information on reliability. We do know, however, from the WISC-R, which also has a maze subtest, that mazes do not correlate well with intelligence and may well be measuring a different ability generally called "perceptual planning."

There are a number of group administered tests that are often given in the schools and therefore can be used for a diagnosis.

8. The Cognitive Abilities Test is a recent revision of the Lorge-Thorndike. It is well standardized, correlates about .70 with school achievement tests and .50 with teacher's ratings. The test yields three scores, and one factor analytic study found that sixty-two percent of the variance could be accounted for by a verbal reasoning factor, five percent by a nonverbal factor, and two percent by the quanitative factor (Goldschmid and Tittle, 1972). The test measures verbal and nonverbal intelligence, but giving the nonverbal portion adds very little to the overall score.

9. The California Mental Maturity Test (CMMT) measures verbal and nonverbal intelligence from kindergarten through college. The test takes about one hour and twenty minutes to administer and is composed of twelve subtests. Traxler (1939) found that silent reading ability correlated about .70 with the verbal IQ and .35 with the nonverbal IQ in the upper grade level. This test has the advantage of a nonverbal section that requires no reading, thus not handicapping the poor reader. McLaulin and Schiffman (1968) gave the CMMT and the WISC to sixty LD children and found the WISC average was 95, while the CMMT was only 79. This suggests that the reading on the CMMT interferes with its score.

10. The Otis-Lennon Intelligence test ranges from kindergarten through twelfth grade. It measures only verbal intelligence and was standardized in all fifty states with about 12,000 students used for each grade level in the norming population. The test from kindergarten through third grade requires no reading, but at the fourth-grade level the child is required to read the problems. The reliabilities for this test are about .85 for children under the age of ten and about .93 for children older than ten. The validity studies show the Otis-Lennon to remain fairly stable from year to year and to correlate well with academic performance.

The Types of Intelligence

One might say that the entire scientific analysis of psychological processes is the stepchild of intelligence testing. The most prominent researchers in intelligence have all become involved in the question of how many psychological processes exist and how these can be measured accurately. Spearman (1927) in his early book on intelligence showed that when large numbers of items now found on many IQ and LD tests are factor analyzed, one single factor emerges that accounts for about eighty percent of the variance. He called this the "g" factor, and this has since been repeatedly identified as verbal reasoning or verbal intelligence. A second clear factor that emerges is a nonverbal factor, which is most clearly identified with the WISC

Performance test and usually accounts for ten to fifteen percent of the variance. Thurstone (1941) in an intensive set of factor analytic studies developed the PMA, which isolated six independent factors, and Guilford has suggested that there are 120 different kinds of intelligence.

The test makers have difficulty agreeing on what intelligence encompasses. There has, however, been one shining light in this field and that is the work of Jean Piaget who to date has published over fifty volumes of original research on how children think and the nature of intelligence. He and hundreds of researchers across the world have been able to establish that intelligence is not a matter of simply teaching the child small increments of knowledge, but that the child almost at birth has a particular view of the world (called a schema) and tries to fit all his experiences into this structure. When they do not fit his schema, he either does not believe it really happened or he asks, "Why?" in the way children do when you cannot give them a satisfactory answer. Children all over the world go through these stages (*see* Goodnow, 1962) and gifted children go through them at a faster rate, while retarded children go through them at a slower rate. There are approximately two dozen stages that are described in most basic child development books (*see* Flavel, 1968).

In the 1960s a county in Virginia closed its public school for five years rather than integrate. The children who did not attend school for this period (mostly poor Black students) were tested on Piaget's tasks, and it was discovered that there were no differences in their performances on these tasks than those who had attended school (Mermelstein and Shulman, 1969). Almy (1970) has also shown that science instruction does not affect the performance on Piaget items. In other words, it appears that Piaget developed a technique for measuring intelligence that is fairly cross-cultural and independent from education.

An interesting historical note is that Piaget worked in Alfred Binet's lab in the early 1900s and after a few years rejected Binet's method of measuring intelligence. Instead the Piaget method presents the child with a problem (e.g. two balls of clay), then asks him questions to establish if he knows the concepts to be asked (e.g. make one larger, smaller, the same), then the child is presented with a problem to establish which schema the child is using (e.g. flatten one ball and ask if more, etc.), and then the child is asked to explain his response (e.g., "Why is it more?") If the child gives the correct answer, but for the incorrect reason, it is scored as a failure which is a radical departure from the standard IQ test where the child usually gives a one-word answer or makes a pattern from some nonverbal material. The result of Piaget's method of investigating intelligence is that one does not just obtain an IQ score, but one finds out exactly what mental operations the child possesses and lacks. Piaget, in the author's view, was able to answer the question of how to best describe what "intelligence" is by amassing a large amount of experimental evidence to show that one can describe a child's progressive intellectual development from birth to the age of about sixteen by using symbolic logic. The first concept a child must grasp is identity ($A = A$) so that when an object reappears, the child recognizes it as the same object. In reading and math, this is measured in discrimination tasks. At preschool age the child develops reversibility ($A + B = B + A$), in the primary grades he learns classification across two dimensions ($A_1 + B_1 + C_1 + A_2 + B_2 + C_2$) and heirarchies, and at junior high level he develops probability strategies. For Piaget, the standard IQ tests are measuring these mental operations with a lot of irrelevant memory attached. For example, the Stanford-Binet at seven years asks the days of the week and then what day comes before Tuesday. The child must have the concept of reversibility as well as know the days of the week to solve this problem.

There are no standardized tests of Piaget items, although the Canadian government has promised to release a standardized Piaget Intelligence test for fifteen years, and soon (?) to be released will be the British Intelligence Test promising Piaget scales. While Piaget is not very helpful in measuring intelligence, he is valuable in understanding what intelligence is and how it is related to academic skills. Piaget (1969) in his book on mental imagery suggests that one can take two views—the mental image may be an internalized imitation and outgrowth of one's cognitive structure or it may be simply an outgrowth of the sensory processes. If the former is true, then the child will only perceive and imitate what he can comprehend. In an experiment Piaget gave wooden rods of various lengths to four- and five-year-old children and asked them to line them up from the shortest to the longest (after they had been shown examples so they understood the terminology). The children were then shown a correctly seriated set of rods, and after this was hidden they were asked to pick out the correct picture of the rods out of a dozen pictures. The children who could not seriate, for the most part selected pictures that were not correct, while those who could seriate picked the correct picture. So far one could explain the results in conventional terms—the children who could not seriate were not as intelligent, it was easier for the child who could seriate to grasp the mental image. But when the same children were shown the same pictures six months later without seeing the rods again almost all children picked out the correct photograph for the rods they had seen six months ago. This included the children who picked out the incorrect picture originally, and the only good explanation for this experiment, which has been replicated, is in Piaget's terms, "It remains an acknowledged fact that the image does not constitute an element of thought itself. It merely accompanies it and serves as a symbol for it." (Piaget, 1950, p. 25).

When the child begins to learn to read, he does not simply acquire visual images one by one. He reads words he does not know sometimes, gets fooled by the word's location in the sentence depending on the syntax of the sentence, misreads simple words he "knows" and gets difficult ones, and is clearly employing crude phonics rules whether he has been taught them or not. When we ask a child to spell, he does not simply visualize the words and then copy down the "picture," because we know good spellers see the words in their own ideosyncratic face type. In other words, visual memory and intelligence are linked to each other in that the visual images of symbolic processes in particular are really outgrowths or visual representations of mental constructs and have little to do with the sensory processes. The author has tried to maintain this point of view throughout the book by characterizing reading and mathematics as "intermodal," which is equivalent to what Piaget calls "intellectual processes" and others call "the ability to abstract."

What then is a child with learning disabilities? The LD child in this view is a child who has not developed the necessary schema for reading, spelling, and mathematics. The reading schema involves correctly observing the letters, breaking them down into syllables or patterns, relating these letters to correct sounds, blending the sounds into words, taking each individual word and drawing meaning out of the sentence, and being able to answer complex comprehension questions about the sentences. The spelling schema involves hearing the words and recognizing them, breaking them up into meaningful letter-word correspondences, writing them either mentally or graphically to see if they "look correct" according to visual memory, and remembering any peculiar letters in the word. This latter step is very interesting in itself, because it raises the question of how one would store in memory unusual spellings—would it be word-by-word, or by groups of words, or by some higher abstract categories? The arithmetic schema involves analyzing the problem, translating it into numerical language (or algorithms), making sure the problem is correct, keeping track of all the steps of the operation, and then judging by estimation if the answer is approximately correct.

It has been the author's experience that skills which LD children use in some situations are not used in others. These children just keep being exposed to words or numbers and just do not seem to grasp the process as a significant, integrated whole. In reading, Piaget's theory would suggest that unless the schema of decoding the word has been developed, the child will not learn to be a very good reader. Children who do not have a strong internal language schema (e.g., having a low verbal IQ) may similarly do poorly in fitting the words they read into sentences and assimilating them enough to derive meaning from them.

The relationship between intelligence and academic ability has already been reviewed, but suffice it to say that of all the psychological processes verbal intelligence correlates highest with academic skills. St. John (Woodrow, 1946), for example, obtained an average correlation of .56 between intelligence and academic achievement in a review of 120 studies. Fronsellow and Gerver (1965) reported the following correlations between reading and the WISC Verbal: age eight, .79; age nine, .58; age ten, .59; age eleven, .44. Briuninks and Lochner (1970) obtained equally high correlations for disadvantaged Black children, and Lohnes and Gray (1971) in a study using 4,000 students found that a general intelligence factor accounted for fifty-three percent of the variance in reading, while an auditory and visual discrimination factor accounted for only eight percent of the variance. Finally, Gates (1930) actually did an experiment in learning where children of various IQs had to learn new words. The children with 120-129 IQ took twenty repetitions to learn a word; the 90-109 IQ students took thirty-five; and the 70-79 IQ students took forty-five repetitions.

Fitting the intellectual evaluation into the process model used in this book we may look at verbal intelligence as a process that is quite necessary for good academic work. Verbal reasoning is the manipulation and coding of language material for meaning. Those students who can listen to the teacher present new information orally and be able to understand it and talk about it, but have great difficulty decoding words and answering questions on reading passages, are the students who are "typical" LD students with normal verbal IQs and reading and spelling difficulties.

Another type of student encountered is the child who has great difficulty understanding oral instructions and explanations, whose speech is often very immature and full of short, choppy sentences, and whose reading comprehension is poor, but who has normal intelligence, but a verbal reasoning deficit that may be accompanied by either normal or deficient visual perceptual skills. The student does poorly in reading and spelling, because these skills above simple word recognition requires a great deal of language. This pattern has often been described as children with "aphasia" or "auditory dyslexia," or in more modern terms, "right-brained children."

A third type of student is one who has fairly good verbal abilities, but whose spatial and nonverbal abilities are poor. These students often have difficulty getting organized, remembering things, finding their way around, and especially in math when spatial concepts such as place value, time, and distance problems are involved.

The mentally retarded student is low in both verbal and nonverbal reasoning and additionally has poor adaptive behavior. His or her perceptual abilities are usually at a level comparable to the mental, not chronological age, and so in some sense most retarded students have "learning" or "perceptual" disabilities. Since there is very little relationship between intelligence and memory (Guilford, 1959), one can see how LD students who cannot seem to remember how to read or spell the simplest words can be very bright, and how some mentally retarded students can do such unusual things as memorize all the dates of calendars for the last thirty years.

Framing intelligence in terms of psychological processes instead of some mystical "learning potential" is much more productive and allows one to plan a remedial program for the low-verbal or low-nonverbal or mentally retarded child rather than trying to find the "typical" LD student. The problem encountered with this approach is that intelligence like other psychological processes is a normally distributed trait, which means the cutoff between LD and retarded is an arbitrary one. The most common cutoffs are at one, one-and-a-half, and two standard deviations.

The Emotional Evaluation

When a student is tested for intellectual or psychological processing deficits, it is assumed that the student is trying to do his or her best on the test, has had enough motivation in school to have tried to learn the academic skills presented, and does not have strong emotional feelings that prevent the student from doing well in the testing situation. For these reasons the emotional evaluation is critical in a diagnosis. The largest problem facing the diagnostician making an emotional diagnosis is that there is no commonly accepted personality theory to work from. In fact the various personality theories cluster mostly around the basic method or test that is used to diagnose the personality functioning. Without understanding the rationale behind personality evaluation, the general theory of personality is hard to present. Therefore some of the evaluation techniques will be discussed.

The most common tools used by psychologists to assess personality are the projective tests. These tests rely on the assumption that when individuals draw a picture, make up a story, describe splotches on an inkblot, they are actually revealing many inner dynamics and functionings of their personality. A large number of personality tests rely on the projective hypothesis, and thousands of articles have been written about them. The four most commonly used projective tests are:

1. The Rorschach test composed of ten inkblots is used to elicit a testee's inner dynamics. This test is used widely by clinical psychologists and less so by school psychologists. The subject describes the objects on the card, and these can be analyzed by several different methods. There are some studies which show that some clinicians using the Rorschach can accurately answer specific questions about individuals (*see* Rabin, 1968, for example). There are, however, a host of investigations for each of these that essentially contradict these findings. Jensen (1965) has reviewed a portion of the 4,000 Rorschach studies and finds this test has very low reliability. In carefully designed investigations having well-known Rorschach experts sort patient's protocols into categories such as normal, neurotic, and psychotic, and answer specific questions about the patients, the experts often do little above chance level (Datel and Gengerelli, 1955; Little and Schneidman, 1959, for example). It is also common knowledge among psychologists that the Rorschach does not work as well in disgnosing the problems of children.

2. The Thematic Apperception Test (TAT) is composed of nineteen outdated pictures, and the testee must make up a story about the picture. Like the Rorschach, the TAT has its strong supporters, and in the hands of some clinicians it can be a very good tool. Shneidman, Juel, and Little (1950) in an interesting book presented the TAT protocols of a real case to fifteen TAT experts and then recoded how they evaluated it along with their predictions. They were able to show that there is no standard way to analyze the TAT, and some clinicians were very accurate about the case. In reviews of other investigations, however, the TAT generally has very low reliability regardless of the scoring method used and has a validity about comparable to the Rorschach. Varble (1970) has reviewed the evidence in this regard and states, "The TAT is not generally considered very well-suited or useful for differential diagnosis."

3. Figure drawings such as the Draw-a-Man, Kinetic Family Drawing, (KFD), or House-Tree-Person (HTP) are popular for personality assessment and rely on essentially Manchover's hypothesis (1949): "The human figure drawn by an individual who is directed to 'draw a person' relates intimately to the impulses, anxieties, conflicts, and compensations characteristic of that individual. In some sense, the figure drawn *is* the person, and the paper corresponds to the environment." There have been numerous challenges to this hypothesis: Swensen (1957) reports fourteen of fifteen figure characteristics did not predict the personality pattern Manchover suggested (e.g. drawing a small figure means the person feels inferior). He reports, for example, figures drawn by hetro- and homosexual soldiers were indistinguishable from each other. Harris (1972), an author of one of the most popular books on human figure drawings, concludes that little research supports the personality hypothesis.

4. The sentence completion technique is a set of incomplete statements, and the testee must finish the statement how he or she feels (e.g. "When I get angry I..."). There are dozens of sentence completion tests, and Murstein (1965) has suggested that this is probably one of the best and most valid projective techniques.

Although there are strong adherents to the projective technique, and many diagnosticians use projectives as a way of supplementing the basic data on personality, there is also a possibility raised by others (e.g., Zubin, Eran, and Schiarer, 1965; Connally, 1969) that when an individual describes an inkblot, tells a story about a picture, draws a man, the individual is for the most part performing an intellectual and cultural task with their inner personality structure being tapped only minimally. The reason more objective tests are not used is that they too are fraught with difficulties. More objective tests rely essentially on having the individual rate statements about how he or she feels or having him or her make choices between two statements such as "I would rather go to a party or I would rather stay home and work on a project."

There are only two major objective tests that cover school age children that describe more than two or three personality variables. These are:

5. The California Test of Personality evaluates fifteen personality variables by asking 480 true-false questions. While the test covers kindergarten through college age, it is written at a fourth-grade reading level and therefore must be read aloud to most elementary age children. Sime (1953) reviewed the test in Buros and suggested that there were many faults with its norming, reliability, and validity,

although it was clearly a step in the right direction by trying to treat a number of personality variables.

6. Cattell's Children's Personality Questionnaire (CPQ), High School Personality Questionnaire (HSPQ), and Sixteen Personality Questionnaire (16 PQ) cover sixteen different personality factors involving about 300 questions (if both forms are given), which takes about two hours to administer. The relationship between these factors and school variables have been well researched. For high school students (Cattell and Butcher, 1968) the following correlations were obtained between certain school variables and IQ, and between these variables and IQ and personality. By squaring these correlations one can see how much of the total variance these skills can be accounted for by IQ and personality.

Variable	IQ alone	IQ and Personality
Social adjustment	.27	.38
Behavior (conduct)	.22	.47
Interest in school subjects	.46	.58
Paragraph meaning (reading)	.46	.58
Spelling	.48	.60
Arithmetic reasoning	.48	.57
Arithmetic Computation	.39	.52

As may be seen from these correlations, intelligence accounts for about fifteen to twenty-three percent of the variance on academic skills, while personality variables account for about ten percent more of the variance. While the Cattell scales are probably the best objective personality tests, they too have many difficulties. The reliability of some of the factors is not very high, and some of the personality variables on the different forms do not correlate well with each other. The test is also difficult to give, and one would have to read it to the average elementary age LD student.

7. One fairly new and promising objective measure of personality is the Personality Inventory for Children (PIC) which consists of 600 items that are filled out by the child's mother (or an adult who knows the child). It takes an hour or longer to fill out and yields sixteen different personality variables. The test was normed on 2,600 children from preschool to adolescence in age. Lachor, Bulkus, and Hryorczuk (1978) report that mother's ratings correlate well with a psychiatric assessment of children referred to a child guidance clinic.

8. Having the teacher or an outsider observe the child and rate his classroom behavior is another technique for assessing his per-

sonality. Since one is interested, for the most part, only in whether the student is motivated and trying in class in an LD assessment, this becomes one of the easiest and most efficient ways to do a personality assessment. A number of investigations (Bower, 1960; McCarthy and Parakevopoulos, 1969; Swift and Spivack, 1969; Balow, 1966; Glavin and Quay, 1969; and Nelson, 1971) have demonstrated that this method accurately discriminates normal from behaviorally disturbed children. Conners (1973) has reviewed a number of children rating scales. Wagonseller (1973) has reviewed a number of children rating scales. Wagonseller (1973) used the Quay and Peterson Behavior Problem Checklist (Quay and Peterson, 1967) to determine if LD students were behaviorally different from students placed in emotionally handicapped (EH) classrooms. He reports that the emotionally disturbed children had significantly more undesirable behaviors; the EH children were higher on the Verbal (but not Performance) WISC IQ; and that the EH children had higher reading and spelling, but not arithmetic scores. Wagonseller concludes that perhaps these three instruments can be used to differentiate these two groups. Barr and McDowell (1972) similarly found that they could distinguish EH from LD students by direct observation of classroom behavior using the Weery and Quay (1969) system of recording behavior. In short, rating scales that have already been discussed in Chapter III seem a fruitful way to evaluate the limited personality assessment one needs for a LD diagnosis.

9. The clinical interview is a very common procedure for evaluating a child's personality functioning. This may be done in an open-ended interview or in a structured interview, where the questions have already been decided upon. There is unfortunately little research on the reliability and validity of interviewing children. Endicott and Spitzer (1972) make a good case that for an interview with adults to be reliable and valid, it has to be a fairly structured interview. The traditional method for interviewing children has been described by Goodman and Sours (1967) in *The Mental Status Examination,* which is the psychiatric interview for fears, anxieties, thought disorders, etc. The only investigation the author has been able to find on the reliability of the clinical interview with children (Rutter and Graham, 1972) reports that a structured interview by a trained clinician can be moderately reliable and that the clinician can usually pick out the EH student with no other information than the interview.

10. One final method for assessing the LD student is by examining his peer relationships and social standing. Sundby and Kreyberg

(1969) have stated that they believe peer relationships are probably the single best indicator of overall adjustment in the school-age child. Bryan (1976) has replicated a study that rated the peer popularity of LD students and found that LD students were more likely to be rejected (eleven percent for LD versus five percent for normal) and less likely to be accepted (four percent for LD and ten percent for normals) by peers. These percentages, however, are not very large, and it is clear from them that many of the LD children did have good peer relationships. Bryan also found that their social status after a year had not changed regardless of whether they were in a stable classroom or one where seventy-five percent of the students changed. The measurement of peer relationships (sociometry) in the classroom has been shown to have a retest reliability as stable as that of IQ and achievement tests (Gronland, 1959) and therefore can be used as a measurement of adjustment.

Reading and Personality

There have been surprisingly few investigations into emotional functioning and reading. There have been some psychoanalytic explanations (Blanchard, 1935; Liss, 1935) which suggest that all reading problems are nothing more than a child's psychological resistance toward his parents or teachers, but anyone who has actually spent time in a LD lab will see that the personalities and psychological defenses employed by LD children are as numerous as those of normal students. Gates (1941) attempted to deal with this issue by reviewing eight previous investigations in which seventy-five percent of "very marked specific reading disability" cases reflected personality adjustment problems, but in only twenty-five of these (or about twenty percent of the total) was the emotional problem the primary cause of the reading defect.

Ellis (1949) examined one hundred cases of reading disabilities severe enough to be sent to a mental health clinic and reported forty-eight percent had no emotional problem while twenty-four had severe emotional problems. He also reported that the amount of tutoring (.62) and intelligence (.46) correlated significantly with increase of reading skill in one year, while the number of psychiatric consultations and social worker visits were nonsignificantly related to progress in reading ability.

There is also one whole issue that plays into the problem of how emotional problems are related to LD problems. In school systems there is a tremendous move to place those children who act up into the LD lab. Ysseldyke and Algozzine (1979), in a whole host of different experiments, have shown that members of diagnostic teams will readily place in a special program children who have normal intelligence and grade level academic scores—if the teacher on the referral form says the child has difficulty. When they compared students in LD labs with underachievers (i.e. students who are low readers with normal intellectual ability, but who are not considered LD candidates), they could find no difference on over two dozen different measures. In other words, those students who are placed in the lab and classified as LD students are the students who are most likely to stick out as problems for the teacher, which usually means undesirable social behavior. The LD labs, then, seem to select for students with behavioral problems.

To try to summarize this field, Connally (1971) has written an interesting article that tries to draw concepts from dozens of psychological theories to explain the social and emotional factors in LD students. He begins by quoting numerous reading experts who say that LD students obviously have emotional problems, but when the actual research is examined, this is not shown to be supported. He says the traditional psychiatric approach to treat academic problems as forms of resistance can be unhelpful, because it often leads to diverting treatment from tutoring in academics to psychotherapy, which has been unproductive in helping LD students. Three factors should also be considered when evaluating a LD student for emotional problems: (a) what is the degree of his academic difficulty, (b) what is the age of the student so that developmental issues can be kept in mind, and (c) what is the sex of the student. Basically, doing poorly in school leads to three psychological problems. First, the student will almost certainly react with frustration, which can show itself in the student being hostile in school, or acting out in such ways as being the "class clown," or in flat refusal to do the work. Second, poor academic skills leads to high anxiety, which expresses itself in a kind of hyperactivity, or in an increasing lack of interest in school because it is so threatening, and to a whole host of avoidance behaviors. Third, low academics often leads to a low self concept, because the student realizes he or she cannot do what comes almost naturally to his or her peers.

The Emotional Evaluation

The emotional evaluation for LD students fortunately does not involve making a complete personality and family evaluation. The clinician is really only trying to answer two questions: Is the student's emotional functioning causing lowered test scores, and would giving the student psychological therapy or counseling improve his or her school functioning more than tutoring in skill areas? If the answer is "yes" to either question, then the diagnosis of learning disabled is probably not appropriate. The decision of how hard a student works on the test can best be determined by observing him closely in testing (especially the body language), examining his test responses for scatter and unusual answers, administering the testing under different conditions such as offering rewards for correcting missed items to see if this improves the score, and comparing the test results with regular classroom behavior. As may be seen, these techniques involve being a careful, sensitive tester, and the use of traditional techniques such as projectives and personality inventories is not so appropriate.

The second question of whether therapy or tutoring is more appropriate is more difficult to answer, but essentially involves deciding if reducing the student's inhibitions, lessening his or her hostility towards school and teachers, channeling his or her fantasies into practical goals, making interpersonal relationships more rewarding and less conflicting, setting up concrete goals to work towards, and reducing his or her anxieties will significantly improve his or her learning. Doing all the above will not appreciably increase the academic skills of a student with a perceptual or intellectual deficit, and therefore one would not recommend psychotherapy as the *primary* form of treatment. The assessment for emotional blocks that would result in poor school and test performance should involve a synthesis of at least some of the following sources of information: (a) a careful interview with the classroom teacher, which goes beyond the basic referral information, (b) the observation of the student in the classroom to see how he or she fits in with the whole classroom environment and reacts to the style of the teacher, (c) a review of classroom interventions attempted to improve the student's motivation and performance, (c) an interview with the student about his feelings and attitudes toward school and the opportunity to work with the student one-to-one on some activity closely related to school work, (d) an interview with the parents to see if class behavior is similar to behavior outside the classroom, and (e) the use of a rating scale that covers emotional, academic, and peer functioning. If one desires to do the evaluation in depth, one may want to use one of the objective personality tests.

One other approach to identifying and classifying emotional problems in children is to use the factor analytic approach. There have been numerous factor studies of children's behaviors and these result in factors that are relatively independent of intelligence and academic factors. Depending on which sample of children was examined and what behaviors were rated, one obtains many different factors. Briefly, one may for convenience consider the following emotional dimensions as separate factors in a LD diagnosis.

1. There is a dimension of social awareness which is how well an individual perceives social situations, body language, and understands others' feelings. A child who has good social awareness is thought of as "perceptive" and regardless of whether he or she has learning problems or is very intelligent will know when to talk in a conversation, how to socialize and make the other person feel at ease, understand when to be close and intimate, be able to reveal feelings directly and so on. Very young and mentally retarded children may have difficulties in this area because they do not intellectually grasp the subtleties of social awareness; but almost all other children lacking social awareness have had poor interpersonal relationships which have difficulties in forming relationships and dealing with others in social situations. Although Guilford (1959) has developed scales to measure this for adults. Social awareness is usually determined through observation and interviewing adults who know the child in question.

2. Another dimension which shows up usually as in independent emotional factor is inhibition. Some children are very shy, withdrawn, have many fears and anxieties and are so bound up in their own emotions that they cannot function productively in school. The primary problem is one of anxiety which may be measured on a children's manifest anxiety scale or through observation and interview.

3. A factor commonly appearing on behavior scales is aggressiveness. The aggressive student, besides being hard to maintain in the classroom, also usually is so involved in fighting authority and defying the system, that there is little energy left to concentrate on the material that is to be learned. Usually resistive behaviors appear in testing with the student saying he or she will not do some part of the test or giving ridiculous answers to see what will happen. These students may often learn to read, but score very poorly on math tests because they essentially refuse to learn their basic facts.

4. The variable of impulsivity has been described extensively in the chapter on hyperactivity. The impulsive student besides usually speaking out in class, touching and bothering his peers, and reacting to small changes in stimuli in an exaggerated manner also has learning styles and strategies that lead to poor and inefficient learning. The impulsive student does not listen to a full explanation or does not examine the possibilities before jumping to an answer or conclusion. In this book, impulsivity has been treated as an attentional variable

although one can see how the impulsive child can be a behavior problem as well.

5. The student whose social values are such that there is little or no emphasis on the value of school and learning has been called the "socialized delinquent" or "unmotivated child." This dimension of motivation is very important because a poorly motivated student will often do poorly on process tests and have "gaps" in his knowledge and skills that could be incorrectly interpreted as genuine perceptual problems. Since motivation fluctuates from situation to situation, the student's overall motivation is best judged by an adult who has known the student over a period of time.

6. There is a large literature in social psychology on achievement motivation. A child with high achievement motivation will try to achieve, enjoy taking on challenges, will have productive strategies in solving difficult problems, will be willing to take risks to learn or accomplish something new and will usually do better in school academically than a child with equal intellectual ability and skills. There have been over 1,000 studies comparing individual achievement in regard to various occupations, job productivity, periods of history, differences in cultures and social class, behaviors in games and competitive activities, child rearing patterns to name just a few (Atkinson and Raynor, 1974). Smith (1969) has reviewed a great deal of the achievement motivation literature of children. The whole area suffers, however, from the problem of measurement of motivation. Usually achievement motivation is measured by presenting the individual with six pictures and having him make up a story about the pictures. The test has good interscorer reliability (.80 to .90) and fair norms, but the retest reliability for even just a week apart is usually very poor (.60 or less). This means that until a better measure is developed, the use of achievement in an individual diagnosis is very shaky.

7. Adaptive behavior is the way in which a child adjusts to his family and community and this adjustment may be very different from adjustment to school which relies heavily on academic ability. This dimension is important because Mercer (1977) has claimed that she can distinguish between "normal" and mentally retarded minority students who score equally low on the WISC-R by looking at the adaptive behavior of the student and using this to calculate a modified IQ score. She suggests that this new Estimated Learning Potential (EPL) is a more accurate measure of the student's academic ability.

Adaptive behavior is usually measured by the Vineland Social

Maturity Scale, the Adaptive Behavior Scale (ABS), or Mercer's Adaptive Behavior Inventory for Children (ABIC) in which a rater interviews an adult who knows the child and asks if the child can do certain tasks. Richmond and Horn (1980) have criticized this approach because these scales were primarily designed for institutionalized children, are cumbersome to administer, and are influenced by the biases of the adult informant (usually the mother). They have developed the Children's Adaptive Behavior Scale which involves asking the child to do certain tasks such as count money. A much more important issue has been raised by Oakland (1980) in an investigation which gave the ABIC and WISC-R to middle and lower class Anglo, Black and Mexican-American children. Oakland reports that IQ predicted school achievement very well (about .70) for all social and ethnic groups and adding adaptive behavior which correlated poorly with school achievement actually reduced the prediction of achievement. These data would suggest that adaptive behavior, at least as measured by the ABIC, may not separate normal from retarded students.

In summary, the emotional dimension adds a number of variables that should be considered in a LD diagnosis. One should first consider the student's general motivation which includes his inhibition, his aggressiveness and resistiveness, his cultural background and values, and achievement motivation. Second, one should consider the persistence and learning strategies at sticking to a task which involves impulsivity and self-concept. For convenience these two factors have been lumped under "concentration" in *Figure 24*. Third, there is social awareness which often influences whether a student will be referred to a diagnostic team, but which isn't usually part of an orthodox LD evaluation. Finally, there is adaptive behavior which is important in a decision of whether a low functioning child who scores poorly on the IQ test is mentally retarded or learning disabled. The evidence of how well adaptive behavior scales can answer this question is not yet clear and this is compounded by the "Larry P." case in California where all psychological testing was banned by the courts for the evaluation of minority students.

The evaluation of emotional functioning does not seem as satisfactory as the evaluation for other processes and relies a great deal on common sense, rather than sophisticated tests. This state of affairs relates to the fact that there is no standard, well-accepted theory of personality functioning, and that the research into the personality functioning of LD students is singularly lacking.

Chapter XIII

The Synthetic Approach to Diagnosing Learning Disabilities

The Scientific Procedure

There have been a number of recent articles suggesting that learning disabilities are simply figments of the clinician's training. The most common criticism is that the LD student is merely the student who does not qualify for any other special program and, therefore, must be simply the product of poor teaching or motivation. These articles also cite the fact that process tests are notoriously unreliable, and every child tested on these tests will come out with a deficit in one subtest if enough are administered. These criticisms are valid in that any LD program could become just that, if left in the hands of poorly trained diagnosticians. These criticisms, however, ignore three facts: human beings do have genuine strengths and weaknesses in their processing of information, and it is clear that some of these weaknesses do lead to intelligent, well-motivated students who are unable to master certain academic skills; there are literally thousands of research studies mostly in western countries for three-quarters of a century which keep reaffirming that students with learning disabilities share the same psychological characteristics and the same academic problems; and although tests developed before 1970 typically had low reliabilities, there are now a number of excellent process tests with good reliabilities and validities.

The combination of new reliable instruments coupled with some very sophisticated research techniques has lead the field of learning disabilities from remedial reading teachers affirming that they have these kinds of students to a solid data base that cuts across many disciplines and now actually is contributing to the whole field of psychology and education in terms of developing hypotheses on how children learn. There are today over 1,600,000 children in LD labs across the United States, and this book is concerned with how one decides if a child qualifies for the program and what direction the remediation should take.

Throughout this book, the difference between labeling and diagnosing has been emphasized. A diagnosis suggests which mode of treatment will be most effective; if there is only one mode of treatment (e.g., place the student in the resource room an hour a day and teach him phonics), then the diagnosis need only to establish if the student can benefit from this treatment. Hopefully, a diagnosis will be more extensive and will be able to specify interventions in the regular classroom, things the parent can do at home, placement decisions such as whether the student should be retained or what group he should be in, the planning of which auxiliary services the student needs, and finally how the student should be taught in the resource room.

One reason this book has been so detailed is that a good clinician must have a good idea "how the mind works," and the more sophisticated this understanding, the better the diagnosis will be. The clinician, for example, who sits in a case staffing and is asked by the teacher how it is possible for the student, who is unable to remember his math facts but to score normally on the digit span and general information scores, can answer this question only by knowing the research on long-term and short-term memory and span of attention; the difference between remembering meaningful and meaningless material; and the difference between remembering symbolic and nonsymbolic material. Since knowledge about individual differences and information processing is constantly increasing, the clinician must also have enough theoretical background to be able to keep up with this research.

This book suggests defining learning disabilities according to the federal government definition (*see* Chapter I), but expands upon this considerably.

First, the student must be shown to have an academic deficit that is not due to poor teaching or poor motivation. Second, the student should have a significant discrepancy between his or her assessed intellectual abilities (verbal reasoning abilities) and one of the following areas: (a) oral expression, (b) listening comprehension, (c) written expression, (d) basic reading skills, (e) reading comprehension, (f) mathematical calculation, (g) mathematical reasoning, and (h) spelling. These are just suggested categories and school districts may want to eliminate oral expression and listening comprehension because they have some other delivery system for communication problems, or eliminate spelling as a criterion because this is such a difficult area to obtain any significant remediation. Third, a severe discrepancy may be defined either in terms of 1 SD or 1½ SD difference between the Verbal IQ and a standardized achievement test (see Chapter XII for a discussion of these cutoffs and when a nonverbal IQ would be more appropriate). The disadvantage of this is that many school districts do not teach the same material that appears on the standardized tests, and they may want to define academic achievement on the basis of basic competencies expected at each grade level similar to what appears in *Figures 19, 21, 22,* and *24,* and to define a discrepancy as a student who is (a) a minimum of a year below on these criteria in kindergarten through second grade, (b) a minimum of two years below in third through sixth grade, (c) a minimum of 2½ years in seventh through ninth grade, (d) and below seventh grade in tenth through twelfth grades.

Finally, this book has stressed repeatedly that there are many different kinds of LD students and no one definition or set of remedial procedures is going to be useful with every student. Therefore, the school district should add to their definition suggested guidelines for dealing with specific kinds of learning disabilities using an Individualized Education Plan (IEP, required by federal law), that includes what should be done with the student at home, in the regular classroom, in the LD lab, and in relation to auxiliary services. The two dozen or so types of LD students are described in *Appendix A* and only a brief example of such an approach is given in *Figure 23*.

Major Diagnostic Dimensions

There have been a number of attempts by other authors to reduce the LD diagnosis to a simple set of variables and then to plug the test scores into a large chart or matrix to make a diagnosis. This approach has met with unfortunate results because of the poor reliability of single test scores, the fact that most LD decisions involve "political" decisions such as the power of the parent, the belief system of the principal and program administrators, and the militancy of the classroom teacher and because a proper diagnostic placement comprises making a decision based on several orthogonal (that is, unrelated) dimensions. In this latter case, we must consider the student's age, the pattern of his strengths and weaknesses, the environmental conditions and previous learning experiences, the narrowness of the deficit, the student's biological makeup, and his motivation and desire to achieve. Only an intelligent, well-informed person could evaluate these simultaneous dimensions and make a good decision with mechanical formulas such as "IQ above 90, 10th percentile on the WRAP," being the equivalent of performing a heart operation based on the patient complaining of chest pains and high blood pressure. These diverse dimensions are summarized in *Figure 15* and are discussed in Chapter III.

Figure 23
An Illustration of a Systematic Definition and Programming for LD Students

Student must meet definition of LD and:

	Type	Handicap	Suggested Individual Education Plan	Service Provider	Program
I A.	2nd or 3rd grade student with normal IQ and who is motivated and reading at preprimer level. Usually has poor auditory skills also.	LD	In classroom student in low group using Benzinger Series with reduced (25%) spelling lists and taken off the Wisconsin Design. If letter formation poor parents do 20 min./day on district visual-motor program. In lab teach intensive decoding skills and criterion ref. skills 1-18. Involve speech and language (S/L) or social work (S.W.) only if language and emotional problems are severe.	LD teacher (S/L and S.W. if needed)	LD resource room 1-2 hrs./day
I B.	4th to 6th grade student with normal IQ and motivation who is reading below 2nd grade in spite of at least 1 year in resource room. Usually poor auditory skills and poor in math also. May have secondary emotional problems, but language is normal.	LD	Integrate in music, art, PE, science, and social studies. For science and S.S. reduce written to minimum, may have to test orally and texts read to student. Use talking books if motivated. Parents may do neural impress and math flash cards 20 min./day. In lab if student had intensive phonics and phonetics switch to linguistic and nonlinguistic methods. Teach math objectives with calculator until memory for facts develops. S/L emphasize oral and language concepts that are missing. (Psych. or S.W. develop better self-concept by emphasizing nonschool activities and performance).	LD teacher with S/L backup (Psych. or S.W. if needed)	LD Self-contained
I C.	Elementary student with verbal and performance IQs in the 80s who is also 1 to 2 years behind in most academic areas, but these match mental age of student.	None	In classroom place in low groups. Suspend more abstract Wisconsin Design objectives. Retain, if appropriate, in K or 1st grade. Have parents drill 20 min./day on word lists and math facts. Emphasize nonacademic skills on projects.	Classroom teacher	None

In addition to the different dimensions of a diagnosis, there is also clearly some hierarchical arrangement of processing skills. One way to look at this is to see a progression of major symbolic systems: oral language, then reading, then written language, with spelling being so difficult that poor spelling might be the only LD trait that remains in adulthood when the student is given good individualized instruction. The other hierarchy is the one suggested by *Appendix A*, in which it is clear that dozens of processes rely on other processes. This leads us to considering a diagnosis in terms of major psychological variables that could lead to the various kinds of learning disabilities.

Major Diagnostic Variables

The functioning of the brain is so complex, with so many overlapping functional areas, that it is unlikely that a student with a deficit in a single, narrow process area such as "discriminating the consonant sounds" will not learn to read in reasonable time and perform well in other academic areas if given good classroom instruction. It is the student who has a broad problem in areas such as general language development, overall auditory or visual processing skills, memory for symbolic material, inability to concentrate for more than a few seconds, and the integration of visual and auditory material that result in long-term learning disability. It is also not uncommon to have students with several of these problems. *Figure 24* gives a summary of the major process areas with representative tests, processes, and given a specific disorder in one of these processes. This can be used to report the information on the LD child, although a more comprehensive form in which the raw scores can be converted directly into percentile scores is available (Johnson, 1981). Taking these individually:

1. Motivation rarely appears as a formal criterion for diagnosing LD students, although it certainly is an important variable and can be measured using rating scales.

2. Equally important is the student's concentration, which is rarely considered as a variable in trying to judge the student's prognosis. Poor attention may be caused by physiological or emotional factors, but whatever the cause, it is an important aspect in programming for the student.

3. Verbal reasoning usually in the form of verbal intelligence is often used to determine the student's "academic potential." It is not really a measure of academic potential, because there are "right-brained" students who have a great deal of potential, but have weak verbal processes. For this reason it is better to think of verbal reasoning as an independent process.

Figure 24
Summary Sheet for the Major Processes
by Clark Johnson, Ph.D.

Student's Name _____ Sex ___ School _____ Grade ___ Program _____

	Processes	Percentiles 0 10 20 30 40 50 60 70 80 90	Subprocesses[1]	Sample Tests
1.	Motivation	+ + + + + + + + + +	1,2	Teacher and Parent Ratings
2.	Concentration	+ + + + + + + + + +	3,10,20	Teacher and Parent Ratings
3.	Verbal Reasoning	+ + + + + + + + + +	35	WISC-R Verbal, Woodcock-Johnson
4.	Nonverbal Reasoning	+ + + + + + + + + +	37	WISC-R Performance, Ravens
5.	Auditory Processing	+ + + + + + + + + +	7,10,11,12,13	GFW, Detroit, ITPA
6.	Visual Processing	+ + + + + + + + + +	17,20,21,22,23	Detroit Motor-Free, Aryes Motor
7.	Visual-Motor Expression	+ + + + + + + + + +	17,20,21,22,23	Beery, Draw-a-Man, Bender
8.	Language Expression	+ + + + + + + + + +	38	Carrow, Northwestern, Sentence scoring
9.	Orientation	+ + + + + + + + + +	27,28,29,30,31,32	Task analysis
10.	Visual Memory	+ + + + + + + + + +	40,41,45,46	Spelling tests, GFW Symbol Memory
11.	Auditory Memory	+ + + + + + + + + +	42,43,51	GFW Auditory Skills
12.	Intermodal Memory	+ + + + + + + + + +	49	By exclusion, task analysis

Degree Limits: Deficient 3% | Weak 16% | Average 17-83% | Good 84% | Superior 97%

[1]See *Appendix A* for these.

4. Nonverbal reasoning is intelligence as it is measured on nonverbal tasks, which some researchers (Bannatyne, 1971; Cattell, 1974) believe is "true" intellectual ability. This is as extreme a position as insisting verbal tests are measures of "academic potential." Nonverbal reasoning is important in the LD diagnosis because it helps determine whether the student will learn best using auditory or visual techniques.

5. Since the evidence that isolated auditory skills lead to major learning problems is very weak, it appears to be more valid to lump all these processes together into a single process. The LD student's word perception, auditory discrimination, figure-ground, closure, and memory are often low, independent of his verbal reasoning. In relatively mild cases one should consider strengthening these processes; in severe cases one may want to try to bypass these processes as much as possible.

6. As with auditory processing, LD students rarely have a deficit in a narrow area such as visual discriminating, closure, or adequate eye movements. These skills can be measured on motor free visual perception tests or on tests that compare visual processing with various levels of motor involvement. The more complex task of remembering which letters go into a word (spelling nonphonetic words) is a combination of visual and auditory processing and is treated later.

7. Deficits in visual-motor expression is almost always found in younger children; with older students this may suggest a neurological dysfunction. Since the treatment in the educational setting of a neurological dysfunction is as a nonneurological weakness, there is no need to add an independent neurological process to this model.

8. There are some students who have normal verbal reasoning and auditory skills who do poorly academically because of language expression difficulties. These students are not usually placed in LD resource rooms, but this is definitely a condition due to a deficient verbal expression process.

9. Specific problems in orientation and sequencing, that is, ordering of material spatially or temporally has been emphasized by Orton. Occasionally, students will have significant problems in this area often with accompanying poor attention span, but more often a deficit in this specific process area is unusual.

10. In contrast to verbal reasoning, which is a process in which verbal information is coded and retrieved for semantic cues, auditory long-term memory relies on coding verbal information with little inherent meaning (e.g., the satellite that photographed Jupiter was

called "Voyager I") or contains epidosic details (e.g., What were you doing yesterday at four?). Students lacking a normal auditory memory often appear dull or slow and have a difficult time in school because they cannot seem to master the large number of facts presented in school.

11. There are LD students who have adequate reading and mathematical skills, but have severe spelling difficulties. These students appear to have a specific deficiency for the letters that go into words. Since these students can usually spell phonetically-spelled words, this process involves remembering the specific letters that go into the word.

12. Finally, there are students with normal auditory and visual processes, their memory for pure auditory material is normal, and they have little visual confusion, but they do not seem to be able to learn to read and write (usually with poor arithmetic abilities as well) even with a great deal of special remedial help. These students are perhaps the "pure" LD students and probably have the poor prognosis for learning to read and spell.

With the introduction of these twelve basic processes, we have come almost full circle and are back to the first few chapters, which delineate learning disabilities in terms of a combination of astute behavioral observations and task analyses, test results, a knowledge of the eitology of learning disabilities, a working knowledge of how psychological processes interact with one another, and some notion of the outcomes of various remedial techniques. Returning to the definition of learning disabilities, one may say that there are at least twelve major characteristics that intimately affect the student's ability to learn. For various reasons, students are high and low in these processes, yielding a theoretical possibility of categorizing students as having deficiencies in one of these twelve areas or of being low in various combinations of these areas, producing several hundred types of LD students. As *Figure 15* suggests, however, strengths as well as weaknesses and environmental conditions affect a student's learning as well. Because of this, each school district must plan its own overall strategy for using diagnostic categories and remediation using an approach such as suggested in *Figure 24*.

The author is well aware that the process theory so strongly advocated in this book, and the idea that one should match the remediation to the deficit, has come under a great deal of criticism lately. One of the best of these attacks is Arter and Jenkins' article (1979), in which they point out that: (a) data documenting difference psychological processes is hard to come by, (b) that existing "process" tests such as the ITPA are not reliable, and (c) that process subtests such as the ITPA Auditory Reception, the WISC Block Design, laterality tests, gross and fine motor measures do not correlate well with reading, spelling, or arithmetic.

The author of this book is in agreement with these assumptions, and this work is actually filled with examples illustrating these three points. Arter and Jenkins go on to essentially say the process theory has no validity, because process subtests do not correlate with academic skills. They present the average percent of discriminating value of various processes such as "visual discrimination" or "auditory memory" for distinguishing various types of readers for about fifteen studies. From these they conclude "neither subtests of the ITPA nor most visual perceptual abilities. . .possess satisfactory diagnostic validity for reading." This is a rather startling conclusion when one considers that visual discrimination, next to IQ, is the best predictor of reading success in the first two grades. The reason for this faulty conclusion is that Arter and Jenkins have averaged together diverse studies, most of which use highly unreliable tests, such as the Frostig, to measure the processing deficit without taking into consideration that the validity of a measure cannot exceed the square root of its reliability. In other words, when one uses tests that have low retest reliability to start with, there is no objective way one can come up with any beneficial or valid treatment. This is why one must, when using processing theory, look at the large, broad psychological processes mentioned in this chapter rather than at narrow subtest scores.

Finally, Arter and Jenkins reviewed the remedial progress made for programs attempting to alleviate specific deficits and found them again, for the most part, negative. There are two errors in judging the whole process model based on this criterion; first, one cannot make a diagnosis of a processing deficit based on unreliable tests, which most of these investigations did; second, a large number of the investigations used a motor program to remediate the academic problem and it is, in fact, the processing theory which has so clearly pointed out that motor abilities and their training are not related to perceptual or academic abilities.

In conclusion, with the wide recognition of the factors that go into learning and the development of very accurate measures of these, the research in learning disabilities will be able to fulfill its original hope of matching the student's weaknesses and strengths to the teaching method that will help him or her the most.

A DIAGRAM OF HYPOTHESIZED PROCESSES

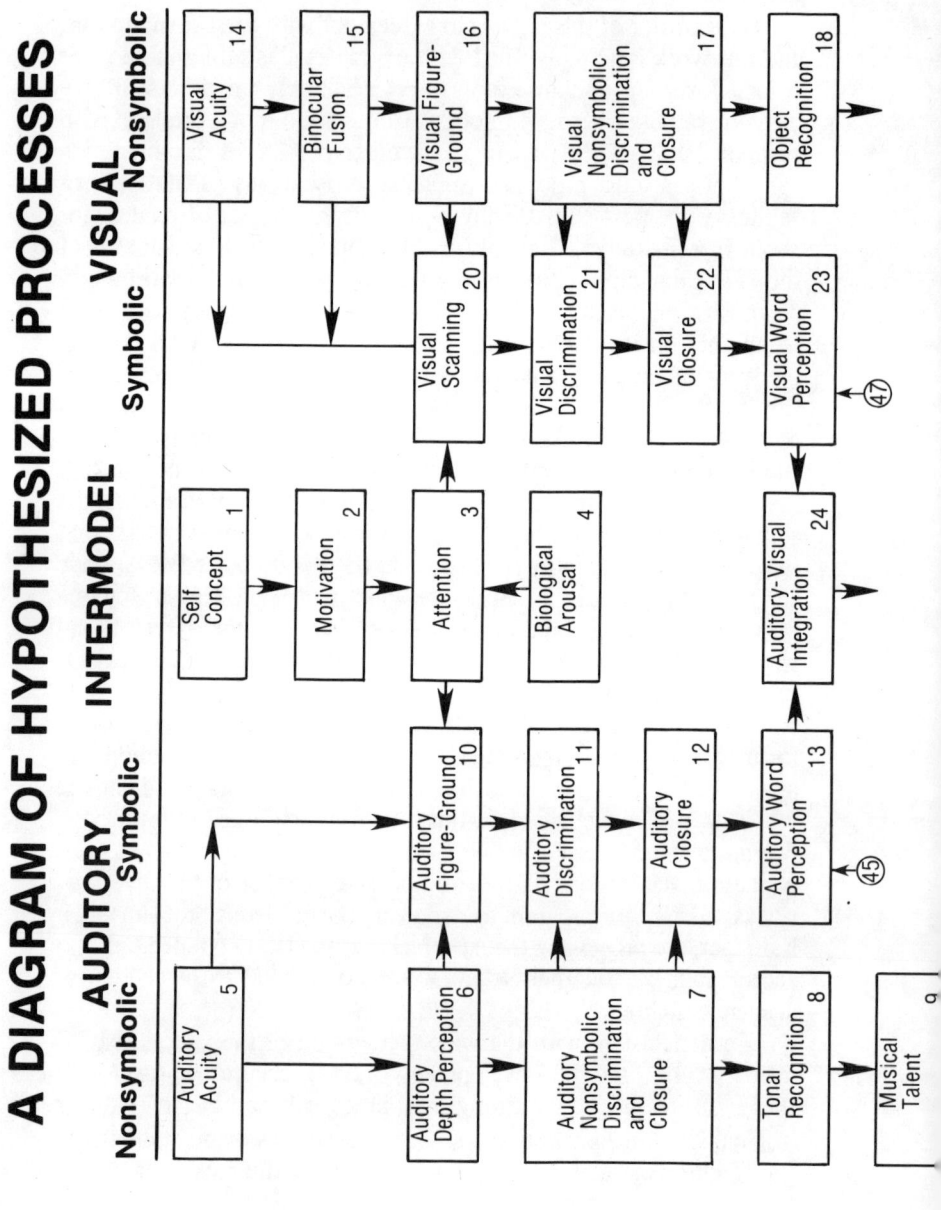

AUDITORY	INTERMODEL	VISUAL
Nonsymbolic Symbolic		Symbolic Nonsymbolic

- 1 Self Concept
- 2 Motivation
- 3 Attention
- 4 Biological Arousal
- 5 Auditory Acuity
- 6 Auditory Depth Perception
- 7 Auditory Nonsymbolic Discrimination and Closure
- 8 Tonal Recognition
- 9 Musical Talent
- 10 Auditory Figure-Ground
- 11 Auditory Discrimination
- 12 Auditory Closure
- 13 Auditory Word Perception
- 14 Visual Acuity
- 15 Binocular Fusion
- 16 Visual Figure-Ground
- 17 Visual Nonsymbolic Discrimination and Closure
- 18 Object Recognition
- 20 Visual Scanning
- 21 Visual Discrimination
- 22 Visual Closure
- 23 Visual Word Perception
- 24 Auditory-Visual Integration

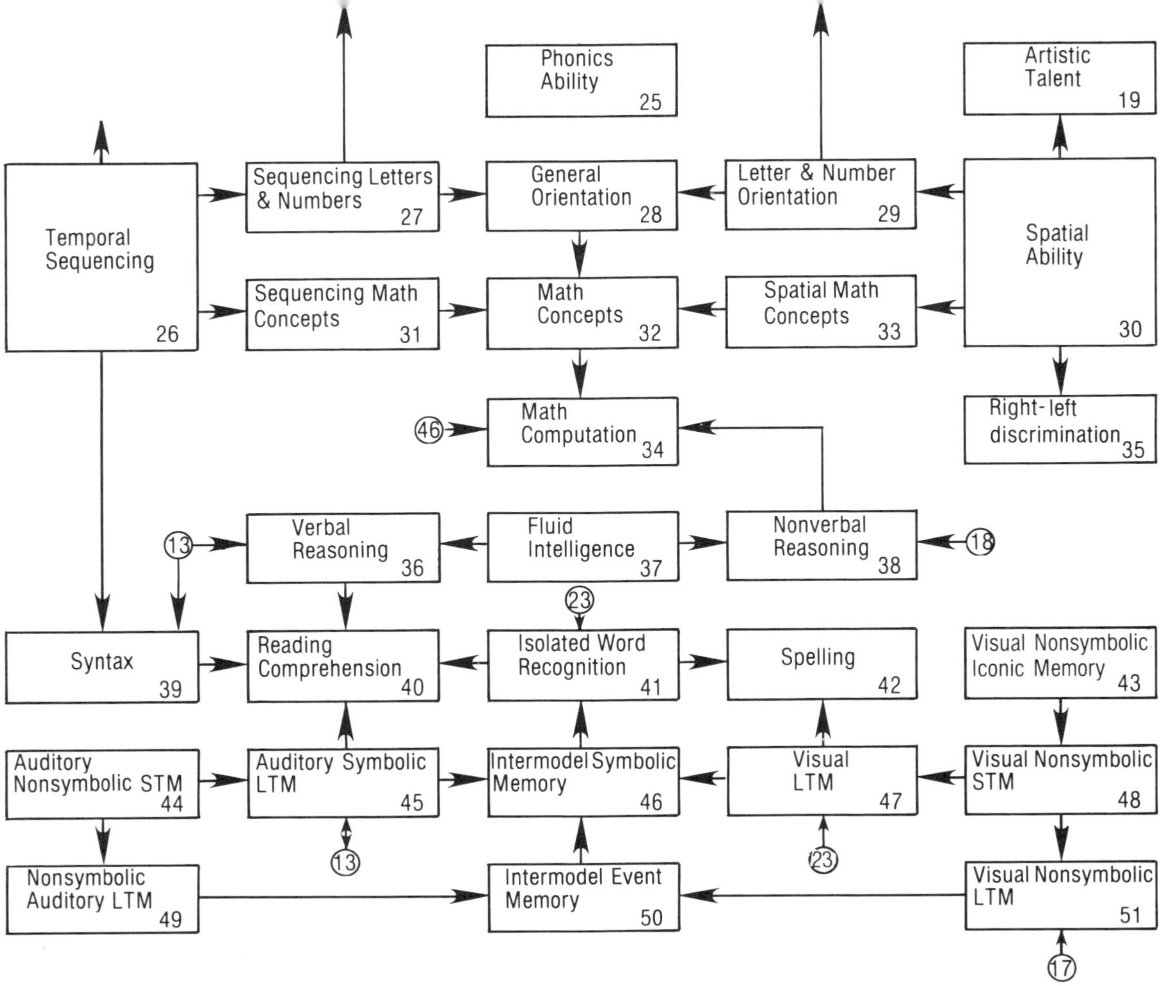
Phonics Ability 25
Artistic Talent 19
Temporal Sequencing 26
Sequencing Letters & Numbers 27
General Orientation 28
Letter & Number Orientation 29
Spatial Ability 30
Sequencing Math Concepts 31
Math Concepts 32
Spatial Math Concepts 33
Math Computation 34
Right-left discrimination 35
Verbal Reasoning 36
Fluid Intelligence 37
Nonverbal Reasoning 38
Syntax 39
Reading Comprehension 40
Isolated Word Recognition 41
Spelling 42
Visual Nonsymbolic Iconic Memory 43
Auditory Nonsymbolic STM 44
Auditory Symbolic LTM 45
Intermodel Symbolic Memory 46
Visual LTM 47
Visual Nonsymbolic STM 48
Nonsymbolic Auditory LTM 49
Intermodel Event Memory 50
Visual Nonsymbolic LTM 51
46
13
18
23
13
23
17

APPENDIX B

List of test, their author and publisher, and some test characteristics

Instructions for using appendix B

This appendix lists the tests mentioned in the text. The name of the test in some cases is shortened to conform to space. The date of the test is the last revised edition known to the author and therefore newer editions may exist. The main author is given to help in locating the test. For example if one cannot find the Wepman test, one can look up the author and find his discrimination test is called the Auditory Discrimination Test. The address of the publisher is listed at the end of the appendix. The type of the test is just a general category to locate tests of similar functions. Some areas that are not directly related to a learning disabilities evaluation or subtests that are already discussed in the text have been omitted. Most manuals list the administration time in terms of minimum and maximum times; this chart usually lists an average of these times. For the norming size and reliabilities only those readily available to the author have been reported and a blank in these columns does not mean that these figures are not available. Buros should be consulted for a complete listing of these data, but this chart should help in allowing the clinician to find tests that might be helpful in a diagnosis.

Name of the Test	Date	Main Author	Publisher	Type of Test	Time to Administer	Grade Level	Norming Size	Reliability Split	Retest
AAHPER Youth Fitness Test	1976		AAHPER	Physical Fitness	15	5-12	9,000		
A O Sight Screening Test	1956	Hunsicker	AOC	Visual Acuity	5	1-12			
AAMD Adaptive Behavior Scale	1974	Nihira	AAMD	Social Behavior	60	2-6	2,600		
American School Reading Read.	1964	Pratt	Bobbs-M.	Readiness	45	K-1	226	.94	
Analysis of Learning Potential	1970	Durost	HBJ	Intelligence	50	1-12	165,000	.95	.87
Anton Brenner Develop. Gestalt	1964	Brenner	WPS	Readiness	10	K-1	750	.88	.65
Arizona Artic. Proficiency Sc.	1970	Fudala	WPS	Articulation	15	P-6	50/gr		
Auditory Discrimination Test	1973	Wepman	Lang. Res.	Aud. Discrimination	10	K-3			.91
Auditory Memory Span Test	1973	Wepman	Lang. Res.	Aud. Memory	5	K-3			
Auditory Sequential Memory Test	1973	Wepman	Lang. Res.	Aud. Sequ. Memory	5	K-3			.82
Bender-Gestalt (Koppitz Method)	1941	Bender	Psych. Corp.	Copying	10	K-6			
Benton Visual Retention Test	1974	Benton	Psych. Corp.	Vis. Memory	10	3-12	600		.85
Bilingual Syntax Measure	1975	Burt	Psych. Corp.	Syntax	10	K-2	1,600		.60
Boehm Test of Basic Concepts	1971	Boehm	Psych. Corp.	Intelligence?	35	K-2			
Bobbs-Merrill Arith. Achievement	1963	Kline	Bobbs-M.	Arithmetic	50	1-9	4,000		
Boston Diagnostic Aphasia Exam.	1972	Goodglass	L&F	Aphasia	60	12+	None		
Burnett Reading Series	1968	Burnett	Scholastic	Reading-Total Word Ident. Reading Comp. Reading Vocabulary	50	1-12	44,025	.93	
California Achievement Tests	1970	Tiegs	CTB	Word Recognition Reading Comp. Arith. Computation Arith. Reasoning Spelling	120	1-12	203,000		.84 .79 .81 .82 .78
California Psychological Inven.	1969	Thorpe	CTB	Personality	60	K-12	14,000		.65
Cal. Test of Mental Maturity	1963	Sullivan	CTB	Verbal IQ Nonverbal IQ	60	K-16	150/gr	.90 .86	.80 .70

Name of the Test	Date	Main Author	Publisher	Type of Test	Time to Administer	Grade Level	Norming Size	Reliability Split	Retest
Child Behavior Rating Scale	1962	Cassel	WPS	Personality	10	K-3	2,000	.73	
Children's Embedded Figures	1971	Karp	Con. Psy.	Figure-Ground	20	P-7		.87	.87
Children's Personality Quest.	1975	Cattell	IPAT	Personality	60	3-7	3,000	.29	.52
Cognitive Abilities Test	1968	Thorndike	Houghton	Verbal IQ	45	K-12	2,000/gr	.93	.86
				Nonverbal IQ	45			.93	.73
				Quantative IQ	45			.93	
Columbia Mental Maturity Sc.	1972	Burgemeister	Psych. Corp.	Intelligence	20	P-4	2,600	.88	.85
Comprehensive Tests of Basic	1975	Staff	CTB	Reading	100	2-12	130,000	.96	.88
				Language	100	2-12			
				Arithmetic	100	2-12		.95	
Culture Fair Intelligence Test	1973	Cattell	IPAT	Intelligence	30	K-12	4,328		
D-K Scale of Lateral Domin.	1969	Dusewicz	FRIMD	Dominance	10	2-6	None		
Deep Test of Articulation	1964	McDonald	Stanwix	Articulation	20	P-12	None		
Del Rio Language Screening Test	1975	Toronto	NEL	Lang. Dominance		K-1			
Dennis Visual Perception Sc.	1969	Dennis	WPS	Embedded Figures	70	1-6	None		
Denver Developmental Screening	1970	Frankenburg	Ladoca	Readiness	20	P-1	1,036		
Detroit Tests of Learning Apt.	1955	Baker	Bobbs-M.	Intelligence		K-12	150/gr		
Developmental Test of Visual-Motor Integration	1967	Beery	Follett	Copying	15	K-10	1,039		.85
Diagnostic Reading Scales	1972	Spache	CTB	Word Recognition	45	1-8		.91	.94
				Oral Reading					.84
				Silent Reading					.88
				Listening Comp.				.91	.88
Diagnostic Reading Tests	1974		CDRT	Word Recognition	30	K-12	11,500		
				Reading Comp.					
				Reading Rate					
				Vocabulary					
				Word Attack					

Name of the Test	Date	Main Author	Publisher	Type of Test	Time to Administer	Grade Level	Norming Size	Reliability Split	Retest
Doren Diagnostic Reading Test	1973	Doren	AGS	Phonics	120	1-4	40/gr		
Durrell Analysis of Read. Diff.	1955	Durrell	HBJ	Reading	60	1-6			
Durrell Listening-Reading Ser.	1969	Durrell	HBJ	Reading Listening Comp.	160	1-9	20,000		
Early School Personality Quest.	1976	Cattell	IPAT	Personality	80	1-3		.50	.48
Embedded Figures Test	1971	Witkin	Con. Psy.	Perceptual		5-12	25/gr	.73	
Emporia Arithmetic Test	1964	Sanders	BEM	Arithmetic	60	1-8	44,000	.89	
Emporia Reading Tests	1964	Sanders	BEM	Reading	50	1-8			
Evanston Early Ident. Scale	1967	Landsman	Follett	Readiness	30	K-1	117		
First Grade Screening Test	1969	Pate	AGS	Readiness	45	1			
Fisher-Logemann Test of Artic.	1971	Fisher	Houghton	Articulation	45	K-12			
Flowers-Costello Test of Central Auditory Abilities	1970	Flowers	PLS	Auditory Fusion		1-6			
Full-Range Picture Vocab. Test	1948	Ammons	PTS	Intelligence?	15	P-12	589	.93	.87
Gates-MacGinity Reading Tests	1972	Gates	Houghton	Word Recognition Reading Comp. Speed and Accuracy	50	1-9	40,000	.93 .93	.81 .86
Gates-MacGinity Read. Readiness	1968	Gates	TCP	Readiness	120	K-1	4,500		
Gates-McKillop Read. Diagnostic	1962	Gates	TCP	Oral Reading	45	2-6			
Gesell Developmental Tests	1964	Ilg	PFE	Readiness	30	P-5	100		
Gilmore Oral Reading Test	1968	Gilmore	Psych. Corp.	Oral Reading Reading Comp.	20	1-8	100/gr	.88 .86	.89 .85
Goldman-Fristoe-Woodcock Auditory Skills Test Battery	1976	Goldman	AGS	Figure-Ground Aud. Discrimination Aud. Memory Sound-Symbol Relat.		P-12	5,773	.85 .85 .85 .85	
G-W-F Test of Aud. Discrim.	1969	Goldman	AGS	Aud. Discrimination	10	P-12		.90	
Goldstein Sheerer Tests	1951	Goldstein	Psych. Corp.	Brain Damage	45	12+	None		

Name of the Test	Date	Main Author	Publisher	Type of Test	Time to Administer	Grade Level	Norming Size	Reliability Split	Retest
Gray Oral Reading Tests	1967	Gray	Bobbs-M.	Oral Reading		1-12	40/gr		
Gray-Votaw-Rogers Spelling	1963	Gray	Steck-V.	Spelling					
Harris Tests of Lateral Dom.	1947	Harris	Psych. Corp.	Lat. Dominance	30	P-5	1,100		
Harrison-Stroud Reading Read.	1956	Harrison	Houghton	Readiness	80	K-1	1,400		
Hiskey-Nebraska Test of Learning Aptitude	1966	Hiskey	Hiskey	Intelligence	50	P-11	2,208	.90	
Houston Test for Lang. Develop.	1963	Crabtree	Houston	Language	30	P-1	215		
Illinois Test of Psycholinguistic	1968	Kirk	U. of Ill.	Perception	50	P-5	See text		
Junior Eysenck Personality Inv.	1965	Eysenck	EDITS	Personality	20	2-10	199		
KeyMath Diagnostic Arithmetic	1976	Connolly	AGS	Arithmetic	30	P-6	1,222	.95	
Keystone Telebinocular	1971		Keystone	Visual Acuity	20	P-12			
Language Faculty Test	1965	Dailey	Allington	Language	10	P-12	4,000		.67
Laradon Articulation Test	1963	Edmonston	WPS	Articulation	30	P-3			
Lee-Clark Reading Readiness	1962	Lee	CTB	Readiness	20	K-1	328	.88	
Leiter International Perf.	1955	Leiter	Stoelting	Intelligence	45	2-12	289	.90	
Lincoln-Oseretsky Motor Dev.	1956	Sloan	Stoelting	Motor	60	1-9	749	.75	
McCullough Word-Analysis Tests	1963	McCullough	Personnell	Phonics	70	4-6	1,856	.89	
McHugh-McParland Read. Readin.	1968	McHugh	Cal-State	Readiness	60	K-1	2,675		.94
Marianne Frostig Developmental Test of Visual Perception	1966	Frostig	Con. Psy.	Vis. Perception	40	K-3	2,116	.83	.80
Massachusetts Vision Test	1959	Staff	Titmus	Visual Acuity	10	K-12			
Meeting Street School Screening	1969	Hainsworth	CCARI	Readiness	20	K-1	494		.80
Memory-For-Designs Test	1960	Graham	PTS	Visual Memory	10	3-12	240	.73	.89
Metropolitan Achievement Tests	1970	Durost	Psych. Corp.	Reading Spelling Mathematics	50 100	1-9 3-9	27,000	.95 .93	
Metropolitan Readiness Test	1976	Nurss	Psych. Corp.	Readiness	60	K-1	12,231	.95	
Minnesota Percepto-Diagnostic	1969	Fuller	Clinical	Brain Damage	15	K-11		.98	

Name of the Test	Date	Main Author	Publisher	Type of Test	Time to Administer	Grade Level	Norming Size	Reliability Split	Retest
Motor-Free Visual Perception	1972	Colarusso	Academic	Visual Perception	10	P-3	883	.85	.80
Murphy-Durrell Reading Readiness Analysis	1965	Murphy	Psych. Corp.	Readiness	60	K-1	12,231	.98	
New Developmental Reading Test	1968	Bond	Lyons	Reading	50	1-6	15,000	.80	
Northwestern Syntax Screening	1971	Lee	NW Univ.	Syntax	15	P-2	344		
Otis-Lennon Mental Ability Test	1969	Otis	Psych. Corp.	Intelligence	30	K-12	144,000		.83
Peabody Individual Achievement Test	1970	Dunn	AGS	Mathematics	40	K-12	200/gr		.68
				Word Recognition					.94
				Reading Comp.					.73
				Spelling					.78
				General Information					.77
Peabody Picture Vocabulary Test	1965	Dunn	AGS	Intelligence?	15	P-12	4012	.85	
Phonics Knowledge Survey	1964	Durkin	TCP	Phonics	20	1-6			
Pictorial Test of Intelligence	1964	French	Houghton	Intelligence	45	P-3	1,830	.96	.88
Picture Story Language Story	1965	Myklebust	G & S	Written Language	25	2-12	747		.70
Primary Visual Motor Scale	1970	Haworth	G & S	Copying	15	P-3	500		.82
Progressive Matricies	1963	Raven	Psych. Corp.	Intelligence	20	P-12			.83
Pupil Rating Scale	1971	Myklebust	G & S	Learning Disabilities		3-4	2,176		
Purdue Perceptual-Motor Survey	1966	Roach	Merrill	Motor	20	1-5	200		.95
Riley Articulation and Language	1966	Riley	WPS	Language	5	K-2	436		
Roswell-Chall Auditory Blending	1963	Roswell	Essay	Auditory Blending		1-4	40/gr	.90	
Sanders-Fletcher Spelling Test	1964	Sanders	Data	Spelling	30	9-12	20,423	.84	
SRA Achievement Tests	1969	Thorpe	SRA	Reading	120	1-9	70,000	.94	.83
				Language				.90	
				Arithmetic	110	1-9		.90	
SRA Primary Mental Abilities	1962	Thurstone	SRA	Intelligence	65	K-12	2,000/gr	.91	.92
SRA Short Test of Ability	1966	Staff	SRA	Intelligence	30	K-12			
School Readiness Test	1974	Anderhalter		Scholastic Readiness	60	K-1		.91	

Name of the Test	Date	Main Author	Publisher	Type of Test	Time to Administer	Grade Level	Norming Size	Reliability Split	Retest
School Vision Tester	1957	Staff	Bausch	Vision	3	P-12		.80	
Screening Deep Test of Artic.	1968	McDonald	Stanwix	Articulation	5	K	700		
Silent Reading Diagnostic Tests	1970	Bond	Lyons	Reading	80	2-7	2,500	.92	.50
Sixteen Personality Factor Quest.	1970	Cattell	IPAT	Personality	60	11-12			.97
Slosson Intelligence Test	1963	Slosson	Slosson	Intelligence	20	P-12			.44
Southern Cal. Figure-Ground	1966	Ayres	WPS	Visual Perception	10	P-3	1,164		
S.C. Kinesthesia & Tactile	1966	Ayres	WPS	Brain Damage	15	P-12	953		.40
S.C. Perceptual-Motor Test	1969	Ayres	WPS	Body Image	20	P-3	1,004		.91
S.C. Motor Accuracy Test	1964	Ayres	WPS	Motor Coordination	10	P-2	280	.80	.40
S.C. Sensory Integration Tests	1972	Ayres	WPS	17 Sensory-motor	90	P-5	30/gr		
Stanford Achievement Test	1973	Kelley	Psych. Corp.	Reading	110	1-9	275,000	.90	.95
				Spelling	35	4-9		.94	
				Language	35	4-9		.86	
				Arithmetic	80	1-9		.90	
Stanford-Binet Intelligence	1973	Terman	Houghton	Intelligence	60	P-12	2,100		
Stanford Diagnostic Mathematics	1968	Beatty	Psych. Corp.	Arithmetic	110	1-12	15,000	.94	
Stanford Diagnostic Reading Test	1966	Madden	Psych. Corp.	Reading & Phonics	150	2-8	150/gr	.90	
Templin-Darley Tests of Artic.	1969	Templin	BER	Articulation	15	P-2	480		
Test of Auditory Comprehension of Language	1973	Carrow	Learning	Language	20	P-1	200		
Test of Language Development	1977	Newcomer	Empiric	Language	40	P-3			
Test of Listening Accuracy	1969	Mecham	CRA	Auditory Discrim.	20	K-3	350/gr	.88	
Titmus Vision Tester	1959	Staff	Titmus	Visual Acuity	5	K-12			
Utah Test of Language Develop.	1967	Mecham	CRA	Language	35	P-9	273	.94	.92
Vineland Social Maturity Scale	1936	Doll	AGS	Social Maturity	50	P-12	20/gr		
Wechsler Intelligence Scale for Children	1974	Wechsler	Psych. Corp.	Intelligence	60	1-10	4,400		.93
Wechsler Preschool & Primary	1967	Wechsler	Psych. Corp.	Intelligence	60	P-1	1,200		.89

Name of the Test	Date	Main Author	Publisher	Type of Test	Time to Administer	Grade Level	Norming Size	Reliability Split	Retest
Wide Range Achievement Test	1970	Jastak	GA	Reading Spelling Arithmetic	25	P-12	1,200	.98	
Woodcock Reading Mastery Tests	1974	Woodcock	AGS	Reading Total Word Identification Word Attack Word Comprehension Paragraph Comp.	30	K-12	5,000	.98 .93	.84

DIRECTORY OF TEST PUBLISHERS

AAHPER	American Association for Health, Physical Education, and Recreation. 1201 Sixteenth St. NW, Washington, DC 20036.
AAMD	American Association of Mental Deficiency. 5201 Connecticut Ave. N.W., Washington, DC 20015.
Academic	Academic Therapy Publ. 1539 Fourth St., San Rafael, CA 94901.
Allington	Allington Corporation. 801 N. Pitt St., Alexandria, VA 22314.
AGS	American Guidance Service. Publisher's Building, Circle Pines, MN 55014.
AOC	American Optical Company. Buffalo 15, NY.
Bausch	Bausch and Lomb. Rochester, NY 14602.
Bobbs	Bobbs-Merrill. 4300 West 62nd St. Indianapolis, IN 46268.
BEM	Bureau of Educational Measurements. Emporia Kansas State College, Emporia, KS 66801.
BER	Bureau of Educational Research and Service. University of Iowa, Iowa City, IA 52242.
Cal-State	Cal-State Book Store. 25776 Hillory St., Hayward, CA 94542.
CTB	California Test Bureau/McGraw Hill. Del Monte Research Park, Monterey, CA 93940.
Clinical	Clinical Psychology Publ. 4 Conant Square, Brandon, VT 05733.
CDRT	Committee on Diagnostic Reading Tests. Mountain Home, NC 28758.
CRA	Communication Research Associates. Box 11012, Salt Lake City, UT 84111.
Con. Psy.	Consulting Psychologists Press. 577 College Ave., Palo Alto, CA 94306.
CCARI	Crippled Children and Adults of Rhode Island. Meeting Street School, 667 Waterman Ave., East Providence, RI 02914.
Data	Data Processing and Educational Measurement Center. Kansas State Teacher's College, 1200 Commercial St., Emporia, KS 66802.

EDITS	Educational and Industrial Testing Service. P.O. Box 7234, San Diego, CA 92107.
Empiric	Empiric Press. 333 Perry Brooks Bldg., Austin, TX 78701.
Essay	Essay Press. P.O. Box 5, Planetarium Station, New York, NY 10024.
Follett	Follett Publishing. 1010 West Washington Blvd., Chicago, IL 60607.
Foundations	Foundations for Research on Human Behavior. Box 1248, Ann Arbor, MI 48106.
FRIMD	Foundation for Research in Mental Development. Box 1483, Wilmington, DE 19809.
G & S	Grune and Stratton. 111 Fifth Ave., New York, NY 10003.
GA	Guidance Associates of Delaware. 1526 Gilpin Ave., Wilmington, DE 19806.
HBJ	Harcourt Brace Jovanovich. 757 Third Ave., New York, NY 10017.
Hiskey	Hiskey, Marshall S. 5640 Baldwin, Lincoln, NE 68507.
Houghton	Houghton Mifflin. 1 Beacon St., Boston, MA 02107.
Houston	Houston Test Company. P.O. Box 35152, Houston, TX 77035.
IPAT	Institute for Personality and Ability Testing. 1602 Coronado Drive, Champaign, IL 61820.
Keystone	Keystone View. 2212 East 12th St., Davenport, IA 52803.
Ladoca	Ladoca Project and Publ. Foundation. East 51st Ave. and Lincoln St., Denver, CO 80216.
Lang. Res.	Language Research Associates. P.O. Box 2085, Palm Springs, CA 92262.
L & F	Lea and Bebiger. 600 Washington Square, Philadelphia, PA 19106.
Lyons	Lyons and Carnahan for Rand McNally College Publ. Co., P.O. Box 7600,
Merrill	Charles E. Merrill. 1300 Alum Creek Dr., Columbus, OH 43216.
NEL	National Education Laboratory Publ. P.O. Box 1003, Austin, TX 78767.

NW Univ.	Northwestern University Press. 1735 Benson Ave., Evanston, IL 60201.
PLS	Perceptual Learning Systems. P.O. Box 864, Dearborn, MI 48121.
Personnel	Personnel Press. Education Center, P.O. Box 2649, Columbus, OH 43216.
Programs	Programs for Education. Box 85, Lumberville, PA 18933.
Psych. Corp.	Psychological Corporation, 757 Third Ave., New York, NY 10017.
PTS	Psychological Test Specialties, Box 9229, Missoula, MT 59801.
Scholastic	Scholastic Testing Service. 480 Meyer Road, Bensenville, IL 60106.
SRA	Science Research Associates. 155 North Wacker Drive, Chicago, IL 60606.
Slosson	Slosson Educational Publications. 140 Pine St., East Aurora, NY 14052.
Stanwix	Stanwix House. 3020 Chartiers Ave., Pittsburgh, PA 15204.
Steck-V.	Steck-Vaughn. P.O. Box 2028, Austin, TX 78767.
Stoelting	Stoelting Co., 1350 South Kostner Ave., Chicago, IL 60623.
TCP	Teacher's College Press, 1234 Amsterdam Ave., New York, NY 10027.
U. of Ill.	University of Illinois Press. Urbana, IL 61801.
WPS	Western Psychological Services. 12031 Wilshire Blvd., Los Angeles, CA 90025.

APPENDIX C

The Conversion of Standard Scores into Percentiles

Standard Score	Percentile	Standard Score	Percentile	Standard Score	Percentile	Standard Score	Percentile
- 2.33	1	- .58	28	+ .13	55	+ .84	80
- 2.06	2	- .56	29	+ .15	56	+ .88	81
- 1.86	3	- .54	30	+ .18	57	+ .92	82
- 1.76	4	- .50	31	+ .20	58	+ .96	83
- 1.65	5	- .47	32	+ .23	59	+ 1.00	84
- 1.56	6	- .44	33	+ .26	60	+ 1.04	85
- 1.48	7	- .41	34	+ .28	61	+ 1.09	86
- 1.41	8	- .39	35	+ .31	62	+ 1.13	87
- 1.35	9	- .36	36	+ .33	63	+ 1.18	88
- 1.29	10	- .33	37	+ .36	64	+ 1.23	89
- 1.23	11	- .31	38	+ .39	65	+ 1.29	90
- 1.18	12	- .28	39	+ .41	66	+ 1.35	91
- 1.13	13	- .26	40	+ .44	67	+ 1.41	92
- 1.08	14	- .23	41	+ .47	68	+ 1.48	93
- 1.04	15	- .20	42	+ .50	69	+ 1.56	94
- 1.00	16	- .18	43	+ .53	70	+ 1.65	95
- .96	17	- .15	44	+ .56	71	+ 1.76	96
- .92	18	- .13	45	+ .58	72	+ 1.89	97
- .88	19	- .10	46	+ .61	73	+ 2.06	98
- .84	20	- .08	47	+ .65	74	+ 2.33	99
- .81	21	- .05	48	+ .68	75		
- .77	22	- .03	49	+ .71	76		
- .74	23	.00	50	+ .74	77		
- .72	24	+ .03	51	+ .77	78		
- .68	25	+ .05	52	+ .81	79		
- .65	26	+ .08	53				
- .61	27	+ .10	54				

Example: If a student had an ITPA subtest score of 28 where the mean of the ITPA is 36 and the standard deviation is 6, then the student would be—1.33 SD (36 minus 28 or 8 divided by 6) or in the 9th percentile.

Bibliography

AAPER. Youth fitness manual. AAHPER-NEA Fitness Department. 1201 Sixteenth St., Washington, D.C., 1958.

Aaronson, D. Temporal factors in perception and short-term memory. *Psychological Bulletin*, 1967, 73, 130-144.

Ackerman, P.T., Peters, J.E., Dykenan, R.A. Children with specific learning disabilities: Bender test findings and other signs. *Journal of Learning Disabilities*, 1971, 4, 437-446.

Adams, R.M., Kacsis, J. & J., and Estes, R.E. Soft neurological signs in learning disabled children and controls. *American Journal of Disabled Children*, 1974, 128, 614-618.

Aiken, L.R. Language factors in learning mathematics. *Review of Educational Research*, 1972, 42, 359-385.

Aiken, L.R. Intellective variables and mathematics achievement: Directions for research. *Journal of School Psychology*, 1971, 9, 201-209.

Aiken, L.R. Nonintellective variables and mathematics achievement directions for research. *Journal of School Psychology*, 1970, 8, 28-36.

Algozzine, R.F. and Sutherland, J. Non-psuchoeducational foundations of learning disabilities. *Journal of Special Education*, 1977, 11, 91-98.

Allen, M.J. The role of vision in learning disorders. *Journal of Learning Disabilities, 1977, 10, 411-415.*

Allen, D. and Ager, J.A. A factor analysis of the ability to spell. *Educational and Psychological Measurement*, 1965, 25, 153-161.

Allingto, R.L., Chados, L., Domaracki, J., and Truex, S. Passage Dependency: Four diagnostic oral reading tests. *The Reading Teacher*, 1977, 30, 369-375.

Almy, M.C. *Logical Thinking in Second Grade.* New York: Teacher's College Press, 1970.

Alwitt, L.F. Attention in a visual task among non-readers and readers. *Perceptual and Motor Skills*, 1966, 23, 361-362.

Anderson, J.E. The limitations of infant and pre-school tests as measurement of intelligence. *Journal of Psychology*, 1939, 8, 351-379.

Anderson, M. and Kelley, M. An inquiry into traits associated with reading disability. *Smith College Studies in Social Work*, 1931, 2, #1.

Anderson, R.P., Halcomb, C.G., and Doyle, R.B. The measurement of attentional deficits. *Exceptional children*, 1973, 40, 534-539.

Anglin, R. Comparison of two tests of brain damage. *Perceptual and Motor Skills*, 1965, 20, 977-980.

Aryes, A.J. Patterns of perceptual-motor dysfunction in children: A factor analytic study. *Perceptual and Motor Skills*, 1965, 20, 335-368.

Aryes, A.J. and Torres, F. The incidence of EEG abnormalities in a dyslexic and control group. *Journal of Clinical Psychology, 1967, 23, 334-336.*

Atkinson, J.W. and Raynor, J.O. *Motivation and Achievement.* Wash., D.C.: V.H. Winston, 1974.

Auxter, D. Reaction time of children with learning disabilities. *Academic Therapy*, 1970-71, 6, 151-154.

Baddeley, A.D. *The Psychology of Memory.* New York: Basic Books, 1976.
Baddeley, A.D. Retrieved rules and semantic coding in short-term memory. *Psychological Bulletin,* 1972, 78, 378-385.
Baddeley, A.D., Effects of acoustic and semantic similarity on short-term paired-associate learning. *British Journal of Psychology,* 1970, 61, 335-343.
Baddeley, A.D. and Levy, B.A. Semantic coding and short-term memory. *Journal of Experimental Psychology,* 1971, 89, 132-136.
Bailey, M.H. The ability of phonic generalizations in grade one through six. *The Reading Teacher,* 1967, 20, 413-418.
Baker, H.J. Personal communication, 1976.
Bakwin, H. Reading disability in twins. *Developmental Medicine and Child Neurology,* 1973, 15, 184-187.
Balow, B. The emotionally and socially handicapped. *Review of Educational Research,* 1966, 36, 120-133.
Balow, B., Rubin, R., and Rosen, M.J. Perinatal events as precursors of reading disabilities. *Reading Research Quarterly,* 1975-76, 11, 36-71.
Bannatyne, A. *Language, Reading, and Learning Disabilities.* Springfield, Ill.: C. C. Thomas, 1971.
Bannatyne, A. Diagnosing learning disabilities and writing remedical prescriptions. *Journal of Learning Disabilities,* 1968, 1, 242-249.
Bannatyne, A. and Wichiarojote, D. Relationships between written spelling, motor functioning, and sequencing skills. *Journal of Learning Disabilities,* 1969, 2, 4-16.
Barr, K.L. and McDowell, R.L. Comparison of learning disabled and emotionally disturbed children on three deviant classroom behaviors. *Exceptional Children,* 1972, 38, 60-62.
Barrett, T.C. The relationship between measures of pre-reading visual discrimination and first grade achievement: A review of the literature. *Reading Research Quarterly,* 1965, 1, 51-76.
Bartel, N.R. Problems in arithmetic achievement. In Hammill, D.D. and Bartel, N.R. *Teaching Children with Language and Behavior Problems.* Boston: Allyn and Bacon, 1975.
Bartel, N.R., Grill, J.J., Bryen, D.N. Language characteristics of Black children: Implications for assessment. *Journal of School Psychology,* 1973, 11, 351-364.
Bateman, B. Three approaches to diagnosis and educational planning for children with learning disabilities. *Academic Therapy Quarterly,* 1967, 2, 215-222.
Beery, J.W. Matching of auditory and visual stimuli by average and retarded readers. *Child Development,* 1967, 38, 827-833.
Beery, K. Westerman, G.S., and Wilkinson, In Westerman, G.S. *Spelling and Writing.* San Rafael, Cal.: Dimension Publishing Co., 1971.
Beiser, H.R. Psychiatric diagnostic inventories with children. *Journal of the American Academy of Child Psychiatry,* 1962, 1, 656.
Belmont, L. and Birch, H.G. Lateral dominance, lateral awareness, and reading disability. *Child Development,* 1965, 36, 57-71.
Bender, L. Problems in conceptualization and communication in children with developmental alexia. In Hoch, P.H. and Zubin, J. (Eds.) *Psychopathology of Communication.* New York: Grune and Stratton, 1958.
Bender, L. A visual motor Gestalt test and its clinical uses. *Research Monographs of the American Orthopsychiatry Association,* 1938, #3.
Benger, K. The relationship of perception, personality, intelligence and grade one reading achievement. In Smith, H.K. *Perception and Reading.* Newark, Del.: International Reading Association, 1968.
Benton, A.L. Right-left discrimination. *Pediatric Clinics of North America,* 1968, 15, 747-758.
Benton, A.L. *Right-left Discrimination and Finger Localization.* New York; Hoeber, 1959.

Benton, A.L. Development of finger-localization capacity in school children. *Child Development,* 1955, 26, 225-230.

Benton, A.L., Hutcheon, J.F., and Seymour, E. Arithmetic ability, finger-localization capacity and right-left discrimination in normal and defective children. *American Journal of Orthopsychiatry,* 1951, 21, 756-766.

Bentzen, F. Sex ratios in learning and behavior disorders. *American Journal of Orthopsychiatry,* 1963, 23, 92-98.

Berko, J. The child's learning of English morphology. *Word,* 1958, 14, 150-177.

Berko, M.J. Psychometric scatter: Its application in the clinical prediction of future mental development in cases of childhood brain injury. *Cerebral Palsy Review,* 1955, 16, 16-18.

Bernstein, B. Elaborated and restricted codes: Their origins and some consequences. In. Smith, A.J. *Communications and Culture.* New York: Holt, Rinehart, and Winston, 1966.

Betts, E.A. *Foundations of Reading Instruction with Emphasis on Differential Diagnosis.* New York: Americn Book Co., 1957.

Biemiller, A. The devlopment of the use of graphic and contextual information as children learn to read. *Reading Research Quarterly,* 1970, 6, 75-96.

Bijou, S.W. and Patterson, R.F. Functional analysis in the assessment of children. In McReynolds, D. (Ed.) *Advances in Psychological Assessment, Vol. II.* Palo Alto, Cal.: Science and Behavior Books, 1971.

Billingslea, F.Y. The Bender-Gestalt: A review and a perspective. *Psychological Bulletin,* 1963, 60, 233-251.

Birch, H. and Gassow, J.D. *Disadvantaged Children: Health, Nutrition, and School Failure.* New York: Grune and Stratton, 1970.

Black, F.W. Cognitive, academic, and behavoral findings in children with suspected and documented neurological dysfunction. *Journal of Learning Disabilities,* 1976, 9, 182-187.

Blanchard, P.J. Reading disability in relation to difficulties of personality and emotional development. *Mental Hygiene,* 1936, 20, 384.

Blank, M. Cognitive processes in auditory discrimination in normal and retarded readers. *Child Development,* 1968, 39, 1091-1101.

Blom, G.E. Sex differences in reading disability. In Calkins, E.O. (Ed.) *Reading Forum: A Collection of Reference Papers Concerned with Reading Disability.* NINDS Monograph #11. Bethesda, Md.: Dept. of HEW, 1972.

Blom, G.E. and Jones, A. Bases of classification of reading disorders. In Calkins, E. O. (Ed.) *Reading Forum: A Collection of Reference Papers Concerned with Reading Disability.* NINDS Monograph #11. Bethesda, Md.: Dept of HEW, 1972.

Boder, E. Developmental dyslexia: A diagnostic approach based on three atypical reading-spelling patterns. *Developmental Medicine and Child Neurology,* 1973, 15, 663-687.

Boder, E. Developmental dyslexia: A diagnostic screening procedure based on reading and spelling patterns. *Academic Therapy,* 1969, 4, 285-287.

Bond, G.L. *The Auditory and Speech Characteristics of Poor Readers.* New York: Columbia Teacher's College Press, 1935.

Bond, E.D. and Partridge, G.E. Postencephalitic behavior disorders in boys and their management in a hospital. *American Journal of Psychiatry,* 1926, 6, 25-103.

Bonner, A. and Healey, W. *A Manual of Individual Tests and Testing.* Boston: Little and Brown, 1929.

Bormuth, J.R. The Durrell Listening-Reading Series. In Buros, O.K. *The Seventh Mental Measurements Yearbook.* Highland Park, N.J.: The Gryphon Press, 1972.

Bormuth, J.R. New data on readability. In Figural, J.A. *Forging Ahead.* Newark, N.J.: International Reading Association, 1967.

Boshes, B. and Myklebust, H.R. A neurological and behavioral study of children with learning disorders. *Neurology,* 1964, 14, 7-12.
Boswell, S.L. A developmental study of immediate memory. Unpublished MA thesis at the University of Colorado, 1971.
Bower, E.M. *Early Identification of Emotionally Handicapped Children.* Springfield, Ill.: C. C. Thomas, 1960.
Bower, G.H., Clark, M.C., Lesgold, A.M., and Winzenz, D. Heirarchical retrieval schemes in recall of categorized word lists. *Journal of Verbal Learning and Verbal Behavior,* 1969, 8, 323-343.
Bower, T.G.R. The object in the world of the infant. *Scientific American,* 1972, 226, 30-38.
Bower, T.G.R. The visual world of infants. *Scientific American,* 1966, 215, 80-98.
Bowerman, M. Syntactic factors in the acquisition of rules for word use and sentence construction. In Morehead, D.M. and Morehead, A.E. *Normal and Deficient Child Language.* Baltimore: University Park Press, 1976.
Boyd, L. and Randall, K. Factor analysis of the Frostig Developmental Test of Visual Perception. *Journal of Learning Disabilities,* 1970, 3, 253-255.
Bray, D.F. *Neurology in Pediatrics.* New York Year Book Med., 1969.
Bradley, C. The behavior of children receiving benzedrine. *American Journal of Psychiatry,* 1937, 94, 577-585.
Bryen, D.N. Special education and the linguistically deficient child, *Exceptional Children,* 1974, 41, 589-599.
Bryan, T.H. Peer popularity of learning disabled children: A replication. *Journal of Learning Disabilities,* 1976, 9, 49-60.
Bryan, T.H. and McGrady, H.J. Use of a teacher rating scale. *Journal of Learning Disabilities,* 1972, 5, 199-206.
Bryant, A.I. Organization of memory in young children. *Archives of Psychology,* 1934, #162.
Bryant, N.D. Some conclusions concerning impaired motor development among reading disability cases. *Bulletin of the Orton Society,* 1964, 14, 16-17.
Broca, P. Sur la facule du language articule. *Bullitin Societie d'Anthropologie (Paris)* 1865, Vol. 6.
Broca, A. Sur le siege de la faculte du language articule avec deux observations d'aphemie (perte de la parole) *Bullitin Societie Anatomie,* 1861, Vol. 6.
Brooks, P.H. Arnold, D.J., and Iacobbo, M. Some cognitive aspects of reading comprehension. *Peabody Journal of Education,* 1977, 54, 146-153.
Bronscom, M.E. Hughs, J., and Oxtalby, E.T. Studies of nonfluency in the speech of preschool children. In Johnson, W. and Leutengger R.R. *Stuttering in Children and Adults.* Minneapolis: University of Minnesota Press, 1955.
Brown, R. Fraser, C. The acquisition of syntax. In Bellugi, U. and Brown, R. *Acquisition of Language.* Monograph of the Society of Research in Child Development, 1964, 29, #1.
Brandis, W. and Henderson, D. *Social Class, Language, and Communication.* Beverly Hills, Cal.: Sage Publ., 1970.
Bray, N.M. and Estes, R.E. A comparison of the PIAT, CAT, and WRAT scores and teacher ratings for learning disabled children. *Journal of Learning Disabilities,* 1975, 8, 519-523.
Bruininks, R.H. Auditory and visual perceptual skills related to the reading performance of disadvantaged boys. *Perceptual and Motor Skills,* 1969, 29, 179-186.
Bruininks, R.H. and Locher, W.G. Change and stability in correlations between intelligence and reading test scores among disadvantaged children. *Journal of Reading Behavior,* 1970, 2, 259-264.
Buckingham, B.R. *Spelling Ability: Its Measurement and Distribution.* New York: Teacher's College Press, 1913.
Burnand, G., Hunter, H., and Haggart, K. Some psychological characteristics of Kleinfeller's syndrome. *British Journal of Psychiatry,* 1967, 113, 1091-1096.

Buros, O.K. (Ed.) *The Seventh Mental Measurements Yearbook.* Highland Park, N.J.: The Gryphon Press, 1972.

Buros, O.K. (Ed.) *The Sixth Mental Measurements Yearbook.* Highland Park, N.J.: The Gryphon Press, 1965.

Buxton, C. The application of multiple factorial methods to the study of motor abilities. *Psychometrika,* 1938, 3, 85-93.

Cahen, L.S., Crown, M.J., and Johnson, S.K. Spelling difficulty—A survey of the research. *Review of Educational Research,* 1971, 41, 281-301.

Cagney, M.A. Children's ability to understand standard English and Black dialect. *The Reading Teacher,* 1977, 30, 607-610.

Camp, B.W. Performance on the children's form of the Train Making Test in a psychiatric population. *Perceptual and Motor Skills,* 1965, 21, 167-170.

Camp, B.W. and Dahlem, N.W. Paired-associate and Serial Learning in Retarded Readers. *Journal of Educational Psychology,* 1975, 67, 385-390.

Cantwell, D.P. Epidemology, clinical picture and classification of the hyperactive child syndrome. In Cantwell, D.P. (Ed.) *The Hyperactive Child: Diagnosis, Management, and Current Research.* New York: Spectrum Publ., 1975.

Cantwell, D.P. Diagnostic examination of hyperactive children. In Cantwell, D.P. (Ed.) *The Hyperactive Child: Diagnosis, Management, and Current Research.* New York: Spectrum Publ., 1975.

Cantwell, D.P. (Ed.) *The Hyperactive Child: Diagnosis, Management, Current Research.* New York: Spectrum Publ. Vol. I, 1973; Vol. II, 1975.

Carroll, J.B. The Illinois Test of Psycholinguistic Abilities. In Buros, O.K. *The Seventh Mental Measurements Yearbook.* Highland Park, N.J.: The Gryphon Press, 1972.

Carter, J.L. and Diaz, A. Effects of visual and auditory background on reading test performance. *Exceptional Children,* 1971, 38, 43-50.

Catania, A.C. and Brigham, T.A. *Handbook of Applied Behavioral Analysis: Social and Instructional Processes.* New York: Irvington Publ.:, 1978.

Cattell, R.B. Personality pinned down. *Psychology Today,* 1973, 7, 40-46.

Cattell, R.B. *Abilities: Their Structure, Growth, and Action.* Boston: Houghton Mifflin, 1971.

Cattell, R.B. and Butcher, H.J. *The Prediction of Achievement and Creativity.* New York: Bobbs-Merrill Co., 1968.

Cavenaugh, L.A. Reading behavior with regard for endocrine inbalances. In *Claremont College Reading Conference Thirteenth Yearbook. Claremont, Cal.: Claremont College Curriculum Lab.,* 1948, 95-102.

Cazden, C.B. *Child Language and Education.* New York: Holt, Rinehart, Winston, 1972.

Chalfant, J.C. Based on lectures given to Education Service Unit #9 at Hastings, Nebraska, 1974.

Chalfant, J.C. and King, F.S. An approach to operationalizing the definition of learning disabilities. *Journal of Learning Disabilities,* 1976, 9, 228-235.

Chall, J.S. *Learning to Read: The Great Debate.* New York: McGraw Hill, 1967.

Chall, J.S. Readability. *Educational Research Monograph,* 1958, #30.

Chall, J.S., Roswell, F.G., and Blumenthal, S.H. Auditory blending ability: A factor in success in beginning reading. *The Reading Teacher,* 1963, 17, 113-118.

Chang, T.M.C. and Chang, V.A.C. Relation of visual-motor skills and reading achievement in primary-grade pupils of superior ability. *Perceptual and Motor Skills,* 1967, 24, 51-53.

Chase, W.G. (Ed.) *Visual Information Processing.* New York: Academic Press, 1973.

Chatton, M.J., Margen, S., and Brainerd, H. *Handbook of Medical Treatment.* Los Altos, Cal.: Lange Medical Pub., 1968.

Chomsky, N. *Syntactic Structures.* London: Mouton, 1957.

Chorost, S.B., Spivack, G. and Levin, M. Bender-Gestalt rotations and electroencephalograph abnormalities in children. *Journal of Consulting Psychology,* 1959, 25, 559.

Clark, M.M. Severe reading difficulties: A community study. *British Journal of Educationall Psychology,* 1971, 41, 14-18.

Clements, S.D. *Minimal Brain Dysfunction in Children.* Public Health Publ., #415. Washington, D.C.: U.S. Dept. of HEW, 1966.

Clements, S.D. and Peters, J.E. Minimal brain dysfunctions in the school-age child. *Archives of General Psychiatry,* 1962, 6, 185-197.

Cohen, J. The factorial structure of the WISC at ages 7-6, 10-6, and 13-6. *Journal of Consulting Psychology,* 1959, 23, 285-299.

Colarusso, D., Martin, H., Harting, J. Specific visual-perceptual skills as long-term predictors of academic success. *Journal of Learning Disabilities,* 1975, 8, 651-655.

Coles, G.S. The learning disabilities test battery: Empirical and social issues. *Harvard Educational Review,* 1978, 48, 313-340.

Colligan, R.C. Concurrent validity of the Myklebust Pupil Rating Scale in a kindergarten population. *Journal of Learning Disabilities,* 1977, 10, 317-320.

The Committee on Child Psychiatry. *Psychopathological Disorders in Childhood: Theoretical Considerations and a Proposed Classification.* New York: Group for the Advancement of Psychiatry, 1966.

Connally, C. The psychosocial adjustment of children with dyslexia. *Exceptional Children,* 196, 36, 126-127.

Conners, C.K. Deanal and behavior disorders in children: A critical review of the literature and recommendations for future studies for determining efficiency. *Psychopharmacology Bulletin,* Dept. of HEW, 1973, 188-195.

Conners, C.K. A teacher rating scale for use in drug studies with children. *American Journal of Psychiatry,* 1969, 126, 152-157.

Conners, C.K., Kramer, K. and Guerra, F. Auditory synthesizers and dicotic listening in children with learning disabilities. *Journal of Special Education,* 1969, 3, 163-169.

Connolly, C. Social and emotional factors in learning disabilities. In Myklebust, H. (Ed.) *Progress in Learning Disabilities, Vol. II.* New York: Grune and Stratton, 1971.

Connor, J.P. Bender-Gestalt test performance as a predictor of differential reading performance. *Journal of School Psychology,* 1968-69, 7, 41-44.

Cooke, B. The relationship between balance, performance, and cognitive abilities. Urbana, Ill.: University of Illinois. Unpublished Ph.D. thesis, 1968.

Copeland, R.W. *How Children Learn Mathematics.* London: The MacMillan Co.: 1970.

Cott, A. Megavitamins: The orthomolecular approach to behavior disorders and learning disabilities. *Academic Therapy,* 1972, 7, 245-258.

Covin, T.M. Stability of the WISC-R for 9-year-olds with learning difficulties. *Psychological Reports,* 1977, 40, 1297-1298.

Cowen, E.L. et. al. The AML: A quick-screening device for early identification of school maladaption. *American Journal of Community Psychology,* 1973, 1,12-35.

Craik, F.I.M. Primary memory. *British Medical Bulletin,* 1971, 27, 232-236.

Craik, F.I.M. and Walkins, M.J. The role of rehearsed in short-term memory. *Journal of Verbal Learning and Verbal Behavior,* 1973, 12, 599-607.

Crain, L. and Werner, H. The development of visuo-motor performance on the marble board in normal children. *Journal of Genetic Psychology,* 1950, 77, 217-229.

Cratty, B.J. *Movement, Perception, and Thought.* Palo Alto, Cal.: Peek Publ., 1969.

Cratty, B.J. and Martin, M.M. Perceptual-motor efficiency in children: The measurement and improvement of movement attributes. Philadelphia: Lea and Feliger, 1969.

Critchley, M. *Developmental Dyslexia.* London: Heinemann, 1964.
Cromer, B. The Cognitive Hypothesis of Language Acquisition. In Morehead, D.M. and Morehead, A.E. *Normal and Deficient Child Language.* Baltimore: University Park Press, 1976.
Crovitz, H.R. and Schiffman, H.R. Visual field and the letter span. *Journal of Experimental Psychology,* 1965, 69, 218-223.
Crowder, R.G. *Principles of Learning and Memory.* Hillsdale, N.J.: Lawrence Erlbaum Assoc., 1976.
Crowder, R.G. The sound of vowels and consonants in immediate memory. *Journal of Verbal Learning and Verbal Behavior,* 1971, 10, 587-596.
Cruiskshank, W.M. *The Brain-Injured Child in Home, School and Community.* Syracuse, N.Y.: Syracuse University Press, 1967.
Culbertson, F.M. and Gunn, R.C. Comparison of the Bender-Gestalt test and Frostig test in several clinical groups of children. *Journal of Clinical Psychology,* 1966, 22, 439.

Dale, E. and Chall, J.S. Formula for predicting readibility. *Educational Research Bulletin,* 1948, 27, 11-20.
Danelson, L.C. and Bauer, J.N. A formula-based classification of learning disabled children: An examination of the issues. *Journal of Learning Disabilities,* 1978, 11, 163-176.
Datel, W.E. and Gengerelli, J.A. Reliability of Rorschach interpretations. *Journal of Projective Techniques,* 1955, 19, 372-381.
Davids, A., Goldenberg, L., and Laufer, M.W. The relation of the Archemedes spiral aftereffect and the Trail Making Test to brain damage in children. *Journal of Counseling Psychology,* 1957, 21, 429-433.
Davidson, H.P. A study of the confusing letters "B," "D," "P," and "Q." *Journal of Genetic Psychology,* 1935, 47, 458-468.
Davis, F.B. (Chairman) *Standards for Educational and Psychological Tests.* Washington, D.C.: American Psychological Association, 1974.
Dearborn, W.F., Ocular and normal dominance in dyslexia. *Psychological Bulletin,* 1939, 28, 704.
DeHirsch, K., Jansky, J.J., and Langford, W.S. *Predicting Reading Failure.* New York: Harper and Row, 1966.
Denhoff, E., Hawsworth, P., and Hawsworth, M. Learning disabilities and early childhood education: An information processing approach. In Myklebust, H.R. *Progress in Learning Disabilities.* New York: Grune and Stratton, 1971.
Denny-Brown, D. The nature of apraxia. *Journal of Nervous Diseases and Mental Diseases,* 1958, 82, 9-32.
Deutsch, D. The organization of short-term memory for a single acoustic attribute. In Deutsch, D. and Deutsch, J.A. (Eds.) *Short-term Memory.* New York: Academic Press, 1975.
Deutsch, D. Music and memory. *Psychology Today,* 1972, 5, 87-120.
Deursch, D. and Deutsch, J.A. (Eds.) *Short-term Memory.* New York: Academic Press, 1975.
Dice, G. and Shearer, W.M. Clinician's accuracy in detecting vocal nodules. *Language, Speech and Hearing Services in Schools,* 1973, 4, 142-144.
DeQueros, J.B. Diagnosis of vestibular disorders in the learning disabled. *Journal of Learning Disabilities,* 1976, 9, 50-58.
Dillard, J.L. *Black English: Its History and Usage in the United States.* New York: Random House, 1972.
Dion, K.K. Physical attractiveness and evaluation of children's transgressions. *Journal of Personal and Social Psychology,* 1972, 24, 207-213.
Dornbush, R.L. and Basow, S. The relationship between auditory and visual short-term memory and reading achievement. *Child Development,* 1970, 41, 1033-1044.

Downing, J. Children's concepts of learning to read. *Educational Research,* 1970, 12, 106-112.

Duffy, O.B. and Clair, T.N. Relationship of IQ, verbal-motor skills, and psycholinguistic abilities with achievement in 3rd, 4th and 5th grades. *Journal of Educational Psychology,* 1972, 63, 358-362.

Dunlap, W.P. and House, A.D. Why can't Johnny compute? *Journal of Learning Disabilities,* 1976, 9, 210-214.

Dunn, J.L. An overview. In Dunn, J.L. (Ed.) *Exceptional Children in the Schools: Special Education in Transition.* New York: Holt, Rinehart, and Winston, 1973.

Dunn, P.J. Orthomolecular therapy: Implications for learning disabilities. In Leisman, G. (Ed.) *Basic Visual Processes and Learning Disabilities.* Springfield, Ill.: C. C. Thomas, 1976.

Durrell, D.D. Phonics problems in beginning reading. In Figural, J.A. (Ed.) *Forging Ahead in Reading.* Newark, Del.: International Reading Assoc., 1967.

Dwyer, C.A. Sex differences in reading: An evaluation and critique of current theories. *Review of Educational Research,* 1973, 43, 455-467.

Dykman, R.A. et. al. Specific learning disabilities: An attentional deficit syndrome. In Mykelbust, H.R. (Ed.) *Progress in Learning Disabilities. Vol. II.* New York: Grune and Stratton, 1971.

Dykman, R.A. and Ackerman, P.T. The minimal brain dysfunction problem: Attention, inattention, and information processing. In Anderson, R.P. and Halcomb, C.G. (Eds.) *Learning Disability/Minimal Brain Dysfunction Syndrome.* Springfield, Ill: C.C. Thomas, 1976.

Dystra, R. Auditory discrimination abilities and beginning reading achievement. *Reading Research Quarterly,* 1966, 1, 5-34.

Eames, T.H. A frequency study of physical handicaps in reading disability and unselected groups. *Journal of Educational Research,* 1935, 29, 1-5.

Eames, T.H. A comparison of the ocular characteristics of unselected and reading disabled groups, *Journal of Educational Research,* 1932, 25, 211-215.

Ebel, R.L. Criterion-referenced measures: Limitations. *School Review,* 1971, 69, 282-288.

Eberle, D.W. An evaluation and analysis of vision studies as they relate to the teaching of elementary reading in current reading textbooks. Unpubl. Doctoral Dissertation, Indiana University, 1974.

Einhart, C.B. et. al. Brain injury in the preschool child: Some developmental considerations: II Comparison of brain-injured and normal children. *Psychological Monographs,* 1963, 77, 17-33. #573.

Eisonson, J. Aphasia in adults: Basic considerations. In Travis, L.E. *Handbook of Speech Pathology.* New York: Appleton-Century-Crofts, 1971.

Eller, W. and Attea, M. Three diagnostic tests: Some comparisons. In Figural, J.A. (Ed.) *Vistas in Reading.* Newark, Del.: International Reading Assoc., 1966.

Ellis, A. Results of a mental hygiene approach to reading disability problems. *Journal of Consulting Psychology,* 1949, 13, 56.

Ellis, W.D. *A Source Book of Gestalt Psychology.* New York: Harcourt and Brace, 1938.

Endicott, J.J. and Spitzer, R.L. The value of the standardized interview for evaluation of psychopathology. *Journal of Personality Assessment,* 1972, 36, 410-417.

Enstrom, E.A. Left-handedness: A cause for disability in writing. *Journal of Learning Disabilities,* 1968, 1, 410-414.

Epstein, W. and Park, J.N. Shape constancy: Fundamental relationship and theoretical formulations. *Psychological Bulletin,* 1963, 60, 265-288.

Espenshade, A.S. and Eckert, H.M. *Motor Development.* Columbus, Ohio: C.C. Merrill, 1967.

Eustis, R.S. The primary etiology of the specific language disability. *Journal of Pediatrics,* 1947, 31, 448.

Farr, R. *Reading: What can be Measured?* Newark, Del: International Reading Association Foundation, 1969.
Farr, R. Burnett Reading Series. In Buros, O.K. *Seventh Mental Measurements Yearbook.* Highland Park, NJ.: Gryphon Press, 1972.
Farr, R. and Anastasiow, N. *Test of Reading Readiness and Achievement: A Review and Evaluation.* Newark, Del.: International Reading Assoc., 1969.
Farrald, R.E. and Schumber, R.G. *A Diagnostic and Perspective Technique: Handbook I.* ADAPT Press, Inc. 1973.
Ferinden, W.E. and Jackobson, S. Early identification of learning disabilities. *Journal of Learning Disabilities,* 1970, 3, 589-593.
Feingold, B.F. *Why Your Child is Hyperactive.* New York: Random, 1974.
Feingold, B.F. Hyperkinesis and learning disabilities linked to the ingestion of artificial food colors and flavors. *Journal of Learning Disabilities,* 1976, 9, 551-559.
Fiedler, M.F. Teacher's problems with hard of hearing children. *Journal of Educational Research,* 1949, 29, 618-622.
Fildes, L.G. Experiments on the problem of mirror-writing. *British Journal of Psychology,* 1923, 14, 57-67.
Fisher, H. A case of congenital word-blindness (inability to learn to read). *Ophthalmic Review,* 1905, 24, 315-318.
Fisher, J.A. The use of out-of-grade tests with retarded and accelerated readers. Unpubl. Doctoral Dissertation, University of Iowa, 1961.
Fisher, S. Body reactivity gradients and figure drawing variables. *Journal of Consulting Psychology,* 1959, 23, 54-59.
Fitzgerald, B.J., Pasework, R.A., and Gloeckler, T. Use of the PPVT with the educationally handicapped. *Journal of School Psychology,* 1970, 8, 296-300.
Flam, M.C. Early experience in the development of visual coordination. In Young, F.A. and Lindsley, D.D. (Eds.) *Early Experience and Visual Information Processing in Perceptual and Reading Disorders.* Washington, D.C.: National Academy of Sciences, 1970.
Flavell, J.H. *The Developmental Psychology of Jean Piaget.* Princeton, N.J.: Van Nostrand, 1964.
Flescher, I. Ocular-manual laterality and perceptual rotation of literal symbols. *Genetic Psychology Monographs,* 1962, 66, 3-48.
Flowers, R.M. The evaluation of auditory abilities in the appraisal of children with reading problems. In Smith, H.K. (Ed.) *Perception and Reading.* Newark, Del.: The International Reading Assoc., 1968.
Flowers, A. and Crandell, R.W. Relations among central auditory abilities, socioeconomic factors, speech delay, phonetic abilities and reading achievement: A longitudinal study. Mimeographed, 1967.
Fog, E. and Fog, M. Cerebral inhibition examined by associated movements. In Box, M. and MacKeith, R. (Eds.) *Minimal Cerebral Dysfunction.* Clinics in Developmental Medicine, #10. London: Heineman Medical, 1963.
Folsom, A.T. The epilepsies. In Haywood, H.C. *Brain-Damage in School Children.* Wash. D.C.: Council for Exceptional Children, 1968.
Forrest, T. Neurological and medical factors discriminating between normal children and those with learning disabilities. Paper read to the Society for Research in Child Development. New York City, 1967.
Forrest, T. Neurological and medical factors between normal children and those with learning disabilities. *Journal of Learning Disabilities,* 1968, 32, 48-55.
Frankenberg, W.F. Speech given to Colorado CEC, Colorado Springs, Colo., 1976.
Franklin, C.C. and Lehsten, N.G. Indiana Physical Fitness Tests for the elementary level (Grades 4 to 8). *The Physical Educator,* 1948, 5, #3.
Fraser, C. Bellugi, U., and Brown, R. Control of grammar in imitation, comprehension, and production. *Journal of Verbal Learning and Verbal Behavior,* 1963, 2, 121-135.

Freud, S. *Zur Auffassung der Aphasian.* Vienna: Franz Beutrake, 1891.
Freeman, F.N. Experimental analysis of the writing movement. *Psychological Monographs,* 1914, 17, 1-46.
Freeman, R.D. Special education and the electroencephalogram. *Journal of Special Education,* 1967, 2, 61-73.
Friedland, S.J. and Shilkret, R.B. Alternative explanations of learning disabilities: Defensive hyperactivity. *Exceptional Children,* 1973, 40, 213-215.
Fristoe M. and Goldman, R. Comparison of traditional and condensed articulation tests examining the same number of sounds. *Journal of Speech and Hearing Research,* 1968, 11, 583-589.
Fronsello, F. and Gerver, D. Multiple regression equations for predicting reading age from chronological and WISC verbal intelligence. *British Journal of Educational Psychology,* 1965, 35, 86-89.
Fry, M.A., Johnson, S.S., and Muehl, S. Oral language production in relation to reading achievement among second graders. In Bakker, D.J. and Satz, S. (Eds.) *Specific Reading Disability, Vol. III.* Rotterdam: Rotterdam University Press, 1970.
Fuller, G.B. and Laird, J.T. The Minnesota Percepto-Diagnostic Test. *Journal of Clinical Psychology Monographs Supplement,* 1963, #16, 1-33.
Furth, H.G. Research with the deaf: Implications for language and cognition. *Psychological Bulletin,* 1964, 62, 145-164.
Furth, H.G. A review and perspective on thinking of deaf people. In Hellmuth, J. *Cognitive Studies, Vol. 1,* New York: Brunner/Mazel, 1970.
Furth, H.G. and Milgren, N.A. Influence of language on comprehension of normal, mentally retarded, and deaf children. *Psychological Monographs,* 1965, 72, 317-335.

Gann, E. *Reading Difficulty and Personality Organization.* New York: Columbia University, 1945.
Gardner, L.I. (Ed.) *Endocrine and Genetic Diseases of Children.* Philadelphia: W.B. Saunders, 1969.
Gates, A.I. The role of personality adjustment in reading disability. *Journal of Genetic Psychology,* 1941, 59, 77.
Gates, A.I. *Interest and Ability in Reading.* New York: Macmillan, 1930.
Gates, A.I. A study of the role of visual perception, intelligence, and certain associative processes in reading and spelling. *Journal of Educational Psychology,* 1926, 17, 433-445.
Gates, A.I. *The Psychology of Reading and Spelling.* New York: Columbia University Press, 1922, #120..
Gearheart, B.R. *Learning Disabilities: Educational Strategies.* St. Louis: C.V. Mosby, Co., 1973.
Gellis, S.S. and Feingold, M. Atlas of mental retardation syndromes: Visual diagnosis of facies and physical findings. Washington, D.C.: U.S. Govt. Printing Office, 1968.
Gentile, A. Academic achievement test performance of hearing impaired students. Washington, D.C.: Office of Demographic Studies, Gallaudet College Bookstore, 1969.
Gerstmann, J. Finger agnosie: eine umschriebene storund der Orientierung am einened Koper. Wein: *klinishe Wochenschrift,* 1924, 37, 1010-1012.
Gesell, A.L. Accuracy in handwriting, as related to school intelligence and sex. *American Journal of Psychology,* 1906, 17, 394-405.
Getman, G.N. *How to Increase your Child's Intelligence.* Luverne, Minn.: Announcers Press, 1962.
Ghent, L. Perception of overlapping and embedded figures by children of different ages. *American Journal of Psychology,* 1956, 69, 575-587.
Gibson, J.J. and Gibson, E.J. Perceptual learning: Differential or enrichment? *Psychological Review,* 1955, 62, 36.

Gittelman-Klein, R. Psychopharmocological approaches to the treatment of learning disabilities: Implications for visual processes. In Leisman, G. *Basic Visual Processes and Learning Disabilities.* Springfield, Ill: C.C. Thomas, 1976.

Glassard, M. The effectiveness of three kindergarten predictors for first grade achievement. *Journal of Learning Disabilities,* 1977, 10, 95-99.

Glavin, J.P. and Quay, H.C. *Behavior disorders. Review of Eduational Research,* 1969, 39, 83-102.

Goetzinger, C.P., Dirks, D.D., and Baer, C.J. Auditory discrimination and visual discrimination in good and poor readers. *Annals of Otology, Rhinology, and Laryngology,* 1960, 69, 121-137.

Goins, J.T. Visual perceptual abilities and early reading progress. *Supplementary Educational Monographs,* 1958, 87, 1-108.

Goldberg, L.R. The effectiveness of clinician's judgements: The diagnosis of organic brain damage from the Bender-Gestalt. *Journal of Consulting Psychology,* 1959, 23, 25-33.

Goldberg, H.K. and Drosh, P.W. ͞thalmologist and the disabled reader. In Hellmuth, J. *Educational T ͞, Vol. 3.* Seattle: Special Child Pub. 1972.

Goldfried, M.R. and Davison, G. *͞nical Behavior Therapy.* New York: Holt, Rinehart, and Winston, 197ı

Goldscheider, A. and Muller, R.F. Zur physiologie and pathologie des lesens. *Zeitschrift fur klinishe Medicin,* 1893, 23, 131-167.

Goldberg, H.K. and Schiffman, G.B. *Dyslexia: Problems of Reading Disabilities.* New York: Grune and Stratton, 1972.

Goldstein, K., Landeau, W.M., and Kleffner, F.R. Neurological observations in a population of deaf and aphasic children. *Annals of Otology, Rhinology, and Laryngology,* 1960, 69, 756-767.

Goleman, D. A new computer test of the brain. *Psychology Today,* 1976, 6, 44-48.

Golinkoff, R.M. A comparison of reading processes in good and poor comprehenders. *Reading Research Quarterly,* 1975-76, 11, 623-659.

Gonzales, G. Language, culture, and exceptional children. *Exceptional Children,* 1974, 41, 565-570.

Goodglass, H. and Barton, M. Handedness and differential perception of verbal stimuli in left and right visual fields. *Perception and Motor Skills,* 1963, 17, 851-854.

Goodglass, H. and Kaplan, E. *The Assessment of Aphasia and Related Disorders.* Philadelphia: Lea and Febiger, 1972.

Goodman, J.D. and Sours, J.A. *The Child Mental Status Evaluation.* New York: Basic Books, 1967.

Goodman, K.S. Reading: A psycholinguistic guessing game. *The Journal of Reading Specialist,* 1967, 6, 15-25.

Goodnow, J.J. A test of melieu effects with some of Piaget's tasks. *Psychological Monographs,* 1962, 76, #555.

Gottschald, K. Uber den Einfluss der Enfahrung aud die Wahrnehnung von Figuren. *Psychol. Forsch.* 1926, 8, 261-317.

Graham, C. Differential markings of two vocabulary tests. *Psychological Reports,* 1963, 12, 421-422.

Graham, F.K. and Kendall, B.S. Memory for Designs Test—Revised general manual. *Perceptual and Motor Skills,* 1960, 11, 147-188.

Gravel, S.R. June reading achievements of first grade children. *Journal of Education,* 1958, 140, 37-43.

Greene, M.C.L. *The Voice and its Disorders.* 3rd Ed. London: Pitman Medical, 1972.

Green, O.C. and Perlman, S.M. Endocrinology and disorders in learning. In Myklebust, H.R. *Progress in Learning Disabilities,* Vol. II. New York: Grune and Stratton, 1971.

Gronland, N.E. *Sociometry in the Classroom.* New York: Harper, 1959.

Groves, P.M. and Thompson, R.F. Habituation: A dual-process theory. *Psychological Review,* 1970, 77, 419-450.

Guilford, J.P. *Fundamental Statistics in Psychology and Education.* New York: McGraw-Hill, 1965.

Guilford, J.P. *Personality.* New York: McGraw Hill, 1959.

Guilford, J.P. Reading comprehension and syntactic responses in good and poor readers. *Journal of Educational Psychology,* 1973, 65, 294-299.

Gutherie, J.T. JFK Institute, 707 N. Broadway, Baltimore, MD, 21205.

Hallahan, D.P. and Cruickshank, W.M. *Psychological Foundations of Learning Disabilities.* Englewood Cliffs, N.J.: Prentice-Hall, 1973.

Hallgren, B. Specific dyslexia (congenital word-blindness). *Acta Psychiatrica Neurologica Scandinavica,* 1950, #65.

Halpin, V.G. and Patterson, R.M. The performance of brain-injured children on the Goldstein-Sheerer tests. *American Journal of Mental Deficiency,* 1954, 59, 91-100.

Halstead, W.C. *Brain and Intelligence.* Chicago: Univ. of Chicago Press, 1947.

Hambleton, R.K. and Novich, M.R. Toward an integration of theory and method for criterion-refferenced tests. *Journal of Educational Measurement,* 1973, 10, 159-170.

Hambleton, R.K. and Norwich, M.R. Toward an integration of theory and method for criterion-referenced tests. *Journal of Educational Measurement,* 1973, 10, 10, 159-170.

Hammill, D. The Slossen Intelligence Test as a quick estimate of mental ability. *Journal of School Psychology,* 1968-69, 7, 33-37.

Hammill, D., Parker, R. and Newcomer, P. Psycholinguistic correlates of academic achievement. *Journal of School Psychology,* 1975, 13, 248-254.

Hannah, L.D. Causative factors in the production of rotations on the Bender Gestalt designs. *Journal of Consulting Psychology,* 1958, 22, 398-399.

Hanna, R.R. et. al. Phoneme-grapheme correspondences as cues to spelling improvement. Office of Education Bulletin #32008. Washington, D.C.: U.S. Office of Education, 1967.

Hanna, R.R. and Moore, T. Spelling from spoken word to written symbol. *Elementary School Journal,* 1953, 53, 329-337.

Harber, J.R. and Bryen, D.N. Black English and the task of reading. *Review of Educational Research,* 1976, 46, 387-405.

Hardy, Factors affecting the growth and development of children. *The Johns Hopkins Collaborative Perinatal Projects.* Baltimore: Johns Hopkins Press, 1970.

Hardy, W.G. and Bordley, J.E. Hearing evaluation in children. *Otolaryngologic Clinics of North America,* 1969, 3-26.

Hare, B.A., Hammill, D.D., and Bartel, N.R. Construct validity of selected subtests of the ITPA. *Exceptional Children,* 1973, 40, 13-20.

Haring, W.G. and Ridgeway, R. Early identification of children with learning disabilities. *Exceptional Children,* 1967, 33, 387-395.

Harris, A.J. *How to Increase Reading Ability.* (5th Ed.) New York: David McKay, 1970.

Harris, A.J. and Jacobson, M.D. Basic vocabulary for beginning reading. *The Reading Teacher,* 1973, 26, 392-395.

Harris, A.J. and Jacobson, M.D. *Basic Elementary Reading Vocabularies.* New York: The Macmillan Co., 1972.

Harris, A.J. Gilmore Oral Reading Test. In Buros, O.K. *The Seventh Mental Measurements Yearbook.* Highland Park, N.J.: Gryphon Pres, 1972.

Hartlage, L.C. and Green, J.B. EEG differences in children's reading, spelling and arithmetic abilities. *Perceptual and Motor Skills,* 1971, 32, 113-134.

Hartlage, L.C. and Lucas, T.L. Differential correlation of Bender-Gestalt and the Beery VMI for Black and White Children. *Perceptual and Motor Skills,* 1976, 43, 1039-1043.

Hawkins, L.F. *Notescript.* New York: Barns and Noble, 1964.

Haynes, J.R. and Sells, S.B. Assessment of organic brain damage by psychological test. *Psychological Bulletin,* 1963, 60, 316-325.

Hayword, P. Evaluating diagnostic reading tests. *The Reading Teacher,* 1968, 21, 523-528.

Hecaen, H. and de Ajuriaguerra J. *Left-handedness, Manual Superiority and Cerebral Dominance.* New York: Grune and Stratton, 1964.

Heller, T.M. Word blindness. *Pediatrics,* 1963, 31, 669-691.

Henderson, N.B., Baller, B.U., and Goffery, B. Effectiveness of the WISC and Bender-Gestalt Test in predicting arithmetic and reading achievement for white and non-white children. *Journal of Clinical Psychology,* 1969, 25, 268-271.

Herbert, M. The concept of testing of brain damage in children: A review. *Journal of Child Psychology and Psychiatry,* 1964, 5, 197-216.

Hermann, K. *Reading Disability: A Medical Study of Word-Blindness and Related Handicaps.* Springfield, Ill.: C.C. Thomas, 1959.

Hermann, K. and Norrie, E. Is congenital word-blindness a heriditary type of Gerstmann's syndrome? *Psychiatric Neurology,* 1958, 136, 59-73.

Hickey, T. Bilingualism and the measurement of intelligence and verbal learning ability. *Exceptional Children,* 1972, 39, 24-28.

Hicks, R.E. and Kinsbournne, M. Human handedness: A partial cross-fostering study. *Science,* 1976, 192, 908-910.

Hinshelwood, J. *Congenital Word-Blindness.* London: H.K. Lewis, 1917.

Hinshelwood, J. Congenital word-blindness with reports of two cases. *Ophthalmic Review,* 1902, 21, 91.

Hodges, R.E. Phoneme-grapheme correspondence in monosyllabic words. In Figural, J.A. *Forging Ahead in Reading.* Newark, Del.: International Reading Assoc., 1968.

Hollingsworth, P.M. Interrelating listening and reading. In Figural, J.A. *Reading and Realism.* Newark, Del.: International Reading Assoc., 1969.

Holmes, J.A. Basic assumptions underlying the substrata factor theory. *Reading Research Quarterly,* 1965, 1, 5-28.

Holmes, J.A. Personality and Spelling ability. *University of Cal. Publ. in Education,* 1959, 12, #4, 213-292.

Honwik, L.J. et, al. Diagnosis of cerebral dysfunction in children. *American Journal of Diseases of Children,* 1961, 101, 364-375.

Hopkins, K.D. and Sitkei, E.G. Predicting grade one reading performance: Intelligence versus reading readiness tests. *Journal of Experimental Education,* 1969, 37, 31-33.

Horn, E. Phonetics and spelling. *Elementary School Journal,* 1957, 57, 425-432.

Hubel, D.H. and Wiesel, T.N. Receptive fields, binocular interaction and functional architecture in the cat's visual cortex. *Journal of Physiology,* 1962, 160, 106-154.

Hubly, S. and Johnson, C. Measuring written language skills: The Written Expression Test. Mimeographed, 1980.

Hughs, J.R. Electroencephlography and learning disabilities. In Myklebust, H.R. *Progress in Learning Disabilities,* Vol. II. New York: Grune and Stratton, 1971.

Ilg, F.L. and Ames, L.B. *School Readiness.* New York: Harper and Row, 1964.

Itard, J.M.C. *The Wild Boy of Aveyron.* New York: Appleton-Century-Crofts, 1962.

Jakobson, R. and Halle, M. *Fundamentals of Language.* S-Gravenhage: Mouton and Co., 1956.

Jeffress, L.A. Masking and biaural phenomena. In Tolvas, J.V. and Schubert, E.D. (Eds.) *Modern Foundations of Auditory Theory.* New York: Academic Press, 1965.

Jensen, A.R. Individual differences in visual and auditory memory. *Journal of Educational Psychology,* 1971, 62, 123-131.

Jensen, A.R. Patterns of mental ability and socio-economic status. *Proceedings of National Academy of Science,* 1968, 60, 1330-1337.

Jensen, A.R. and Rohwer, W.D. The Stroop Color-Word Test: A review. *Acta Psychologica Amsterdam,* 1966, 25, 36-93.

Johnson, C. The Hyperactivity Kit. Can be obtained by writing the author c/o the publisher. 1981.

Johnson, C. The Synthetic Profile of Learning Problems. Can be obtained by writing the author c/o the publisher, 1981.

Johnson, C. The Oral Language Test. Can be obtained by writing the author c/o the publisher, 1981.

Johnson, C. Print the Alphabet Test (PTA). Can be obtained by writing the author c/o the publisher. 1977.

Johnson, C. The effect of frequency, pronounceability and word length on word recognition ability of elementary school children. Unpubl. Ph.D. Thesis, University of Colorado, 1973.

Johnson, C. and Hubly, S. The Written Expression Test. Can be obtained by writing the author c/o the publisher, 1979.

Johnson, C. and Olds, A.E. The Academic Screening Test. Can be obtained by writing the author c/o the publisher, 1981.

Johnson, D.D. The Dolch list reexamined. *The Reading Teacher,* 1971, 24, 449-457.

Johnson, D.J. and Myklebust, H.R. *Learning Disabilities: Educational Principles and Practices.* New York: Grune and Stratton, 1964.

Johnson, W. (Ed.) *The Onset of Stuttering.* Minneapolis: University of Minnesota Press, 1959.

Johnson, W., Darley, F.L., and Spieslershack, D.C. *Diagnostic Methods in Speech Pathology.* New York: Harper and Row, 1963.

Jones, J.W. Blind Children, Degree of Vision, Mode of Reading. Washington, D.C.: U.S. Office of Education, #24, 1961.

Jones, R.R., Reid, J.B., and Patterson, G.R. Naturalistic observation in clinical assessment. In McReynolds, P. *Advances in Psychological Assessment,* Vol. III. San Francisco: Jossey-Bass Publ., 1975.

Jordan, D.R. *Dyslexia in the Classroom.* Columbus, Ohio: Charles E. Merrill, 1972.

Julez, B. *Foundations of Cyclopedia Perception.* Chicago: University of Chicago Press, 1971.

Kagan, J. Body build and conceptual impulsivity in children. *Journal of Personality,* 1966, 34, 118-128.

Kahneman, D. Method, findings, and theory in studies of visual masking. *Psychological Bulletin,* 1968, 69.

Kasl, S.V. Are there any primary biochemical correlates of achievement behavior and motivation? The evidence for serum aric acid and serum cholesterol. *Review of Educational Research,* 1974, 44, 447-462.

Kass, C.E. Psycholinguistic disability of children with reading problems. *Exceptional Children,* 1966, 32, 533-539.

Kassmore, H. Effects of meaningful auditory stimulation on children's scholastic performance. *Journal of Educational Psychology,* 1972, 63, 526-530.

Katz, J. and Illmer, R. Auditory perception in children with learning disabilities. In Katz, J. *Handbook of Clinical Audiology.* Baltimore: Williams and Wilkins, 1972.

Kaufman, A.S. *Intelligence Testing with the WISC-R.* New York: John Wiley & Sons, 1979.

Kaufman, M. Figure-ground in visual perception. In Spache, G.D. *Reading Disability and Perception.* Newark, Del.: International Reading Assoc., 1969.
Kay, B.R. Intra-individual differences in sensory channel performance. *Journal of Applied Psychology,* 1958, 42, 166-167.
Keele, D.K., et. al. Role of special pediatric evaluation in the evaluation of a child with learning disabilities. *Journal of Learning Disabilities,* 1975, 8, 40-45.
Kennedy, H. A study of children's hearing as it relates to reading. *Journal of Experimental Education,* 1942, 10, 238-251.
Keogh, B.K. Hyperactivity and learning disorders: Review and speculation. *Exceptional Children,* 1971, 38, 101-108.
Keogh, B.K. and Margolis, J. Learn to labor and to wait: Attentional problems of children with learning disorders. *Journal of Learning Disabilities,* 1976, 9, 276-286.
Kephart, N.C. *The Slow Learner in the Classroom.* 2nd Ed. Columbus, Ohio: Charles E. Merrill, 1971.
Keppel, G. Verbal learning and memory. *Annual Review of Psychology,* 1968, 19, 169-202.
Kermonian, S.B. Teacher appraisal of first grade readiness. *Elementary English,* 1962, 39, 196-201.
Kerr, Howard Prize Essay. *British Royal Statistical Society,* 1896.
Killgallon, P.A. A study of relationships among certain pupil adjustments in language situations. Unpubl. Doctoral Dissert., Pennsylvania State U., 1942.
Kimura, D. Speech lateralization in young children as determined by an auditory test. *Journal of Comparative and Physiological Psychology,* 1963, 56, 899-902.
Kimura, D. Cerebral dominance and the perception of verbal stimuli. *Canadian Journal of Psychology,* 1961, 15, 166-171.
Kinsbourne, M. and Warrington, E.K. A study of finger agnosia. *Brain,* 1962, 85, 57-66.
Kirby, C.L. Using the Cloze procedure as a testing technique. In DeBoer, D.L. *Reading Diagnosis and Evaluation.* Newark, Del.: International Reading Assoc., 1970.
Kirk, S.A. Ethnic differences in psycholinguistic ability. *Exceptional Children,* 1972, 39, 112-118.
Kirk, S.A. Learning disabilities: The view from here. In Kirk, S.A. *Progress in Parent Information, Professional Growth, and Public Safety.* San Rafael, Cal.: Academic Therapy, 1969.
Kirk, S.A. and Elkins, J. Characteristics of children enrolled in the child resource demonstration centers. *Journal of Learning Disabilities,* 1975, 8, 630-637.
Kirk, S.A. and Kirk, W.D. *Psycholinguistic Learning Disabilities: Diagnosis and Remediation.* Urbana, Ill.: University of Illinois Press, 1971.
Kirk, W.D. A tentative screening procedure for selection of bright and slow children in kindergarten. *Exceptional Children,* 1966, 32, 235-241.
Klare, G.R. *The Measurement of Readability.* Iowa City: Iowa State University Press, 1963.
Klluver, R. Mental attributes and disorders of learning. In Myklebust, H.R. *Progress in Learning Disabilities.* New York: Grune and Stratton, 1971.
Klopfer, W.G. *The Psychological Report.* New York: Grune and Stratton, 1960.
Knapp, M.L. *Nonverbal Communication in Human Interaction,* 2nd Ed. New York: Holt, Rinehart, and Winston, 1978.
Knox, G.E. Classroom symptoms of visual difficulty: Clinical studies in reading, II. *Supplemental Educational Monographs,* 1953, #77, 9-101.
Koehler, W. *Gestalt Psychology.* New York: Horace Liveright, 1929.
Konfer, F.A. and Saslow, G. Behavioral analysis. *Archives of Psychiatry,* 1965, 12, 529-539.

Konigsmark, B.W. Genetic hearing loss with no associated abnormalities: A review. *Journal of Speech and Hearing Disorders,* 1972, 37, 89-99.

Koppotz, E.M. *Children with Learning Disabilities: A Five Year Follow-up Study.* New York: Grune and Stratton, 1971.

Koppitz, E.M. The Bender-Gestalt test for children: A normative study. *Journal of Clinical Psychology,* 1960, 16, 432-435.

Kraus, H. and Hirschland, R.P. Minimum muscular fitness tests in school children. *Research Quarterly,* 1954, 25, 178-188.

Kraus, H. and Hirschland, R.P. Minimum muscular fitness tests in school children. *Research Quarterly,* 1954, 25, 178-188.

Kroth, J. *A Programmed Primer in Learning Disabilities.* Springfield, Ill.: C.C. Thomas, 1971.

Kupietz, S., Bailer, I., Winsberg, B.G. A behavior rating scale for assessing improvement in behaviorally deviant children: A preliminary investigation. *American Journal of Psychiatry,* 1972, 128, 1432-1436.

Kusmaul, A. Disturbances of speech. In Buck, A.H. *Zeimisen's Cyclopedia of the Practice of Medicine,* Vol. XIV. New York: William Wood, 1877.

Kwai, A.A. and Pasananik, B. Association of factors of pregnancy with the development of reading disorders in childhood. *Journal of the AMA,* 1958, 166, 1420.

Labov, W. Psychological inflection in Negro language behavior. *American Journal of Orthography,* 1971, 41, 636-637.

Labov, W. The logic of nonstandard English. *Report of the 20th Annual Round Table Meeting in Languages and Linguistics.* Washington, D.C.: Georgetown University Press, 1969.

Lachor, D., Butkas, M., and Hryorczuk, L. Objective personality assessment of children: An exploratory study of the personality inventories for children (PIC) in a psychiatric setting. *Journal of Personality Assessment,* 1978, 42, 529-537.

Lansdell, J.P. The caratid amytal test. *Journal of Speech and Hearing,* 1964, 3, #1.

Langman, M.P. and Rabinvitch, R.D. The Hawthorn Center longitudinal reading study. In Figural, J.A. *Forging Ahead in Reading:* Newark, Del.: International Reading Association, 1967.

Lerner, J.W. *Children with Learning Disabilities.* Boston: Houghton Mifflin, 1971.

Lee, L.L. and Canter, S.M. Developmental sentence scoring: A clinical procedure for estimating sytactical development in children's spontaneous speech. *Journal of Speech and Hearing Disorders,* 1971, 36, 315-340.

Leisman, G. The role of visual processes in attention and its disorders. In Leisman, G. *Basic Visual Processes and Learning Disbility.* Springfield, Ill.: C.C. Thomas, 1976.

Lerman, J.W. Voice disorders. In Weston, A.J. *Communicative Disorders: An Appraisal.* Springfield, Ill.: C.C. Thomas, 1972.

Leton, D.A. A factor analysis of ITPA and WISC scores of learning disabled pupils. *Psychology in the Schools,* 1972, 9, 31-36.

Leton, D.A. Computer program to convert word orthography to phoneme equivalents. Hawaii University Research and Development Center, 1969, ERIC ED 038-266.

Levy, J. and Reid, M. Variations in writing, posture and cerebral organization. *Science,* 1976, 194, 337-339.

Lewis, F.D., Bell, D.B. and Anderson, R.P. Relationship of motor proficiency and reading retardation. *Perceptual and Motor Skills,* 1970, 31, 395-401.

Lewis, R.S., Strauss, A.A., and Lehtinen, L. *The Other Child: The Brain-Injured Child.* New York: Grune and Stratton, 1960.

Liebert, R.E. and Sherk, J. Three Frostig visual perception subtests and specific reading tasks for kindergarten, first, and second grade children. *Reading Teacher,* 1970, 24, 130-137.

Liebert, R.E. Some differences between silent and oral reading responses on a standardized reading test. In Figural, J.A. *Forging Ahead in Reading.* Newark, Del.: International Reading Assoc., 1967.

Littie, K.B. and Shneidman, E.S. Congruences among interpretation of psychological test and anamnestic data. *Psychological Monographs,* 1959, 73, 6, 1-42.

Lohnes, P.R. and Gray, M.M. Intelligence and the cooperative reading studies. *Reading Research Quarterly,* 1971, 7, 466-476.

Lott, I.T., Wheelden, J.A., and Levy, H.L. Speech and histidenemia: Methodology and evaluation of psychology cases. *Developmental Medicine and Child Neurology,* 1970, 12, 596.

Lovell, K. and Woolsey, M.E. Reading disability, nonverbal reasoning, and social class. *Educational Research,* 1964, 6, 266-229.

Lovell, K., Shapton, D. and Warren, N.S. A study of some cognitive and other disabilities in backwards readers of average intelligence as assessed by a non-verbal test. *British Journal of Education,* 1964, 34, 58-64.

Lowen, A. *The Language of the Body.* New York: Macmillan, 1971.

Luchsinger, R. and Arnold, G.F. *Voice-Speech-Language.* Belmont, Cal.: Wadsworth Publ., 1967.

Luria, A.R. *The Mind of a Mnemonist.* New York: Basic Books, 1968.

Lutey, C.L. *Individual Intelligence Testing.* Greeley, Colo.: Carol L. Lutey, 1977.

Lyle, L.G. Certain antenatal, perinatal, and developmental variables and reading retardation. *Child Development,* 1970, 41, 481-491.

Maccoby, E.E. and Bee, H.L. Some speculation concerning the lag between perceiving and performing. *Child Development,* 1965, 36, 367-378.

Maccoby, E.E. and Jacklin, C.N. *The Psychology of Sex Differences.* Stanford, Cal.: Stanford University Pres, 1974.

Machover, K. *Personality Projection in the Drawing of the Human Figure.* Springfield, Ill.: C.C. Thomas, 1949.

MacKinnon, A.R. *How Do Children Learn to Read?* Vancouver, Canada: Copp Clark, 1959.

Mae, I.L. Measuring listening skills to predict reading potential. In Dukker, S. *Listening: Readings.* New York: Scarecrow Press, 1966.

Malmquist, E. *Factors Related to Reading Disabilities in the First Grade of Elementary School.* Stockholm Sweden: Almquist and Weksell, 1958.

Mann, P.H. and Suiter, P.A. *Teacher's Handbook of Diagnostic Screening.* Rockleigh, N.J.: Allyn and Bacon, 1974.

Moray, N. *Listening and Attention.* New York: Penguin Books, 1969.

Mardock, J.B., Terrill, P.A., and Novik, E. The Bender-Gestalt Test in differential diagnosis of adolescents with learning difficulties. *Journal of School Psychology,* 1968-69, 7, 11-14.

Marks, L.E. Diary on a Synesthete. *Psychology Today,* 1975, 9, 50-52.

Marwitt, S.J. and Stenner, A.J. Hyperkinesis: Deliniation of two patterns. *Exceptional Children,* 1972, 39, 401-406.

Marzano, R.J. and DiStefano, P.D. *DiComp.* Indian Rocks Beach, Fla.: Relevant Prod., 1977.

Matheny, A.P. Comparability of WISC and PPVT scores among young children. *Exceptional Children,* 38, 147-150.

Mattingly, I.G. Speech cues and sign stimuli. *Amerian Scientist,* 1972, 60, 327-337.

Maurer, D.M. and Maurer, C.E. Newborn babies see better than you think. *Psychology Today,* 1976, 10, 85-88.

McCarthy, J.M. and Paraskevopoulos, J. Behavior patterns of learning disabled, emotionally disturbed, and average children. *Exceptional Children,* 1969, 36, 69-74.

McCready, A.B., Wordblindness as a cause of backwardness in school children: A report of a case associated with stuttering. *The Pennsylvania Medical Journal,* 1910, 13, 278-284.

McGlannman, F.K. Familial characteristics of genetic dyslexia: Preliminary report of a pilot study. *Journal of Learning Disabilities,* 1968, 1, 185.

McGrady, H.J. and Olson, D.A. Visual and auditory learning processes in normal children and children with specific learning disabilities. *Exceptional Children,* 1970, 36, 581-589.

McLaulin, J.C. and Schiffman, G.B. A study of the relationship between the CTMM and the WISC test for retarded readers. (mimeo) Board of Education, Bulfine County, Cal.

McLeod, J. Prediction of childhood dyslexia. *Bulletin of the Orton Society,* 1966, 16, 14-23.

Meehl, P.W. Seer over sign: the first good example. *Journal of Experimental Research in Personality,* 1965, 1, 27-32.

Meehl, P.E. *Clinical versus Statistical Prediction.* Minneapolis: University of Minnesota Press, 1954.

Meek, L.H. *A Study of Learning and Retention in Young Children.* New York: Columbia University Press, 1925.

Meir, J.H. Prevalence and characteristics of learning disabilities found in second grade children. *Journal of Learning Disabilities,* 1971, 4, 1-16.

Meltzer, N.S. and Herse, R. The boundaries of written words as seen by first graders. *Journal of Reading Behavior,* 1969, 1, 3-14.

Menyuk, P. *Sentences Children Use.* Cambridge, Mass.: MIT Press, 1969.

Mercer, J. System of Multicultural Pluralistic Assessment Conceptual and Technical Manual. Riverside, Cal.: U. of Cal., 1977.

Mermelstein, E. and Meyer, E. Conservation training techniques and their effects on different populations. *Child Development,* 1969, 40, 471-490.

Merwin, J.C. The Wide Range Achievement Test. In Buros, O.K. *Seventh Mental Measurements Yearbook.* Highland Park, N.J.: Gryphon Press, 1972.

Meyers, P.I. and Hammill, D.D. *Methods for Learning Disorders.* New York: John Wiley and Sons, 1969.

Miller, G.A. The magical number seven, plus or minus two: Some limits of our capacity for processing information. *Psychological Review,* 1956, 63, 81-97.

Millichap, I.G. Drugs in management of hyperkinesis and perceptually handicapped children. *Journal of the AMA,* 1968, 206, 1527-1530.

Millman, J. Criterion-referenced tests. In Dopham, J. *Evaluation in Education: Current Practices.* Berkeley, Cal.: McCutchin, 1974.

Milner, B. Memory and the medial temporal regions of the brain. In Pribram, K.H. and Broadbent, D.E. *Biology and Memory.* New York: Academic Press, 1970.

Minskoff, E.H. Research on psycholinguistic training: Critique and guidelines. *Exceptional Children,* 1975, 42, 136-147.

Money, J. (Ed.) *Reading Disability: Progress and Research Need in Dyslexia.* Baltimore: Johns Hopkins Press, 1962.

Monroe, M. *Children Who Cannot Read.* Chicago: University of Chicago Press, 1932.

Morehead, D.M. and Ingram, D. The development of base syntax in normal and linguistically deviant children. *Journal of Speech and Hearing Research,* 1973, 16, 330-352.

Morency, A. Auditory modality and reading. In Smith, H.K. *Perception and Reading.* Newark, Del.: International Reading Association, 1968.

Morgan, E.F. Efficiency of two tests in differentiating potentially low from average and high first grade achievers. *Journal of Educational Research,* 1960, 53, 300-304.

Morgan, W.P. A case of congenital word-blindness. *British Medical Journal,* 2, 1612-1614.

Morley, M.E. *The Development and Disorders of Speech in Childhood.* London: Churchill Livingston, 1972.

Mosenthal, P. Psycholinguistic properties of aural and visual comprehension as determined by children's ability to comprehend syllogisms. *Reading Research Quarterly,* 1976-77, 12, 55-92.

Mulder, R.L. and Curtan, J. Vocal phonic ability and silent reading achievement: A first report. *Elementary School Journal,* 1953, 56, 121-123.

Mumpower, D.L. Sex ratios found in various types of referred exceptional children. *Exceptional Children,* 1970, 36, 621-623.

Munn, N.L. and Steining, B.R. The relative efficiency of form and background in a child's discrimination of visual patterns. *Journal of Genetic Psychology,* 1931, 39, 73-90.

Murphy, A.T. *Functional Voice Disorders.* Englewood Cliffs, N.J.: Prentice-Hall, 1964.

Murphy, H.A. The spontaneous speaking vocabulary of children in primary grades. *Journal of Education,* 1957, 140, 1-14.

Murstein, B.I. *Handbook of Projective Techniques.* New York: Basic Books, 1965.

Myklebust, H.A. (Ed.) *Progress in Learning Disabilities.* New York: Grune and Stratton, 1968.

Myklebust, H.R. *Development and Disorders of Written Language,* Vol. I (1965); Vol. II (1973). New York: Grune and Stratton.

Naidoo, S. *Specific Dyslexia.* New York: John Wiley & Sons, 1972.

Neligan, G. and Prudham, D. Norms for four standard developmental milestones by sex, social class and place in family. *Developmental Medicine and Child Neurology,* 1969, 11, 413-422.

Nelisen, R. and Johnson, W. A comparative study of stutters. *Archives of Speech,* 1936, 1, 61.

Nelson, C.M. Techniques for screening conduct disturbed children. *Exceptional Children,* 1971, 37, 501-507.

Nelson, W. *Textbook of Pediatrics.* Philadelphia: W.B. Saunders, 1964.

Nettleship, E. Cases of congenital word-blindness (inability to learn to read) *Ophthalmic Review,* 1901, 2, 61-67.

Neville, D. and Bucke, B. The effect of meaning on the measurement of the ability to auditorially discriminate sounds contained in words. In Figural, J.A. *Reading and Readiness,* Newark, Del.: International Reading Assoc., 1969.

Newcomer, P.L. and Hammill, D.D. *Psycholinguistics in the Schools.* Columbus, Ohio: Charles E. Merrill, 1976.

Newcomer, P. and Hammill, D. The ITPA and academic achievement: A survey. *The Reading Teacher,* 1975, 28, 731-741.

Norman, D.A. Memory while shadowing. *Quarterly Journal of Experimental Psychology,* 1969, 21, 85-93.

Obersteiner, H. On allochiria: a peculiar sensory disorder. *Brain,* 1881, 4, 153-163.

Oakland, T. An evaluation of the ABIC, pluralistic norms, and estimated learning potential. *Journal of School Psychology,* 1980, 18, 3-11.

O'Connor, W.J. The relationship between the Bender-Gestalt test and the Frostig Test of Visual Perception. In Spache, G.D. *Reading Disability and Perception.* Newark, Del.: International Reading Assoc., 1969.

O'Donnell, P.A. and Eisenson, J. Delacato training for reading achievement and visual motor integration. *Journal of Learning Disabilities,* 1969, 2, 441-446.

Orton, S.T. *Reading, Writing, and Speech Problems in Children.* New York: W.W. Norton, 1937.

Orton, S.T. Specific reading disability—strephosymbolia. *The Journal of the AMA,* April, 1928.

Ott, J.N. Influence of florescent lights on hyperactivty and learning disabilities. *Journal of Learning Disabilities,* 1976, 6, 417-422.

Otto, W. and Chester, R. Sight words for beginning readers. *The Journal of Educational Research,* 1972, 65, 435-443.

Otto, W., McNenemy, R.A., and Smith, R.J. *Corrective and Remedial Teaching,* 2nd Ed. Boston: Houghton Mifflin, 1973.

Ouadfasel, F.A. and Goodglass, H. Specific reading disability and other specific disabilities. *Journal of Learning Disabilities,* 1968, 1, 590-600.

Owen, F.W. Learning disability—a family study. *Journal of Learning Disabilities,* 1968, 18, 33-39.

Paine, R.S. and Oppe, T. *Neurological Evaluation of Children.* London: Heineman, 1966.
Paine, R.S., Werry, J.S., and Quay, H.C. A study of "Minimal Cerebral Disfunction." *Developmental Medicine and Child Neurology,* 1968, 10, 505-520.
Park, G.E. Reading difficulty (dyslexia) from the ophthalmic point of view. *American Journal of Ophthalmology,* 1948, 31, 28-34.
Park, G.E. and Burri, C. The relationship of various eye conditions and reading achievement. *Journal of Educational Psychology,* 1943, 34, 290-299. (a.)
Park, G.E. and Burri, C. The effect of eye abnormalities on reading difficulty. *Journal of Educational Psychology,* 1943, 34, 420-430. (b)
Peacher, W.G. The etiology and differential diagnosis of dyarthria. *Journal of Speech and Hearing Disorders,* 1950, 15, 252-265.
Penfield, W. and Roberts, L. *Speech and Brain Mechanisms.* Princeton: Princeton University Press, 1959.
Peterson, R.D. *The Clinical Study of Social Behavior.* New York: Appleton-Century-Crofts, 1968.
Phillips, M. et. al. Analysis of results from Kraus-Weber test of minimal muscular fitness in children. *Research Quarterly,* 1955, 26, 314-323.
Piaget, J. *Mechanisms of Perception.* New York: Basic Books, 1969.
Piaget, J. *Child's Construction of Reality.* New York: Basic Books, 1954.
Piaget, J. *The Psychology of Intelligence.* London: Routledge and Kegan, 1950.
Piaget, J. *Judgement and Reasoning in the Child.* New York: Harcourt and Brace, 1926.
Piaget, J. *Language and Thought of the Child.* London: Harcourt and Brace, 1926.
Pond, D. Psychiatric aspects of epeleptic and brain damaged children. *British Medical Journal,* 1961, 2, 1377-1382.
Pihl, R.O. and Parkes, M. Hair element content in learning disabled children. *Science,* 1977, 198, 204-206.
Poole, I. Genetic development in articulation of consonant sounds in speech. *Elementary English,* 1934, 11, 159-161.
Popp, H.M. Visual discrimination of alphabet letters. *The Reading Teacher,* 1964, 17, 221-226.
Poppen, R.J., et. al. Visual sequencing performance of aphasic children. *Journal of Speech and Hearing Research,* 1969, 12, 288-300.
Porteus, S.D. *The Maze Test and Clinical Psychology.* Palo Alto, Cal.: Pacific Books, 1959.
Posner, M.I. and Boises, S.J. Components of attention. *Psychological Review,* 1971, 78, 391-408.
Poston, F. and Patrick, J.R. Evaluation of word and picture tests for first and second grades. *Journal of Applied Psychology,* 1944, 28, 142-152.
Pyfer, J.L. and Carlson, B.R. Characteristic motor development of children with learning disabilities. *Perceptual and Motor Skills,* 1972, 35, 291-296.
Prechtl, H.F.R. and Stemmer, C.J. The choreiform syndrome in children. *Developmental Medicine and Child Neurology,* 1962, 4, 119-127.
Quay, H.C., Morse, W.C. and Culter, R.L. Personality patterns of pupils in special classes for the emotionally disturbed. *Exceptional Children,* 1966, 32, 297-301.
Quay, H.C. and Peterson, D.R. Manual for the Behavior Problem Checklist. Champaign: University or Illinois Children Research Center, 1967.
Rabe, E.F. Neurological evaluation. In Paine, R.S. et. al. *Minimal Brain Dysfunction in Children.* Washington, D.C.: Dept. of HEW, 1969.
Rawson, M.B. Prognosis in dyslexia. *Academic Therapy Quarterly,* 1966, 1, 164-173.
Read, M.S. Anemia and behavior. *Modern Profiles in Pediatrics,* 1975, 14, 189.
Rechner, J. and Wilson, B.A. Relation of speech sound discrimination and selected language skills. *Journal of Communication Disturbances,* 1967, 1, 26-30.
Reed, J.C. Lateralization, finger agnosia and reading achievement at ages six to ten. *Child Development,* 1967, 38, 213-220.

Reed, S.K. *Psychological Processes in Pattern Recognition.* New York: Academic Press, 1973.

Reese, H.W. and Lipsitt, L.P. *Experimental Child Psychology.* New York: Academic Press, 1970.

Reitan, R.M. Methodological problems in clinical neuropsychology. In Reitan, R.M. and Davidson, L.A. *Clinical Neuropsychology: Current Status and Applications.* New York: John Wiley and Sons, 1974.

Reitan, R.M. Cerebral lesions in young children. In Reitan, R.M. and Davidson, L.A. Clinical Neuropsychology: *Current Status and Applications.* New York: John Wiley and Sons, 1974(b).

Reitan, R.M. and Ball, T.J. Neuropsychological correlates of minimal brain damage. *Annals of the N.Y. Academy of Science,* 1973, 205, 65-88.

Reynolds, M.C. A study of the relationship between auditory characteristics and silent reading abilities. *Journal of Educational Research,* 1953, 46, 439-449.

Rich, J. *Interviewing Children and Adolescents.* New York: St. Martin's Press, 1968.

Richardson, S.A., Dahrenwend, B.S., and Klein, D. *Interviewing: Its Forms and Functions.* New York: Basic Books, 1965.

Richmond, B.O. and Horn, W.R. Children's Adaptive Behavior Scale: A new measure of adaptive functioning. *Psychology in the Schools,* 1980, 17, 159-162.

Roach, R.E. and Rosecrans, C.J. Verbal deficit in children with hearing loss. *Exceptional Children,* 1972, 39, 395-399.

Roback, H.B. Human figure drawings: Their utility in the clinical psychologist armamentarium for personality assessment. *Psychological Bulletin,* 1968, 70, 1-19.

Robbins, M. and Glass, G.V. The Domain-Delacato rationale: A critical analysis. In Hellmuth, J. *Educational Therapy,* Vol. II. Seattle, Special Child Pub., 1969.

Robinson, H.A. The metropolitan reading test. In Buros, O.K. *The Sixth Mental Measurements Yearbook.* Highland Park, N.J.: Gryphon Press, 1965.

Robinson, H.M. *Why Pupils Fail in Reading.* Chicago: University of Chicago Press, 1946.

Robinson, M.E. and Schwartz, L.B. Visuo-motor skills and reading ability: A longitudinal study. *Developmental Medicine and Child Neurology,* 1973, 15, 281-286.

Rose, F.C. The occurance of short-term memory span among school children referred for diagnosis of reading difficulty. *Journal of Educational Research,* 1958, 51, 459-464.

Rosvold, H.E., et. al. A continuous performance test of brain damage. *Journal of Consulting Psychology,* 1956, 20, 343-350.

Routh, D.K. and Roberts, R.D. Minimal brain dysfunction in children: Failure to find evidence for a behavioral syndrome. *Psychological Reports.* 1972, 31, 307-314.

Rogers, F.R. *Physical capacity tests in the administration of physical education.* New York: Columbia Teacher's College, 1925.

Rubin, S.S. *A reevaluation of figure-ground pathology in brain damaged children.* American Journal of Mental Deficiency, 1969-70, 74, 111-115.

Russell, D.H. A second study of characteristics of good and poor spellers. *Journal of Educational Psychology,* 1955, 46, 129-141.

Russell, D.H. A diagnostic study of spelling readiness. *Journal of Educational Psychology,* 1943, 37, 276-283.

Russell, D.H. *Characteristics of Good and Poor Spellers.* New York: Columbia University Teacher's College, 1937.

Rutter, M. (Ed.) *Infantile Autism: Concepts, Characteristics and Treatment.* London: Churchhill, 1971.

Rutter, M. and Graham, P. The reliability and validity of the psychiatric assessment of the child. *Acta Psychiatrica Scandanavica,* 1972, 48, 2-21.

Rutter, M., Graham, P., and Birch, H.G. Interrelations between the choreiform syndrome, reading disability and psychiatric disorder in children of 8-11 years. *Developmental Medicine and Child Neurology,* 1966, 8, 149-159.

Rutter, M., Graham, P., and Yule, W. *A Neuropsychiatric Study in Childhood.* London: Spastics International Medical Pub., 1970.

Ryckman, D.B. and Weigerink, R. The factors of the ITPA: A comparison of 18 factor analysis. *Exceptional Children,* 1969, 36, 107-113.

Rystrom, R. Dialect training and reading: A further look. *Reading Research Quarterly,* 1970, 5, 581-599.

Rystrom, R. Evaluating letter discrimination problems in primary grades. *Journal of Reading Behavior,* 1969, 1, 38-48.

Sabatino, D.A. The construction and assessment of an experimental test of auditory perception. *Journal of Learning Disabilities,* 1974, 6, 115-121.

Sabatino, D.A., Abbott, J.C. and Becker, J.T. What does the Frostig DTVP Measure? *Exceptional Children,* 1974, 35, 453-454.

Sabiruna, A. The relationship between handedness and language function. *International Journal of Neurology,* 1964, 4, 215-234.

Sadanand, S. *Distinctive Features: Theory and Validation.* Baltimore: University Park Press, 1972.

Safer, D.J. and Allen, R.P. *Hyperactive Children: Diagnosis and Management.* Baltimore: University Park Press, 1976.

Sammuels, S.J. Word recognition and beginning reading. *The Reading Teacher,* 1969, 23, 159-161.

Samuels, S.J. and Anderson, R.H. Visual recognition memory, paired-associate learning, and reading achievement. *Journal of Educational Psychology,* 1973, 65, 160-167.

Salva, J. and Clark, J. The use of deficient scores to identify learning disabled children. *Exceptional Children,* 1973, 39, 305-308.

Sander, E.K. When are speech sounds learned? *Journal of Speech and Hearing Disorders,* 1972, 37, 55-63.

Sandoval, J. The measurement of hyperactive syndrome in children. *Review of Educational Research,* 1977, 47, 293-318.

Sattler, J.M. *Assessment of Children's Intelligence.* Philadelphia: W.B. Saunders, 1974.

Schain, R.J. *Neurology of Childhood Learning Disorders.* Baltimore: Williams and Wilkins, 1972.

Schields, J. *Monozygous Twins.* London: Oxford University Press, 1962.

Schilder, P. *The Image and Appearance of the Human Body.* New York: International Universities Pres, 1950.

Schilder, P. Congenital alexia and its relation to optic perception. *Journal of Genetic Psychology,* 1944, 65, 67-88.

Schmitt, C. Developmental alexia: congenital word-blindness, or inability to learn to read. *Elementary School Journal,* 1918, 18, 680-700.

Schulman, J.L., Kasper, J.C., and Throne, F.M. *Brain Damage and Behavior: A Clinical Experiment.* Springfield, Ill.: C.C. Thomas, 1965.

Seashore, H.G. The development of a beam-walking test and its use in measuring development of balance in children. *Research Quarterly,* 1947, 18, 246-259.

Seguin, E. *Idiocy: and Its Treatment by the Physiological method.* (1868). Albany, N.Y.: Brandow Printing, 1907.

Semel, E.M. and Wiig, E.H. Comprehension of syntactic structures and critical verbal elements by children with learning disabilities. *Journal of Learning Disabilities, 1975, 8, 46-53.*

Shallice, T. and Warrington, E.K. Independent functioning of verbal memory stores: A neuropsychological study. *Quarterly Journal of Experimental Psychology,* 1970, 22, 261-273.

Shearer, W.M. Diagnosis and treatment of voice disorders in school children. *Journal of Speech and Hearing Disorders,* 1972, 37, 215-221.
Sheehan, J.G. *Stuttering: Research and Theory.* New York: Harper and Row, 1970.
Shephard, R.N. Recognition memory for words, sentences and pictures. *Journal of Verbal Learning and Verbal Behavior,* 1967, 6, 156-163.
Schneidman, E.S., Joel, W., and Little, K.B. *Thematic Test Analysis.* New York: Grune and Stratton, 1951.
Shneour, E.A. *The Malnourished Mind.* Garden City, N.Y.: Doubleday, 1974.
Shores, J.H. and Yee, A.H. Spelling achievement tests: What is available and and needed. *Journal of Special Education,* 1973, 7, 301-309.
Shuy, R.W. Some language and cultural differences in a theory of reading. In Goodman, K.S. and Fleming, J.T. *Psycholinguistics and the Teaching of Reading.* Newark, Del.: IRA, 1969.
Silberberg, N.E. Silberberg, M.C. A note on reading tests and their role in defining reading difficulties. *Journal of Learning Disabilities,* 1977, 10, 100-103.
Silberbeg, N.E. and Silberberg, M.C. Case instances in hyperlexia. *Journal of School Psychology,* 1968-69, 7, 3-7.
Silver, A. Psychological aspects of pediatrics: Diagnostic value of three drawing tests for children. *Journal of Pediatrics,* 1950, 37.
Silver, A. and Hagin, R.A. Specific reading disability: Follow-up studies. *American Journal of Orthopsychiatry,* 1964, 34, 95-102.
Simon, D.P. and Simon, H.A. Alternative used of phonemic information in spelling. *Review of Educational Research,* 1973, 43, 115-137.
Simon, M. Body configuration and school readiness. *Child Development,* 1959, 30, 493-512.
Simmons, J.E. *Psychiatric Examination of Children.* Philadelphia: Lea and Febiger, 1969.
Sims, V.M. The California Personality Test. In Buros, O.K. *The Fifth Mental Measurements Yearbook.* Highland Park, N.J.: Grython Press, 1959.
Singer, H. *Theoretical Models and Processes of Reading.* Newark, Del.: International Reading Association, 1970.
Singer, R.N. and Brink, J.W. Relation of perceptuo-motor ability and intellectual ability in elementary school children. *Perceptual and Motor Skills,* 1967, 24, 967-970.
Sivaroli, N.J. *Classroom Reading Inventory,* 2nd Ed. Dubuque, Iowa: Wm. C. Brown, 1965.
Skinner, B.F. Critique of psychoanalytic concepts and theories. *Scientific Monthly,* 1954, 79, 300-305.
Sladen, B.K. Inheritance of dyslexia. *Bulletin of the Orton Society,* 1971, 20, 30-40.
Sloan, W. The Lincoln-Oseretsky Motor Development Scale. *Genetic Psychological Monographs,* 1955, 51, 183.
Slupinski, L. Drawing the obtuse angle. *Research Review of Durham University,* 1955, #6, 54-56.
Smith, A. Objective indices of severity of chronic aphasia in stroke patients. *Journal of Speech and Hearing Disorders,* 1971, 36, 167-207.
Smith, C.E. and Koegh, B.K. The group Bender-Gestalt as a reading readiness screening instrument. *Perceptual and Motor Skills,* 1962, 15, 639-645.
Smith, C.P. (Ed.) *Achievement-related motives in Children.* New York: Russel Sage Foundation, 1969.
Smith, H.P. and Dechant, E.V. *Psychology in Teaching Reading.* Englewood Cliffs, N.J.: Prentice-Hall, 1961.
Smith, R.F. Diagnosis of pupil performance on place-value tasks. *The Arithmetic Teacher,* 1973, 403-408.
Sowell, V., Larsen, S., and Parker, R. The efficiency of psycholinguistic training through the MWM program. Unpub. Dept. of Special Education, Un. of Texas, 1975.

Spache, G.D. *Reading in the Elementary School.* Boston: Allyn and Bacon, 1964.

Space, G.D. A new readability formula for primary grade reading materials. *The Elementary School Journal,* 1953, 53, 410-413.

Space, G.D. A comparison of certain oral reading tests. *Journal of Educational Research,* 1950, 43, 411-452.

Spache, G.D. Spelling disability correlates: I. Factors probably causal in spelling disability. *Journal of Educational Research,* 1941, 34, 561-586.

Spache, G. The role of visual defects in spelling and reading disabilities. *American Journal of Orthopsychiatry,* 1940, 10, 229-238.

Spache, G. Testing vision. *Education,* 1939, 59, 623.

Spearman, C.E. *The Abilities of Man.* New York: Macmillan, 1927.

Squire, L.R. Short-term memory as a biological entity. In Deutsch, D. and Deutsch, J.A. (Eds.) *Short-term Memory.* New York: Academic Press, 1975.

Spring, C. and Sandoval, J. Food additives and hyperkinesis: a critical evaluation of the evidence: *Journal of Learning Disabilities,* 1976, 6, 560-569.

Stark, J. Reading Failure: A language-based problem: American Speech and Hearing Association, Dec., 1975.

Steuler, E. and von Neumann, A. Methylpenidate in the treatment of hyperkinetic children. *Clinical Pediatrics,* 1974, 13, 19-24.

Steer, M.C. and Drexler, H.G. Predicting later articulation ability from kindergarten tests. *Journal of Speech and Hearing Disorders,* 1960, 25, 391-397.

Steiner, R.R., Weiner, M. and Cramer, W. Comprehension training and identification for poor and good readers. *Journal of Educational Psychology,* 1971, 62, 506-513.

Stephenson, S. Six cases of congenital word-blindness affecting three generations of one family. *Ophthalmoscope,* 1907.

Sterritt, G.M. and Rudnick, M. Auditory and visual rhythm perception in relation to reading ability in fourth grade boys. *Perceptual and Motor Skills,* 1966, 22, 859-864.

Stevens, G.D. and Birch, J.W. A proposal for clarification of the terminology used to describe brain-injured children. *Exceptional Children,* 1957, 23, 346-349.

Stoer, L., Corotto, L.V., and Curnutt, R.H. The role of visual perception in the reproduction of Bender-Gestalt designs. *Journal of Projective Technique and Personality Assessment,* 1965, 29, 473-478.

Storey, A.G. *The Measurement of Classroom Learning.* Chicago: Science Research Associates, 1970.

Stouffer, R.G. Certain psychological characteristics of retarded readers. Doct. Diss. Philadelphia: Temple University, 1947.

Strang, R. *Reading.* San Rafael, Cal.: Directions Publ., 1968.

Strauss, A.A. and Kephart, N.C. *Psychopathology and Education of the Brain-injured Child,* Vol. II. New York: C.C. Thomas, 1955.

Strauss, A.A. and Lehtinen, L.A. *Psychopathology and Education of the Brain-injured Child,* Vol. I. New York: Grune and Stratton, 1947.

Strauss, A. and Werner, H. Deficiency in the finger schema in relation to arithmetic. *American Journal of Orthopsychiatry,* 1938, 8, 719-728.

Street, R.F. *A Gestalt Completion Test.* New York: Columbia University Teachers' College, 1931.

Stroud, J.B. Rate of visual perception as a factor in rate of learning. *Journal of Educational Psychology,* 1945, 34, 495-496.

Stuart, I. Perceptual style and reading ability. *Perceptual and Motor Skills,* 1967, 24, 135-138.

Stuart, M. *Neurophysiological Insights Into Teaching.* Palo Alto, Cal.: Pacific Books, 1963.

Sundby, H. and Kreyberg, P. *Progress in Child Psychiatry.* Baltimore: Wiliam and Wilkins, 1969.

Swanson, R. and Benton, A.L. Some aspects of the genetic development of right-left discrimination. *Child Development,* 1955, 26, 123-133.

Swensen, C.H. Empirical evaluation of human figure drawings. *Psychological Bulletin,* 1957, 54, 431-466.

Swift, M.S. and Spivack, G. Clarifying the relationship between academic success and overt classroom behavior. *Exceptional Children,* 1969, 36, 99-104.

Talent, N. *Psychological Report Writing.* Englewood Cliffs, N.J.: Prentice-Hall, 1976.

Templin, M. *Certain Language Skills in Children.* Minneapolis: University of Minnesota Press, 1957.

Terman, L.M. *The Measurement of Intelligence.* Boston: Houghton Mifflin, 1916.

Thomas, C.J. Congenital word-blindness and its treatment. *Ophthalmoscope,* Aug. 1905.

Thorndike, E.L. Reading as reasoning: A study of mistakes in paragraph reading. *Elementary School Journal,* 1917, 18, 98-114.

Thursone, T.G. Primary mental abilities in children. *Educational Psychological Measurement,* 1941, 1, 105-116.

Tiffin, J. and McKinnis, M. Phonic ability: its measurement and relation to reading ability. *School and Society,* 1940, 51, 190-192.

Timmons, B.A. and Boudreau, J.P. Auditory feedback as a major factor in stuttering. *Journal of Speech and Hearing Research,* 1972, 37, 476-484.

Tinker, M.A. *Basis for Effective Reading.* Minneapolis: University of Minnesota Press, 1965.

Tinker, M.A. Recent studies of eye movements in reading. *Psychological Bulletin,* 1958, 54, 215-231.

Tinker, M.A. Reliability and validity of eye-movement measures of reading. *Journal of Educational Psychology,* 1939, 19, 732-746.

Tinker, M.A. Eye movements in reading. *Journal of Educational Research,* 1936, 30, 241-277.

Tinker, M.A. and McCullogh, C.M. *Teaching Elementary Reading.* 2nd Ed. New York: Appleton-Century-Crofts, 1962.

Tonwen, B.C.L. and Prechtl, H.F.R. *The Neurological Examination of the Child with Minor Nervous Dysfunction.* New York: Lippincott, 1970.

Town, H.C. Congenital aphasia. *The Psychological Clinic,* 1911, 5, 167-179.

Townsend, E.A. A study of copying ability in children. *Genetic Psychological Monographs,* 1951, 43, 3-51.

Traxler, A.E. Value of Controlled Reading: Summary of opinions and research. *Journal of Experimental Education,* 1943, 11, 280-292.

Tulkin, S.R. and Kagan, J. Mother-child interaction: Social class differences in the first year of life. Cited in Cazden, C.B. *Child Language and Education.* New York: Holt, Rinehart and Winston, 1972.

Tulving, E. and Donaldson, W. (Eds.) *Organization of Memory.* New York: Academic Press, 1972.

Varble, D.L. Current status of the Thematic Apperception Test. In McReynolds, P. *Advances in Assessment.* Palo Alto, Cal.: Science and Behavior Books, 1970.

Vellutino, F.R., et. al. Has the perceptual deficit hypothesis led us astray? *Journal of Learning Disabilities,* 1977, 10, 375-385.

Vernon, M.D. *Reading and Its Difficulties.* London: Cambridge University Press, 1971.

Vogel, S.A. Syntactic abilities in normal and dyslexic children. *Journal of Learning Disabilities,* 1974, 7, 103-110.

Wadhaugh, R. Theories of language acquisition in relation to beginning reading instruction. *Reading Research Quarterly,* 1971, 7, 168-194.

Wagenberg, R. and Blau, H. Hyperlexia: The problem of the wordy child. *Academic Therapy,* 1971, 6, 411-413.

Wagonseller, B.R. Learning disability and emotional disturbance: Factors relating to differential diagnosis. *Exceptional Children,* 1973, 39, 205-206.

Waldrop, M.F., Bell, R.Q., and Jacob, D.G. Minor physical abnormalities and inhibited behavior in elementary school girls. *Journal of Child Psychology and Psychiatry,* 1976, 17, 113-122.

Waldrop, M.F. and Goering, J.D. Hyperactivity and minor physical anomolies in elementary school children. *American Journal of Orthopsychiatry,* 1971, 41, 602-607.

Waldrop, M. and Haverson, C. Minor physical anomolies and hyperactive behavior in young children. In Hellmuth, J. (Ed.) *The Exceptional Infant,* Vol. II. New York: Brunner-Mazel, 1971.

Walker, M. Perceptual, coding, viso-motor and spatial difficulties and their neurological correlates: A progress report. *Developmental Medicine and Child Neurology,* 1965, 7, 543-548.

Walker, L. and Cole, E.M. Familial patterns of expression of specific reading disability in a population sample. Part I: Prevalence distribution and persistance. *Bulletin of the Orton Society,* 1965, 15, 12-24.

Wallach, M.A. Perceptual recognition of approximations to English in relation to spelling achievement. *Journal of Educational Psychology,* 1963, 54, 57-62.

Walters, R.H., Loan, M.V., and Crofts, I. A study of reading disability. *Journal of Consulting Psychology,* 1961, 25, 277-283.

Warren, R.M. and Warren, R.P. Auditory illusions and confusions. *Scientific American,* 1970, 223, 30-36.

Washington, E.D. and Teska, J.A. Relations between the Wide Range Achievement Test, the California Achievement tests, the Stanford-Binet, and the ITPA. *Psychological Reports,* 1970, 26, 291-294.

Watkins, M.J. Locus of the modality effect in free recall. *Journal of Verbal Learning and Verbal Behavior,* 1972, 11, 644-648.

Waugh, N.C. Retrieval time in short-term memory. *British Journal of Psychology,* 1970, 61, 1-72.

Waugh, N.C. and Norman, D.A. Primary memory. *Psychology Review,* 1965, 72, 89-104.

Weber, R.M. The study of oral reading errors: A survey of literature. *Reading Research Quarterly,* 1968, 4, 96-119.

Wechsler, D. *Manual for the Wechsler Intelligence Scale for Children.* New York: Psychological Corp., 1974.

Weiner, P.S. Auditory discrimination and articulation. *Journal of Speech and Hearing Disorders,* 1967, 32, 19-28.

Weiner, M. and Feldman, S. Validation structures of a reading prognosis test for children of lower and middle socio-economic status. *Educational and Psychological Measurement,* 1963, 23, 807-814.

Weiner, E.E., Simonian, K., and Smith, R.S. Reading achievement, language functioning, and perceptual-motor development of ten-and eleven-year-olds. *Perceptual and Motor Skills,* 1967, 25, 409-420.

Weins, A.N. The assessment interview. In Weiner, I.B. *Clinical Methods in Psychology,* New York: Wiley, 1976.

Weiss, D.A. *Cluttering.* Englewood Cliffs, N.J. Prentice-Hall, 1964.

Wellman, B. et al. Speech sounds of young children. *University of Iowa Studies in Child Welfare,* 1931, 5, #2.

Wenar, C. The reliability of developmental histories: Summary and evaluation of evidence. *Psychosomatic Medicine,* 1963, 25, 505-509.

Wender, P.H. *Minimal Brain Dysfunction in Children.* New York: John Wiley and Sons, 1971.

Wepman, J.M. Auditory discrimination: Its role in language comprehension, formulation and use. *Pediatrics Clinics of North America,* 1968, 15, 721-727.

Wepman, J.M. and Haas, W. *A spoken word Count: Children Five, Six and Seven.* Chicago: Language Research Association, 1969.

Werdelin, I. *The Mathematical Ability: Experimental and Factorial Studies.* Copenhagen: Ejnar Munksgaard, 1958.

Werkman, S.L. The psychiatric diagnostic interview with children. *American Journal of Orthopsychiatry,* 1965, 35, 764.

Werner, H. and Strauss, H.H. Pathology of the figure-ground relationship in the child. *Journal of Abnormal and Social Psychology,* 1941, 36, 236-247.

Werry, J.S. The diagnosis etiology, and treatment of hyperactivity in children. In Hellmuth, J. *Learning Disorders.* Vol. III. Seattle: Special Child Publications, 1968.

Werry, J. and Quay, H. Observing the classroom behavior of elementary school children. *Exceptional Children,* 1969, 35, 461-470.

Werry, J.S., Weiss, G., and Douglas, V. Studies on the hyperactive child I: Some preliminary findings. *Canadian Psychiatric Association Journal,* 1964, 9, 120-134.

Westerman, G.S. *Spelling and Writing.* San Rafael, Cal.: Dimension Publ. Co., 1971.

Wheller, L.R. and Wheeler, V.D. A study of the relationship of auditory discrimination to silent reading abilities. *Journal of Educational Research,* 1954, 48, 103-113.

Wickelgran, W.A. The long and short of memory. *Psychological Bulletin,* 1973, 80, 425-438.

Wiig, E.H., LaPointe, C., and Semel, E.M. Relationship among language processing and production abilities of learning disabled adolescents. *Journal of Learning Disabilities,* 1977, 10, 292-299.

Williams, F. (Ed.) *Language and Poverty.* Chicago: Markham, 1970.

Willard, L.S. A comparison of culture-fair test scores with group and individual intelligence test scores of disadvantages Negro children. *Journal of Learning Disabilities,* 1968, 1, 584-589.

Wilson, D.K. *Voice Problems of Children.* Baltimore: Williams and Wilkins, 1972.

Wilson, G. and Nias, D. *The Mystery of Love: The Hows and Whys of Sexual Attraction.* New York: Quadrangle, 1976.

Wilson, F.T. et. al. Reading progress in kindergarten and primary grades. *Elementary School Journal,* 1938, 38, 442-449.

Wissink, J.F., Koss, C.E., and Ferrell, W.R. A bayesian approach to the identification of children with learning disabilities. *Journal of Learning Disabilities,* 1975, 8, 158-166.

Wolfe, L.S. An experimental study of reversals in reading. *American Journal of Psychology,* 1939, 52, 533-561.

Winkley, C.K. What do diagnostic reading tests really measure? In Leibert, I.R.E. *Diagnostic Viewpoints in Reading.* Newark, Del.: International Reading Association, 1971.

Wolf, W.W. An experimental investigation of specific language disability (dyslexia). *Bulletin of the Orton Society,* 1967, 17, 32-40.

Wood, L. and Schulman, E. The Ellis Visual Designs Test. *Journal of Consulting Psychology,* 1940, 31, 591-602.

Woodrow, H. The ability to learn. *Psychological Review,* 1946, 53, 147-158.

Woodward, H. and Lowell, F. Children's association frequency tables. *Psychological Monographs,* 1916, 22, #97.

Woody, C. and Phillips, A.J. The effects of handedness on reversals in reading. *Journal of Educational Research,* 1934, 27, 651-662.

Index

Adaptive behavior 363-364
Additive weakness theory 41
Age 191-194, 324, 325
Agnosia 163, 245
Agraphia 37, 245
Alexia 5
Aphasia 26-27, 48, 225, 334-335, 340, 345
Apraxia 243-244
Arithmetic 90, 162-173
  diagnosing 165-168
  emotional factors 164
  reading 164
  research 163-165
  tests 172-173
Articulation 105, 208, 320, 322-327
Attention 71-75
  span 68, 71-73
Auditory
  acuity 298-302, 325, 339
  blending and closure 39, 308-310, 311
  discrimination 124, 148, 306-308
  dyslexia 129, 141
  figure-ground 304-306
  perception 298-318

Behavioristic analysis 80-81
Binocular fusion 267-268
Birth history 60
Birth order 194
Body image 258-259
Brain damage 30, 32, 36, 38, 44, 45, 219-227, 311, 318
  also see Minimal Brain Damage

Case study 83-87
Cerebral Dominance 36-37

Chess 91, 286-287
Choreiform movements 216-217
Composition *see* written language
Congenital aphasia *see* aphasia
Copying figures 293-296
Criterion referenced tests 145

Definition of learning disabilities 4-9
Detroit Tests of Learning Aptitude 111-113
Developmental Interruption 47-48
Diagnosis 17-23, 25, 56, 365-373
  academics 178-183
  behavioral 18-21
  brain damage 219-227
  definition 17
  etiological 21
  hyperactivity 204-207
  mathematics 165-168
  medical 17-18
  milestones 60
  motor abilities 228-248
  neurological exam 207-213
  phonics 146-149
  physical description 194-198
  reading 118-146, 150-151
  spelling 156-162
Diagnostic report 80-87
Directionality 91, 217, 219
Distinctive features 303, 330-331
Distractibility 44-45
Dominance *see* Laterality
Dyscalculia 5, 163
Dysgraphia 5, 36

Dyslexia 5, 33, 48, 50, 129, 162-163, 166, 177, 181, 191, 258
Electroencephlograph 45, 213-215, 220
Embedded figures 39, 279-281
Emotional problems 332, 340, 354-364
Ethical standards 23-24
Etiology 21, 25-55
Expectancy formula 9
Eye dominance 248-252
Factor analysis 13-17, 44, 107-110
Family Rights and Privacy Act 24
Family Information form 56
Figure-ground 39, 72, 75, 90, 278, 303-306
Finger agnosia 163, 167, 209, 212, 217-219
Fluency disorders 327-329
Form constancy 275-276

Genetic variables 46, 51-52, 185-188
Gerstmann's syndrome 163, 218, 255
Gestalt perception 37-39

Handedness 91, 163, 233, 241, 248-255
Handwriting 244-245
Hyperactivity 44-45, 69, 73-74, 201-207, 219, 222, 234, 241
Hyperlexic 127-128
Hypoactive 75

Illinois Test of Psycholinguistics (ITPA) 102-111, 156
Informal reading inventories 132-134
Inheritance 46, 51-52, 185-188
Intelligence 10-11, 226, 307, 342-360
  definition 342-344
  drawing 293
  measurement 344-349
  motor ability 247
  phonics 149
  Piaget 350-352
  reading 34, 120, 353
  spelling 34
  syntax 335
  tests 33-34, 338-339
  visual perception 34
Interposition 275
Interviews 62-69, 76-80, 358

Kinesthetic memory 30

Labeling 20
Language 48, 50, 122, 177, 319-341
Laterality 91, 163, 233, 241, 248-255
Learning disabilities
  Act 9
  articulation 324
  attention 71-75
  auditory perception 51, 315-317
  brain damage 30, 32, 44-45
  conditioning 75
  definition 4-9, 352-353
  right-left discrimination 256
  motor abilities 228-248
  sex linked 30
  personality 42-44
  visual acuity 264-267
Letter and word discrimination 277
Letter reversals 37, 40, 106 251-252, 278

Mathematics *see* Arithmetic
Maturational lag 290
Megavitamins 200-201
Memory
  auditory 90, 310-316
  visual 90, 124, 284
Milestones 60-62, 210

Minimal brain damage 45-46, 51, 213-219
Minority testing 105
Motivation 71, 73
Motor ability 91, 228-248
Musical ability 90-91

Neurological exam 207-213, 233, 253, 270
Norming 94-95

Observation 75-76
Overlapping figures 38

Perseveration 44-45
Phonics 31, 32, 94, 146-150, 155, 305, 317
Physical characteristics 194-198
Piaget 350-352
Prenatal and natal 198-200, 215
Processes *see* Psychological processes
Process tests 150
Projective tests 355-357
Psycholinguistic training 109
Psychological processes 21, 48-49, 89-91, 107, 115-117

Rating scales 69-71, 357-359
Ratings, teacher 137-138
Reading 118-151
  and arithmetic 164
  blending 309, 317
  closure 283
  comprehension 126-128
  diagnosis 118-119, 150-151
  diagnostic tests 136-139
  discrimination 306-307
  errors 121-122, 140-141
  figure-ground 278-282, 305-306
  inheritance 186-188
  intelligence 353
  IRIs 132-134
  memory 285, 288-289
  personality 42-45, 359-360
  phonics 146-150
  processes 128-131
  readiness 134-136
  sex differences 188-191
  spelling 153
  silent reading 136-139
  visual perception 34, 277-278
  word lists 132
Reliability 97-101, 110-111, 113, 137, 140, 211
Reversals 106, 251-252, 278
Right-left discrimination 252-258

Self-concept 71
Sequencing 36-37
Sex differences 188-191
Sex linked traits 30
Seizures 203-204
Size constancy 275
Sound blending 105
Spatial ability 162-163, 190
Speech 310-311
Spelling 152-163, 194, 352
  inheritance 186, 194
  ITPA 107, 156
  research 153-159
  skills 161-162
  tests 159-160
  visual perception 34
Standard deviation 96-97
Standardized testing 22-23, 137-138
Standardized tests *see* Appendix B
Strauss syndrome 45
Strephosymbolia 35-36, 40
Symptoms and signs 17-18
Syndrome 17, 53

Task analysis 80-82
Testing, informal 22
Tests
  criterion referenced 94
  individual vs. group 93

norming 94
reliability 97-101
standardized 90-102
validity 101-102

Validity 101-102
Visual 260-297
  acuity 262-267
  binocular fusion 270-271
  closure 106, 123-124, 282
  depth perception 273-276
  discrimination 242, 276-278
  dyslexia 129, 141
  eye movements 268-270
  interposition 273-274
  memory 180, 283-292
  optical problems 260-271
  perceptual learning 272-273
  reading 34-35, 123
  size and form constancy 275-276
  spelling 153
Voice disorders 320-322

Word-blindness 27-30, 32, 36, 40, 187
Written language 108, 173-178

DISCHARGED APR 5 1990
DISCHARGED MAR 16 1993
AUG 1 6 1993

DISCHARGED

MAY 27 1994
JUN 27 1995
DISCHARGED OCT 0 9 1995
DISCHARGED

DISCHARGED
OCT 2 3 1984

DISCHARGED

DISCHARGED
MAR 0 5 1997
DISCHARGED

DISCHARGED
MAR 3 1 1988

DISCHARGED
MAR 1 0 1989

DISCHARGED
OCT 1 4 1986

DISCHARGED
NOV 1 3 1986

OCT 1 5 1987
DISCHARGED

AUG 1 1 1992